Regina Williams Davis

Andrea Patterson-Masuka

Intercultural Communication for
GLOBAL ENGAGEMENT

Kendall Hunt
publishing company

Cover image © Shutterstock, Inc.

Kendall Hunt
publishing company

www.kendallhunt.com
Send all inquiries to:
4050 Westmark Drive
Dubuque, IA 52004-1840

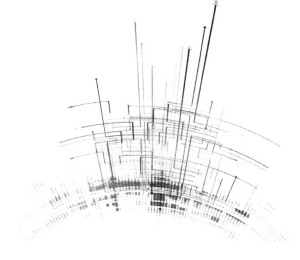

Contents

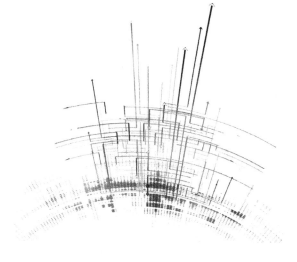

Foreword

Omar Swartz, Ph.D.
University of Colorado, Denver

Fundamental to the inclusive society envisioned by many intercultural communication scholars, such as those who have contributed to this innovative and practical text, is a sense of individual and collective empowerment that enables us to relate to one another in ways that are often precluded by our current identifications (gendered, racial, religious, sexual, etc.). Such empowerment involves the ability to help others achieve their goals by providing them with resources, facilitating actions, and using our power for cross-cultural community building. Central to this is the *moral imagination*, our ability and willingness to understand and to engage the subjectivity and situatedness of others. Another way of seeing this is as a "double vision," one allowing those of us with privilege to contextualize that privilege and, ultimately, to use it on behalf of others to create more comfortable physical and cultural space for themselves. Enacting this power comes from an awareness of how communication operates to create and sustain culture.

It is of fundamental importance to be able to see the study of communication—and, in particular, of intercultural communication—as embracing the presence, parameters, and importance of critical and empathetic thought and action in our society. It is communication—the hierarchies and distinctions that we make through communication and commitment—that bring us together or tear us apart. Engaging such communication critically and compassionately, however, is not easy. Although it is crucial that we change as a culture and become more inclusive of others both within and outside of our borders, it is much more comfortable to simply accept things as they appear to be, and to take comfort in the intoxications that society readily offers us. We are in, in this country, an intoxicated people in many ways. By *intoxication*, I mean to suggest that we are overwhelmed by the stimuli that are intended to distract us, to define us, and to limit us in fundamental ways, giving us the impression that all is as it should be. However, all is *not* as it should be. We do not love our neighbors and we often hate the people who live on the other side of the world from us.

The moral imagination is an orientation by which individuals possess a heightened state of awareness of the influences of communication on their lives and its effect on their attitudes. Humans communicate through systems of verbal and nonverbal symbols, and the overall picture of what is considered to be "reality" is comprised of these symbol systems. Kenneth Burke's description of human beings as the "symbol-using, symbol-making, and symbol-misusing animal" aptly points out that humans cannot separate themselves from the symbolic; we live within a symbolic world created by us.[1] Like breathing, symbols are such an integral part of human experience that individuals forget that symbols exist, and they forget that symbols, and the meanings they take from them, are human creations. Thus, it becomes easy to delineate between "us" and "them" when, in actuality, we are all one.

A moral imagination, however, goes beyond a general awareness of the symbolic to a study of the *competence* needed for using symbols effectively to build human relations, to repair the sense of difference created by culture when it harms us. It requires movement from individual to collective imagination. This discursive aspect of imagination operates as both a background and as an active process; rather than functioning as transmission, it acts as a constitutive force. In other words, as individuals, we discursively use a moral imagination to strengthen our connection to others and to envision and articulate ideologies that reflect common social goods. When we are involved collectively in this creative process, we begin to see others as being more similar to ourselves than different with their interests and well-being inherently coupled with our own. This is what philosopher Martha Nussbaum calls the *narrative imagination*—the ability to imagine the experiences and perspectives of others different from oneself, and to suspend one's worldview and judgment to open oneself to the experience of another. Such ability allows individuals to increase their capacity to see others as human and as not so different from ourselves. This ability also paves the way for the development of *moral intelligence*, a quality possessed by human beings who recognize their connections to others and understand the power of language to reify or reject human connectedness. Moral intelligence is not only comprised of this intellectual understanding but also incorporates acts of compassion and respect for others through the careful and considerate use of our interactions with others.

The world that we live in is one that we have inherited; it was constructed to serve certain interests. Communication is central to understanding that construction and to learning to do something about it; after all, an inherited world is not one of our making, stripping us of the creativity that makes us human. The sense of agency that comes from understanding the power of language is evident in the following quote from author James

---

1. *Language as Symbolic Action* (Berkeley, CA: University of California Press, 1966), 16.

Baldwin. As he argues, we must resist being forced "to live according to the world's definitions: one must find a way, perpetually, to be stronger and better than that."[2] To do so is to become, in the sense established by the philosopher Richard Rorty, a "strong poet." As strong poets, we accept responsibility for the power of communication to make a difference in our lives and in the world around us. Strong poets seek out opportunities to engage the world creatively and humanely.

The essays collected in this *Intercultural Communication for Global Engagement* consist of practical, tangible examples of moral intelligence in the sense that I have been describing it. In each of their own ways, they are examples of strong poetry, strategic interventions in cultural life. Collectively, the essays consist of a type of antidote to our cultural intoxications that weaken us as a society. Students who use this book—indeed all of us—can learn to see that the power to make the world better by developing our skills as intercultural communicators is the power to redefine and remake the world in our image and in the image of our collective humanity.

---

2. *The Evidence of Things Not Seen* (New York: Holt Paperbacks, Anniversary Edition, 1995), 86.

Introduction

Dr. Regina Williams Davis
North Carolina Agricultural & Technical State University

Dr. Andrea Patterson-Masuka
Winston-Salem State University

When we first began this project, we wanted to help our readers develop an understanding of the interconnectivity of intercultural communication, global engagement, and globalization. We wanted to explore how our own intercultural journeys and experiences impact ourselves, our community, and today's world. Having the opportunity to prepare a reader who is themed about intercultural communication and global engagement has been one of our most favorite projects thus far. As professors of communication, we teach these massive communication concepts in the classroom, but rarely find that "right" text that radiates the magnitude as well as the essence of intercultural communication. So, what is this concept of intercultural communication, and how, when, where, and why does it occur?

It starts with the ambiguous nature of culture. The "what is intercultural communication" is even more abstruse than the ambiguous nature of culture. It is confusing when expressing the notion of "interculture" as an adjective to describe communication. The prefix, "inter" suggests the idea of being among, mutual, or in a reciprocal relationship. A great analogy may resemble biological relationships characterized as "symbiotic," which means a potentially long-term interaction between two or more different biological species, relationships which become interdependent. Assuming that we understand that culture refers to the beliefs, customs, and ways of being for a particular society's norms, then intercultural communication becomes an act of expression among two or more cultures promoting a long-term collaboration of educational growth and understanding of the other, be it formal or informal connections.

You will explore in this reader "when" intercultural communication occurs. You will read about a variety of events that were pivotal moments in the authors' lives. These events were educational, often informal, life-changing, explorative, disturbing, and exciting. You will read about historical activities and current events that make intercultural communication necessary from the messages sent from pop culture and the media to political misunderstandings from a global perspective. You will see the need for global engagement and the need for understanding the culture of others as well as the recognition and reflection of an author's personal "aha" moment of growth from the obliviousness of the challenges of others.

When it comes to "how" intercultural communication occurs, a moment of enlightenment ensues when readers recognize a point of connection. They begin to see where their cultures intersect. Once someone's eyes are opened, they tend to have epiphanies that the more we are different, the more we may be the same. Then the "how" progresses and is passed along. Individuals who experience these moments of epiphanies start to desire to learn more, to seek understanding, and to become more understood by others. To enhance knowledge and have the desire to share it with others assist with the unravelling of the complexities that keep the walls of ignorance as barriers to successful long-term relationships.

The "why" can be recognized from the microcosm of a diverse kindergarten classroom to the macro-issues of global engagement. You will read about reflections an author had when pondering cultural nuances from their childhood regarding intercultural communication. And yet this reader is written at a time when the United States Government is struggling to find a comprehensive solution that cuts off all of Iran's pathways to creating an atomic bomb and verifiably ensure the peaceful nature of Iran's nuclear program going forward. Yet, Israeli leader Benjamin Netanyahu is distrustful of the success the United States may have with the details of the "deal" with Iran and that its framework will threaten the survival of Israel. Young kindergarten students need to understand intercultural communication because they will grow to become the policy-makers of tomorrow.

Scaffolding is an educational approach that moves students progressively toward skill building, learning, and understanding. This reader is designed to provide students with a broad-based knowledge of intercultural communication and a variety of tools for the enhancement of intercultural understanding. The goal for us as educators is to produce a culturally competent communicator. We begin our scaffolding approach in Chapter 1 by "**Laying the Foundation**." In this chapter students will be introduced to the idea of engaging intercultural communication and a dialogical approach to intercultural communication. Key foundational terms and concepts will be presented throughout the chapter and interwoven themes.

After laying the foundation it is time to frame the student's learning. Culture is strongly connected to identity which is a person's conception and expression of themselves. In Chapter 2, students will explore "**Identifying the Self**." This reader is packed with personal experiences from various authors who will force college and graduate-level students to self-reflect. This chapter has amazing essays from a case study perspective of viewing identity and culture to identity conflict and negotiating with one's knowledge of the self. Most students find connections with themselves and the stories these authors share.

As communication professors, we find it absolutely necessary to recognize that communication is happening in unintentional ways; hence Chapter 3: "**Communicating Verbally and Nonverbally.**" This phenomenon is acknowledged in the basic fundamentals of communication course; therefore, it must be addressed in terms of intercultural communication. After reading the essays in this chapter, students will have an understanding of the relationship between culture and language, verbally and nonverbally.

When we speak of inter-culture in terms of communication crossing boundaries, pop-culture transcends. Chapters 4 and 5 are about "**Living the Pop Culture**" and "**Reviewing the Media**," respectively. These chapters profoundly bring intercultural communication to a relevant space for students to see the inescapable blending, growth, and crossing of cultural boundaries. What better way to see the shifting of connotations and the assimilation of symbolic communication than in popular music, art, literature, drama, film, radio, television, and most recently, social media. Networked media influences the masses and promotes the exposure of a wide variety of cultures and provides context for individuals to make connections and find points where different cultures intersect.

In Chapter 6, "**Surviving the Culture Shock**," and Chapter 7, "**Experiencing Global Engagement**" are experiences some of the authors shared that propelled their thoughts and ideas of the other culture to unexpected heights. These chapters offer a pragmatic and ethical framework for providing the purpose to educate ourselves and others for international understanding.

Chapter 8, "**Making the Intercultural Connection in the Workplace**" provokes some necessary conversations around workplace diversity. Students are becoming aware of living in the age of globalization and the workplaces where they will eventually grow their professions will most likely be places without boundaries. Inevitably, in interpersonal communication there is potential for conflict. If it is likely that conflict may arise in interpersonal conversations, then the likelihood is greater in intercultural communication. Chapter 9, "**Meeting the Challenges and Barriers**," presents several examples of encounters and obstacles met by the authors and how they managed to find resolutions. These authors shared their inner feelings and emotions when going through these pivotal moments in their lives.

Because we are professors who believe in experiential learning, Chapter 10, "**Engaging Intercultural Communication**," is a set of activities in which students can participate to simulate many of the experiences shared by the authors. Taking the time to participate in any of these activities may enhance the comprehension of each student to the nuances of intercultural communication and global engagement.

We finally want to leave you with the idea that this project is about voices. These essays were not written as a collection of politically correct stories, but rather an invitation to conversation that reflects the real challenges and joys of engaging with diverse groups of people. Let us be certain that we hear each other before we determine we do not agree with each other. Open your minds and hearts as you read these essays. We hope you will be transformed.

Chapter 1

Laying the Foundation

1. Engaging Intercultural Communication

Andrea Patterson-Masuka

One does not have to necessarily travel outside the United States to experience intercultural communication and global engagement. Imagine unpacking a new laptop and you need technical assistance. You make a phone call and whether you realize it or not, you are speaking with someone in Bangalor, India. You are engaging in intercultural cultural communication.

You may want to know why you as a student need to learn about intercultural communication. How can learning about communicating with other cultures be an advantage? In this chapter, we will explore why we need to study intercultural communication, define intercultural communication, explore the various meanings of culture, and finally examine the concept of communication flexibility.

The Need to Study Intercultural Communication

The act of communicating across cultural boundaries is as old as humanity itself, whereby different ethnic cultures encountered and communicated with one another. In fact, for nearly 3,000 years Europeans have traversed sand and seas to buy and trade with silk and satin. Although there has been a long history of communicating with other cultures, the formal study of intercultural communication only began during the last half of the twentieth century.

In today's world, because of the economic, social, political, cultural, and environmental dimensions of globalization, we need to envision new intercultural ways of thinking and approaching communication. This need is even more intensified in the context of **globalization**. Thomas Palley, from the Economics for Democratic and Open Societies, defines globalization as the general concept incorporating the diffusion of ideas and cultures (Perkovich, 2006).

Perhaps one of the major imperatives to studying the intercultural communication process is the realization that we as humans must learn to understand each other and that our world depends on it to avoid self-destruction. Think about the tragic shooting deaths of African Americans Eric Gardner of New York, and Michael Brown of Ferguson, Missouri, by law enforcement officers. The racial tensions and riots that followed remind us that intercultural communication and conflict are part of our everyday lives but they can be prevented. It is important to remember that there is also a level of responsibility that comes with gaining intercultural knowledge. As you embark upon your journey of learning more about intercultural communication, ask yourself the following questions: Do you listen to the voice of others from different cultural backgrounds? Do you listen carefully to learn about their culture and what matters to them? Do you explore ways you can contribute to positive change? Are you also developing a sense of social justice?

As a student, it is important to realize that regardless of your major or field of study, effective intercultural communication is essential to help you prepare for an increasingly complex and diverse community, workplace, and world. Allen Goodman, the President and CEO of the Institute of International Education (IIE), contends that all students' careers "will be global ones, in which they will need to function effectively in multinational teams" (Institute of International Education, 2014b, para. 6). Goodman contends that in today's world students will need to understand the cultural and historical differences among people as well as the commonalities of value and humanity that connect human beings. Different cultural groups impact the way their members view the world. Members of a culture develop a worldview, which subsequently influences communication.

As a future employee, you may become a nurse, global manager, a media specialist, or a sales team member. You and others around you can benefit from learning and mastering intercultural competencies (J. M. Bennett, 2009, 2014; Gupta, 2009; Hyatt, Evans, & Haque, 2009). J. M. Bennett (2014) describes **intercultural competence** as those attitudes, behaviors, and skills that enable you to engage effectively and appropriately in

maxstockphoto/Shutterstock.com

multiple intercultural contexts. Intercultural scholars Stella Ting-Toomey and Leeva C. Chung (2012) believe that any individual or organization that interacts with culturally-diverse clients, customers, or co-workers can benefit from becoming flexible intercultural communicators. Now that we have discussed various reasons to explore intercultural communication, it is important to define intercultural communication and examine its relationship to culture.

Defining Intercultural Communication and Culture

For communication scholars Judith Martin and Thomas Nakayama (2014), **intercultural communication** happens when persons of different cultures and backgrounds communicate and interact. While this definition may sound simplistic, elements such as culture and communication are essential. Culture is often viewed as the core concept of intercultural communication. **Culture** is learned, and involves the perceptions, values, feelings, shared cultural patterns, and expressed behaviors, which are dynamic and varied. Essential to our understanding of intercultural communication is examining the concept of culture from an interdisciplinary perspective. Next we will explore the various definitions of culture from the anthropological, cultural studies, and globalization perspectives.

Culture

The concept of culture itself has been contested and challenged. There is no one agreed-upon definition of culture, and there are many different meanings to the word culture. Anthropologists Arthur Kroeber and Clyde Kluckhohn (1952) identified more than 150 definitions of culture in the 1950s. Scholars have varied definitions of **culture**. Intercultural researcher J. M. Bennett (2014) describes culture as "the learned and shared values, beliefs, and behaviors of a group of interacting people" (p. 2).

The concept of culture is critically integral to the way we see, interpret, sense, and experience the world in which we live. Consequently, our definitions of culture are influenced by the political, social, and historical era in which we live. In fact, historically the term "culture" was closely related in its use and meaning to the process of colonization (Sorrells, 2008). During the nineteenth century European anthropologists wrote depictions of the life of "others," and their descriptions mainly described non-European cultures as uncivilized and lacking "culture." This viewpoint of "culture" provided grounds for colonization. By the beginning of World War I, European powers had colonized approximately nine-tenths of the world. Young (2001) argues that this legacy of imperialism and colonization influences the field of intercultural communication even today.

Anthropologic definition of culture. The field of communication studies and the area of intercultural communication have been influenced by a variety of disciplines including psychology, sociology, philosophy, and anthropology. Clifford Geertz (1973) states that culture historically involved patterns of meaning that were embodied in symbols. He further describes it as a system of concepts and symbolic forms "by means of which men communicate, perpetuate, and develop their knowledge about attitudes towards life" (p. 89).

At the core of this definition is the concept of symbols and symbol systems. **Symbols** stand for arbitrary, abstract representations of phenomena. Ideas, objects, actions, and people can all be symbols to represent other things.

Cultural anthropologist Goodenough (1981) reserved the term culture for "what is learned, for the things one needs to know in order to meet the standards of others" (p. 50). He expressed a view that places culture in the minds and hearts of men. He viewed culture as a product of human learning and summarized its content as the way people organize their experiences, their past efforts, and how they make sense of those experiences. Goodenough's model of culture consists of standards for deciding one's feelings, actions, and how to proceed.

Goodenough's concept of culture is an interpretive process that includes the central elements of interacting with others (conversation) and aligning groups of people (community). These central elements of conversation, community, and code are thus connected with a sense of identity. Cheng (2007) contends that people communicate through the use of **codes**, which is the system used to transmit meaning. Codes can be letters or numbers, verbal or nonverbal, formal or informal.

Therefore, culture from a traditional anthropological perspective is a system of shared meanings that are transmitted from generation to generation through symbols that allow us to communicate and sustain how we see our lives. In essence, culture allows us to engage in sense making and expression.

Cultural studies definition: Culture as a site of contested meaning. In contrast, while traditional anthropologists view culture as a system of shared meaning, the cultural studies perspective informed by Marxist theories of class, struggle, and exploitation see culture as a site of contested meaning, whereas meaning is always negotiated (Grossberg, Nelson, & Treichler, 1992). Simon During (2001) contends that as England's working class became more dispersed and affluent during the 1950s and mass-produced culture started to loom over more local and community cultures, the old concept of culture as a shared way of meaning and life became less applicable.

Hall (1997) argues that culture is the "actual grounded terrain" of our everyday lives from the clothes we buy, the food we eat, the movies we watch, and music we hear, and the news that we select to inform us about our world—are all grounds where meaning can be created and challenged.

The concept of culture from an idea of shared meaning and lives shifts to a view of culture as an apparatus of power within a larger system of domination. A cultural perspective reveals how culture operates as a form of hegemony, or domination through consent. Meanings are constantly challenged or negotiated, or produced (Sorrells, 2008).

This concept that takes the view of culture being challenged and negotiated appeals to individuals who view themselves as marginalized or disenfranchised from the center of power. In contrast, viewing culture as system of shared meaning from the dominant culture's perspective is more aligned with the anthropological view of culture. From a cultural studies perspective, culture is a subject of analysis—something that needs to be reviewed and critiqued, but it is also a site of intervention that we can use to work toward making the world more equitable and just.

Pressmaster/Shutterstock.com

Culture in the context of globalization. Guided by cultural studies, George Yudice (2003) contends that culture, in the context of globalization, should be understood as a resource or commodity. It plays an even larger role based upon how it is linked to community, local, national, and transnational economies and politics. In the context of globalization, culture is being exploited, commodified, and appropriated; an example is the controversial use of the "Redskin" name by one of the NFL franchises. In this sense, culture is being used as a resource or a brand.

Culture can also be viewed as a tool for empowerment and resistance. Consider how Black youth in the favelas—poverty-ridden areas of Rio de Janeiro in Brazil—use funk music to protest against racial discrimination and as a platform for advocacy while they access funding from organizations that support cultural empowerment. Yudice (2003) stresses that today, in the context of globalization, "the understanding and practice of culture is quite complex, located at the intersection of economic and social justice agendas" (p. 17). The second element we will consider in studying intercultural communication is the concept communication.

Communication

There is a distinct relationship between culture and communication. Julia T. Wood (2014) contends that **communication** can be viewed as a systemic process whereby people use symbols to create, interpret, share, and negotiate meaning. Intercultural researcher D. C. Barnlund (1989) believes that "It is through communication that we acquire culture; it is in our manner of communicating that we display our cultural uniqueness" (p. xiv).

Intercultural communication happens when persons of different cultures and backgrounds communicate and interact (Martin & Nakayama, 2014). **Intercultural communication** can be defined as a systemic process in which people from two or more cultural communities simultaneously encode and decode symbols to negotiate, interpret, and share meanings within an embedded social system (Ting-Toomey & Chung, 2012). The major characteristics of this definition include the following concepts: process, encoding, decoding, system, meaning, and embedded social systems.

The first essential element of our definition is process. Communication is a **process**, meaning it is ongoing and dynamic. It is very difficult to determine when communication begins and ends. An African American businessman meets a South Korean businessman at a business conference in Brazil. The African American businessman may be extending his hand to shake the South Korean businessman's hand. The South Korean may bow. In a brief awkward moment, the two businessmen may quickly change their nonverbal gestures, creating another awkward moment of greeting. This quick reversal of greeting leads us to our concept of symbolic exchange, which refers to the verbal and nonverbal symbols between at least two individuals to communicate a shared meaning.

The transactional nature of communication refers to the **simultaneous encoding** (the person choosing the messages to send) and **decoding** (the person translating the words or nonverbal cues into a comprehensible message). Unfortunately, intercultural encounters are filled with misunderstandings and missteps because of cultural communication differences, language barriers, nonverbal communication miscues, and different value orientations. Furthermore, it is important to keep in mind that communication is also an irreversible process. Two American businessmen may be impatient due to the length of time their Japanese co-workers may be taking to give them a decision on a project-related matter. Frustrated, one of the American businessmen rushes into the other American businessman's office and blurts, "Those damn people take too long!" He did not realize that their Japanese co-worker was in the office. He mutters "sorry" and immediately retreats from the room. This intercultural encounter may have repercussions far into the future. He notices that the people in his office begin avoiding him. His duties are slowly reassigned. He is subsequently demoted and transferred to another division in another city. He eventually leaves the company in frustration due to his lack of promotion.

Communication also happens within the context of a **system** of interdependent and interrelated components, which require consistent adaptation to each other to maintain its balance and wholeness (Galanes & Adams, 2013). The central principle of a system is **interdependence**, which is the concept that all interrelated parts affect each other as well as the entire system. For example, in order for an extended family reunion to occur without any major obstacles, the publicity committee has to create fliers, newsletters, and emails to inform and update the family members, and the logistics committee has to identify, select, and secure the reunion hotel and conference center. The event coordinator has to determine and plan the events during the weekend, and the budget committee has to collect family dues for rent, the venue, etc. All of these tasks and more must be completed to have a successful family reunion.

Our definition of communication also involves **symbols**, which include arbitrary, abstract, representations of reality; we bestow the meaning using symbols. Our symbols can be verbal and nonverbal and can include art and music. We express our affection to someone we love by hugging them and crying when we depart on a journey. We may say the words "I love you" and give them a kiss. **Symbolic exchange** refers to the use of verbal and nonverbal symbols between at least two or more individuals or groups from different cultural backgrounds. Kendra, an African American female college student meets Adrien, an international male student from France at her university in her international business class. The two become study partners, begin dating, and are engaged the following year. The French student invites his new fiancée home during the Christmas break to meet his family. When they meet at the airport, Kendra extends her hand to the father as a greeting. Adrien's father quickly glances at him in confusion, the father draws Kendra close to him, gives her a hug and gives her a kiss on both cheeks. She immediately stiffens, but quickly realizes the future father-in law is transferring the closeness and acceptance from his son to her to welcome her to France and to their family. Later, her fiancée explains that his parents were very happy to have her in the family.

Another element of communication is **meaning**, which is at the heart of communication. Meaning is the importance we bestow on a phenomenon of what it actually means to us. Meaning grows out of our interactions with symbols that we interpret through verbal and nonverbal communications. There are two levels of meaning in communication. One level of meaning is the content level of meaning, which is the literal message. For example, if you walk into a room unannounced and someone says "get out of here" and slams the door in your face, the content level of this message is that you should leave the premises immediately. The relationship level of meaning expresses the relationship between the individuals. The preceding scenario indicates there is no relationship at all. The message is clear and simple. In another scenario, a person tells a friend a joke. The friend laughs and smiles. They shake their head and say "get out of here." The receiver of the message can probably interpret the relationship level of meaning and that the person is joking with them.

The final element is **embedded societal systems**, which refers to multiple layers of politics, history, society, privilege, class, race, eco-

Gustavo Frazao/Shutterstock.com

nomics, policies, and customs, and more that shape the context, process, and outcome of an actual intercultural interaction (Oetzel, Ting-Toomey, & Rinderle, 2006; Ting-Toomey & Chung, 2012). Transactional communication always takes place within an interactive situation and is subjected to the influences of these multiple layers. The next characteristic is **cultural community** or **group**, which is broadly defined as a group of individuals interacting together who uphold sets of traditions, beliefs, or systems. In the broadest sense, a cultural group can be referred to as an ethnic group, gender group, or hold some type of group membership together. The boundaries of a cultural group may include more than geographic or national boundaries. I encourage you to think of additional examples and questions to clarify your understanding of the intercultural communication process.

Flexible Communication

As the world gets smaller and boundaries become blurred, it is important that we always become more aware of and develop **flexible communication,** which emphasizes the importance of "integrating knowledge and an open-minded attitude and putting them in adaptive and creative practice in everyday communication" (Ting-Toomey & Chung, 2012, p. 28). Inflexible communication, on the other hand, involves using our own cultural values, judgments, and worldviews when we communicate with someone who is different from us. Inflexible communicators have an **ethnocentric mindset,** which means they believe their culture or way of life is superior or the best and they will use their own culture as the baseline to evaluate other cultures' behaviors, values, beauty, or belief system. In contrast, an **ethno-relative mindset** strives to comprehend the other person's frame of reference (M. J. Bennett, 1993). In an ideal state of ethno-relativism, a flexible mindset, sensitive emotional awareness, and cultural interactions come together for successful flexible intercultural communication. In order to participate in flexible communication behavior, one must acquire the knowledge, content, and intercultural communication skills.

Knowledge refers to the intentional learning of the critical themes and concepts in intercultural flexibility. Developing cultural knowledge requires engaging in cultural self-awareness, acquiring cultural general knowledge, cultural-specific knowledge, and analyzing our interactions (J. M. Bennett, 2014). Conscious learning can be achieved through formal studying and informal cultural learning experiences. Formal experiences include enrolling in an intercultural communication class, a foreign language class, or a world history class. Informal study includes studying abroad, international traveling or vacations, developing a friendship with someone from another culture, attending international festivals, viewing international movies, or participating in international volunteer experiences such as serving in the Peace Corps. You may also read an international magazine. In order to comprehend the knowledge we have acquired, we must approach our cultural learning with an open mind and a willing heart.

Attitude can include cognitive and affective dimensions of our behavior. The cognitive dimension refers to how much we desire to suspend our ethnocentric behavior and judgment and be willing to immerse ourselves in intercultural issues (Ting-Toomey & Chung,

2012). In contrast, the affective layer of attitude refers to our emotional willingness to engage in cultural dual perspective taking, cultivating an open mindedness, and opening our hearts to culturally diverse groups and contexts. In developing a culturally flexible attitude, we are able to participate in ethno-relative thinking to understand someone else's worldview. We take a moment and reflect upon whether we are making hasty cultural judgments. Once we have acquired knowledge, reflected upon our attitudes, we can then develop our skills.

Skills are our acquired and operational behaviors and abilities we use once we acquire our knowledge and attitudes. We apply those to the communication process in our daily lives. Many interpersonal skills can be applied when engaging in flexible communication including listening skills, relationship building, empathy, and engaging in dual perspective (Ting-Toomey & Chung, 2012).

In summary, this chapter discussed several reasons why you should study intercultural communication; we defined culture(s), communication, intercultural communication, and explored the concept of flexible communication. To be a culturally competent communicator you must begin practicing some of the ideas that you have read about in your everyday intercultural encounters.

Discussion Questions

1. What are the various definitions of culture? Compare and contrast the different definitions.
2. What are some of the reasons why we need to study intercultural communication?
3. How do you define intercultural communication?
4. How can you engage in flexible communication in your daily interactions? Give an example.

References

Barnlund, D. C. (1989). *Communication styles of Japanese and Americans images and realities.* Belmont, CA: Wadsworth.

Bennett, J. M. (2009). Cultivating intercultural competence: A process perspective. In D. K. Deardoff (Ed.), *The Sage handbook of intercultural competence* (pp. 121–140). Thousand Oaks, CA: Sage.

Bennett, J. M. (2014). *Intersecting pathways: Global diversity and inclusion.* Conference presentation and unpublished manuscript from NAFSA Conference, San Diego, CA.

Bennett, M. J. (1993). Towards ethnorelativism: A developmental model of intercultural sensitivity. In R. M. Paige (Ed.), *Education for intercultural experience* (pp. 21–71). Yarmouth, ME: Intercultural Press.

During, S. (2001). *The cultural studies reader* (2nd ed.). New York, NY: Routledge.

Galanes, G., & Adams, K. (2013). *Effective group discussion: Theory and practice.* New York, NY: McGraw-Hill.

Geertz, C. (1973). *The interpretation of culture: Selected essays.* New York, NY: Basic Books.

Goodenough, W. (1981). *Culture, language, and society.* New York, NY: Benjamin/Cummings.

Grossberg, L., Nelson, C., & Treichler, P. (1992). *Cultural studies.* New York, NY: Routledge.

Gupta, S. R. (2009). Beyond borders: Leading in today's multicultural world. In M. A. Moodian (Ed.), *Contemporary leadership and intercultural competence: Exploring the cross-cultural dynamics within organizations* (pp. 145–158). Thousand Oaks, CA: Sage.

Hall, S. (1997). The work of representations. In S. Hall (Ed.), *Representation: Cultural representations and signifying practices* (pp. 13–74). Thousand Oaks, CA: Sage.

Hyatt, L., Evans, L. A., & Haque, M. M. (2009). Leading across cultures: Designing a learning agenda for global praxis. In M. A. Moodian (Ed.), *Contemporary leadership and intercultural competence: Exploring the cross-cultural dynamics within organizations* (pp. 111–123). Thousand Oaks, CA: Sage.

Institute of International Education. (2014b). *Open Doors 2013: International students in the United States and study abroad by American students are at all-time high.* Retrieved from http://www.iie.org/Who-We-Are/News-and-Events/Press-Center/Press-releases/2013/2013-11-11-Open-Doors-Data

Kroeber, A., & Kluckhohn, C. (1952). *Culture: A critical review of concepts and definitions.* New York, NY: Vintage Books, a division of Random House.

Martin, J., & Nakayama, T. (2014). *Experiencing intercultural communication: An introduction.* New York, NY: McGraw-Hill.

Oetzel, J. G., Ting-Toomey, S., & Rinderle, S. (2006). Conflict communication in contexts: A social ecological perspective. In J. G. Oetzel & S. Ting-Toomey (Eds.), *The Sage handbook of conflict communication* (pp. 575–594). Thousand Oaks, CA: Sage.

Perkovich, G. H. (2006). *Is globalization headed for the rocks?* Carnegie Endowment for intercultural peace (pp. 1–6). Washington, DC: Carnegie Endowment for International Peace.

Sorrells, K. A. (2008). *Linking social justice and intercultural communication in the global context.* Portland, OR: Intercultural Communication Institute.

Ting-Toomey, S., & Chung, L. (2012). *Understanding intercultural communication.* New York, NY: Oxford University Press.

Young, R. (2001). *Postcolonialism: An historical introduction.* Malden, MA: Blackwell.

Yudice, G. (2003). *The expediency of culture: Uses of culture in the global era.* Durham, NC: Duke University.

Wood, J. (2014). *Communication in our lives.* Stamford, CT: Cengage Learning.

2. Intercultural Communication

Stephanie Sedberry Carrino

I would *never* talk to my mother like she does.
Married people shouldn't act like that!
Why do "they" live like that? Talk like that? Dress like that?
How can he *eat* that? Nasty!
Why is he looking at me that way?

What Is Intercultural Communication?

Have you ever heard someone ask a question like one listed above? If so, you have probably witnessed a breakdown in intercultural understanding. Intercultural communication occurs when people from different cultural groups communicate to try to co-create meaning or negotiate a shared understanding. The purpose of this communication might be to gather information, influence the other, establish a personal relationship, or just acknowledge the presence of another human being, and can occur in many settings. To be an effective, successful communicator, you'll need to add intercultural communication competence to your list of skills.

Like all communication, intercultural communication is complex and multi-faceted, and can be best understood by examining the principles, or foundational elements. Intercultural communication is:

- ▶ **Transactional:** Communicators send and receive messages simultaneously, through numerous channels and by using both language and nonverbal symbols.

- ▶ **A Process:** Communication is ongoing, meaning that we are communicating even if we do not intend to communicate. As long as there is another person around who attaches meaning to what we say or do, communication occurs.

- ▶ **Systemic:** All communication is part of a larger system in that what happens between people is affected by what has happened in the past. One aspect of your life affects others aspects and impacts your communication with others.

- ▶ **Dynamic:** Communication is not static, meaning that it is ever changing. Even the exact same phrase, stated in the same way to the same person, can mean something different every time.

- ▶ **Contextual:** All communication occurs within a context—a place and time—that influences the way we interpret what is communicated.

- ▶ **Symbolic:** All messages are symbolic, meaning that both the words we choose and the nonverbal signals are symbols we use to represent our ideas to others. We encode our thoughts and feelings into verbal and nonverbal messages and hope the other person decodes them in the way we intended.

Globalization, Immigration, and Technology

In past generations, intercultural communication was not as common as it is today. For many reasons, populations are shifting, resulting in the greater likelihood that we will encounter others who are culturally different. In fact, it may well be impossible to live in the United States today without having to connect with others from a variety of cultural backgrounds. *Globalization* refers to the increased connectedness of people from different cultural backgrounds. This connection can

J. Lekavicius/Shutterstock.com

be economic, through goods and natural resources, or informational. Certainly, increased international and intercultural business and trade have had a significant impact on globalization.

The greatest force in expanding globalization is, of course, technology. The many ever-expanding digital technologies, including the Internet, have enabled many global citizens to connect with others despite physical distance. Satellites broadcast TV stations from all over the world giving us access to the perspectives of other cultural groups. Much of our experience with others is now mediated through technology rather than based on face-to-face personal experience.

Immigration and travel have allowed people more freedom to move from place to place, often locating diverse people right next door. Many colleges and universities encourage students to study abroad for a semester or a year and welcome students from all over the world.

What Are Cultural Groups?

I have used the term *cultural group* to refer to any group of people who share a set of values, beliefs, attitudes, practices, traditions, and norms. In other words, any group of people who share "a way of life." Your cultural groups teach you what is right and wrong, good and bad, and how people are supposed to communicate with others. Cultural groups share *fields of meaning*, and these shared meanings give us our identities.

This broad definition allows a cultural group to refer to more than just people of different nationalities. Using this broad definition, a cultural group includes people who identify themselves as belonging to:

- A country or nationality: French, Sudanese, American, etc.

- Specific regions in a country: South, North, West Coast, USA; North Korea

- Generations: your grandparents, parents, and your age group

- A lifestyle: air heads/ potheads, emos, jocks, dramas, preps, hippies, gangsters, etc.

Alexander Image/Shutterstock.com

- Race/ethnicity: People of different racial groups can be seen as distinct cultural groups if you consider that racial groups share cultural history and present-day life experiences.

- Socio-economic status: poor, middle class, wealthy

- Gender: male, female, lesbian, gay, transgender

Obviously, we each belong to multiple cultural groups, all of which influence the way we see the world and communicate with others.

Components of Culture

So far we have discussed intercultural communication and cultural groups, but have not yet defined culture. *Culture* is a set of beliefs, values, attitudes, practices, traditions, speech patterns, and norms that are passed down from one generation to another and sustains a particular way of life. In short, a culture *is* a way of life—a guidebook for who you are and how you should relate to others. Your cultural groups form the basis for who you are by providing a *worldview*, or a way of thinking about the world and the people in it.

Cultures are by no means static—they can and do change—although they tend to be relatively stable. Listed below are some components or influences on culture:

- History (slavery, colonialism, etc.)
- Religion (core values and principles for living)
- Geography (temperature, climate, food availability, etc.)
- Institutions and organizations (education, the justice system, media, etc.)
- Major events (9/11, a tsunami, etc.)

Though cultures can differ widely, there are a number of orientations or values that can be used to compare and contrast cultures. As you read through the following list, try to think of examples to share with the class.

- ▶ Individualistic vs. collectivistic orientation . . . Is the focus on the individual or the group?
- ▶ Values equality for all people vs. accepts power inequality.
- ▶ Definitions of work and play and the balance between them.
- ▶ How conflict is managed . . . overtly? Covertly? Directly? Indirectly?
- ▶ How time is viewed . . . Is the focus on the past, present, or future? Is time measured by a clock or by other means, like the cycle of the day or season?
- ▶ How the ideas of "progress and change" are viewed . . . positively or negatively.
- ▶ Gender roles vary greatly across cultures, as do attitudes toward homosexuality and transgender people.

Our cultural orientations provide us with a basic understanding of the world and with challenges when we attempt to communicate with people who have different cultural understandings. One can be a more effective intercultural communicator just by being aware of these basic differences in worldview.

Language and Culture

Language and culture are interconnected. We learn about culture through language. When we listen to others' stories, we learn about their cultural understandings. One of the best ways to learn about a culture that is different from your own is to listen to the narratives—the fables, myths, news, histories, and other stories. You can also pay attention to the popular culture (like music, fashions, media, etc.) and artifacts (items or things).

In addition, language actually shapes culture as well. For example, the structure of language provides a framework for understanding. In some romance languages like Spanish and French, there are two different verbs for "to be": one indicates a temporary state and the other indicates a permanent state. In English, we only have one verb. Also, some cultures use much nonverbal communication to transmit meaning, while others rely primarily on words.

A professor of mine used to say: "My enemy is someone whose story I do not yet know." What he meant is that our conflicts often come from a place of cultural misunderstanding. If we listen to the stories of others with an open mind, we might find our commonalities beneath the difference in culture.

Nonverbal Communication and Culture

Just as with language, nonverbal communication is also culture-bound. What this means is that nonverbal signs and signals can be interpreted differently across cultural groups. Eye contact, gestures, physical distance, turn-taking practices, sounds, and other body movements can be understood differently based on cultural context.

Business Communication and Culture

In the business world, as in all contexts, there are rules for how people are supposed to communicate. In a typical American business interaction, we shake hands to greet the other, keep a foot or two of distance between us, make direct eye contact, smile, and exchange business cards. However, this code of conduct is very American! Other cultures have their own rules for conducting business, and your success in *intercultural business* is dependent on your knowledge of the cultural practices and norms. A friend of mine was asked to work in an office in Japan for a few weeks, and he was required to study the Japanese "way" before he went. His company wanted to make sure he would not inadvertently offend his new coworkers.

Words of Caution

As with most ideas, understanding culture and intercultural communication strategies have both benefits and limitations. The obvious benefit is that you can be more effective in your interactions and experience richer relationships with others from distinct cultural backgrounds. However, you need to be careful not to oversimplify or overgeneralize the cultural characteristics of individuals you meet. While cultural groups strongly influence who we are, they do not determine who we are. Individuals have the ability to change, create, and recreate themselves, and we need to keep an open mind about the possibilities.

While having categories for people makes a complex world easier to understand, it can also exaggerate the differences between people, rather than focus on the similarities. In the end, human beings do share the common experience of being human! Our shared fields of meaning are often larger than we might initially think.

The major problem with fixed or rigid views on culture is stereotyping, which can lead to prejudice and ethnocentrism. *Ethnocentrism* is the belief that your culture is superior to others. Often, our ethnocentric tendencies lead us to avoid interacting with others who are culturally distinct, or we become intolerant and reject them. Everyone deserves the chance to define himself or herself and be seen as an individual.

Developing Intercultural Communication Competence

Sometimes intercultural communication goes well with little effort. When there are shared fields of meaning, then intercultural understanding is easy. However, more often than not, when intercultural communication is successful, it is because one or more of the people in the transaction has intercultural communication competence.

Communication competence refers to the ability to communicate effectively with others. Intercultural communication competence is the ability to communicate effectively with others from different cultural backgrounds, and it is a skill that can be developed.

Self-awareness is the first step toward becoming an effective intercultural communicator. Remember, we have all been socialized to see the world from a particular point of view and to communicate in a particular way. How has your cultural background shaped who you are? How might others have been shaped differently?

The next step in becoming an effective intercultural communicator is to develop a *dual-perspective*, or empathy toward others. This is the ability to temporarily step outside your own worldview so you can try to understand the worldview of another person.

Developing good listening habits is another way to enhance your intercultural competence. *Active listening* is a process where you really attend to the messages of another person and interact with them to check your understanding. This involves your ears, eyes, body, and mind!

Finally, remember that effective intercultural communication is based on the *recognition of cultural differences* and a respect for cultural differences. Just because someone or something is different, it does not have to be judged as "bad." Try to adopt an "I'm OK, you're OK" approach to others, and you will be amazed at the connections you can make with people from a variety of cultural groups.

Discussion Questions

1. Select a scene from a movie or novel that depicts intercultural communication. Discuss how well (or poorly) the characters managed the transaction.
2. Write an "I am from . . ." poem. The only guideline is that the first line has to start with the words "I am from . . ." This exercise will help you to see how your cultural background has influenced who you are today.
3. Create a list of the cultural groups you identify with and some that you do not identify with. Are there any commonalities between the two lists?
4. Imagine what your life might have been like had you been born into a different cultural group. How might you be different today?

3. Dialogic Communication: A Foundation for Authentic Intercultural Communication

Joe DeCrosta, Ph.D.
Andrea Patterson-Masuka, Ph.D.

Courtney's frustration and impatience began the moment she landed at the airport in Rio de Janeiro, Brazil, to make her connecting flight to Belo Horizonte, Brazil, to begin her summer study abroad program at the Universidade Federal de Minas Gerais. She could barely understand the speaker's Portuguese over the intercom. To say the least, she was frustrated as there were only minutes to spare to make her connecting flight because she stood in the wrong line for over an hour. When she arrived in Belo Horizonte, Courtney was relieved to see a familiar sign with her name held by one of the professors from the university. She had been traveling for 24 hours, there was a three-hour time difference from home and she had had enough—she was extremely tired and confused. Why was she doing this? When her host professor dropped her off at her new residence hall—if that is what you call it—she told her that she would be back in a few hours and all of the new students would go to dinner at a famous Brazilian churrascaria, *a typical Brazilian steakhouse, around 9 p.m. The dinner lingered for several hours and Courtney barely attempted to speak any Portuguese, eat any of the food, or get to know any of the other American study abroad or Brazilian students. She thought that having dinner at such a late hour was ridiculous; how could anyone expect her to digest all this heavy beef at such a late hour after traveling for an entire day? She quickly declined when they offered to take her to a nightclub after dinner. Courtney only wanted to go back to her room and call her parents and best friend, Lisa. Oh wait . . . she could not contact anyone until she purchased a SIM card for her phone or bought a new phone; no one even offered to help her figure that out yet. Courtney's response of her first day was indicative of the rest of her time in Brazil. During her first week, she spent more time on the video chat and SMS with her friends being critical of her new environment and her hosts. Nothing made sense and it was all rather annoying. Little did she know that time was quickly running out to explore one of the loveliest cities in Brazil, a world-class university, and to immerse herself in a culture that might be considered one of the warmest and most welcoming in the world.*

Three hours away in the city of Rio de Janeiro, Courtney's classmate Tasha had just arrived to study abroad at the Universidade Federal do Rio de Janeiro. Tasha's curiosity about her new home was overwhelming as she would inquire about every detail that flashed across her radar. During her layover in Sao Paulo, she sat beside a young Brazilian woman named Renata. Tasha, aware that her Portuguese was far from fluent, took a deep breath and introduced herself. The student smiled broadly and told Tasha in English that she was a student enrolled at the same university. Tasha took a big sigh of relief; although she was nervous she was glad she took the time to engage in dialogue and open up the conversation with someone from a different culture—her new host culture. Her host professor from the

Federal University of Rio de Janeiro invited her out to dinner that evening. Although Tasha was tired—no, exhausted—she took a shower to refresh herself and shake off her long travels. She realized how important it was to connect with the Brazilian students and the other study abroad participants if this experience was going to be as transformative as they say it could be. Unlike Courtney in Belo Horizonte, she welcomed the invitation to go to a Brazilian nightclub that same night. Although she was tired the next day, she accepted yet another invitation to take the bus and go shopping, and she even ventured on the public transportation known as the local metro. The Brazilian students warmed up to her personality and enthusiasm so much that she was invited to her new Brazilian friend's, Ana Lucia's, home as early as her second weekend. She was so excited and nervous the night before that she could barely sleep. Tasha could not wait to leave the college campus and have local dinner with a real Brazilian family; how would she interact with them in Portuguese, what questions should she ask, what would they ask her, and what would the conversation be like? How was she going to do this while being herself at the same time? Tasha finally drifted off to sleep, looking forward to her new informal learning experience, and soon would learn that Ana Lucia's family would welcome her with open arms and "adopt" her as a new honorary member of the family even after she would leave Brazil. Needless to say, Tasha's willingness to be vulnerable, open herself up to new, sometimes intimidating, experiences, and engage in authentic dialogue with new people from a different culture would undoubtedly open the door to a semester of informal learning experiences and intercultural dialogue that would affect her for a lifetime, and even shift her professional goals into the future.

After "seeing" these two contrasting experiences above, we invite you to investigate intercultural communication framed in what communication scholars call a "dialogic approach." In this chapter, we will explore the concept of dialogue as it relates to intercultural communication and the model/concept of Intercultural Praxis in particular. These approaches are interesting alternatives to traditional approaches to human communication and offer new perspectives on how we interact and engage the world around us. It is important to remember that there is "no universally accepted approach within the social sciences, although there are rich traditions that cannot be ignored" (Rudestam & Newton, 2011, p. 23); dialogue and intercultural praxis are two orientations to communication that have become legitimate approaches to human interaction that should not be ignored when exploring

CREATISTA/Shutterstock.com

ways to engage the world around us. A dialogical approach to intercultural communication will inspire you to use your voice to challenge the disparities and injustices you see throughout the world all too often. By engaging ideas of dialogue framed within intercultural communication, we are called to imagine and create a world where the sound of each voice is welcomed, heard, and empowered—it can open doors to new worlds that we never knew existed.

Dialogue and Intercultural Communication

Brazilian educator and philosopher Paulo Freire (1970) believed that "Without dialogue there is no communication, and without communication there can be no true education" (p. 93). In this sense, dialogue is viewed as a way of knowing, viewing, and understanding the world. Although we are familiar with the word "**dialogue**" in a general sense, and we assume that we participate in it regularly, it is helpful to consider its linguistic and philosophical origins as we examine how dialogue is used in intercultural communication today.

The word dialogue is derived from the Greek word "dialogos." The term "dia" means "through," "between," or "across," and "logos" refers to "word" or "the meaning of the word," as well as "speech" or "thought." Philosopher and physicist David Bohm (1996) contends that the "picture or the image that this derivation suggests is a stream of meaning among and through us and between us" (p. 6).

Hence, according to Freire's concept of liberation, we ultimately form a critical consciousness through dialogue that is formed in utterances and words and achieve liberation through dialogue in the way it manifests itself in words and phrases. Freire (1970) states that "constant dialogue and awareness must be self-guarded to avoid the relationship of the oppressor-oppressor and it is existential necessity" (p. 87). Engaging in dialogue allows us to listen to other voices as well as to speak openly. Effective dialogue allows us to have authentic conversations about issues of culture, race, disabilities, homelessness, poverty, war, and peace, to name a few. The practice of dialogue can help us develop a sense of critical consciousness and hear our own voices; our identity is formed in relation to the self and other individuals. In this sense, dialogue can be viewed as a way of knowing, or *epistemology.*

Dialogue and the Human Connection

Traditionally, dialogic communication is viewed as a form of communication theory that explains how meaning and relationships emerge interpersonally through discussion of existence (existential) and what it means to be human (ontological). Scholars such as Bakhtin (1981), Levinas (2004), and Buber (1988, 1996, 2002), among others, have all grappled with existential questions of ethics and being through the act of human dialogue and how it affects the ways in which we communicate, create meaning, structure thought, and exist as human beings in community. Although dialogic theory from this perspective has been readily appropriated to studies of interpersonal and intergroup communication, there are direct linkages to discussion of intercultural communication. We turn to Jewish philosopher Martin Buber because of his detailed treatment of dialogue not only as a philosophy of communication, but also as a practical application for human communicative acts. Buber's ideas may open up particular lines of inquiry that emerge from our experiences of communicating with "the Other" as well as a communication ethic that leads us to build bridges with our communication partners as well as with the communication experience itself.

For Buber, dialogue is a quintessential element of community that involves a connection between communication partners. As he explored the nature of human life, and more importantly our communion with each other, Buber believed it was the roles of speech and dialogue that truly made us human. He believed that dialogue enables us to have an "I-Thou relationship," which is perhaps the most sacred and precious of all human relationships. "I" and "Thou" were not two separate concepts, but rather one "primary word," emphasized by the connective hyphen which transforms the two concepts into one. The I-Thou relationship occurs when people are not referred to or treated as objects, but rather full participants in the communication act and therefore participants in acts of being—ontological acts. Conversely, when we objectify our communication partners in one-directional, non-interactive methods, we are engaging in monologue—a "talking-at" form of communication. "[M]onologue [is] disguised as dialogue, in which two or more men . . . speak each with himself in strangely tortuous and circuitous ways" (Buber, 2002, p. 22). Authentic dialogue, as opposed to monologue, thus allows us to forge mutual understanding and meaningful relationships in the deepest manner; listening then becomes a critical communication act. It is through dialogic communication that we engage the world and respond to the Other; meaning emerges "between Man and Man," in the communities in which we live, not in a vacuum of solitary confinement (p. 23).

This notion of dialogic versus monologic communication has been appropriated to describe what we might popularly call not only "effective" communication, but also meaningful communication guided by an ethical orientation (Anderson, Arnett, & Cissna, 1994; Anderson, Baxter, & Cissna, 2004; Arnett, 2004). Although monologue is important and has its place in the realm of human life and action in appropriate contexts (Arnett, Fritz, & Bell, 2009), dialogic communication provides a space for us to speak about effective communication that takes the human element into consideration. Dialogue is not simply about two people exchanging ideas, rather it is about people exchanging ideas that will transform them and ultimately make a difference for issues that may otherwise be considered insurmountable.

Given the above discussion, one might readily assign this notion of communication, but Buber's understanding of dialogic communication is not confined to the interpersonal; rather, it is a modality of turning toward existence, an embodied communicative approach that influences all other modes of communication whether they are interpersonal, intergroup, intercultural, or international, essentially because it is "interhuman." In Buber's world, the "voice of the particular" must be heard above the various political institutions and conversations that take place in a larger context. In short, Buber's dialogue is not only an ontological explanation of the interpersonal relationship, but it is a vehicle for allowing voices to connect to each other substantively on a much larger scale—socially, interculturally, and internationally. However, we must understand Buber's philosophical anthropology—a philosophy focused on the whole human being—and how it offered credence to the interpersonal relationship, the necessity of "turning towards" the Other, to offer his philosophy as an overlay to our discussion about intercultural communication.

Anderson and Cissna (1997) situate Buber as an important, although perhaps less evident, contributor to the postmodern conversation on dialogue. They investigate how his philosophy helps us explore alternative philosophical standpoints for human communication at every level of interaction—"the interpersonal, intergroup, inter-social, or intercultural, and international"—what Buber coins "interhuman." Buber's anthropological philosophy is significant in the conversation about dialogic theory because it encourages us to explore "how to turn toward, address, and respect otherness" (Anderson & Cissna, 1997, pp. 109–110). Arnett and Arneson (1999) point out that Buber sets himself apart from other dialogic theorists in the way he views the self as deeply situated in the narratives of the historical moment. Buber recognized the embeddedness of these individuals in narratives and their existence as communicative, dialogic beings that emerge out of intersubjective consciousness—the "interhuman"—and the meaning that emerges "between" those persons engaged in dialogic communication. The self does not exist in a self-reliant vacuum for Buber, but rather a relational, ontological realm where meaning and responsibility emerge (Arnett & Arneson, 1999). The concept of the "between" becomes a consistent metaphor in Buber's work (Buber, 1996, 2002). In a need to address "the between," Buber addresses our disillusionment with institutions that are constructed to support human activity, and most importantly, human relations. Buber distinguishes between emotions and the self, and that the human communicative relationship builds community through reciprocity. Strong, functional communities are the results of a dialogic relationship that emerges in the "between," not an egotistical focus on developing one's self without the guidance of the narrative, or what he refers to as the "center" (Buber, 1996, p. 94). Buber recognizes that the reality of shifting meaning and multiple narratives which lack a guiding metanarrative does not have to mean that we are lost in a world of individualism and personal emotions; rather, community is still possible when we find this "center."

Buber's dialogic theory also speaks about the "quality" of contact through instrumental and objective means (Stewart, Zediker, & Black, 2004, p. 33). Arnett (2004) explains that this "quality" in dialogic communication is inherently ethical and elicits what he calls a "responsive ethical I" (p. 87). A "responsive ethical I" is one that understands that responsibility rests in our true dialogic relationships with the Other—relationships that acknowledge a "decentered self" who is committed to the Other and also responsive to the historical moment (p. 88). The "I" cannot exist without the "Other," as the "I" finds itself emerging out of responsiveness to the "Other" while recognizing the narratives that live around them and within which they dwell.

This "responsive ethical I" also leads us to engage dialogics in terms of community. Arnett's work on Buber and what dialogic theory means for community (Arnett, 1986) actually preceded his work on the "responsive ethical I" (Arnett, 2004), but it seems that this "I" is a requirement of dialogic communication and applies to the formation of healthy, productive communities. Communities are a result of this "fuzzy clarity" or "communicative poetic" because they emerge from what Arnett refers to as "dialogic tension." "[C]ommunity . . . is not rooted in a precise definition, but in an attitude sensitive to the dialogical tension between self, other, and . . . a group or organization" (Arnett, 1986, p. 17). However, we must be careful not to conceptualize community as collectivism. Buber warns, "Modern collectivism is the last barrier raised by man against a meeting with himself" (Buber, 2002, p. 239). In other words, man is not dialogically joined with man in a collective; otherwise, he is embedding himself in a collective that masks his true relationship with the other and himself. In community, there is a dialogic tie that recognizes and acknowledges the other as an embedded other and all that comes with her—uncertainty, tension, agreement, disagreement, and cooperation—a full menu of life's experiences. However, living in community requires a thoughtful response to everyday communication, or what Buber called the "narrow ridge"—an alternative to the dualistic form of oppositional communication that we are often accustomed to, particularly in contemporary Western culture. The "narrow ridge" depolarizes our communication recognized through multiple viewpoints, "as an alternative to absolute positions that characterize communication in a polarized community" (Arnett, 1986, p. 31). The "narrow ridge" is also an ontological communicative space where contingency thrives as a positive element of human communication, where answers are reached and solutions are discovered. A linear, rational methodology for problem-solving may not always be the solution; instead, through a constructive conversation of opposing viewpoints, answers emerge in the "between," textured even more by the diacritic of what has been described as Buber's "unity of contraries" (Arnett, 1986, p. 65; Arnett & Arneson, 1999, p. 142). It is important to note, however, that Buber referred to the "unity of contraries" when discussing mankind's tendency to escape individual responsibility under the protection of the collective. Not until the individual was able to achieve a sense of unity would she be able to emerge from the collective to engage in dialogic communication and, therefore, the productive, meaningful construct of community (Buber, 2002, pp. 137–138). Buber sets himself apart from other philosophers of communication, and scholars of dialogue in particular, because he believes that dialogic communication is deeply rooted in and between people. His theory is a practical approach to intersubjectively lived experiences that address real, daily problems. In essence, it is through dialogue that we begin to know and understand the other. The process of learning about the other cultures, their lifestyles, their stories of family, struggles, and how they define themselves and their world is critical to the process of becoming more culturally competent global citizens.

Unfortunately, we can see that even in the college classroom dialogic communication is often difficult to achieve when the main method of instruction—lecturing—is pervasive. Such an approach threatens to infect us with what Freire would call "narration sickness," and the idea of "monologue" dominates the communicative act. Like Martin Buber, Russian philosopher Mikhail Bakhtin (1984) was concerned with this idea of **monologism.** Bakhtin (1984) believed that, "Life by its very nature is dialogic. To live means to participate in dialogue" (p. 293); it is through this process that we learn about other people, reflect, and eventually create a critical consciousness. Bakhtin was concerned about what he considered to be the oppressive character of monologue, the monopolization of meaning, and the ruling out and suppression of all competing voices. These philosophers' hatred of monologue became the driving force for the development of his concept of dialogue. He viewed life as an ongoing, unending dialogue taking place at every moment of our existence. Dialogism is Bakhtin's attempt to counteract pervasive monologism because dialogue can cut across cultural, religious, national, and political boundaries.

Buber (2002), Bakhtin (1984), and Freire (1970) all contend that it is through the process of dialogue that we achieve importance and meaning as human beings; dialogue enables us to name and thus transform our universe. "Dialogue is thus an existential necessity" (Freire, 1970, p. 88). Dialogue can create authentic, truthful, and meaningful discussion among students over issues such as immigration, affirmative action, legislation before Congress, climate change, same-sex marriages, and global social and political issues. A dialogic approach to intercultural communication can help transform the culture of silence and injustice that pervades our world. According to Bakhtin, language cannot be separated from ideology; he uses this term to mean a socially-determined idea system. He distinguishes between a nation's unitary language and its stratification into dialects and various socio-ideological languages past and present among social groups. Bakhtin's concept of *heteroglossia*, or a multitude of voices, helps us understand why it is essential to develop intercultural competencies in an ever-changing world. The increasing need for multicultural awareness and intercultural engagement in our society—in schools, universities, government, as well as social and political institutions—has placed a new emphasis on dialogue in all academic disciplines, even those outside of the liberal arts and social sciences (Mangano, 2015).

A dialogic approach to intercultural communication can help us as global citizens envision how we will live, negotiate, and participate in a multicultural society with a sense of ethics, social justice, and purpose. Dialogue becomes the foundation for understanding the importance of communication in our intercultural world. Intercultural Praxis (Sorrells, 2008) is one theoretical/conceptual construct through which we can put dialogic communication into action.

Intercultural Praxis

One innovative approach for studying intercultural communication is the theoretical framework of *Intercultural Praxis*, developed by Sorrells (2008). It was initially developed for understanding intercultural communication in the context of globalization and provides strategies and methods for interrogating power that pervades the globalization debate in terms of culture, communication, and economics. The integration of *Intercultural Praxis* as a pedagogical framework is grounded in critical theory, the philosophy of Paulo Freire, and a combination of intercultural theories. This framework can aid in our understanding of our intercultural encounters and perspectives and hence help us become more effective communicators in a global society. Sorrells (2008) describes *Intercultural Praxis* as the process of "critical, reflective, engaged thinking and action" that enables us to comprehend "other cultures, find their voice, engage in critical dialogue, and become empowered to use communication to advocate for social justice" (Sorrells, 2008, p. 206).

In this section we will briefly explain this model or concept of Intercultural Praxis and how it can be applied as a pedagogical framework for our study in intercultural communication. The six points of entry for intercultural praxis include *inquiry, framing, positioning,*

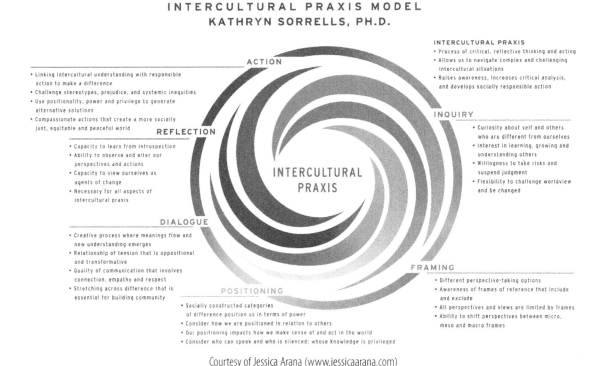

INTERCULTURAL PRAXIS MODEL
KATHRYN SORRELLS, PH.D.

INTERCULTURAL PRAXIS
- Process of critical, reflective thinking and acting
- Allows us to navigate complex and challenging intercultural situations
- Raises awareness, increases critical analysis, and develops socially responsible action

ACTION
- Linking intercultural understanding with responsible action to make a difference
- Challenge stereotypes, prejudice, and systemic inequities
- Use positionality, power and privilege to generate alternative solutions
- Compassionate actions that create a more socially just, equitable and peaceful world

INQUIRY
- Curiosity about self and others who are different from ourselves
- Interest in learning, growing and understanding others
- Willingness to take risks and suspend judgment
- Flexibility to challenge worldview and be changed

REFLECTION
- Capacity to learn from introspection
- Ability to observe and alter our perspectives and actions
- Capacity to view ourselves as agents of change
- Necessary for all aspects of intercultural praxis

INTERCULTURAL PRAXIS

DIALOGUE
- Creative process where meanings flow and new understanding emerges
- Relationship of tension that is oppositional and transformative
- Quality of communication that involves connection, empathy and respect
- Stretching across difference that is essential for building community

FRAMING
- Different perspective-taking options
- Awareness of frames of reference that include and exclude
- All perspectives and views are limited by frames
- Ability to shift perspectives between micro, meso and macro frames

POSITIONING
- Socially constructed categories of difference position us in terms of power
- Consider how we are positioned in relation to others
- Our positioning impacts how we make sense of and act in the world
- Consider who can speak and who is silenced; whose knowledge is privileged

Courtesy of Jessica Arana (www.jessicaarana.com)

dialogue, reflection, and action. The intent of Intercultural Praxis is to increase our awareness, critical reflection, and development of a socially responsible way of taking action. One is not required to enter intercultural praxis from inquiry, but rather may enter the process at different points and times during the intercultural encounter.

Inquiry

Inquiry as a place of entry for Intercultural Praxis means a wish and willingness to know, ask, find out, and learn. Exploratory inquiry about those who are unalike leads us to engage seriously with others. We are willing to take risks and be open to other perspectives. In other words, inquiry is viewed as an invitation to question; it is used as a space for interrogation. Questions are asked such as: "Whose knowledge is presented?" and "What ideologies are reinforced?" For instance, inquiry may inspire you to learn more about your classmate from another country or cultural background. It may also increase your desire to invite this person to join your group for a class project.

Framing

The term and action of framing suggests that our perspectives—our views of ourselves, others, and the world around us—are ultimately limited by frames. Framing as a point of entry in Intercultural Praxis means that we are able to zoom in and to focus on the particular and very situated details of a specific exchange or interaction. Engaging in framing allows us to become more aware of the perspective of others. In the beginning of the chapter, Courtney engaged in the dominant framing of the U.S. cultural standpoint by being critical of the cultural norms surrounding dinner on her first night in Brazil. In developing a class assignment, you may consider developing a presentation or conducting research from the standpoint of an immigrant group in our society—as a homeless person or someone afflicted with an incurable disease.

Positioning

Sorrells (2010) contends that it is critical to be able to locate "knowing" in one's body/experience. This embodiment makes one mindful of the material, intellectual, and practical consequences of the curriculum and what we observe in the world. Moreover, it allows you to develop an authentic way of knowing—other than from a textbook. Once students are able to make connections between reality and their experiences, we can move to engage in meaningful dialogue.

Dialogue

As discussed earlier through dialogic theory, there is no doubt that dialogue provides a significant point of entry into intercultural praxis as well. This entry point of dialogue invites you to view intercultural communication as a site of "dynamic meaning-making."

Engaging in dialogue allows us to stretch ourselves and communicate different ways of thinking, being, and knowing, and accepting other cultures' differences while acknowledging that we may not fully understand another person's point of view or position. Here, we hear echoes of Freire's, Buber's, and Bakhtin's deep philosophical analyses of dialogue and how it takes us to even more meaningful and substantive forms of communication.

Reflection

Reflection allows us to ponder upon our experiences, encounters, and thoughts, what was effective that day, and what was not effective. It affords us to consider our interactions for areas of synergy and growth. In participating in reflection as a communicator, you are better able to step back and think about your encounters with other people, and to make connections with what you are learning in your classes and readings. Engaging in this reflective process can help you in utilizing your newly-developed communication tools for action.

Action

Intercultural Praxis not only challenges us to move beyond curious inquiry, framing, positioning, and reflecting, but to also take action. In intercultural communication, action is a site for engagement, as it invites us to look at what actually is the connection, what is our involvement and responsibility in the entire learning process. Communication for global engagement involving action looks at how we can encourage and engage to make significant differences in society. In engaging in *Intercultural Praxis*, we are able to push beyond the boundaries of the classroom, community, culture, and country. By becoming mindful of what the process of intercultural communication entails and engaging this idea of dialogue and Intercultural Praxis in particular, we may become more flexible intercultural communicators.

Moving Forward

If we begin to analyze Courtney's and Tasha's approaches to communication in their new intercultural experiences through a lens of Intercultural Praxis, we can see how Tasha's experience appears richer and more transformative because of the way she *inquired* about her new surroundings, *framed* or oriented her experience to benefit more from a challenging situation, *positioned* herself in the new situation, *engaged in authentic dialogue* with those around her, *reflected* on her transformation as someone who was actively learning from a new culture, and *acted* on the challenges that were placed before her. Philosophical and practical dialogue, although an element of Sorrell's intercultural praxis, also serves as the foundation for that which would follow in each of their experiences. Where they wished to take the experience depended on how they chose *to communicate* and thus *live* their shifting cultural boundaries.

As we learn about intercultural communication in the context of globalization, a dialogical approach requires us to examine the complexities of power dynamics and to understand the significance of culture, history and politics, to see how we can increase our understanding of ourselves and others' cultures, as well as the larger world we inhabit. According to Freire, only when teachers and students come together as critical co-investigators can we move beyond simply interpreting our world and engaging it in meaningful and productive ways. Ultimately, communication is not only about persuasion and the exchange of ideas and information, but it is a call to action that piques our curiosity and seduces our very being to know more. For these reasons, this book is a collaborative effort between interdisciplinary scholars as well as students who have experienced authentic instances of intercultural communication. In the spirit of dialogue, and Bakhtin's concept of *heteroglossia*—we all can learn from each other with the contribution of multiple voices.

Discussion Questions

1. Does dialogue seem like a practical approach to dealing with intercultural problems or does it seem overly theoretical and out of reach for the everyday practitioner of communication? Why or why not?
2. What are some practical examples of how we can apply the concept of dialogue to everyday life, and in particular, other relevant intercultural situations?
3. Dialogue often seems like a communication that can be readily applied to interpersonal and small group communication, but how might we apply this idea to larger issues like political, social, cultural, and economic forms of globalization? Give some examples.
4. Was there a time in your life when you think this concept of dialogue might have been applied more effectively to help you resolve a communication challenge? Explain.
5. Identify a case of intercultural communication in your life or in the world at large at this moment. How might you frame the situation according to Sorrells's model of Intercultural Praxis and the six points of entry?

References

Anderson, R., Arnett, R. C., & Cissna, K. (1994). *The reach of dialogue: Confirmation, voice and community.* New York, NY: Hampton Press.

Anderson, R., Baxter, L., & Cissna, K. (2004). Texts and contexts in dialogue. In R. Anderson, L. Baxter, & K. Cissna (Eds.), *Dialogue: Theorizing differences in communication studies* (pp. 1–19). Thousand Oaks, CA: Sage.

Anderson, R., & Cissna, K. N. (Eds.). (1997). *The Martin Buber–Carl Rogers dialogue: A new transcript with commentary.* Albany, NY: State University of New York Press.

Arnett, R. C. (1986). *Communication and community: Implications of Martin Buber's dialogue.* Carbondale, IL: Southern Illinois University Press.

Arnett, R. C. (2004). A dialogic ethical "between" Buber and Levinas: A responsive ethical "I." In R. Anderson, L. A. Baxter, & K. N. Cissna (Eds.), *Dialogue: Theorizing difference in communication studies* (pp. 75–90). Thousand Oaks, CA: Sage.

Arnett, R. C., & Arneson, P. (1999). *Dialogic civility in a cynical age: Community, hope and interpersonal relationships.* Albany, NY: State University of New York.

Arnett, R. C., Fritz, J. H., & Bell, L. M. (2009). *Communication ethics literacy: Dialogue and difference.* Thousand Oaks, CA: Sage.

Bakhtin, M. (1981). *The dialogic imagination* (M. Holquest, Ed.). Austin, TX: University of Austin Press.

Bakhtin, M. (1984). *Rabelais and his world* (H. Iswolsky, Trans.). Bloomington, IN: Indiana University Press.

Bohm, D. (1996). *On dialogue.* New York, NY: Routledge.

Buber, M. (1988). *The knowledge of man: Selected essays.* Atlantic Highlands, NJ: Humanities Press International.

Buber, M. (1996). *I and thou* (W. Kaufmann Trans.). New York, NY: Touchstone.

Buber, M. (2002). *Between man and man* (R. Gregor-Smith, Trans.). London: Routledge.

Freire, P. (1970). *Pedagogy of the oppressed.* New York, NY: Continuum.

Levinas, E. (2004). *Otherwise than being, or beyond essence* (A. Lingis, Trans.). Pittsburgh, PA: Duquesne University Press.

Mangano, M. F. (2015). *Dialogue, a space between, across and beyond cultures and disciplines: A case study in transcultural and transdisciplinary communication.* In N. Haydari & P. Holmes (Eds.), *Case studies in intercultural dialogue* (pp. 73–86). Dubuque, IA: Kendall Hunt.

Rudestam, K., & Newton, R. (2011). *Surviving your dissertation: A comprehensive guide to content and process.* Thousand Oaks, CA: Sage.

Sorrells, K. A. (2008). *Linking social justice and intercultural communication in the global context.* Portland, OR: Intercultural Communication Institute.

Sorrells, K. A. (2010). *Towards a politics of locations: Relationships and ruptures in the multicultural curriculum and classroom.* Northridge: Unpublished Manuscript.

Stewart, J., Zediker, K., & Black, L. (2004). Relationships among philosophies of dialogue. In R. Anderson, L. Baxter, & K. Cissna (Eds.). *Dialogue: Theorizing differences in communication studies* (pp. 21–38). Thousand Oaks, CA: Sage.

4. Globalization and Intercultural Communication: Interwoven Themes

Andrea Patterson-Masuka, Ph.D.

Lisa, an American student at a university in North Carolina, was extremely frustrated. She could not install the software for her printer on her new laptop. After several failed attempts, she called the 1-800 phone number for the printer.

The technical support person was extremely helpful and spent half an hour walking her through each step of the installation process. Lisa was relieved and grateful. She had her section of the group PowerPoint due for her intercultural communication class. The project focused on popular culture. Lisa's section highlighted the influence of Bollywood and India on popular culture. Lisa wanted to print her slides to preview and edit before submitting them to her group.

Without realizing it, Lisa experienced the interwoven relationship of intercultural communication and globalization in a digital world. Her laptop was manufactured by a Japanese company, her printer was manufactured by an American company assembled in China. The technical support person was sitting in a cubicle in Bangalore, India. Her research focused on another part of the globe—India. What factors shaped the interaction described above? The scenario demonstrates the impact of globalization in today's world society. With advances in technology from communications (the cell phone, the Internet) to global transportation technology and open global markets, intercultural communication and interaction have become a common occurrence.

This chapter begins with an introduction of the critical role history plays in the context of intercultural communication and globalization. To understand the complexity of globalization, we will examine the aspects of social/cultural, economic, and political globalization. Following this section, we will analyze the role of power and the popular resistance to globalization. Our study will conclude with a discussion of the imperative to balance the explosion of technology in the context of globalization with intercultural sensitivity.

The Role of History in Intercultural Communication and Globalization

Stephanie Carrino (2012) refers to globalization as the "increased connectedness of people from different cultural backgrounds. These connections can be economic, through goods and natural resources, or informational" (p. 73). In fact, people have traveled around the globe exchanging cultural goods, practices, and ideas, and have consequently been involved in intercultural communication for centuries. For nearly 3,000 years, Europeans have traversed sand and seas to buy from, and trade with, the Far East for silk and satin. It is important to note that Islamic and Mongol empires had far reaches. European domination and conquests, beginning in the sixteenth century, changed global migration patterns and have a profound impact on our world today. Authors Held, McGrew, Goldblatt, and Perraton (1999) note in the book *Global Transformation: Politics, Economics, and Culture* that during the European colonial period, people migrated not only from Spain, Europe, Portugal, and England, but also France, Belgium, and Holland to Asia, Africa, and Oceania with the goal of economic gain, territorial conquest, and religious conversion. Settlers from these countries formed colonies in these conquered countries. As we know from our study of history, between the 1600s and the 1850s, nine to 12 million Africans were forcibly moved, mainly to the Americas during the transatlantic slave trade. In the nineteenth century, Indians were forced to live under British colonial rule and some were subjected to relocate to colonies in Africa and Oceania (Young, 2001). This process of colonization, based upon the stripping and exploitation of natural and human resources, established Europe as a central world power and the colonies as the borders.

Further into the nineteenth century, after the British and Spanish colonies had gained independence in the Americas, a massive migration erupted with the working class and poor people from economically and war-distressed countries of Europe to the United States of America and other countries including Brazil, Chile, Argentina, and others (Young, 2001). The migration of indentured laborers from Asia—mainly Japan, China, and Phillipines to the United States, Canada, and other former European colonies, made the number of migrants explode to more than 40 million people before World War II (Sorrells, 2013).

The Second World War ushered in the unparalled restriction of national borders and the development and enactment of immigration legislation and border controls in the United States of America in recent history. The unprecedented ethnically-motivated violence, mass murder, and genocide of WWII led to the exodus of Jews from Europe to the United States, Latin America, and Israel. In response to the devastation of human lives, political structures, economies, and natural resources across Europe, Japan, and Russia, first organizations of economic and world political governing bodies were created, including the World Bank (WB), the International Monetary Fund (IMF), and the United Nations (UN) (Sorrells, 2013).

Consequently, since the 1960s, with the rise of economic power in the United States and the rebuilding of Europe as an economic power, there is a migratory pattern shift. The migration of immigrants from Europe to the United States at the beginning of the twentieth century is mirrored today by the influx of immigrants from Asia and Latin America to the United States.

In addition to this stream of people was the flow of people from Africa and Asia to the oil-rich countries of the Middle East, as well as regional migration patterns within Latin America, Africa, and East Asia (Young, 2001). During the latter part of the twentieth century, the increase of people looking for asylum and refugees fleeing for a variety of reasons including war, famine, and natural distasters has risen substantially (Held et al., 1999).

Sorrells and Nakagawa (2008) argue that the current wave of globalization, deeply rooted in European colonization and Western imperialism, have thrust people from different countries and cultures together in physical and virtual spaces. All the facets of globalization including social/cultural, political, and economical depict the interwoven connection of people, culture, market, and the connection to power that is rooted in history and is evident in today's world. The intent of this chapter is not to highlight history and globalization. However, it is important to note that history plays a profound role in intercultural communication within the context of globalization.

In recent years, significant developments in governance, economics, politics, and educational institutions have combined with changes in communication technology and transportation to have exponentially increased the interaction and relations of humans from different religious, ethnic, social, national, and international cultures around the world (Sorrells, 2008).

Many people around the world, however, regard globalization with suspicion, apprehension, and trepidation. They worry about its impact on humanity. Some people view it as a threat to jobs, livelihood, and culture. It increasingly leads to inequality between countries—wealth for a few, and mounting poverty for many. Globalization is complicated and means many things to different people.

Rawpixel/Shutterstock.com

Globalization

In India, China, or Vietnam, globalization may be viewed as economic prosperity and opportunity, while in Afghanistan or Iraq, globalization may be viewed as occcupation and "democratic" terrorism and imperialism. Globalization may be seen on one hand as "the increase in worldwide networks of interdependence" (Nye, 2009, para. 3), whereas Thomas Palley, from the Economics for Democratic and Open Societies, defines globalization as the general concept incorporating the diffusion of ideas and cultures (Perkovich, 2006).

Although globalization is often viewed as the world economy and markets, it has, in fact, several dimensions—each impacting our lives. And while the term globalization became common in the 1990s, the various factors that constitute globalization have been in existence for thousands of years. Regardless of how one may view globalization, the one element that is ubiquitous involves communication. Author Kirk St. Amant believes that "in every instance, however, globalization involves one central factor—communication" (St. Amant & Olaniran, 2013, p. 2). In the following section, we will examine the social/

cultural, political, and economic dimensions of globalization.

Social/Cultural Globalization

The first type of globalization is social/cultural globalization, which includes the dissemination, infusion, or exchange of ideas, images, artifacts, customs, cultures, and interaction of people. The dimensions of social/cultural globalization impact people's ways of thinking, believing, and behav-

erichon/Shutterstock.com

ing and communicating. As people travel across the world, whether for work, military service, tourism, family, economic survival, or opportunity, they take their culture with them. People make efforts to recreate a sense of the familiar or home. In addition, people returning home from their travels take artifacts or reminders of the places they have visited. While the complicated notion of culture cannot be reduced to an item packed in a suitcase, the mementos we take or leave are important in representing our cultures, the languages we speak, the beliefs we hold, and the practices we carry out (Sorrells, 2008).

One specific example of social/cultural globalization is migration. During the nineteenth century, more than 80 million people crossed continents, oceans, and borders to new homes. In America, at the start of the twenty-first century, more than 11.5% of the population, or 32 million people residing in the United States, were born in another country (Nye, 2009). Consequently, the lives of people from various cultural backgrounds—ethnic/racial, religious, class, national, and regional cultures—are increasingly intertwined and interconnected.

Political Globalization

The second type of globalization we will discuss is political. There is a growing trend toward political globalization. Following the toppling of the Berlin Wall in 1989 and the collapse of the former Soviet Union in 1990, there has been a growing assumption that capitalism and democracy together will bring about global prosperity and peace. Many observers suggest there has been a global trend toward democracy since World War II, and this move of "democratization" has been highly contested in different parts of the world (Fukuyama, 1992; Leys, 2001; Nsouli, 2008; Nye, 2009; Palley, 2006). Some observers and skeptics of globalization conclude that the political agendas associated with "democratization" are closely related to the free-trade agreements of the World Trade Organization (WTO), the World Bank, and the International Monetary Fund (IMF).

The impact of political globalization is also felt by women in the Kingdom of Saudi Arabia. According to CNN commentator Mohammed Jamjoom (2013), Saudi Arabian women face many restrictions—including driving. An interior minister spokesperson in Saudi Arabia issued a warning that women caught driving or participating in driving demonstations during the Women's Driving Campaign slated for October 26, 2013, would be punished. The spokesperson went on to state that punishment for defiance of the ban on women driving would not only occur on October 26, but anytime before or after. According to Jamjoom (2013), there is no specific law which bans women from driving; however, "religious edicts there are often interpreted to mean women are not allowed to operate a vehicle" (para. 20). Saudi religious leaders warn that driving could negatively impact women's ovaries.

Despite repeated arrests, Saudi Arabian women have been practicing civil disobediance in relation to driving out of symbolic protest and practicality. News reports state that there have been several staged protests, and women have posted videos of themselves driving on YouTube. Women have also used social media to help organize demonstrations. An electronic petition was launched in September 2013 stating opposition to the stance of probiting women drivers. The movement has gained more than 16,000 signatures (Jamjoom, 2013). The Arab Spring, the political revolts in Tunisa, Iran, Egypt, Syria, and other Arabic nations are indicative of how technology has helped initiate social changes through the use of social media including YouTube, Twitter, and Facebook.

Economic Globalization

Think about the coffee you drink that was harvested in Brazil, the chocolate you eat, grown in the Ivory Coast, the pants you wear, designed in Italy and assembled in China, and the tennis shoes you wear, produced in Indonesia—all of these items are indicators of economic globalization. These examples point to the intercultural economic dimensions of globalization.

Many economists, businesspeople, and journalists view economic globalization and the world economy as one (Nye, 2002). Thomas Friedman views economic globalization as the international system that replaced the one established by the Cold War. It is perceived as the integration of capital, technology, and information across national borders, and in a manner that is creating a single global market—or in essence, a global village (Friedman, 2007).

But for some observers and skeptics, the ideology of globalization is deceptive and destructive. It represents imperialism, global capitalism, and inequity of power. It also appears shrouded in economic greed, corporate gain, captialistic consumerism, and Western imperialism. The World Bank, in a report released in September of 2009, states that poorer countries face a $11.6 billion shortfall in key areas such as education, health, social protection, and infrastructure. The private capital flows to the poorest countries are projected to plummet. This represents a decrease from $21 billion in 2008 and $30 billion in 2007 (World Bank, 2009).

However, Kenya has infused technology into mobile banking and transformed its global economy with this innovation. The Economist Newspaper Limited ("Why does Kenya," 2013) reported that Kenya leads the world with mobile banking. Kenya uses a mobile money operating system M-PESA which allows over 17 million Kenyans to use their mobile phones as a banking system. With the stroke of a few keys, Kenyans are able to pay for services from taxicab fares to transferring cash with their phones.

Although economists, scholars, world leaders, businesspeople, and others distinguish between the variations in globalization. Critical theorist Peter McLaren and Ramin Farahmandpur (2005) contend that they are all interconnected. The dimensions of globalization—economic, social, political, and environmental—have shaped conditions in our world society. Essential to our understanding of globalization is also the role of power in intercultural communication.

Power in the Context of Intercultural Communication and Globalization

The term power can be viewed as something that is imposed on or held over someone that other people do not have. In this sense, power can be seen as coercion, control, or manipulation through language, thought, or action. In some cases, people are rendered helpless, defenseless, and unable to respond or escape—physically or mentally.

In his writings, philosopher Michel Foucault (1977, 1984) challenges us to critically examine the relationship between power and the way it is understood, how it develops, its intricacy, how it functions, and how it is formed. Foucault notes that power is not something that is only hierarchical in nature, uniform or top down only in its approach; it is something that is pervasive, insidious, that grows, and manifests itself within society. Power not only rests on the elements of repression and ideology, but goes further. Power can also be understood in terms of discipline and the function of rules, norms, and regulations, reified through policies and procedures. It is through this normalization of power that it becomes a process, it is enforced, and the language becomes codified (Swartz, Campbell, & Pestana, 2009).

An example is Barber's (1992) concept of *McWorld,* which he describes as the capitalistic spell that mesmerizes consumers for fast food like McDonald's to MTV, fast computers, fast music, and glamorous makeup and clothes. George Ritzer (2000, 2004) discusses the concept of "McDonaldization." He refers to it as the development of a formal prototype originated from a few principles that can be duplicated anywhere around the globe. This view also extends to mainstream America where "McMansions" are becoming more prevalent in the suburbs—a sign of progress and affluence. The McDonalds mentality has become embedded in American culture. The McDonaldization mentality has been compared to the policies, procedures, operations, and marketing of the Disney theme parks, whose practices are being adopted across America as well as around the globe. Disney's amusement parks consist of fantasy worlds that transport the visitor to a different global location, and even to outer space.

The bigger-than-life theme is also evident in oversized malls such as the Mall of America in Bloomington, Minnesota. The casinos and hotels of Las Vegas, also often built around a theme, transport the visitor into another world. Hotel visitors can travel around the globe: Caesar's Palace becomes Italy; New York, New York becomes a cosmopolitan city; Circus Circus becomes the ultimate children's three-ring circus event. Visitors are constantly surrounded by merchandise, food courts, casinos, and amusement.

While intercultural encounters can be entertaining, delightful, and even memorable, they can also be contentious, challenging, and filled with protest. In the next section, I discuss the global protest and resistance to globalization.

Protest, Resistance, and Defiance

The debates over globalization are passionate and fierce. The resistance to globalization and its adverse effects are erupting around the globe. Protestors are angry about the inequities between rich and impoverished countries, the policies of the Group of Eight (G-8), International Monetary Fund (IMF), and the World Bank, the lack of intervention from the United Nations, and the increasing militarization and domination of foreign countries in the name of "democracy" and "freedom." In recent decades, anti-globalization protests have disrupted meetings around the world, including those of the IMF, World Bank, and World Trade Organization (WTO), among others. Demonstrations were held during the annual meetings of the IMF and the World Bank in 1988 in West Berlin, then a part of the German Democratic Republic. Many view these protests as a foreshadowing of the anti-globalization movement.

Since then, protesters against globalization have marched faithfully during WTO, IMF, and World Bank meetings. The first mass anti-capitalist, anti-globalization protest took place on June 18, 1999, when thousands of militant protesters took to the streets in more than 40 cities around the world, including London, England, and Eugene, Oregon, in a mass movement known as The Global Carnival against Capital. This event also came to be known as J-18.

The second major anti-globalization protest, known as the Battle of Seattle or N30, occurred some five months later on November 30, 1999, in Seattle, Washington. With an estimated 50,000 to 100,000 protesters in attendance, the massive gathering turned violent; more than 600 people were arrested, and opening ceremonies of the WTO meeting were cancelled. The protest, however, continued throughout the four-day meeting.

On September 26, 9,000 protesters in Prague voiced their fury and frustration over economic globalization. The *Seattle Times* ("Prague protests," 2000) reported at least 69 people were injured and 44 hospitalized. News reports called Prague a "smoky battle zone" (para. 4), filled with the chants of demonstrators yelling "London, Seattle, continue the battle" (para. 3) as they converged on Prague's Wenceslas Square, where peace protesters had gathered more than 10 years earlier to speak out against communism.

Since 2001, additional protests held in Quebec, Canada, Davis, Switzerland, and other places have become symbols of the festering and growing feelings of frustration and resentment about the unfair gap between rich and poor and the power inequities that exemplify globalization (Sorrells, 2008).

Meetings, rallies, and protests are being held around the world to develop programs, strategies, and oppositional forces to combat the various forms of globalization. The patchwork quilt of forces has formed a loosely-woven blanket of resistance. Activists have been energized across the globe.

The energy of activism was evident in Porto Alegre, Brazil, during the 2003 World Social Forum (WSF) where as many as 40,000 activists gathered to discuss the conference's two main themes: global justice and life after capitalism. More than 15,000 attendees packed a local soccer stadium to hear the keynote address of Scholar Noam Chomsky. Harsh criticism of the United States dominated the conference.

In his speech "Confronting the Empire," Chomsky (2003) said, "the most powerful state in history has proclaimed, loud and clear, that it intends to rule the world by force" (p. 1). During the course of the speech, Chomsky told the audience that many of them already knew how to combat the empire—through their own lifestyles. The best choice is to "create a different world, one that is not based on violence and subjugation, hate and fear" (p. 2).

The local TV station reported that the fans cheered like "it was a rock concert" during Chomsky's speech. Organizers said the heavy turnout during the conference proved the anti-corporate globalization movement had regained some of the energy lost after September 11. On the final day of the conference, thousands of protestors marched and danced through the city carnival style, waving red flags and banners. This demonstration and the World Economic Forum in New York occurred simultaneously.

In our study of globalization in relation to intercultural communication, it is important to think about how people, businesses, products, and global movements are shaped, influenced, and in some instances controlled by relationships of power.

Who is controlling these policies, positions, and relationships of power? How have these relationships been formed and maintained? How does the media impact and influence power? Who are the media giants that control the flow of information, news, and popular culture? How is this power disseminated in the context of globalization? Through innovations in communication technology, transportation technology, and economic technology, people around the world with different cultures, identities, ideologies, and beliefs are becoming more connected in the workplace, home, and community. Obviously, intercultural encounters are becoming a more everyday experience. One of the elements that connects globalization is technology.

Technology and Globalization

Carrino (2012) contends that one of the most significant impacts on globalization is technology. Technology, including the Internet, computers, and mobile phones all impact globalization and consequently, intercultural communication. The current wave of globalization has thrust people from different countries and cultures together into shared physical and virtual homes, workplaces, schools, and communities in unprecedented ways. High school students in Senegal can SKYPE with a group of students learning French at an American high school.

A businessman from Brazil may participate in a virtual conference call in Spain. An activist in Egypt may organize a protest on Facebook. People also no longer have to rely on traditional media outlets such as television, newspaper, or radio. Social media including Twitter, Tumblr, YouTube, Flickr, and Facebook have also opened up many avenues for communication.

Unfortunately, not all people benefit from globalization. The inequities in our society are evident in how communication technology is allocated in our world. Sorrells (2008) reports that while technological advances enable about 15% of the earth's inhabitants to connect to the world via the Internet on wireless laptops at home or in our favorite coffee spots, more than 50% of the earth's population live below the poverty line. These people start their day without the basic necessities of decent food, clean water, and safe shelter. These inequities point out that there is also a digital divide in relation to globalization.

Technology and Intercultural Sensitivity

It is also imperative that communicators in a digital age balance this explosion of technology in the context of globalization with intercultural sensitivity. On December 13, 2013, CNN reported an American public relations executive sent a tweet shortly before boarding a 12-hour flight to South Africa. Justine Sacco's tweet read: "Going to Africa. Hope I don't get AIDS. Just kidding. I'm white!" However, by the time Sacco landed in South Africa, Sacco's tweet was the biggest Internet story of the week. Sacco received countless negative tweets condemning her comments. The public relations executive did release an apology a few days later. Subsequently, 53 characters caused her to lose her job. CNN commentator Brandon Griggs observed that one should consider the consequences before you send a tweet. "It only takes a few seconds to compose a dumb tweet. The damage can last much longer" (Griggs, 2013, para. 4).

This example highlights how ethnocentrism, the belief that your culture is superior to another culture, can be instantly communicated in a digital age. In essence, whether you realize it or not, with only a few keystrokes and characters you have created attitudinal and behavioral barriers to intercultural communication in the context of globalization via social media.

Understanding culture is imperative to success in the modern world of globalization. Therefore, successful interaction in the context of globalization, especially with online media, demands that communicators understand and respect the "other" culture (Kalafatoğlu, 2013). In a digital age, social media blunders can have an immediate and profound impact. Developing communication competence in the context of globalization requires one to not only develop intercultural competence skills, but also to learn how to use these skills responsibly and successfully in connection with technology.

Conclusion

In this chapter, we explored the social/cultural, economic, and political influences of globalization. We defined globalization as an increased connectedness of people from different cultural backgrounds. These connections can be social/cultural, economic, and political. While in reality it is unrealistic to divide globalization into facets, we recognize it is an extremely complex concept that is interrelated and interwoven, with the elements of history and power playing significant roles. We also looked at a few of the debates and resistance to globalization. Our discussion concluded with how technology is a driving force in intercultural communication in the context of globalization. We stressed that developing intercultural communication competence in the context of globalization requires one to understand and respect other cultures and learn how to use these skills in a complex, challenging, and rapidly-changing digital age.

Discussion Questions

1. How has globalization had a direct impact upon your life? Provide an example.
2. How does the media impact and influence power?
3. What is an example of the technological impact of globalization?
4. What is one way you can improve your intercultural sensitivity in relation to intercultural communication and technology?
5. Who are the media giants that control the flow of information, news, and popular culture? How are people of color portrayed in many media outlets? What is an example of a negative and a positive portrayal?

References

Barber, B. (1992). Jihad vs. McWorld. *The Atlantic Monthly, 269*(3), 53–65.

Carrino, S. (2012). Intercultural communication. In R. W. Williams, D. L. McQuitty, & T. Snipes (Eds.), *ttyl…The fundamentals of speech communication in the digital age.* Dubuque, IA: Kendall Hunt.

Chomsky, N. (2003, February 5). *Confronting the empire—Noam Chomsky speech.* Retrieved from Scoop New Stories: www.scoop.co.nz.stories

Foucault, M. (1977). *Discipline and punishment: The birth of the prison.* New York, NY: Vintage.

Foucault, M. (1984). Power/knowledge: Selected interviews and other writings, 1972–1977. In P. Rabinow (Ed.), *The Foucault reader* (pp. 51–75). New York, NY: Pantheon Books.

Friedman, T. (2007). *The world is flat.* New York, NY: Picador.

Fukuyama, F. (1992). *The end of history and the last of man.* New York, NY: Avon Books.

Griggs, B. (2013). *7 social media resolutions for 2014.* Retrieved from http://www.cnn.com/2013/12/31/tech/social-media/social-media-resolutions/

Held, D., McGrew, A. G., Goldblatt, D., & Perraton, J. (1999). *Global transformations: Politics, economics, and culture.* Stanford, CA: Stanford University Press.

Jamjoom, M. (2013). *Saudi Arabia issues warning to women drivers, protesters.* Retrieved from http://www.cnn.com/2013/10/24/world/meast/saudi-arabia-women-drivers/

Kalafatoğlu, T. (2013). *The spread of culture under the umbrella of globalization.* In K. St. Amant & B. Olaniran (Eds.), *Globalization and the digital divide.* Amherst, NY: Cambria Press.

Leys, C. (2001). *Market-driven politics: Neoliberal democracy and the public interest.* London: Verso Books.

McLaren, P. L. & Farahmandpur, R. (2005). *Teaching against global capitalism and the new imperialism.* New York: Roman & Littlefield.

Nsouli, S. (2008). *Ensuring a sustainable and inclusive globalization.* Speech delivered at Universal Postal Union Congress (pp. 1–4). Geneva: International Monetary Fund.

Nye, J. (2002, April 15). *Globalism vs. globalization.* Retrieved from http://www.theglobalist.com

Nye, J. (2009, April 12). *Which globalization will survive?* Retrieved from http://www.realclearworld.com/articles/2009/04/nye_globalization_will_survive.html

Palley, T. (2006, April 13). *Could globalization fail?* Retrieved from http://yaleglobal.yale.edu

Perkovich, G. H. (2006). *Is globalization headed for the rocks? Carnegie Endowment for International Peace* (pp. 1–6). Washington, DC: Carnegie Endowment for International Peace.

Prague protests renew 'Battle of Seattle.' (2000, September 27). *The Seattle Times.* Retrieved from http://community.seattletimes.nwsource.com/archive/?date=20000927&slug=4044799

Ritzer, G. (2000). *The McDonaldization of society.* Thousand Oaks, CA: Pine Forge.

Ritzer, G. (2004). *The globalization of nothing.* Thousand Oaks, CA: Pine Forge.

Sorrells, K. A. (2008). *Linking social justice and intercultural communication in the global context.* Portland, OR: Intercultural Communication Institute.

Sorrells, K. A. (2013). *Intercultural communication: Globalization and social justice.* Thousand Oaks, CA: Sage.

Sorrells, K. A., & Nakagawa, G. (2008). Intercultural communication praxis and the struggle for social responsibility and social justice. In O. Swartz (Ed.), *Transformative communication studies: Culture, hierarchy, and the human condition* (pp. 23–61). Leicester, UK: Troubador.

St. Amant, K., & Olaniran, B. A. (Eds.). (2013). *Globalization and the digital divide.* Amherst, NY: Cambria.

Swartz, O., Campbell, K., & Pestana, C. (2009). *Neo-pragmatism, communication, and the culture of creative democracy.* New York, NY: Peter Lang.

Why does Kenya lead the world in mobile money? (2013, May 27). *The Economist Newspaper Limited.* Retrieved from http://www.economist.com/blogs/economist-explains/2013/05/economist-explains-18

World Bank. (2009, September 22). *World Bank.* Retrieved from http://www.worldbank.org/financialcrisis/bankinitiatives.htm

Young, R. (2001). *Postcolonialism: An historical introduction.* Malden, MA: Blackwell.

Chapter 2

Identifying the Self

5. Peeling Back the Layers: Understanding and Negotiating Identity

Soncerey L. Montgomery Speas

Introduction

An identity would seem to be arrived at by the way in which
the person faces and uses his experience.

—James Baldwin

. . . effective cross-cultural communication has more to do with releasing the right
responses than with sending the 'right' message.

—Edward Hall

Christopher is from a small town in eastern North Carolina. Since his childhood, he was encouraged by his mother (his father was absent from his life) to pursue higher education. He is now enrolled at a predominantly white institution (PWI) and majors in business administration. Christopher is an avid reader and golfer who aspires to be a bank manager.

Christopher is a dark-skinned African American male who is 6'1" with an athletic build. His typical daily attire consists of plaid shirts, loose-fitting jeans, and timberland boots.

He walks with a slight limp (from injuries he sustained in a car accident) and has dimples that dance across his face. Christopher describes himself as a family-oriented, God-fearing Christian who is focused and ambitious. He is an openly gay male who has a magnetic personality and who loves watching sports.

Christopher's profile reflects several negotiated identities that will impact his interactions with others. Like Christopher, our daily communication encounters and identity structures transcend one-dimensional boundaries and affect our intercultural interactions. In order to be effective and competent in our intercultural interactions, however, we must peel back the layers, explore varied negotiated identities (e.g., gender, race/ethnicity, sexual orientation, class, religion, age, physical disability, etc.), and participate in communication encounters that can strengthen our cultural relations.

Arguably, intercultural interactions are part of our everyday life. These interactions play an important role in how various people and groups react when they encounter each other in specific contexts and engage in intercultural communication (Martin & Nakayama, 2014). Ideally, the intercultural interactions would foster deeper understanding of different groups. However, undergirding many of these interactions are misunderstandings and barriers that become communication obstacles or lead to communicative prejudices. Two of the most prevalent barriers are ethnocentrism and assumed similarity. **Ethnocentrism** is the belief that one's culture is better than any other or the assumption that the experience of one's own culture is "central to reality" (Bennett, 2004). **Assumed similarity** occurs whenever we ignore differences and assume that everyone is exactly the same. Many educational institutions, however, are trying to overcome these types of barriers through **adaptation**, the state in which the experience of another culture yields perception and behavior appropriate to that culture, and **integration**, the state in which one's experience of self is expanded to include the movement in and out of different cultural worldviews (Bennett, 2004). Common approaches of adaptation and integration for educational institutions include exposing students to diverse individuals or groups through campus programs (e.g., Office of International Programs, Center for Multicultural Affairs) and incorporating more culturally responsive content into the curriculum. For example, Loyola College offered a course titled *The Theology of Eating*. The course centered on complex religious aspects associated with eating and explored texts to expound the intricacies of etiquette in a canonical context. Granted, these types of deliberate attempts at suitable cultural integration may not be a panacea for all educational woes but they do provide a springboard to help frame deeper conversations about identity, cultural connections, and educational experiences. Since it is the goal of most educational institutions to broaden knowledge and increase appreciation of global exchanges, *intercultural communication* seems to be the most viable mechanism through which institutions of higher learning promote a healthy climate across cultural boundaries.

At its core, **intercultural communication** serves as a prism for helping individuals concretely articulate their experiences and configure their sense of the world. Further, it occurs as a result of the knowledge and perceptions that people have about one another, their motivations to engage in meaningful interactions, and their ability to communicate in ways that are regarded as appropriate and effective (Lustig & Koester, 2000). As stated by Trenholm and Jensen (2004), "communicating interculturally means communicating with people who are different, and people who are different often make us feel uncomfortable" (p. 377). Arguably, in a theoretical context, intercultural communication functions as a conceptual container that promotes

Brocreative/Shutterstock.com

healthy micro- and macro-level exchanges. Moreover, it invites multiple ways of seeing/knowing and offers varied accounts in ways that open up new possibilities for critical discourse and intellectual engagement. So as we assess approaches to intercultural communication and explore frailties related to this concept, we must look at obstacles and possibilities at every turn. We must also consider fundamental and philosophical differences in students' identity development. And as we strategically construct pathways for diverse student learners in the twenty-first century, we should use intercultural communication as the proverbial building block for strengthening historically complex relations and multifaceted identities.

Many factors affect one's conception or adoption of an identity. As noted by Blumer (1969), identity may be construed differently depending on personal interactions with the social environment. Cornel West (1994) echoes this sentiment in his comments that how people act and live is shaped by the larger circumstances in which they find themselves. Since students bring multiple realities and multi-dimensional identities to college campuses, intercultural communication serves as a clear lens through which various notions of identity (gender, race/ethnicity, sexual orientation, socioeconomic status, special abilities, physical disabilities, etc.) can be explored. Intercultural communication can also stimulate awareness that improves cultural relations and enhances social and cultural experiences. Consciously or unconsciously, intentionally or unintentionally, our attitudes are developed through communication with both **in-group** members (people who share a common group identity) and **out-group** members (people who come from a different social group). When communicating with in-group members or familiar cultural groups, people typically experience more security, inclusion, and connection. But when interacting across cultures or with out-group members, individuals experience vulnerability, unpredictability, and differentiation (Littlejohn & Foss, 2011). With this in mind, this chapter will explore various aspects of identity and highlight ways in which intercultural communication is affected by socially constructed identity structures.

Understanding and Negotiating Identity

According to Littlejohn and Foss (2011), **identity** is a "code" that defines one's membership in various communities. This code consists of symbols (e.g., clothes and artifacts), words (e.g., self-description and language), and meanings (e.g., individual understandings and group perceptions) that individuals ascribe to certain things or people. The act of negotiating identity is an all-encompassing, multi-dimensional, fluid process that consists of a subjective dimension (personal sense of self) as well as an ascribed dimension (what others say about you) (Littlejohn & Foss, 2011). As theorized by Stella Ting-Toomey (1988), there are many ways in which we explore and negotiate our identity when interacting with others, especially across cultures. **Negotiation skill** refers to the ability to negotiate identities through careful observation, listening, empathy, nonverbal sensitivity, politeness, reframing, and collaboration (Littlejohn & Foss, 2011).

Darrin Henry/Shutterstock.com

Martin and Nakayama (2014) further note, "Identity plays a key role in intercultural communication, serving as a bridge between culture and communication" (p. 91). People identify with multiple groups based on social interactions and cultural influences. Our individual identities help shape and affect our communication to some degree (Martin & Nakayama, 2014). So let's look more closely at some of the most salient identities that most affect our perceptions and influence our communication patterns: personal identity, racial/ethnic identity, class identity, religious identity, gender identity, age identity, sexual identity, and physical ability identity.

Personal Identity

Personal identity is based on an individual's "unique character, which frequently differs from those of others in their cultural and social groups" (Lustig & Koester, 2000, p. 4). It connotes an individual psychological relationship to particular social category systems (Frable, 1997). Julia Wood (2013) furthers this point, stating that communication is "both an important influence that shapes personal identity and a primary means by which we express who we are" (p. 327). Fundamentally, personal identity is multidimensional and affects one's connection to other identity constructs. More specifically, it refers to a person's self-concept, or notions of self. We internalize perspectives on our identity from various sources (media, family, social comparisons, etc.) and they become part of who we are and how we see ourselves (Wood, 2013). For example, you may take a selfie then ask yourself, *who am I?* Your response would most likely be compiled of an extensive list of personal descriptors. Your list may include qualities like tall or short, right-handed or left-handed. Or it may include certain traits like attractive, intelligent, or trustworthy. Additionally, your list may consist of roles you have like mother or father, student or friend. Further, it may contain positions you occupy like president or secretary, manager or cashier, or hobbies you have like singing, drawing, or playing basketball. With personal identity, we negotiate a portrayal of self we want others to know.

Racial and Ethnic Identity

Identifying with a particular racial or ethnic group reflects our racial or ethnic identity. Although the terms race and ethnicity are often used interchangeably and may be interrelated, there are cultural differences in their socio-historical constructions. **Race** refers to biological characteristics and distinctions drawn from physical appearances (skin color, eye shape, hair texture, etc.) and racial identities are constructed in fluid social contexts (Martin & Nakayama, 2014). **Ethnicity**, on the other hand, refers to shared experiences and distinctions based on natural origin, language, religion, food, and other cultural markers (Frable, 1997). As such, ethnic identity reflects a set of ideas about one's own ethnic group members (Martin & Nakayama, 2014). It consists of an association with ancestry or a group history across generations connected to national origin, race, religion, and/or language (Littlejohn & Foss, 2011). For example, the term "African American" may be used to describe those of African descent with prominent, distinctive physical features while simultaneously recognizing that group's American citizenry. Unique to this ethnic group and in honor of its African heritage is the observance of Kwanzaa from December 26 to January 1. This celebration of family, community, and culture is based on seven principles that center on reconnecting the African American community with African culture and traditions.

One's racial or ethnic identity is clearly affected by social interactions, external appearances, cultural experiences, and differing views. Increasingly, some people self-identify with multiple racial categories depending on social and historical influences. Tiger Woods, for example, coined the term "Cablinasian," thus creating and embracing a distinct racial identity. This term expresses and classifies Tiger's background as a person of multiracial ancestry—Caucasian, Black, Indian, and Asian. In the twenty-first century, President Barack Obama's rise to prominence has sparked deeper conversations about racial identity in the United States. Though he identifies proudly as an African American, he is candid in acknowledging his mother was a White woman from Kansas and his father was a Black man from Kenya. Clearly, people process identity in different ways and express who they are according to their level of comfort in particular environments. As noted by Aumer-Ryan, Li, and Hatfield (2010), many mixed race individuals adopt a racial identity that is most congruent with their environment and/or most rewarded. This statement rings true for Jasmine Yi, a student of African and Asian descent (her father is

African American, her mother is Korean) who attends a local HBCU (Historically Black College or University). Jasmine identifies most with her African American heritage while in her college setting but sees herself as Korean when interacting with her mother's family in her home environment.

Even though race and ethnicity are often seen as vague concepts, they are typically the most recognizable identities as socially constructed across multiple dimensions. And though racial/ethnic identity is one of the most salient aspects of who we are, some still struggle to understand and negotiate their identity within this social category. Moreover, still in 2014, race and ethnicity are often at the center of many heated debates and social justice movements. For instance, recent incidents of "racial profiling" in which protesters march in Ferguson, Missouri, in response to a police shooting of an unarmed teen, Michael Brown, reflect the ongoing country's challenges and views surrounding notions of race and/or ethnicity.

Class Identity

Class identity, which often has strong implications for one's perceived or expected level of attainment, manifests in both tangible and intangible ways. Whether people live in a trailer park, public housing, a house with a white picket fence, or a deluxe apartment in the sky, there are disparities and inequities in income, assets, and resources. Clearly, disparities and inequities in class distinctions relate to one's socioeconomic status. **Socioeconomic status (SES)** is the position of a person or family in the power hierarchy of a society based on income, education, and occupation (Verberber, Sellnow, & Verderber, 2015). The three generalized class categories include low, middle, and upper—variations within each category inform the social, political, and economic well-being of its members.

Undeniably, class identity has both positive connotations and negative associations and impacts on how issues are dealt with for certain groups. Because of differences in each group's history and sociopolitical interaction in society, certain limitations are imposed and boundaries are placed on members of particular groups. I recently saw a news story about a 17-year-old teenager named Akintunde Ahmad. At a glance, this "street dude" from a tough neighborhood in Oakland, California, may likely be overlooked, judged, and stereotyped by his appearance—he has locks and wears gold chains. However, Ahmad, a senior at Oakland Tech High School, has a 5.0 GPA and earned 2100 on the SAT. As a result of his outstanding academic achievements, Ahmad has been accepted into an impressive list of colleges and universities, including Ivy League institutions like Yale, Brown, and Columbia. A product of the Oakland Public School System, Ahmad is both academically gifted and athletically skilled. But both of these qualities may be overlooked by someone assessing his identity based solely on his class category or SES.

Moreover, certain material goods, for example, are signs that people use to denote class association. For instance, when we meet someone new we often classify him or her as a member of a particular class based on differences in his or her attire, appearance or language (e.g., a black male wearing sagging pants and timberland boots may be perceived as a member of a lower socioeconomic class, while a white male in dockers and loafers is perceived as being in the middle or upper class). These differences encourage a more distant approach to communication (Trenholm & Jensen, 2004) and may result in different classes devaluing one another.

Religious Identity

Religion is a belief system with a set of rituals and ethical standards based on a common perception of what is sacred or holy (Verberber et al., 2015). Thus, racial identity is typically anchored in one's spiritual and moral values, and is influenced by what certain religious communities establish as divine truth. Examples of one's religious identity include self-identification as a Christian, Muslim, Catholic, Buddhist, Jew, etc. It is worth mentioning that religious identity, which frames certain behaviors of religious groups, may be expressed through one's dress, food, practices, etc. For example, in terms of dietary restrictions, Hindus do not eat beef and Muslims do not eat pork. In line with expected dress codes for their respective religions, Muslim women cover their hair with a *hijab*; Jewish men wear a *kippah*. Easter and Christmas are important holidays for Christians while Vesak signifies a major celebration for Buddhists.

It is also worth noting that one's religious identity may be one of the most passionately-charged identities that individuals have. Globally, nationally, and locally, intercultural conflict often stems from one's religious identity. Rampant terrorist threats by ISIS (term used to refer to the Islamic militant group named Islamic State of Iraq and Syria) who seized parts of Syria and Iraq reflect challenges and conflicts related to religious identity. On a local level, some magistrates in North Carolina quit their jobs, based on religious beliefs, when federal judges ruled North Carolina's ban on same sex unions unconstitutional in October 2014. In response, a bill is being crafted to protect state officials who choose not to issue licenses for religious reasons or feel forced to give up religious liberties by marrying same-sex couples.

Gender Identity

The identification of gender is defined as a personal conception of oneself as a man or woman. Gender identity is constructed as a result of a combination of inherent and extrinsic environmental factors (Ghosh, 2012). For example, newborn baby boys are wrapped in blue blankets and newborn baby girls are swaddled in pink blankets. The colors blue and pink signify the gender of the newborn as a boy or girl, respectively.

Historically, gender identity is typically congruous with gender roles (e.g., boys play with toy cars and girls play with dolls). However, significant progress has been made toward equal rights for the sexes. For instance, women now function effectively in male-dominated jobs like construction workers, sports analysts, and public officials. Men have made progress in occupations historically relegated to women such as nurses, secretaries, and teachers. Granted, gender takes on different meanings in different cultures. Nevertheless, these changes in gender roles suggest that "as a culture changes, so do notions of what is masculine or feminine" (Martin & Nakayama, 2014, p. 100).

Age Identity

In the context of certain cultural conventions, age underlies some of our societal responsibilities, expectations, and roles, and influences many of our social interactions and activities. Age identity refers to how individuals act, think, feel, and behave according to their age. According to Westerhof (2008), age identity is an inner expression of a person's age and the aging process. It is the "outcome of the processes through which one identifies with or distances oneself from different aspects of the aging process" (p. 10). Clearly, the perceptions and meanings attached to certain ages and generations can positively or adversely affect our intercultural interactions.

Undeniably, different generations often have different philosophies, values, and ways of speaking (Martin & Nakayama, 2014). For example, in the United States, generations are named according to certain characteristics and values of the age groups: 1900–1924—G.I. Generation; 1925–1945—Silent Generation; 1946–1964—Baby Boomers; 1965–1979—Generation X; 1980–2000—Millennials or Generation Y; 2001–Present—New Silent Generation or Generation Z (Rosenberg, 2014). Each cohort or population group is distinguished by both its conservative and progressive ideals as well as traditional and contemporary perspectives. So while the Millennials are technologically savvy and obsessed with self-achievement, Baby Boomers tend to be more financially secure and consumer-oriented.

Sexual Identity

At a fundamental level, sexual identity refers to one's concept of sexuality as well as notions of being gay or lesbian. Although sexual identity is a self-identified, inherent construct, there are strong cultural stigmas and physical contradictions associated with this identity. As noted by Wood (2013), historically and today, heterosexuality is viewed as normal sexual orientation and some regard gays, lesbians, bisexuals, trans-sexuals, etc., as abnormal. Underscoring this point is the current controversy surrounding same-sex unions. Although 32 states have legalized same-sex unions, 18 states have banned same-sex unions. As recent as October 2014, courts in North Carolina and Alaska have overturned bans on gay marriage. So while many same-sex couples lined up to get their licenses outside of the register of deeds office, opponents protested the issuing of licenses and performing of ceremonies (Chappell, 2014).[1]

---

1. As a point of clarification, according to the Human Rights Campaign website (2014), "gender identity" and "sexual orientation" are distinct terms. Gender identity refers to a person's innate, deeply felt psychological identification as a man or woman, which may or may not correspond to the sex assigned to them. Sexual orientation is the preferred term used when referring to an individual's physical and/or emotional attraction to the same and/or opposite gender.

Physical Ability Identity

According to Martin and Nakayama (2014), knowledge of self based on characteristics related to the body (e.g., sight, hearing, weight, mobility, cognitive processes, etc.) underlies our physical ability identity. "And our physical ability, like our age, changes over a lifetime" (p. 107). Just as our physical abilities change over time, so do our perceptions of and responses to individuals with physical abilities. In other words, our perceptions and responses impact our social judgment about certain physical ability identities. These judgments are further influenced by our assessment of an individual's identity which is shaped in part by the person's abilities or disabilities. So that the communication encounter can be psychologically safe for those with physical limitations, Wood (2013) offers guidelines for effective and confirming communication with people with disabilities. She recommends, for example, that we respect the space of people with disabilities by not leaning on someone's wheelchair or touching someone's cane.

To prohibit discrimination based on physical disabilities, the Americans with Disabilities Act (ADA) was enacted in 1990. Designed to protect individuals with physical limitations from inequities and help such individuals lead a productive life, the ADA prohibits discrimination against people with disabilities in employment, transportation, public accommodation, communications, and governmental activities. For example, effective March 2012, laws required that newly constructed buildings were handicap accessible for individuals with mobility disabilities. Buildings must also be in compliance and services must be available for individuals with hearing and visual disabilities (e.g., braille labels are available on button panels in elevators; ATMs are equipped with headphone jacks for those who are hearing-impaired). Fortunately, the ADA regulates actions and guarantees that appropriate measures are being taken to strengthen communication with those who embrace their physical ability identity.

Summary

Communication is "the means by which identity is established and mechanism by which it changes as well" (Littlejohn & Foss, 2011, p. 103). At the intersection of our political, social, cultural, and historical communication encounters is our identity. Though identity is seemingly a simple term, it is a deeply complex, socially defined construct. Each identity in our repertoire contributes to who we are and influences how we communicate across cultural lines. To be effective intercultural communicators we must be sensitive to varied identities and adapt socially to a wide range of communication interactions. One of the most challenging things for people to do is communicate effectively and successfully with different cultures and co-cultures. Understanding and negotiating multiple identities constructs add an additional layer of complexity to this challenge. Still, deliberate steps must be taken if we are going to be effective intercultural communicators and make a difference in the lives of others in meaningful ways.

Discussion Questions

1. Briefly define personal identity. Which aspects of your personal identity do you embrace? Which aspects do you resist?
2. Share an instance when your identity was confirmed/validated. Give an example of when your identity was disconfirmed/challenged.
3. What do you think can be done to increase intercultural understanding in our society?
4. Why is it important for society to promote intercultural competence in different learning environments (e.g., school, church, home, etc.)?
5. How do media and social media affect your identity?

References

Aumer-Ryan, K., Li, N. P., & Hatfield, E. (2010). *The multiracial experience in redefining race.* Retrieved from http://www.elainehatfield.com/113.pdf

Bennett, M. J. (2004). Becoming interculturally competent. In J. Wurzel (Ed.), Toward multiculturalism: A reader in multicultural education (2nd ed., pp. 62–77). Newton, MA: Intercultural Resource Corporation.

Blumer, H. (1969). *Symbolic interactionism: Perspective and method.* Englewood Cliffs, NJ: Prentice-Hall.

Chappell, B. (2014). NC and Alaska issue same sex marriage licenses. *The two-way.* Retrieved from http://www.npr.org/blogs/thetwo-way/2014/10/13/355891757/north-carolina-and-alaska-issue-same-sex-marriage-licenses

Frable, D. E. S. (1997). Gender, racial, ethnic, sexual and class identities. *Annual Review of Psychology, 48*(24), 1–18.

Ghosh, S. (2012, June 1). Gender identity. *Medscape.* Retrieved from http://emedicine.medscape.com/article/917990-overview

Human Rights Campaign. (2014). *Sexual orientation and gender identity definitions.* Retrieved from http://www.hrc.org/resources/entry/sexual-orientation-and-gender-identity-terminology-and-definitions

Littlejohn, S. W., & Foss, K. A. (2011). *Theories of human communication* (10th ed.). Long Grove, IL: Waveland Press, Inc.

Lustig, M. W., & Koester, J. (2000). Negotiating intercultural competence. In M. W. Lustig & J. Koester (Eds.), *Among us: Essays on identity, belonging and intercultural competence* (pp. 197–212). New York, NY: Longman.

Lustig, M. W., & Koester, J. (2000). The nature of cultural identity. In M. W. Lustig & J. Koester (Eds.), *Among us: Essays on identity, belonging and intercultural competence* (pp. 3–8). New York, NY: Longman.

Martin, J. N., & Nakayama, T. K. (2014). *Experiencing intercultural communication: An introduction* (5th ed.). New York, NY: McGraw-Hill.

Rosenberg, M. (2014). Names of generations. *About education.* Retrieved from http:// geography.about.com/od/populationgeography/qt/generations.htm

Ting-Toomey, S. (1988). Identity negotiation theory: Crossing cultural boundaries. In W. B. Gudykunst (Ed.), *Theorizing about Intercultural Communication* (pp. 211–34). Thousand Oaks, CA: Sage.

Trenholm, S., & Jensen (2004). *Interpersonal communication* (6th ed.). New York, NY: Oxford University Press.

Verberber, K. S., Sellnow, D. D., & Verderber, R. F. (2015). *COMM3.* Stamford, CT: Cengage Learning.

West, C. (1994). *Race matters.* New York, NY: Vintage Books.

Westerhof, G. J. (2008). Age identity. In D. Carr (Ed.), *Encyclopedia of the life course and human development.* (pp. 10–14). Farmington Hills, MI: Macmillan.

Wood, J. T. (2013). *Interpersonal communication: Everyday encounters.* Boston, MA: Wadsworth.

6.   Maybe the World Is Flat

J. Maria Merrills, Ph.D.
Winston-Salem State University

Key Terms
Fat Studies, globalization, digitization, media, culture

****

Maybe the World Is Flat

"I like your fat," he said in his deep Jamaican accent as if he were telling me that he liked my scarf, shoes, hat, or something like that. I immediately looked up from the jewelry stand; I had been eyeing a table of turquoise necklaces. Beside me stood a Jamaican man with dark skin, a slim build, and long dread-locks. "What?" I asked in shock as if I did not hear what I knew I heard. "I like your fat," he repeated in his a matter of fact baritone voice just as he had said seconds before. The waves from the beach on which we stood swelled and crashed loudly.

stoupa/Shutterstock.com

I know I should have been offended and upset by his use of that word *fat*. I had heard that word too many times getting off of the school bus. It was the word that I had heard from loved ones in attempts to "motivate" me to fit into pretty dresses.

Throughout the years, the word *fat* had become my own personal f-bomb, so much so that when I heard it, my mind would explode into instant depression. When people called me fat, it was a reminder of what I am but should not be. It was one other characteristic of me other than being black and a female that would be used as a strike against me in not only social situations but academic and career as well.

I had to admit that my last memories of that word came from a high school English teacher. She was short, pale, and petite. Her hair was jet black, and I was always scared of her as she was strict and seemed to enjoy letting the students know when they were wrong about their class assignments. One day upon returning an assignment to her desk, she noticed how I had lost some weight. It was 30 pounds to be exact, part of the hundreds of pounds that I had lost crash dieting. She called me out in the hall and was quick to let me know that I was still fat and had a ways to go. "With fifteen or twenty more pounds, you will be perfect," she grinned. In my mind, I was happy with my weight for once. That day was the last day of that particular crash diet and that was 80 pounds south ago.

Once in college, I had bumped into a group of guys at a college gym jam. They were locals who had somehow made their way onto our college campus. They were huddled in a group, making audible comments about the young women at the party. Walking past them, I accidently brushed one of the guy's shoulders. "Get out the way, fat ass," the rude boy shouted. I did not look back, I kept walking. I acted as if I had not heard that word.

The last time an adult had talked to me about my weight, I was talking to a woman at least 20 years my senior. She was giving me the "advice for the best life" talk, the kind of wishful conversation a middle-aged woman has with a younger woman whom she does not wish to repeat the same mistakes that she had made in life. In her motherly voice, she told me that I had such a pretty face and that I would be so beautiful if only I lost "the weight"; so much for finishing one's education, finding a good job, and living life as a responsible adult. The message was loud and clear that when one is a woman, looks are what matters and being thin was a huge part of a woman's overall perception and accep-tance by others.

But this time, on that beautiful sunny day, on that sandy Caribbean beach hearing the word fat was different. Did he say he liked my fat? Did he embrace that word that would have sent me on days of crash dieting, only to rebound by days of binging? He was waiting on me to respond to his statement, but I was still a bit puzzled.

"You like my fat?" I asked him with more curiosity in my voice than shame. "Yes," he nodded. Then he moved towards me a bit closer, pressing the boundaries of personal space. "You do?" I continued to question, "Why?" "Because it is sexy," he added, as if I should have known. Did he just say sexy? Fat as sexy, now there was a first for me. I had never heard of such a thing.

Every day I awake in America, I am told that I must lose the fat. On the morning radio alarm, I am greeted by announcers who talk about smoothies that promise to help me lose a dress size in only one week. When I watch television, I learn how big women lead miserable lives until they lose "the weight." I am told that I too would find newfound self-esteem and "live" again once the weight is gone. I hear about "scientific" diet pills that would block the stress in my life, and I would lose weight while I slept, all while eating whatever I want. When I go to my favorite bookstore, I can pass shelves upon shelves of diet advice books that have countless pages of ways to lose weight and to get rid of the "ugly" fat.

When this Jamaican man told me that he liked my fat, I wanted to know what was so "sexy" about it. Just before I got a chance to interview him further, my husband walked up and the slim Jamaican man with dark skin, deep voice, and long dreads quickly stepped away and disappeared as fast as he had appeared.

Somehow, after that encounter, I kept being reminded how my size was a benefit on this Caribbean island instead of a disadvantage. While walking with my spouse down the street in Ocho Rios, a man called out, "Don't have her walk so much, I don't want her to lose that beautiful figure of hers." I feared that my husband would become indignant and have a "chat" with the man with the remarks, but he did not. These complimentary calls had become commonplace and expected for the remainder of our stay. My husband and I actually had to learn to adjust to the way that Jamaican men vocalized their affections in front of any and every one. Weird interactions with Jamaican men whom I did not know included them approaching me and sharing their income, the jobs that they had, and lands and farms that they owned.

Thinking back, I could not help but to chuckle about the contrasts between American and Jamaican culture. In America, men that I don't know approach me with the latest diet products that they are selling. In Jamaica, I was adored in ways that I could only imagine Halle Berry must be accustomed. Needless to say, Jamaica is one of my favorite countries to visit. In Jamaica, I was not inundated with the message that I must lose weight at whatever cost. There were no media and social pressures to move toward the thin ideal we have in the U.S. Though I am aware of the health risks of the extra pounds and still wish to rid myself of them, it has been one of the only places that I could go and feel truly comfortable with myself.

Still, I could not help but think about the man who directly told me that he liked my fat. It left me with the question that I did not have the opportunity to answer while I was there: Why do Jamaicans like voluptuous women? It was a question that I would intend to answer, even now, six years later.

Through my initial online research, I discovered that my interest in knowing more about attitudes toward big people is actually a discipline that is studied at some universities. It is called of all things, Fat Studies (Saguy, 2013). Fat Studies is a sub-discipline of Women's Studies and is an interdisciplinary field of study similar to African American Studies or Lesbian, Gay, Bisexual, and Transgender Studies. Fat Studies explores the social, cultural, political, medical, and economic impact of people of size. Though fat impacts both male and female alike, Fat Studies is housed in feminist programs because people put more emphasis on the way that a woman looks (Saguy, 2013).

Last year, I contacted some Jamaican scholars and arranged for interviews with them, along with volunteer students and focus groups so that I could conduct some research about Jamaicans' perceptions about girth. Interestingly, the University of West Indies scholars were also questioning the impact of societal standards of beauty as there was a conference in June 2014 called the "Dying to Be Beautiful" conference that I attended. The conference was designed to explore international beauty ideals and the medical, psychological, and social implications of them. Luckily I was able to contribute to the conversation at the conference as I had recently completed production of a film that I had written and produced called *Seeing Faith*, a web movie about a plus-size woman who finds love and acceptance in Jamaica.

Travelling around Jamaica, I noticed how the country was different than it was six years before. All the streets were paved; there were no dirt roads as there once were. KFC,

Pizza Hut, and Burger King were on major street corners. Jamaican women appeared plumper than I had remembered. While watching television, health advocates talked about avoiding diabetes, high cholesterol, and high-blood pressure by reducing carbs. I saw a commercial for Curves, the exercise franchise. Radio announcers talked about smoothies designed to regulate one's digestive system and stave off health problems, code for weight loss.

The conference was telling. The thick of it (pun intended) was that fat was out and thin was in, at least for Jamaicans below the age of 30. However, when I spoke to focus groups, discovering size ideals proved complex. I interviewed groups of young Jamaican men, ages 18 to 25 to discover the ideal body type for women and discovered that Meager girls, girls whose bones could be seen, were considered repulsive, but so too were young women whose fat jiggles. While some men preferred thick girls who were firm, many preferred slender women. One group even went on to proclaim that Meagan Good, the African American actress, was the ideal body size. Miss Good is probably less than a size six.

The Jamaican women in the group seemed to indicate a different perspective. I interviewed young women who could not find dates in their desired age range because they were told that they were too fat, though at most they would be a size 14. Other women I interviewed nearing the end of their child-bearing age could not find suitable husbands because economically successful men desired thin women on their arms as a sign of their financial success. Conflicting perspectives and new social ideals now come with familiar health concerns in Jamaica just as we face in the U.S. Young Jamaican women are now developing anorexia, bulimia, and binge eating disorders. But why, why the rapid change?

Time and time again, interview after interview, I uncovered two common threads—the Internet and cable television. Apparently five years ago, one year after my initial visit, the Internet and American cable moved into Jamaica, bringing American media images and our standards of beauty with it. Sad to say, Jamaicans are becoming more and more Americanized, forever changing its culture, making it more difficult for me to answer my initial question and now demanding that I instead look at the direct influences for the change.

And I am saddened by this, just as sad as I was when I visited the Louvre in Paris, France, last year only to discover that there are two Starbucks and a McDonald's restaurant in this world-famous museum. Still to this day, I cannot wrap my mind around how people from all over the world would come to the Café capital to order coffee from an American company.

In fact, France today deeply contrasts from the France of 20 years past when I could look at the people on the street and based on their fashion would know who was European, African, or American. Today, I can no longer look at a sea of people and identify their nationality just by looking at them. Unfamiliar French boutiques are surrounded with stores like H&M, Clarks, the Gap, and Bloomingdales, even on famous French streets. Black women wear weaves in France, just as they do in America.

I saw more American films on the marquees in France than I did French films. I listened to cars as they drove by with booming systems, blasting American rap songs. If it weren't for popular landmarks like the Eiffel Tower and the Arc De Triomphe, along with the six-hour flight, the outskirts of Paris could be any town U.S.A. to me.

Maybe, just maybe the people from Christopher Columbus's day were right all along, "the world is flat." Thanks to the Internet which gives the world access to American shows and music at the touch of a button, American culture is spreading beyond the national borders even more rapidly than before. Digitization is creating new colonies. These virtual colonies are not the ones that we knew of yesteryear that required colonizers to physically conquer and control new territories; instead, the spread of American values and culture happens unintentionally, perhaps. Regardless of its intent, the U.S. is forming digital colonies which now dictate socially acceptable ways of being based on American standards, diluting and impacting cultures all over the world.

Ironically, this morning, I noticed that my four-year-old daughter left an unusual amount of cereal in her breakfast bowl. I asked her why she did not finish it. "Because I don't want to get fat mommy," she replied. My heart just floated to the edge of the world, leaped over, and then sank.

Discussion Questions

1. What are American standards of beauty? What evidence from the media can you find to substantiate your opinion?
2. Are standards of beauty different depending on race and ethnicity? What evidence do you have to support this opinion?
3. Is it a benefit or disadvantage to have American franchises worldwide?
4. Does media from other countries impact American culture? How so?
5. Complete a web search to understand beauty ideals in other places. How do these international standards of beauty differ from the U.S.?

Reference

Saguy, A. (2013). *What's wrong with fat?* New York, NY: Oxford University Press.

7.   Peeling Back My Layers

Ronell Miller

"There's nothing more dangerous than a closed mind." When first attending North Carolina Agricultural & Technical State University I thought I had a lot figured out when it came to life. Coming in to college with that kind of attitude I blocked out many of my peers. When discussing sensitive topics, I would always remove myself from the conversation. Sure, I would still be in the environment where the conversations took place, but I wouldn't participate beyond absorbing the information. Sometimes I felt as if I was just taking up space because this was cutting my form of self-expression. I was often labeled as the stuck-up type—I always seemed to be the "odd ball" when I spoke my mind.

Within a month or so of attending North Carolina Agricultural & Technical State University, I met my best friend. This person is very interesting to me because he challenged my thinking, and to this day he continues to do so. At the time, my sense of ***diversity*** was somewhat developed being raised in Southern California my whole life. ***Diversity*** is a variety of things, from race, environment, and religion; it is everything that makes the world rotate (Martin & Nakayama, 2011). So, growing up from a young age, I recognized different underlying issues that people had against one another. I had a lot of time to think on my own being raised in a single parent household. As a child I was either at some type

of sport practice or just thinking about life. That was the foundation with which I met my best friend. When we met, I could tell he just wanted a friend to connect with. We were from totally different backgrounds, and parts of the globe as well. By this time, I had already established a base of friends while he was still looking for people with whom to associate. As I started to get to know him, I thought I knew a lot about Africa, but I was very wrong. My problem was that I was trying to give everyone a certain ***ethnic identity***. ***Ethnic identity*** is a set of ideas about one's own ethnic group, a sense of belonging to a particular group, and knowing something about the shared experience of a group (Martin & Nakayama, 2011). Sharing my perspective on Africa, I was coming from a western European perspective. I was categorizing Africa as a whole when in reality it is such a diverse place that you can't put it into a box.

Daniel M Ernst/Shutterstock.com

He taught me many things, such as the diversity of countries and cultures in Africa. It was interesting that when the subject of slavery came about, we came from such different viewpoints and our passion differed in so many ways. Ethiopia was the only nation in Africa not conquered by Europeans. When trying to piece issues together he was confused almost as much as I was. I understood more issues on slavery, being from America and a descendant of the slave. His perspective was interesting to me because he was completely disconnected from the issue.

Revolutionary discussions began to arise, with my friend asking, "How are you going to revolutionize if you're not willing to die for the brother next to you?" Sure, you might not know that man next to you, but he is a *cosmopolitan* in your struggle. A *cosmopolitan* is a citizen of the world, so he is retrospectively in the same position as you are (Martin & Nakayama, 2011). Cosmopolitan mentality recognizes the value of human life, and never forgets that each human being has responsibilities to one another. Regarding this topic, I started to understand that we have to work together, try to understand one another, and work together or at least be willing to empathize. Africans have been spread across the globe and tricked into not adopting or identifying themselves for who they are. The first key thing in releasing yourself from slavery is to love yourself and the others around you who were enslaved as well. Without love, and being content with embracing you for you, then it will be hard to lead others around you who don't love themselves. Another big problem we discussed in our first encounter was that I had a subliminal stigma to Africans on how they looked or expressed themselves. Back home I was used to conversing with Nigerians and people from Congo. At first I was trying in some way to *ethnically identify* my friend to Nigerians and Congolese. That was a big wakeup call because these people were affected by slavery and imperialism as well. Listening to his perspective was refreshing to me—we began to have talks related to these subjects almost every day, and yes we did clash at times. Then I started to realize that we were more the same than we actually thought. We both came from the same *religious identity*, which was instilled in us by our families. *Religious identity* is an important decision in many people's identities, and a common source of intercultural conflict (Martin & Nakayama, 2011). My friend and I first met at a Bible study, which was held here on campus. As we grew apart from others in the Bible study, we continued to grow closer because we felt as if some people were only trying to restrict us from other communities on campus. Also, we both love to express ourselves by the clothes we wear; it might not make sense to others how we dress, but as long as we are comfortable then we are content.

One of the greatest experiences in my life was meeting his family. They took me in as if I was their own. I have some family members today who would be skeptical if I even spent a couple of hours in their home. These people let me spend a night, fed me, and took me out around the nation's capital. It was hilarious because some people started to think I was Ethiopian; it was real intriguing. Girls would talk to me in Amharic, which is the official national language of Ethiopia. It was interesting to listen to all the different languages I was encountering. I learned that Africa has over tens of thousands of languages across the entire continent. That is amazing. Then, it clicked with me that we all come from diverse backgrounds, experiences, and perspectives, but we all want our voices to be heard.

In a way, I think of Africa as the heart of the world, and if we want to answer a lot of wrongs, we have to change our hearts first. With that being said, we have to reform the concept that this continent isn't valuable, because at the root of it, is life. From the first human being born there, to the infinite natural resources, to the building of the pyramids, there is so much to learn in Africa.

Reference

Martin, J., & Nakayama, T. (2011). *Experiencing intercultural communication: An introduction* (4th ed.). New York, NY: McGraw-Hill.

8. There's a Redneck in My Backyard, HELP!
A Case Study Perspective

Sheila M. Whitley, Ph.D.

When you hear the term redneck, many different stereotyped images may pop into your head. Maybe you have a definite image and behavior in mind, because your stereotyped image has held true for every redneck you have ever met. When I hear redneck, one stereotyped image pops into my head—southern white male. Let me clarify, I don't think all southern white men are rednecks and not all rednecks are the same. My stereotype may differ from your stereotype. Humor me as I label and poke fun at my stereotyped image of a redneck. I place rednecks on a continuum. On one side of the continuum is the friendly redneck. He is country-talking, gregarious, blue-jean wearing, never met anyone he couldn't get along with, will help anyone, and in general—just a nice guy.

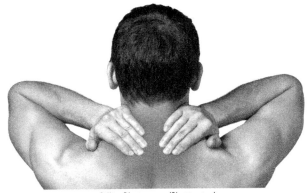

www.BillionPhotos.com/Shutterstock.com

The other side of the redneck continuum is the extreme opposite of our friendly redneck. He is the guy you don't want living next door. He out-cusses a sailor, guzzles beer, favors collecting unemployment money over a job, owns aggressive dogs, scurries off in his mufflerless car, is always itching for a good fight (especially in a bar), is overly proud of his race and sees all other races as inferior, has had at least one clash with the law before he could legally acquire intoxicating beverages, and in general is someone his friends won't turn their backs on out of fear or lack of trust. I almost forgot, he picks a woman with the same qualities.

Some guys on both ends of the continuum proudly proclaim their redneck status, while others distress if you call them a redneck. I know many self-acknowledged and in denial rednecks. I adore and appreciate the friendly redneck. They are good guys to have as friends and neighbors. But on the other side of the continuum, well . . . I rather only hear stories and be thankful it didn't happen to me. Sit back, 'cause I'm about to tell you a story that happened to me, and you can be thankful it wasn't you. I need to give you a bit of background so you can fully understand my befuddlement. The names have been changed to protect the guilty.

I was about six years old when Mr. and Mrs. Smith moved into the house on the left side of our home. Karen, their only child, was married and about to have her first baby. Her husband was away in the military, so she moved in with her parents so they could help with the new baby. Around Thanksgiving, Karen had a baby boy. For satirical emphasis, I'll call him Bubbbbba. His real name doesn't fit the stereotype and he's guilty. Bubbbbba was a cute baby and another neighborhood playmate. I don't remember how long Karen lived with her parents after the baby was born. Eventually, she joined her husband in another town. Bubbbbba visited his grandparents often and some of the visits were for extended periods of time. All the neighbors grieved when Bubbbbba was about three or four years old, and his grandfather was beaten to death in a convenience store robbery. It was about this time that Karen started her marrying and then divorcing spree. Mrs. Smith was financially stable and she paid the bill every time Karen got into a predicament. Karen was engrossed with her life and didn't devote time to raising Bubbbbba. The end result was that Bubbbbba lived off and on with his grandmother. Looking back, I wonder if this shuffling back and forth was the birth of what would become his adult value system.

I know Bubbbbba loved his grandfather. It is possible that his grandfather was the only positive male role model in his life. Years after his grandfather's death, Bubbbbba told me he thought his grandfather was the only person who really loved him. Wow! I didn't know what to say then and I still don't know what to say. I think he was wrong. I believe his mother and grandmother loved him. He obviously didn't receive love the way he perceived it should be given. I can only speculate how Bubbbbba's life would have been different if his grandfather lived.

To sum up my relationship with Bubbbbba, we grew up together and had an amicable relationship. I'm told he looked up to me as an older sister. His grandmother affirmed to my mother many times that I was a good influence on Bubbbbba. I didn't see Bubbbbba much after he reached junior high school. I was away in college and he wasn't spending as much time with his grandmother. His high school years completed his transformation to a new value system. He converted into the type of redneck you don't want living beside you. Bubbbbba didn't try in high school and frequently got into trouble. His grandmother kept us updated on his ins and outs of trouble during this time, mainly traffic violations. My father is a barber, so what wasn't told, he heard through the proverbial barber shop grapevine—gossip.

Throughout high school, Bubbbbba's grandmother bought him several cars. He wrecked, destroyed, or maimed every car. Mrs. Smith bailed him out of trouble every time he drove or walked into it. She lamented many times to my mother about how much it worried her the way Bubbbbba was living his life. I think she believed buying him things and bailing him out of trouble would wake him up. Conversely, it fueled his lifestyle and reinforced an absence of love. He knew her money was available to fix his mess with no parental discipline attached. So he messed and messed and messed. I saw Bubbbbba for the first time in many years at his grandmother's funeral. He was about 23 years old. Noticeably, he wasn't the same person as my childhood friend. We had a pleasant visit and relived some of the good ole days. It was obvious to both of us that we didn't have any common interests or the necessary foundation for a friendship. Our value systems were too different. Even so, I continued hoping his childhood heart would resurrect. My mother had no doubts. She heard way too much from his grandmother and knew the type of person he had become. He was someone you didn't want in your neighborhood.

For the first time in two decades, Mrs. Smith's house was vacant. Hopefully, Karen would sell the house. The neighborhood's worst possible nightmare would be for Karen to allow Bubbbbba to move into the house. The neighbors prepared for the worse. I was living at home and would be affected by Karen's decision. I really didn't think Karen would let Bubbbbba move in because surely she knew the problems he would cause the neighbors. Not to mention, he would probably destroy the house. Karen wasn't like her mother; she wanted all the money for herself.

I was sure she would sell the house for the money—if for no other reason. We all woke up to a nightmare. Bubbbbba moved into the house with several of his friends and his seven-month pregnant soon-to-be wife. Initially, it was difficult to see the intensity of his hostility because it was masked in lightheartedness. It wasn't long before Bubbbbba and I discovered we had nothing in common and no relationship. He no longer respected me as a friend, looked up to me as an older sister, or even talked to me.

Gregory Johnston/Shutterstock.com

I won't even talk about how he approached my parents and the rest of the neighbors. Bubbbbba and his live-in friends worked occasionally, but by far, spent most of their time messing around the house. They competed in front yard cussing episodes in the early morning, midmorning, noon, night, and late night; drove noisy cars; kept an aggressive pit bull and chow inside the fenced-in backyard; hosted beer guzzling parties that encouraged their propensity for outdoor bladder relief and ended with empty beer cans all over the yard; and performed many other openly defiant behaviors aimed at upsetting the neighborhood old fogies. One peaceful Sunday afternoon sticks out in my mind and confirmed where Bubbbbba's belief system ended up. I had just returned from Baton Rouge and was trying to take a nap since my early morning flight robbed me of a good night's rest. My bedroom was about 15 feet from Bubbbbba's driveway and the side entrance into his basement. The driveway ran the length of his house and continued beyond the driveway-width chain-linked-fence gate, which wrapped around to the back of the house into the basement garage.

I was awakened from my nap by the jocularity of Bubbbbba and three or four of his friends in the driveway trying to fix his stentorian, but at the moment, broken car. I tried to ignore all the commotion and go back to sleep. Yeah, right! What was I thinking?

Suddenly, the mood changed. I heard an anguished, "No! . . . NO! . . . BUBBBBBA!" OK, that didn't sound promising. Could be a problem? Probably not! Drama was commonplace when they were messing around outside. I'm a bit upset. It's beginning to look a lot like I'm not going to get my nap. I'm soooooo sleepy. Why today, Bubbbbba? You planned it this way, didn't you? Oh my, what's that? Surprise, surprise! The engine started. VAROOM, VAROOMMMMM, VAROOMMMMMROOM. Great! He got the strident engine started. The verdict's in. I lost my nap attempt. Can't sleep with that cacophony! I knew the usual routine. Race the engine in an attempt to break the sound barrier or annoy the peace and quiet out of the neighbors. Success, Bubbbbba! You drove my peace and quiet into the next county. No nap for this very tired gal.

A flash later . . . CRASH, KABOOM! . . . "OH . . . !" Sorry. I didn't quite catch that last part. Hummmmmm? I wondered what that was all about. Was that a whoops? Sort of sounded like damage. I knew I wasn't dreaming because I couldn't nap with all that racket! A split second later, my curiosity mounted beyond restraint. I sprang out of bed—interrupting my insomnia—with an inquiring mind. I was about to take the big risk and look out the window to see what they destroyed. Took a deep breath . . . Held it! Exhaled! Braced for the worse. Prayed! "Please, don't let it be our house." Looked out the window. Opened my eyes! Sighed with relief—"NOT our house." Sort of chuckled—"HIS house!!!!!" Based on visual scrutiny and what I heard, I surmised the chain of events. No one was behind the wheel of the car. The boys were all in or near the driveway close to my bedroom window. The hood was up. Bubbbba and maybe one of his dudes worked on the engine while the rest joked around and made a lot of needless noise.

Stunner! Bubbbba got the car started. Based on all the joking, I'm guessing his ability to start the engine took his buddies by surprise. After all, Bubbbbba wasn't a mechanic. Now for the whoops. . . . If you aren't a mechanic, it is in your best interest not to be under the hood trying to fix the engine. Even more so, it really isn't in your best interest to be under the hood with the engine running. You could blow up the engine, electrocute yourself, or accidentally put the car into gear. What? You think you know where I'm going with this?

For the second time that Sunday afternoon, Bubbbba had success. He didn't blow up the engine or electrocute himself. That's right, he got the car in gear and it took off down the driveway. I'm guessing this evoked the: "No! . . . NO! . . . BUBBBBBA!!" The car traveled about ten feet and ran through the double gates, busting them off the fence post hinges. It traveled another ten feet and rested after hitting the corner of the freestanding garage. Needless to say, there was a lot—and I mean a superfluity—of cussing. I could only shake my head in bewilderment over his accidental mechanical achievement. Shoot. This was more entertaining than television. Even my dreams aren't this whacked. Could my afternoon get any more entertaining? Could he appease for terminating my nap? Yea, he could and did! Bubbbbba decided to fix the gates. After all, he needed to keep his pernicious pit bull and chow incarcerated. Resourcefully, he got the necessary supplies to reattach the twisted gates. With twine in hand, he was ready to repair. Luckily, his friends were there for him and willing to help. You know, drink beer and laugh at him . . . I mean . . . laugh with him.

Each gate was half the width of the driveway. The two gates met in the mid-point of the driveway. One gate had a rod that anchored into the driveway. The other gate latched to the anchored gate to ensure the gates closed securely. Anyway, that was the design prior to the "whoops." Bubbbbba diligently worked to secure the mutilated gates back in place—original design in mind. He took his sturdy twine and wove the twine around each gate, reattaching it to its respective fence post. His comrades offered copious encouragement with each weave—laughter. Wonderful. Beautiful. Most excellent. Finished. Bubbbbba had a puff of pride. At last, the gates were shabbily tied to the fence posts. You ask, "What about the gate with the anchoring rod so the gates close securely?" Twine was used to hold the two gates closed. "Securely?" you ask. Get real. Of course, not! Bubbbbba's friends agreed with me. With mockery in their voices, they pronounced their judgment on Bubbbbba's workmanship. Bubbbbba retorted, "I ain't no nigger! I'm a white man and don't do no nigger job!" Ergo, Bubbbbba proved beyond a shadow of a doubt where he resided on my redneck continuum. In addition to exhibiting all the other extreme end criteria (cussing, drinking, loud cars, vicious dogs, no job, police difficulty, and so forth), he announced to the world his racist stance. In doing so, he implied other races can't match his mastery—inferior to his white supremacy. In reality, race has nothing to do with quality of work. Quality of work is determined by knowledge, ability, skill, and talent. In this case, Bubbbbba was not qualified to fix the gate. Hence, I had to contemplate Bubbbbba's promulgation. I wondered why the "pride of the race" couldn't process that he didn't have the skill or knowledge to fix the fence. My first thought was, "You goof. You ran the car through the fence and into the side of the garage. The fence shouldn't be broken, and you park the car . . . in the garage." Perhaps, the best solution would have been to call the fence repair man. Needless to say, the gates fell off the "hinges" every time they tried to open the gates. Twine just doesn't work as well as steel bolts and an anchoring rod. Bubbbbba's broken-down repair job kept the dogs inside the fence. We were thankful his dogs weren't smart enough to figure out they could push down the gates. He never fixed the garage. Bubbbbba, his wife (Bubbbbbett), their son (Bubba, Jr.), and friends lived next door to us for many more months. During his remaining time, Bubbbbba continued to do an array of things that reinforced his position on the extreme end of the redneck continuum.

Just as he was born with his mother living in that house, his oldest son was born with him living in that house. I only saw his son from a distance. Neither one of us made any attempts to rebuild our previous relationship. In telling this true story, I've used my redneck stereotype satirically. We all have stereotypes and use them daily. Is this fair? How often do you label a person and then judge him by that label? Was Bubbbbba a redneck? His attitudes and behaviors fit nicely into my extreme-end redneck continuum. Our strife had nothing to do with a label. It was all about our opposing value systems.

I can only wonder why our lives took such drastically different paths. I know my family structure and situation was more stable. More importantly, my belief system prohibits me from viewing anyone as inferior or superior. Undoubtedly, our perceptions of a person greatly influence the way we interact with that person. I know attitude and behavior determines the type of relationship I cultivate with anyone. My perceptions and the time I spent with Bubbbbba as a baby and young boy were harmonious. Our opposing adult attitudes and behaviors shattered our childhood relationship. In spite of the challenges in Bubbbbba's life, he had the opportunity to take a different path. His grandmother was an elementary school teacher. She graduated from college when women were told and expected to stay home and have babies. She would have gratefully paid for him to go to college. What happened, and why did he choose the path of slothfulness instead of opportunity?

In retrospect, I regret I didn't encourage him more when we were growing up. He was six years younger which translated into light years away from my peer group. When I was with my friends, we didn't want him around us all the time—especially when boys entered the picture. It was difficult for 12-year-old girls to woo the boys with a six-year-old boy hanging around. When I wasn't with my friends, I spent a lot of one-on-one time with him. Let me tell you the end of the story. Bubbbbba moved out of his grandmother's house about a year after moving in. His sister, Chick, moved in after he vacated. She is six years younger than Bubbbbba and I barely knew her. She was a better neighbor and cared—at least superficially—how the neighbors reacted to her shenanigans. Just like two peas in a pod, Chick had the same belief system. Consequently, she had conflicts with the neighbors. She lived in the house less than a year and moved out. Karen sold Mrs. Smith's house soon after Chick skedaddled. Once again, my parents have a real neighbor. The new neighbors put up a new gate and tore down the detached garage. After Bubbbbba moved, we didn't hear much about him until a neighbor heard his obituary on a local radio station. We found out Bubbbbba committed suicide in his mother's house in Charlotte. He died somewhere around his 30th birthday, the father of three boys, and divorced. His mother buried him in our hometown beside his grandfather and grandmother. I never told my parents, but I visited his grave shortly after he died. I think my parents did too.

After seeing Bubbbbba's lifestyle and attitude when he moved in next door, I'm not surprised he died young. I really thought he would die in a bar room fight or a car wreck. He had two serious car accidents—alcohol related—a few years before he moved in next door. I never thought about suicide because he had a gregarious personality and appeared to have a positive self-image. Shortly after Bubbbbba moved in next door, my father had his only serious conversation with him. My father asked him if he learned anything from his two near-death experiences. He responded, "Yeah, I'll do the driving next time we are all drunk." My father told him he was headed for a short life if he didn't get it together. He blew off my father's prophetic warning. I hadn't really thought about the potential reasons Bubbbbba became the person he was until now. I thought writing this essay would be easy, but it wasn't. I've told and laughed about the Sunday afternoon escapade many times. Bubbbbba was a friend. I remember him fondly as a child and cherish those days. I still think about him around Thanksgiving. As an adult, he became pure misery in our lives for a short period of time. I didn't like or respect him at all. His metamorphosis from friend to nemesis is why writing the complete story wasn't easy. As a matter of fact, it was downright painful.

There is no happy ending for this story. A wasted friendship. A wasted life. After this experience, I hope I never say, "There's a redneck—on the unenviable end of the c ontinuum—in my backyard, HELP!"

Key Terms
Perception, Prototype, Mental Yardsticks, Stereotyping

9.   Family, Faith, and a Fish Fry

Daniel Richardson

Being a Caucasian professor at a predominantly African American university affords many interesting opportunities to relate and connect with my students. One opportunity occurs when I discuss the role of identity scripts in shaping our self-concepts to my fundamentals of speech classes. Identity scripts reflect the values and heritages of our families, defining our roles, how we play these roles, and the basic elements in the plot that defines our lives (Wood, 2009). I explain that the identity script I was given by my father centered on our family history of being small farmers in the rural South who valued manual labor, an insular world view, and had little use for education and for people who, quite frankly, did not look like us.

pavla/Shutterstock.com

My follow-up question after making this startlingly disclosure is how did I escape the identity script my father did his best to instill within me, obtain an advanced degree as well as a teaching position at the premier HBCU in Greensboro, and be generally well-liked by my students? The answer, I say, started when I was a small boy with the three F's of Family, Faith, and a Fish Fry.

My mother did not share all aspects of my father's identity script as she had grown up in a family where service, not farming, was prized. Two of her brothers were career military, and she had been a nurse before leaving the profession to wed my father who needed her at home to help raise his three children from a prior marriage. Mom believed in education and in the fundamental decency of people without regard to their ethnicity, gender, or socioeconomic status. She insisted on subscribing to the local newspaper published in a nearby city and on having a television or at least a radio in the house for entertainment and to keep up with the outside world. My father had a particular disdain for television with its suspect influences and required much convincing to buy a new set or to have our existing one repaired. In fact, had it not been for his enjoyment of a small number of programs like "The Porter Wagoner Show" I doubt we would have ever had a TV to watch.

Another aspect of mom's character was her steadfast belief in helping people and in her general sympathy for the church, even though she rarely attended services. I remember seeing a strange car turn into our gravel driveway one Saturday afternoon. My father was not at home (he worked second shift most Saturdays at a textile mill), and my mom told me to stay inside until she had a chance to speak to the people in the car. I peeked out a window and observed her conversing with two African American men, an unusual sight to say the least at our small farm. After speaking with them for a few minutes, she came back inside to get her purse, and I asked what was happening. She explained that the two men were members of a local Baptist church and that they were selling tickets for an upcoming fish fry.

I protested that father would not approve and that he would not, under any circumstances, go pick up the fish plates she was about to purchase. The local community remained heavily segregated in the 1970s despite the start of forced busing and integrated schools in the early part of the decade. While we all prayed to the same God, Caucasian believers did not go to the African American churches, and African American believers did not go to the Caucasian churches. The morning of the Sabbath remained the most segregated time of the week.

My mom sat me down and said she knew we would not get the food but was going to buy the tickets anyway because the proceeds would help the church. I was puzzled as to why she would support a church we would never visit and why she would give her money away with no hope of getting the product she was buying. She replied that the church is the church and God does not care about denominations or other artificial constructs of man, and she added that she had told the two African Americans she would buy two tickets, but because she did not drive (one quirk of her family's identity script), she did not have the means to pick up the fish and that they should consider the purchase a donation.

Still, I was not thrilled about paying for food we would never eat as I walked outside with mom. What happened next surprised and delighted me. One of the African American men said something like,

> Ma'am, we've been talking while you were inside, and we've decided to deliver the plates to you on the Saturday of the fish fry. That's not something we normally do, but if you don't drive and want the fish for you and your little one, we'll bring them to you. We appreciate you so much for being willing to help the church.

The second gentleman, who may have been the pastor, added something about how the Lord commanded us to be fishers of men and how this situation gave them an opportunity to fulfill the Lord's command. Reflecting back on his words today, I wonder if he was referencing the courageous outreach they were doing on the Caucasian side of our segregated community. Indeed, as my paternal grandmother might say, I am sure they received their share of being "mean-mouthed, door slammed, and dog bit." I wish I could remember what he said more clearly as it sounded profound to my young ears, but alas, the words have faded over the decades.

I remember being so excited the day of the fish fry and asked my mother multiple times what we could expect for dinner and when our food would be delivered. She must have grown weary of telling me what all came on the plate, and she also cautioned me gently that weeks had passed since she purchased the tickets, that organizing and running a fish fry is a big job, and that I should not think less of the men if they forgot to bring our plates.

To pass the time, I loaded a stack of 45s on our record player and wondered how many of these songs I would hear before our plates were delivered. I went through one stack, a second stack, and by the time I was halfway through the third stack, I heard pots and pans banging in the kitchen and resigned myself to the disappointment of having been forgotten. But before that last record on the third stack dropped down, I heard the unmistakable crunch of gravel and knew a vehicle was coming up the driveway. I became almost as excited as I would have been on Christmas morning when I saw a car I did not recognize pull up near the back door and an African American man get out carrying two fish plates.

Mom called me into the dining room after bringing the plates into the house, and we had supper together. The fish turned out to be some type of white fish, the sides were coleslaw, french fries, and hush puppies. I think a dessert and sweet tea was also included. Standard fare is how I would probably rate it today, but for a young boy who had never experienced fish fry dining and who had never had a meal delivered to his house, I thought the food on my plate was the best I had tasted in a long time.

Members of this African American church would return about every six months with tickets for the next fish fry. My mom would always buy two, and the plates were delivered with clockwork precision. This cycle continued for a couple of years, and my excitement about these special suppers never waned. When the men did stop coming, I missed them.

How do you start to break the cycle of a narrow, limited/limiting, racist identity script passed down from one generation of your family to the next? Everyone has to find his or her own exit ramp I suppose, but for me, my journey was marked by the signposts of family from my mother, faith from the church, and a fish fry as the special supper I enjoyed as a boy.

Discussion Questions

1. How do family and faith work together to imprint a new identity script on the young boy?
2. How does faith influence the way the mother perceives the two African American men?
3. What did the African American pastor mean when he said this situation gave them an opportunity to fulfill the Lord's command of being "fishers of men"?
4. What is significant about the mother referring to the African American Baptist Church as being simply "the church" and why did the African American man use this same construction when speaking with the mother?

5. While the media is not discussed to a significant degree in the essay, what role might it have played in the young boy choosing to adopt a different identity script than the one offered by his father? Why did the father have a particular disdain for 1970s television?

Reference

Wood, J. T. (2009). *Communication in our lives* (5th ed.). Boston, MA: Wadsworth Cengage Learning.

10. Minorities Scorned

Sydney M. Silverthorne

Identity is *a core issue for most people. It is about who we are and who others think we are* (Martin & Nakayama, 2012). *How do we come to understand who we are? And how do we communicate our identity to others?* Conflicts emerge when there are sharp differences between who we think we are and who others think we are.

There are several shades to my identity: I am a full-time, non-traditional undergraduate student at North Carolina Agricultural and Technical State University. I am also a single mother, a military veteran, a Black woman, and a housekeeper. I never imagined issues regarding identity would come into question in my role as a housekeeper.

Last December I accepted a position as a housekeeper for a local apartment management company. My goal was to earn money to help pay for my college education and support my six-year-old son. At the beginning of my employment the staff consisted of 13 employees: six leasing agents, five maintenance technicians, a groundskeeper, and me as the housekeeper.

Rob Marmion/Shutterstock.com

On the first day of work, I realized that the staff was predominantly White. One of the maintenance technicians appeared to me to be bi-racial, with Black and White ancestry. He seemed a little standoffish, which I thought was kind of unusual, but I didn't think too much of it. Eventually, we started speaking to each other casually at work and very early on he made the statement, "You know I'm not Black, right?" I was extremely taken aback by his comment, and was not sure if there was an appropriate response to give in return. As previously stated, I thought that he was partially Black and identified with the Black race. I made assumptions about his **racial identity** or what *particular racial group with which he identified* based upon my perception of his appearance. I quickly realized he was not joking and was very serious about what he said. I felt he already knew that I thought he was Black, and he needed to make clarification. His follow up statement was "I'm

Native American." The look on my face was probably one that was accepting, but showed confusion. Our brief conversation was disconcerting and unsettling. My coworker made me feel as though I offended him, and somehow I was feeling the same—offended. It was very obvious that he wanted to make it clear that he identified as Native American and not Black. Naturally, my issue is the "not Black" aspect. I honestly don't know whether he knows his statement could be seen as offensive and that he could have just as easily stated that he was Native American without being so adamant about not being Black.

The conversation set the tone for our casual work relationship and on my end, the conversation actually put up a barrier. I was offended because I got the impression that in his mind being Black is inferior and undesirable. Another reason for the communication barrier is because I could see that he could be potentially offended by something I might say, and in return I could be easily offended by something he might say in reference to our respective races.

Most people can recall a time when they felt discriminated against by someone of the opposite race or remember racist remarks that were made toward them. However, this was the issue of two minorities in a workplace where White employees were the majority. Maybe he had been offended in the past for being considered a Black male. The issue raised a few questions for me: Was he offended because he felt like his race was not being acknowledged? Another question arose: Was he offended because being considered Black was demeaning in some way, or could it have been both? Could it be a different issue? My initial perception was that he felt that identifying as a Black male was beneath him.

We worked together for another six months and held many conversations in which interestingly enough *he* discussed his declaration he made within our first interactions. Later on he made the comment to me, "you know my people had it worse than your people." With this comment I was not taken aback like I was with the first comment. By this time I had come to understand some of his thought processes and views on certain issues, this one in particular. However, I politely let him know that I was not going to argue about which race "had it worse." I did not think it was necessary or appropriate. We shared the **minority identity**; *the sense of belonging to a non-dominant group* (Martin & Nakayama, 2012). And yet he was ready to have a battle of the minorities with staff, which at that time consisted of just the two of us. I gathered that his passion about this issue was from something personal. As far as I was concerned, we still needed to avoid conversation on the subject—especially since our only communication is in the workplace.

Later, the issue arose again among my White employees. My Native American coworker also made it clear to our White coworkers that he was not Black. One day, the White employees decided to ask me, the Black employee, whether or not the Native American coworker was Black. I simply told them that he was Native American. They reacted in a joking manner, implying that he was Black and wondering why I would say different. Their response was no big deal to them, but it showed me a lot about their character and I was offended as the minority, personally, and for my Native American coworker. It was moments like that which helped me to somewhat understand why this coworker chose to personally share his identity with me.

Communication scholar Julia T. Wood (2002) believes that our self and identity is a "multidimensional process that involves importing and acting from social perspectives . . . Communication is essential to developing a self" (p. 53), and hence our identity. Wood believes that once we form our sense of self and identity we communicate with others our perspective of who we are. This experience helped me realize that there are multiple dimensions of identity. It is important that we acknowledge and respect everyone's perception of self and identity.

References

Martin, & Nakayama, T. K. (2012). *Intercultural communication in contexts* (5th ed.). New York, NY: McGraw-Hill Higher Education.

Wood, J. T. (2002). *Interpersonal communication: Everyday encounters* (3rd ed.). New York, NY: Wadsworth Publishing Company.

11. My Historically Black University Experience

Matt Parmesano

While sitting in my first class as a college student on the first day of school back in the fall of 2012, I was asked by my professor to tell the class one thing that made me unique. My answer was simply, "I'm White." This instantly made my professor and the entire class laugh out loud. I'm a White male, and I go to Winston-Salem State University. WSSU is a historically Black university, and only 18% of students at the university are White.

Throughout my three years at WSSU, I've been asked dozens of times by various people why, as a White male, I chose to attend an HBCU.

I decided to go to WSSU because I'm a local kid from Walkertown with a passion for sports journalism who works at the Winston-Salem Journal. By choosing WSSU, I have been able to keep my job at the Journal while earning a degree in mass communications at the same time. It also didn't hurt that I'm here on a full academic scholarship.

Another question I'm asked often is whether I like going to an HBCU. To be honest, I didn't know what to expect when I first made the choice to attend WSSU. Prior to my coming here, I had always gone to predominately White schools and most of my friends were White.

Although I didn't know what to expect, I still had my own expectations and fears. Aside from the usual freshman jitters and nerves, I was worried I would be looked at as an outsider or be treated differently by other students as a result of me not being African American. Boy, was I wrong.

I'm an honors student, and the freshman honors students at WSSU arrive on campus a week earlier than the rest of the freshmen to go through their own separate orientation called "Jumpstart" before also participating in the usual "Ramdition" for all freshmen the following week.

To my surprise, I was immediately accepted as just another student. I quickly learned it didn't matter to anybody else that I was White because just like my African American peers, I was a college student looking to further my education and make something out of myself.

Now a junior, I can honestly say I love my HBCU. These past three years have helped me see that even though there are set stereotypes about every race, we as humans are really all the same. We all just want to be happy and successful.

If I had to choose all over again, I'd still choose WSSU. Just as I would at any college or university that offers a journalism or mass communications degree, I've received a higher education and I'm working toward earning a degree that will help me with my career. But that's not all college is about. College is about discovering oneself, making lifelong friends, and learning about life. Attending WSSU has given me the opportunity to do all of these things to a greater extent than I would have had had I attended a predominately White institution because I've made many African American friends.

These friends have taught me about African American culture, and I've taught them about White culture. The greatest lesson I've learned in my time here, though, is that while our cultural backgrounds may be quite different, we all want the same thing—an opportunity to achieve our dreams.

michaeljung/Shutterstock.com

Discussion Questions

1. In your opinion, what is the biggest difference between African American and White culture?
2. Describe a situation where you were the minority and you had a positive experience. What did you learn from this encounter?
3. How have your various interactions over the years with peers of different ethnicities from your own affected who you are today?
4. What's your dream?

12.   Identity, Conflict, and Intercultural Communication

Anna K. Lee

Psychology, the study of behavior and mental processes, is a discipline in which identity and conflict have been examined (Barken & Snowden, 2001). **Identity** may be defined as a distinctive characteristic belonging to any given individual that is also shared by other people in a particular social category or group. A person's identity may be ascribed in different ways, such as race, nationality, religion, gender, etc. (Turner, 1982). **Conflict** is a form of intercultural communication in which there are differences in intentions, goals, values, and beliefs between individuals or groups. Intercultural conflict may occur between groups with different identities (Gaertner, Mann, Murrell, & Dovidio, 1989). For example, conflict may exist between groups from different racial groups, nationalities, or religions. We tend to view people who share our identity more positively and those who do not more negatively.

For instance, the U.S. has had a history of racial tension and violence since its inception. In this discussion, the term **race** is used to distinguish between recognized groups whose members share certain physical (e.g., skin color, hair texture, facial features) and cultural characteristics (e.g., ancestry). In contrast, the term **ethnicity** is used to refer to groups whose members' shared traits are limited to features such as language, religion, dress, and nationality. Of course, there are problems with using either of these types of classification systems (Yee, Fairchild, Weizmann, & Wyatt, 1993) because there are more differences among individuals within a racial or ethnic group than between different racial or ethnic groups (Zuckerman, 1990).

Although race is a social concept rather than a scientific one, it has been used to separate people into groups around the world. Due to a group's desire for social, economic, and political power, conflict between groups may arise. Conflict is sometimes expressed through **aggression**, which refers to the intent to harm another individual or group, or through **violence**, which refers to the unjust or unwarranted exertion of force. Intercultural conflict can lead to the infliction of harm and use of force toward an

PathDoc/Shutterstock.com

individual or group (Krahé, 2001). Therefore, intercultural conflict is sometimes motivated by extreme bias or prejudice (McDevitt, Levin, & Bennett, 2002). When the behavior in question is also illegal (e.g., assault), it may be called a "hate" crime (Craig, 2002), which is an alternative term that puts the focus on racial/ethnic bias, and which characterizes much of the contemporary intercultural conflict that occurs (Ehrlich & Pincus, 1999).

Not a Uniquely American Problem

Conflict because of differing identities is not a uniquely American problem (Alexseev, 2003; Duckitt, 2004). Many other countries have experienced incidents of intercultural conflict. For example, Krahé (2001) refers to the aggressive behaviors of right-wing German youths targeting Turkish immigrants and Jewish memorials as "ethnocentric violence." In the United Kingdom, reports of racist and ethnic violence are also not unusual. Indeed, because of the extent of racial victimization in Britain, Bowling (1993) concludes that racial harassment and victimization is a widespread problem. Furthermore, in Scotland, rates of racially motivated attacks upon people of color who may or may not be immigrants occur often enough to have warranted establishing a distinct annual review by Scotland's government (Audit Scotland, 2004). The Middle East has seen a number of struggles over the years in differences between nationalities and religions, and there continues to be significant intercultural conflict between the Palestinians and Israelis, as well as between the Sunni and Shia Muslims of Iraq (Sørli, Gleditsch, & Strand, 2005). Furthermore, the global community continues to mourn the Rwandan genocide in which ethnically-similar Hutus murdered scores of Tutsis in 1993 (Uvin, 1996). Assuredly, the problem of intercultural conflict is widespread and shows no signs of fading.

Examples of Racially Motivated Conflict

In the U.S., research on conflict has generally studied conflicts between Black and White Americans (Wright, 1990). Specifically, researchers have actively studied conflict in the pre-civil rights era of the 1940s and 1950s, and then again during the social upheaval of the 1960s, the 1970s, and to a lesser degree in the 1980s (Allport, 1954; Struch & Schwartz, 1989). For example, until late in the 1950s, racism and physical violence directed at Black Americans by White Americans was normative, and well entrenched within the social fabric of American society. Whereas some blamed the collective violence directed at the newly-freed Black slaves or on White fears about intercultural sex (Myrdal, 1944), others attributed the problem to the expanding rights of Black Americans (Bobo, 1983; Park, Burgess, & McKenzie, 1925). Today, a renewed interest in the topic is evident among researchers around the world who are addressing issues related to hate crime and terrorism (Bar-Tal & Teichman, 2005).

There are many examples of racial conflict that have caught national attention in the media. In 2003, Kendra James, an unarmed 21-year-old Black American woman was shot and killed by a White police officer in Portland, Oregon (Ritchie, 2011). In 2007, six Black American youth who became known as the Jena 6 were charged with assault for attacking a young, white male (The Washington Times, 2007). In 2011, an unarmed Black American teenager, 17-year-old Trayvon Martin, was shot and killed on his way home from a convenience store by a White Hispanic American male (Blow, 2012). Renisha McBride, an unarmed Black American 19-year-old was shot by a White male homeowner while asking for help after a car accident in 2013 (Alexander-Floyd, 2014). Also, after seeking help after a car accident, Jonathan Ferrell was shot ten times by a police officer (Troutman, 2013). In 2014, Michael Brown, an 18-year-old Black American unarmed teenager was shot and killed by a police officer in Ferguson, Missouri, while walking down a public street (Newburn, 2014). These tragedies captured the public's attention primarily because of the lack of weapons on behalf of the victims and the race of the victims and perpetrators.

The Persistent Nature of Intercultural Conflict

Intercultural conflict continues to exist because of **internal** (i.e., reasons within the individual) or **external** (i.e., reasons outside the individual) factors. For instance, it has long been recognized that conflict is strongly influenced by the **attitudes**, meaning one's internal positive or negative evaluations of an object, person, or thing of the persons involved (Baron & Richardson, 1994). It is in this way that attitudes can serve as both causes and effects of intercultural conflict. Consequently, in a number of studies, researchers have investigated the role of **prejudice**, or one's internal negative feelings toward a racial group as a factor in the likelihood of committing an act of intercultural conflict (Beal, O'Neal, Ong, & Ruscher, 2000).

External factors such as the integration of racial groups, physical closeness, competition over important resources (i.e., land, food, politics), and trespass of geographical boundaries may explain intercultural conflict (Tolnay & Beck, 1995). Moreover, conflict between groups may stem from the groups' desire for social, economic, or political benefits (Bar-Tal, 1997). Finally, some external explanations for intercultural aggression have considered the role of socialization, meaning the messages one receives from society, family, and friends regarding racial groups (Altmeyer, 1996), as well as the spectrum and likelihood of continued racial conflicts within and outside of the U.S. (Yang, Power, Takaku, & Posas, 2004).

PathDoc/Shutterstock.com

The problem of intercultural conflict continues to occur within the U.S. and across the globe. Although it is inevitable that people will associate themselves with group identities, the intercultural communication of conflict does not have to persist. Tolerance of various identities may lead to less conflict between groups and reduce negative intercultural communication. Also, the elimination of unequal and unfair treatment and establishment of fair and equitable treatment between groups would improve intercultural communication and reduce instances of intercultural conflict.

Discussion Questions

1. What is conflict? How is conflict related to intercultural communication?
2. What is the difference between race and ethnicity?
3. How is identity related to intercultural conflict?
4. What is the difference between internal and external factors?
5. How can intercultural conflict be reduced?

References

Alexander-Floyd, N. G. (2014). Beyond superwomen: Justice for Black women too. *Dissent, 61*(1), 42–44.

Alexseev, M. A. (2003). Economic valuations and interethnic fears: Perceptions of Chinese migration in the Russian Far East. *Journal of Peace Research, 40*(1), 89–106.

Allport, G. W. (1954). *The nature of prejudice.* Cambridge, MA: Addison-Wesley.

Altemeyer, R. (1996). *The authoritarian specter.* Cambridge, MA: Harvard University Press.

Audit Scotland. (2004). *Performance indicators: Racially motivated incidents.* Edinburgh, Scotland: Audit Scotland.

Barken, S., & Snowden, L. (2001). *Collective violence.* Boston, MA: Allyn & Bacon.

Baron, R. A., & Richardson, D. R. (1994). *Human aggression.* New York, NY: Plenum Press.

Bar-Tal, D. (1997). Formation and change of ethnic and national stereotypes: An integrative model. *International Journal of Intercultural Relations, 21,* 491–523.

Bar-Tal, D., & Teichman, R. (2005). *Stereotypes and prejudice in conflict: Representations of Arabs in Israeli Jewish society.* Cambridge, MA: Cambridge University Press.

Beal, D., O'Neal, E., Ong, J., & Ruscher, J. (2000). The ways and means of interethnic aggression: Modern racists' use of covert retaliation. *Personality and Social Psychology Bulletin, 26,* 1225–1238.

Blow, C. M. (2012). The curious case of Trayvon Martin. *The New York Times.* Retrieved from http://www.nytimes.com/2012/03/17/opinion/blow-the-curious-case-of-trayvon-martin.html?pagewanted=all&_r=0

Bobo, L. (1983). Whites' opposition to busing: Symbolic racism or realistic group conflict. *Journal of Personality and Social Psychology, 45,* 1196–1210.

Bowling, B. (1993). Racial harassment and the process of victimization: Conceptual and Methodological Implications for the Local Crime Survey. *British Journal of Criminology, 33*(2), 231–250.

Craig, K. M. (2002). Examining hate-motivated aggression: A review of the social psychological literature on hate crimes as a distinct form of aggression. *Aggression and Violent Behavior, 7*(1), 85–101.

Duckitt, J. (2004). The cultural bases of ethnocentrism: Comparing white Afrikaners and European New Zealanders. In Y. T. Lee, C. McCauley, F. Moghaddam, & S. Worchel (Eds.). *The Psychology of ethnic and cultural conflict* (pp. 155–173). Westport, CT: Praeger.

Ehrlich, H. J., & Pincus, F. L. (Eds.). (1999). *Race and ethnic conflict: Contending views on prejudice, discrimination, and ethnoviolence*. Boulder, CO: Westview Press.

Gaertner, S. L., Mann, J., Murrell, A., & Dovidio, J. F. (1989). Reducing intergroup bias: The benefits of recategorization. *Journal of Personality and Social Psychology, 57*(2), 239.

Krahé, B. (2001). *The social psychology of aggression*. Philadelphia, PA: Taylor and Francis.

McDevitt, J., Levin, J., & Bennett, S. (2002). Hate crime offenders: An expanded typology. *Journal of Social Issues, 58*(2), 303–317.

Myrdal, G. (1944). *An American dilemma: The Negro problem and modern democracy*. New York, NY: Harper.

Newburn, T. (2014). Civil unrest in Ferguson was fuelled by the Black community's already poor relationship with a highly militarized police force. *LSE American Politics and Policy*. Retrieved from http://blogs.lse.ac.uk/usappblog/2014/08/29/civil-unrest-in-ferguson-was-fuelled-by-the-black-communitys-already-poor-relationship-with-a-highly-militarized-police-force/

Park, R., Burgess, E. W., & McKenzie, R. D. (1925). *The city*. Chicago, IL: University of Chicago Press.

Ritchie, L. D. (2011). Justice is blind: A model for analyzing metaphor transformations and narratives in actual discourse. *Metaphor and the Social World, 1*(1), 70–89.

Sørli, M. E., Gleditsch, N. P., & Strand, H. (2005). Why is there so much conflict in the Middle East? *Journal of Conflict Resolution, 49*(1), 141–165.

Struch, N., & Schwartz, S. H. (1989). Intergroup aggression: Its predictors and distinctness from in-group bias. *Journal of Personality and Social Psychology, 56*, 364–373.

Tolnay, S. E., & Beck, E. M. (1995). *An analysis of southern lynchings, 1882–1930*. Champaign, IL: University of Illinois Press.

Troutman, A. (2013). Leading the movement for health equity, social justice, human rights. *The Nation's Health, 43*(9), 3.

Turner, J. C. (1982). Towards a cognitive redefinition of the social group. In H. Tajfel (Ed.), *Social identity and intergroup relations* (pp. 15–40). New York, NY: Cambridge University Press.

Uvin, P. (1996). Tragedy in Rwanda: The political ecology of conflict. *Environment: Science and Policy for Sustainable Development, 38*(3), 7–29.

Washington Times. (2007). *Civil rights activists join fight of 'Jena Six' charges.* Retrieved from http://www.washingtontimes.com

Wright, G. C. (1990). *Racial violence in Kentucky, 1865–1940: Lynchings, mob rule and "legal lynchings."* Baton Rouge, LA: Louisiana State University Press.

Yang, P. Q., Power, S., Takaku, S., & Posas, L. (2004). Immigration and ethnic conflict in comparative perspective. In Y. T. Lee, C. McCauley, F. Moghaddam, & S. Worchel (Eds.), *The psychology of ethnic and cultural conflict* (pp. 89–112). Westport, CT: Praeger.

Yee, A. H., Fairchild, H. H., Weizmann, F., & Wyatt, G. E. (1993). Addressing psychology's problems with race. *American Psychologist, 48,* 1132–1140.

Zuckerman, M. (1990). Some dubious premises in research and theory on racial differences: Scientific, social, and ethical issues. *American Psychologist, 45,* 1297–1303.

Chapter 3

Communicating Verbally and Nonverbally

13. You Don't Have to Say a Word!

Dr. Regina M. Williams Davis
North Carolina A&T State University

My teenage daughter loves to use emoticons to help explain her text messages. At her emotional age, she seems to be fully aware that I tend to receive messages from her facial expressions and other nonverbal behaviors more than anything she says. I will see her dreadfully sad, "my life is over . . ." look on her face often, and hear her words, every time I ask her, "Are you okay?" respond to me with, "I'm fine!" All of her nonverbal behaviors say otherwise. Therefore, in spite of the digital way we communicate, it is apparent that some method of reinforcing a text or an email with an emoticon symbol, be it J or L, is a valued part of nonverbal communication.

Different textbooks and studies in communication will suggest there are more non-verbal categories, but the following eight are consistently addressed: aesthetics, artifacts, chronemics, haptics, kinesics, oculesics, paralanguage, physical appearance, and proxemics. These categories are broad, with subcategories included. Figure 13.1 provides the behavioral emphasis that clarifies the nonverbal category.

Nonverbal behavior typically accompanies our verbal messages, but not always. Often we send nonverbal messages unintentionally. Aesthetics includes atmosphere and ambiance. Having your boyfriend over for dinner, setting your table with candles lit, playing soft sultry music, and dressing slightly provocative can send an intentional message. However, folding your arms across your chest, in concert with a serious look of concern, may send a message of judgment unintentionally.

PunyaFamily/Shutterstock.com

Nonverbal Category	Behavioral Emphasis
Aesthetics	Environmental Factors
Artifacts	Personal Objects
Chronemics	Time
Haptics	Physical Touch
Kinesics	Body Movements
Oculesics	Eye Movement
Paralanguage	Vocal Variations
Physical Appearance	Personal Presentation
Proxemics	Physical Space

FIGURE 13.1   Behavioral emphasis of nonverbal category.

When my students hear "artifacts," they immediately think of ancient artifacts. **Artifacts** can be something as simple as earrings or a belt buckle. **Chronemics** is the use of time. Arriving to an interview for employment, 10 to 15 minutes late, sends the interviewer the message that you either have no respect for another's time, or that you are not truly interested in the job. On the other hand, arriving early to the same interview will send a message that shows interest and eagerness for the position.

Haptics deals with physical touch. If a male brushes against a woman's body and she perceives it to be inappropriate, then negative interactions can result. Waving a fist purposefully through the air until it touches another person, hitting them sends a belligerent message. Nonetheless, the human touch is powerful, and a genuine hug or a congratulatory handshake can take positive messages a long way.

Kinesics is body movement and includes hand gestures. It can enhance or hinder a message. It can simply be walking away from the podium to become more engaged with the audience. However, pacing can annoy your audience and excessive gestures can be a distraction to your audience. Most people are not always conscious of their body movements. Becoming aware of it will aid in effective communication.

We can send nonverbal messages using our eyes. **Oculesics** is eye movement. Did your mother ever ask you to stop "rolling your eyes"? If or when you did this, it sent her a message that you had a negative attitude about something. In **neuro-linguistic programming (NLP)**, the study of eye movement and its meaning posits that when eyes move up and to the right, the person is trying to recall or remember an event. If their eyes move up and to the left, the person is constructing a new idea. Some people who ascribe to this philosophy suggest that this is a way to tell if a person is telling the truth or not.

Paralanguage is considered nonverbal communication even though words are stated. It is not always what you say, but how you say it. For example, the way I say, "Whatever" and the way my teenager says, "Whatever" seems to provide two completely different connotations. Practice all of the different ways you can state the same sentence and see how many different meanings can be understood.

Physical appearance is a major form of nonverbal communication; hence, "dress for success." Your "self" presentation will speak to your knowledge of appropriateness and respect for others. Physical appearance will include your hair or haircut. So many college students are disappointed that they may need to cut the dreadlocked hair they had grown fond of over the four years they were in school in order to land that first job after graduation. Fortunately, many companies currently are less judgmental about such things than they have been in the past.

Proxemics is really nothing more than respecting personal space. However, I do recall living in Europe and felt that my personal space was violated. It was common for individuals in Germany to ask you questions or dialogue with another with less than five inches between you. In this country, the United States of America, it is important to respect each other's personal space.

There are times when words are not used because we believe that actions will speak for themselves. However, it is important that an effective communicator not assume that their audience or the individual you are in dialogue with will comprehend nonverbal messages the way they are intended. Please be mindful of your words, actions, and nonverbal behaviors.

Key Terms

Aesthetics, Artifacts, Chronemics, Emoticons, Haptics, Kinesics, Neuro-linguistic Programming, Oculesics, Paralanguage, Physical Appearance, Proxemics

14. Experiencing Nonverbal Communication Between Cultures

Dongjing Kang
Nathaniel Simmons
Yea-Wen Chen

Nonverbal communication plays an important role in understanding intercultural interactions in our increasingly globalized world. Cultures are different in spoken languages, just as they have unique nonverbal codes and cues. Nonverbal communication, to most people, refers to communication effected by means other than verbal communication, but it is impossible to separate them (Knapp, Hall, & Horgan, 2013; Mehrabian, 2009). Both verbal and nonverbal interactions communicate meaning and are governed by rules and norms in a particular situation and context (Martin & Nakayama, 2010). On one hand, verbal communication could provide a semantic context for nonverbal interactions to evolve. On the other hand, nonverbal communication is powerful and indispensable because our verbal communication would be ineffective if our nonverbal messages were inconsistent (Giri, 2009). Along with our verbal languages, our appearance, facial expressions, emotions, and gestures all convey meaning within complex cultural systems, shaping and reshaping our experience (Sorrells, 2013).

Nonverbal interactions are the embodied human experience. They are highly ambiguous, relational, and cultural, and often function at a subconscious level. Misunderstandings could rise when the same non-verbal behaviors symbolize different meanings across cultural contexts. The following incident occurred to Dongjing when she first studied in the U.S.:

> Two friends from Italy invited me to dinner at their house when I just landed in the U.S. from China. When the dinner was over, I tried to shake hands to thank them for their hospitality. Two male Italian friends ignored my hands, hugged me and quickly kissed me on my cheek. I immediately pushed them away and run to the door. I felt extremely embarrassed and wasn't able respond in the moment. Seeing me standing in astonishment at the door, the two new friends from Italy apologized with embarrassment.

When such moments of discomfort arose, we could possibly find ways to explain verbally what we meant. It was a learning experience for persons from two different cultures in this particular context. First, the meaning of the nonverbal codes such as "hugging" and "kissing" can be interpreted differently between persons from Italy and China. Second, the event of interaction was embedded in an American cultural context. Third, the varied cultural criteria of a "comfortable" physical distance can be perceived as problematic in communicating gender. Thus, *to whom* and *in what situation* we are communicating our nonverbal codes matter. Such relational/contextual dimensions are important for us to explore in terms of how we send, interpret, and respond to each other in intercultural communication.

The first part of the essay will provide an overview of why nonverbal communication matters in communicating between cultures. Second, we will introduce the theory of the coordinated management of meaning (CMM) to further explore how we coordinate our responses and create meaning with cultural others. Then, each of the three authors will reflect upon their individual experiences with nonverbal communication within an intercultural context where the meaning of nonverbal codes is highly dynamic and ever-changing when coordinating and negotiating intercultural relationships.

Experiencing Nonverbal Cues Across Contexts

Gregory Bateson (1972) suggested that our words and actions will have no meaning without context. Intensified globalization has created various situations for encounters to occur between persons from different cultures. Following Bateson's rendering on context and meaning in the pragmatics of human communication, the authors will engage *coordinated management of meaning (CMM)* in examining the meaning of nonverbal codes across diverse intercultural situations. The core of CMM centers on coordination, coherence, and mystery (Cronen, 1991; Cronen & Pearce, 1992; Pearce, 1989, 2005; Pearce & Pearce, 2000).

Coordination deals with how we create social worlds and coordinate our action (send, receive, interpret, and respond, etc.) together in particular contexts. In *Communication and the Human Condition*, Pearce (1989) defined coordination as a process by which individuals collaborate with each other with intentions to bring what they see as "necessary, noble, and good," and make an attempt to turn away from what they "fear, hate, or despise" (pp. 32–33). These collaborated actions are highly situated and imperfect. In communicating across cultures, nonverbal codes are highly ambiguous and "imperfect" in our interaction. We must constantly negotiate meaning(s) with others and coordinate our responses with individuals from a variety of cultures in particular situations.

Coherence designates human activity as a meaning-making endeavor. In other words, coherence is not only a dynamic pattern of our ever-changing life world, but a partnered process that is created within communicating with others. Coherence refers to the process by which individuals make sense of the world by creating, telling, and/or testing story to themselves and others as well as giving accounts for their successes and failures in coordinating with others (Pearce, 1989). The meanings of nonverbal codes can be created by persons from different cultures by story-telling. When we are actively listening to the others verbally elaborating and explaining the meaning of their nonverbal codes in their cultural stories, we can seek potentials to collaborate meaning for particular codes and (re)produce more favorable patterns of communication in intercultural relationships.

Mystery illuminates the uncertainty and potentials that we might escape negative social worlds and create new realities. Pearce (1989) engaged Chinese Taoist *Lao Tze*'s philosophy to explain mystery as the uncertain and the unfinished nature of human activity, "the Tao that can be spoken is not the true Tao" (p. 77). To understand nonverbal communication, the principle of mystery in CMM helps us to understand that there is always more to life than the mere facts of daily existence.

Guided by CMM, the three authors will share how we experience nonverbal communication across three particular contexts. In the context of disability/ability, the first author will narrate her volunteer experience in an international non-governmental organization working with Tibetan students with disabilities. Coordinating the nonverbal behaviors between able-bodied persons and persons with disabilities enhanced a relationship with respect and trust. Within the context of intercultural relationships, the second author will narrate his intercultural work experiences as an assistant language teacher in Japan. Within the context of higher education and immigration, the third author will unpack how relevant nonverbal behaviors such as silence can affect classroom interactions between U.S. students and international faculty members.

Context One: Nonverbal Codes and Disabilities/Abilities

In the summer of 2012, I (Dongjing) volunteered to teach within an international non-governmental organization that worked toward educating young Tibetans with disabilities (particularly eye impairments) living in an extremely under-resourced condition across the Tibetan plateau. I experienced firsthand and observed the significance of nonverbal elements in persons' interactions across cultures. I particularly reflected on the moments of interaction with Tibetan students with eye impairments and how such coordinated interactions communicated meaning and created the potential to transcend the barrier of intercultural difference.

The most memorable moment between my students and I occurred after my first day of teaching. "Teacher, can I see your face?" said a male Tibetan student with eye impairment. Hearing the request, I hesitated and did not know how to respond—I knew that the student was not able to *see*. I felt frustrated as I said to him, "Ok, but how . . ." After my verbal confirmation, he first placed two hands on my forehead, then moved the hands towards my chin and said to me, "Teacher, thank you! Now, I know how you look." From numerous moments like this, volunteering and working with students with disabilities has proven to be an embodied experience. During this month of volunteering, not only through face-touch, but I enacted other nonverbal interactions with my students, such as holding hands while walking and directing my students' hands to touch objects (e.g., chopsticks during lunch). Sometimes my students would request to "see" my facial expressions which produced both less favorable and favorable communication outcomes. I described this very memorable experience and will provide in-depth analysis of how persons from different cultures coordinated their nonverbal interactions in the context of ability/disability.

Primarily, this particular nonverbal element—haptics, played an important role to *coordinate* interactions in the context of communication ability/disability. **Haptics** refers to a type of nonverbal interaction involving bodily touch. It served as the first step for an able-bodied person and a person with eye impairment to *coordinate* their actions to understand each other's worlds.

J. Lekavicius/Shutterstock.com

Sometimes while my students with eye impairment and I were sitting together, they put their hands on my hands to "feel" each other's presence. Trust sprouted at the very first moment of touch. Being an able-bodied person, I had imaged the worlds of the *other* as well as the unspoken words of worlds through nonverbal interactions.

This scenario of face-touch also reflected an interaction between low contact and contact culture. Edward Hall (1990) noted that persons from **contact cultures** tend to stand close together and touch frequently when they interact, while persons from **low contact cultures** maintain more space and touch less often. Persons from low contact cultures (e.g., America) could be frustrated in this very first bodied contact. For Tibetan volunteers (from contact cultures), it was much easier to work with students with disabilities. I observed that Tibetan volunteers tapped each other's hands softly while talking with students with eye impairments.

I also reflected upon the social and cultural context in which my identity forms—the **cultural spaces** I lived in the Midwest towns of America for the past eight years. Acculturated in America, I usually keep a comfortable distance (an arm's length) with the other person (regardless of a perceived gender) while walking together in public spaces. When experiencing face-touch, I first felt a moment of discomfort. The less favorable communication outcome was highly interconnected with my perception of comfortable personal space, **proxemics**. Personal space norms vary from culture to culture. It is very different that personal physical distance in both private and public spaces became much closer when communicating in the context of ability/disabilities.

During volunteering, the American volunteers and I had a similarly shared body experience with our students with eye impairment—face-touch. By telling and sharing stories, the cultural meaning of the nonverbal behavior became more *coherent* to volunteers. We discussed ways in which how our perception of comfortable spaces had been changed due to this experience. Sometimes we tried to make sense of such moments that came up as "surprising" in this particular context. In CMM, the principle of *mystery* states that human interactions are inherently uncertain and unfinished (Pearce, 1989). To further understand the interplay between uncertainty and expectation in our communicative practices, the moments that we responded to the unanticipated violation of cultural norms could be well explained by **expectancy violations theory**. Expectancy violations theory holds the view that when one's behavior violates our expectations, the person and/or the action will be perceived positively or negatively depending on the specific context and behavior (Burgoon & Hale, 1988; Burgoon & Hubbard, 2004). To American volunteers, the new experience first appeared to be awkward, but was eventually perceived as rewarding in retrospect. Travelling between cultures enables us to think of the ever-changing nature of nonverbal interaction in different contexts. To maintain a distance or space with other persons symbolizes the respect of individuality in America. In Tibetan culture,

Juriah Mosin/Shutterstock.com

living together with closer space means more connection, trust, and closeness in relationships between persons (Norberg-Hodge, 2009).

More often, we *coordinated* our nonverbal choices around our verbal behaviors. From the very memorable moment I described, the student with eye impairment said that he would like to "see" my face; I was confused as to how he could *see* without eyesight. In coordinating and managing meaning in such a context, the language *see* represented different world views. What a person with eye impairment meant by "see" was different from my (an able-bodied person's) interpretation, a privileged, "normalized" understanding—being able to see by my abled eyes. While coordinating our nonverbal interactions around verbal cues, it is quite important to understand the study of **semiotics**, how we create meaning(s) by interpreting signs. According to Martin and Nakayama (2009, 2010), the meanings of **signs** emerge from the combination of the signifier and the signified (**signifiers** are culturally constructed arbitrary words or symbols we used to refer to things, whereas **signified** refers to anything that is expressed in arbitrary words or signifiers). In the context of ability/disability interaction, the word "see" (as a signifier) signified different expectations of nonverbal actions: (a) the action of seeing by abled eyes, and (b) the *bodily* touching as seeing. In this context, verbal and nonverbal interactions were inseparable and *coordinated* with each other to convey meaning. Next, the second author will discuss nonverbal codes within intercultural relationships in light of his work experience as an assistant language teacher in Japan.

Context Two: Nonverbal Codes Within Intercultural Relationships

To discount nonverbal codes within intercultural relationships is to negate dyadic meaning-making opportunities. In other words, by not attending to nonverbal codes we not only run the risk of miscommunicating, but leave a story half-told. As a former English teacher at a Japanese junior high school and researcher of intercultural workplace relationships (Simmons, 2012, 2014a), I (Nathaniel) walked the pages of my undergraduate and graduate intercultural texts in several instances, which I discuss below. In this section, I not only highlight and define key intercultural elements, but do so as I reflect upon my intercultural workplace relationships in Japan. However, first, I will provide you with a bit of a background of my experiences.

As a Japan Exchange & Teaching (JET) Programme participant, I lived in a small town of roughly 8,000 people in Japan's Kansai area. There, I taught English and American culture courses within a small, rural junior high school. I was not only the sole foreigner in the town, but was the only individual I met who spoke English fluently, including my coworkers. I moved to Japan a bit naïve regarding Japanese culture and language. In fact, I *only* knew how to say *konnichiwa* (Good afternoon), but with an accent that most people could not understand. However, with the help of a Sunday morning tutor, I began to learn about Japanese language and culture. Despite the help I received, no tutor could have prepared me entirely for what I encountered. It was within encounters and instances with nonverbal communication that I realized the importance of attending to particular ways of speaking—or speech codes—and nonverbal elements within intercultural communication.

Speech Codes

Speech codes theory (SCT) is a communication theory that examines culturally specific ways of speaking. Within SCT, a **code** refers to a particular way of speaking deemed significant by a particular community (or culture). For example, SCT has been used to expose what it means to speak honorably "like a man" (Philipsen, 1975, 1976), how drag queens should uphold sisterly bonds when competing against each other (Simmons, 2014b), highlighted the importance of listening amongst Blackfeet American Indian speech (Carbaugh, 1999, 2005), as well as how Lebanese American identity is (re)constructed through food and tradition (Homsey & Sandel, 2012). Each of these studies examined communicative conduct in a particular time and space through interviews, observation, and/or ethnography. Such research not only highlights Philipsen's (1997) propositions within SCT, but provides a general understanding of how members of various cultural communities create shared meaning, rules of conduct, and identity via communication.

Based off six propositions, or beliefs, SCT states: (a) distinct speech codes exist within every culture; (b) each culture maintains multiple speech codes; (c) speech codes reveal culturally distinct ways of speaking, thinking, and interacting with one's self and others; (d) the significance or salience of a culture's speech code(s) is (re)created through interaction amongst a culture's participants; (e) speaking speech codes reveals rules and terms of the speech code; and (f) speech codes help predict, control, and explain what is considered appropriate, common sense, sound judgment, and moral communicative conduct. Verbal interaction constructs a space for nonverbal elements to evolve and create meaning as nonverbal elements simultaneously influence verbal interaction. In addition to CMM, SCT is important to consider within intercultural relationships due to ways in which nonverbal elements may hold particular meanings for certain cultures.

g-stockstudio/Shutterstock.com

Nonverbal Elements

At the beginning of this chapter we defined nonverbal communication as communication effected by means other than verbal communication. Within such, various elements exist that compose nonverbal messages. Nonverbal elements are important in both high- and low-context countries. However, the ways in which such cultures rely upon such nonverbal statements vary. For instance, high-context cultures, such as Japan, place meaning within indirect communication contexts, whereas low-context cultures, such as the United States, place meaning within direct verbal statements. In other words, high-context cultures typically have fewer "signs" or verbal statements to explicitly *coordinate* meaning, rules, and regulations when compared with low-context cultures. Whether a culture is high or low context, nonverbal elements are valued.

As an example, one day after working on a lesson plan regarding American holidays, I needed to obtain my team-teacher's approval prior to printing handouts for class. I approached him in the staff room and asked, "Sensei, is this lesson plan ok?" "Hmm," my team-teacher responded as he read. "Is this ok for first-year students?" I asked. The response was none other than what I referred to as the "teeth-suck," in which he tilted his head to one side, clenched his teeth together, and inhaled which created an audible sound. At this point in my time living and working in Japan, I learned that this was a polite, *coherent* way of saying "No!" To make sense of this instance via CMM, I reminded myself of nonverbal elements I learned within my intercultural studies.

First, **facial expressions** refer to various facial features, or expressions, such as a raised eyebrow, an "inquisitive look," and even something as simple as a smile, etc. As my sensei, team-teacher, examined my lesson plan for approval, his facial expressions included a raised eyebrow, a crinkled brow, and a lack of smiling which I interpreted as signaling disapproval. Second, **eye contact** refers to the amount of gaze that an individual exerts when speaking with another. This was a particular challenge in my Japanese workplace, as I attempted to diminish my American cultural training to have eye contact to be polite, my co-workers increased eye contact with me to be polite. In other words, we both adapted in some ways to the other's culture. As my co-worker and I were talking we had reasonably good eye contact, but as he teeth sucked he removed eye contact which further led me to believe my lesson plan was too difficult for early language learners. Third, **emblems** refer to signs or signals such as an "ok" gesture, a smile, shaking one's fist at someone, or bowing. Fourth, **illustrators** emphasize verbal speech. For instance, saying something is "this big" and then demonstrating how big an item was with one's hands serves the function to illustrate just "how big" big is. As a further example, I noticed my Japanese junior high students pointed to their nose when asking, "Me?" when called upon to practice English in class. This moment opened my eyes to ways in which different cultures use illustrators to indicate the same meaning. Whereas I would put my hand on my chest and ask, "Me?" to clarify if someone was speaking with me, my Japanese students pointed to their nose.

Fifth, **haptics** is another way of discussing "touch." Some cultures will value touch while communicating, such as holding hands with one's conversational partner, while others will prefer minimal touching. To extend the first author's understanding of haptics within intercultural relationship, the extent to which one touches or does not touch is in the eye of the beholder. As I prepared for my sojourn in Japan, I read a book about Japanese culture that explained that Japanese do not touch. However, I quickly learned this book was inaccurate as my junior high students were continuously touching, hitting, kicking, tackling, and hugging their friends and classmates just as I witnessed within the U.S. (or perhaps even more so!).

Sixth, **regulators** serve to continue or discontinue speech from one's participant(s). For instance, gazing into one's eyes while speaking with someone in conversation might signal as a message that one needs to leave the conversation. One day, after bringing what I later learned was a receipt from a routine medical visit, my sensei held up a finger and said, "Wait," as he went to speak with others about the letter's contents, which I later learned was my *private* medical information (see Simmons, 2014a). Similarly, holding one's hand to signal "stop" may also serve as a more direct regulator that one must discontinue conversation. In such moments, an individual is using a regulator to dictate the amount of appropriate speech in a given moment.

Seventh, **paralanguage** refers to vocal elements such as **quality** or **tone**, or the clarity of one's voice, **rate**, how quickly or slowly one speaks, and **pitch**, the highness or lowness of one's voice. Keeping paralanguage in mind, it is often important to remember how things are said versus what is said. The ways in which things are said may lead to a variety of interpretations and perceptions that may either positively or negatively influence one's relationship. Eighth, **gestures** refer to bodily movements which are sometimes referred to as "body language" within popular culture. Gestures may include head or hand movements.

Ninth, **chronemics** refers to a culture's orientation to how time is spent, acknowledged, and claimed. All cultures maintain a set, or standard, sense of time that is shared.

However, one's "punctuality" varies across a culture. Cultures may generally be defined as **polychronic** or **monochronic**. A polychronic orientation to time refers to cultures in which multiple timeframes are perceived. For instance, in a polychronic culture, meeting friends at noon for lunch may very well mean meeting at 1, 2, or 3 p.m. On the other hand, a monochronic orientation to time refers to a singular shared perception of time. For instance, meeting friends at noon for lunch means meeting at noon. To arrive at 1, 2, or 3 p.m. may mean one is late, missed lunch, or "stood someone up," thus potentially harming a relationship. It is important to remember that cultures vary in terms of how monochronic or polychronic they are. For example, even if two cultures are both monochronic they will vary in how "monochronic" they are.

For instance, one day when I was working on a lesson plan for an English class in Japan, my supervisor came into the shared staff room and informed me that we had a meeting at 3 p.m. for all teachers. I looked at the clock, and noticing it was 15 minutes till 3 p.m., I said, "Ok," and continued working. However, shortly afterward I noticed it was eerily quiet in the normally chaotic staff room. This struck me as odd, so I went to the conference room where I found everyone waiting for me to join the meeting! As soon as I sat down, the meeting began. I felt embarrassed, wondering if somehow my watch was incorrect. I glanced at two clocks within the room and both revealed that it was ten minutes till 3 p.m. This experience and others led me to believe that if I was not ten minutes early in Japan, I was late! However, as a graduate student I once went to a faculty member's office ten minutes early and was asked to wait as my professor "was counting on that time to work." These two moments struck me as seeing that both the U.S. and Japan are monochronic countries, but how being "monochronic" exists in each culture is different from the other.

Masumoto (2004) exposed ways in which time was perceived differently between American interns in Japan and their Japanese coworkers. Masumoto (2004) found that American interns expected to be able to "hit the ground running" once they joined their organization. In other words, they expected to be able to contribute to the organization by submitting new ideas and making what they perceived to be substantive contributions to the organization through performing work duties that capitalized from their job skills. Japanese coworkers, on the other hand, believed that it took "time" to be an effective organizational workgroup member. In other words, Japanese coworkers thought it was hasty to "hit the ground running" when one was a newcomer. Instead, Japanese coworkers believed that the American interns should use time to observe the atmosphere of the high-context culture of their workplace. It was only through such observation that one could start to understand how the organization functions and then begin to "make a difference" by contributing ideas and perform certain job functions. Masumoto's (2004) research highlighted that time is not necessarily a matter of being late to a dinner party with friends or a workplace meeting, but rather deepens understanding to showcase that even expectations as to how time should be spend at work is culturally based. Next, to enrich our understanding of nonverbal communication, the third author will discuss nonverbal codes within the context of higher education.

Context Three: Nonverbal Codes Within Higher Education

Higher education is another rich context through which to explore the interrelationships between cultures and nonverbal codes. To meet global challenges, many colleges and universities in the U.S. seek to "diversify," "internationalize," or "globalize" their campuses. As a result, the number of international, or foreign-born, faculty, staff, and students has been rapidly increasing (e.g., Robbins, Smith, & Santini, 2011). As a former graduate teaching assistant and a current international faculty member, I will unpack how I have come to experience nonverbal codes inside and outside classroom interactions. Specifically, I will reflect on my experiences as they relate to issues of relationship, power, and micro-aggression.

To help contextualize my experiences, I will briefly explain my academic journey in the U.S. In the fall of 2004, I found myself teaching for the very first time in the U.S. as a teaching assistant. Despite my robust educational training from Taiwan, I experienced one of the most challenging semesters of my career as a teacher—teaching in an unfamiliar cultural context, teaching a brand new subject matter, and teaching U.S. American students for the first time. That semester, I had many unexpected encounters such as students challenging their grades. Between the fall of 2004 and fall 2014, I have come to teach a wide range of communication courses at three different institutions in three different states (i.e., Texas, New Mexico, and Ohio), including two historically White universities and one Hispanic-serving university. Through critical reflections, I have come to realize how nonverbal codes do not just enable and constrain instructional communication interactions, but also shed light on unequal power relations as they relate to status, silence, and identity positions (e.g., race, gender, immigration status) (Chen, 2014; Lawless & Chen, 2015).

Relational Message, Status, and Nonverbal Behaviors

In general, relational messages are more often communicated through nonverbal behaviors than verbal ones. **Relational messages** communicate particular feelings toward others and particular relationships to them. Yet, members of different cultural groups often subscribe to varying rules for enacting, interpreting, and assigning meanings to nonverbal behaviors. As an example, I had a memorable encounter with a (White) male student during my first semester teaching in the United States. One sunny afternoon, as I walked toward the classroom, a male student caught up to me. I honestly could not recall what he said to me or what we talked about in that moment, but I vividly remembered one of his nonverbal behaviors. I recalled sharing a pleasant conversation with him. Maybe we smiled at each other about something. As our conversation continued, he suddenly put one of his arms on my shoulder. He was much taller than me so it was easy for him to do that. Out of politeness and *coherence*, I tried to carry on the conversation without appearing surprised. But I very quickly moved away from him. In that moment, I understood this (White) male student as using nonverbal behaviors (e.g., smiling and putting his arm on my shoulder) to communicate a positive feeling toward me, which was consistent with our pleasant verbal conversation. Nevertheless, I—as his teacher—was shocked and offended by his putting his arm around my shoulder. If we had been in Taiwan, I would have talked to him about inappropriate behaviors toward one's teacher. On that particular day, I felt out of my cultural space and I did not react. In hindsight, it would have been a great teachable moment to engage this student in thinking about cultural differences and nonverbal communication.

Besides relational messages, status is also more often communicated through nonverbal behaviors. **Status** refers to the relative influence and position that an individual holds within a social or organizational setting such as a university, a department, or a classroom. Throughout my career as a teacher, I have mixed experiences with my status as the course instructor. On one hand, as a non-native English speaker, I have had native speakers question or challenge my authority (e.g., giving me certain looks, not taking my instructions as seriously, etc.). On the other hand, as a cultural other, I have struggled to establish a rapport with my students and become a more immediate teacher. **Teacher immediacy** describes communication behaviors that a teacher enacts to reduce the perceived distance between teacher and students such as conveying warmth, approachability, and availability for communication. Thus, I have constantly been negotiating the contradictions between gaining authority and establishing rapport with my students. When I transitioned from the status of a teaching assistant to an assistant professor, I could feel the perceived distance between my students and myself widening even more. At the same time, many of my students have had little awareness of Asian/Asian American professors and/or female international faculty members. Overall, my status has been one of instability, open to negotiations, coordination, and disruptions.

Silence and Micro-Aggressions

Moments of silence in the classroom have been both productive and unproductive for me. In moments of silence, a lot is said without actual words, such as agreement, consent, distrust, resistance, pensiveness, etc. Here, I will focus on moments of silence that function to cast me as an *other*—racially, ethnically, or culturally. In other words, silence can function as **micro-aggressions** as brief and commonplace acts that communicate subtle yet persistent everyday discriminations based on race, gender, immigration status, etc. The term "micro[-]aggressions" was first coined by Chester Pierce to describe subtle, incessant, and cumulative assaults—verbally, behaviorally, and environmentally—targeted at racial minorities. As Pierce (1974) put it, the primary "vehicle for racism in this country is offenses done to blacks by whites in this sort of gratuitous never-ending way" (p. 515). For me, there have been particular moments of silence within classroom interactions that cumulatively construct indignities for me as a foreign other and an immigrant woman. Of course, I know that most of those acts have been done without intent, malice, or hatred. Nevertheless, cumulatively those acts communicate hostility and can make a cultural other like me question if I belong. Some examples include but are not limited to silence to my questions regarding race, racism, and racial inequalities; silence to my warm questions of concerns; and silence following a stereotypical comment about a presumed incompetent immigrant other (e.g., "My math teacher from XXX cannot speak English"). The concept of micro-aggression reminds us that when we *coordinate* communication interactions, unequal power relations affect how we make meanings with others.

Conclusion: Globalizing Nonverbal Communication

The three authors engaged CMM and examined the nonverbal behaviors, codes, and cues within the context of ability/disability, intercultural workplace relationships, and higher education. We also provided explanations of how we *coordinated* (negotiate, interpret, respond, etc.) our actions (nonverbal behaviors in particular) with *others* to understand and co-create meaning in intercultural communicative practices. The authors believe that understanding self-reflexivity and situationality serves as imperatives in better experiencing nonverbal communication between cultures in this increasingly globalized world. Self-reflexivity is a *bodymindful* practice, the integral experience of one's body, emotion/feeling, mind, and spirit (Nagata, 2004). It can help us become more attentive to, and conscious of, the moment of intercultural interaction: the contexts (constraining and/or enabling), the communicators' relationships, and the messages to which we receive and/or respond. Thus, understanding nonverbal codes in the particular situationalities provided grounds to coordinate our actions to communicate meaning as well as to create meaning between persons from different social/cultural backgrounds.

Discussion Questions

1. From your observation, how are nonverbal codes/behaviors similar and different across cultural and/or relational contexts?
2. Describe a particular nonverbal code/behavior in your culture. Explain what it means to you.
3. Reflect upon your intercultural experience, describe a context (cross-cultural and/or relational) where your particular nonverbal code/behavior you described in the previous question has created favorable or less favorable communication outcomes. What did you do in the particular context?
4. What is your "comfortable" distance in everyday interaction? How will you make attempts to adapt a different perception of cultural space when you are in another culture?

5. How is your nonverbal communication interconnected with your verbal interactions? Have you ever walked away in silence when you felt uncomfortable toward a cultural other's nonverbal codes/behavior? If you have another chance, what will you do to change the outcome in that situation?
6. Describe an experience with violating a nonverbal code of which you were previously not aware. What happened? Who was there? What have you gained from this experience?

References

Bateson, G. (1972). *Steps to an ecology of mind; collected essays in anthropology, psychiatry, evolution, and epistemology*. San Francisco, CA: Chandler.

Burgoon, J. K., & Hale, J. L. (1988). Nonverbal expectancy violations: Model elaboration and application to immediacy behaviors. *Communication Monographs, 55*(1), 58–79. doi:10.1080/03637758809376158

Burgoon, J. K., & Hubbard, A. S. E. (2004). Cross-cultural and intercultural applications of expectancy violation theory and interaction adaptation theory. In W. B. Gudykunst (Ed.), *Theorizing about intercultural communication* (1st ed., pp. 149–171). Thousand Oaks, CA: Sage.

Carbaugh, D. (1999). "Just listen": "Listening" and landscape among the Blackfeet. *Western Journal of Communication, 63*, 250–270.

Carbaugh, D. A. (2005). *Cultures in conversation*. Mahwah, NJ: Lawrence Erlbaum.

Chen, Y.-W. (2014). "Are you an immigrant?": Identity-based critical reflections of teaching intercultural communication. *New Directions for Teaching and learning, 2014*(138), 5–16. doi:10.1002/tl.20091

Cronen, V. E. (1991). Coordinated management of meaning theory and postmodern ethics. In K. Greenberg (Ed.), *Conversations on communication ethics* (pp. 21–53). Norwood, NJ: Ablex.

Cronen, V. E., & Pearce, W. B. (1992). Grammars of identity and their implications for discursive practices in and out of academe: A comparison of Davies and Harre's views to coordinated management of meaning theory. *Research on Language and Social Interaction, 25*, 37–66. doi:10.1080/08351819109389356

Giri, N. V. (2009). Nonverbal communication theory. In S. W. Littlejohn & K. A. Foss. (Eds.), *Encyclopedia of communication theory* (pp. 690–694). Thousand Oaks, CA: Sage.

Hall, E. T. (1990). *The hidden dimension*. New York, NY: Anchor.

Homsey, D. M., & Sandel, T. (2012). The code of food and tradition: Exploring a Lebanese (American) speech code in practice in Finland. *Journal of Intercultural Communication Research, 41*, 59–80. doi:10.1080/17475759.2011.649513

Knapp, M., Hall, J., & Horgan, T. (2013). *Nonverbal communication in human interaction* (8th ed.). Boston, MA: Cengage Learning.

Lawless, B., & Chen, Y.-W. (February, 2015). *Immigrant women, academic work, and agency: Negotiating identities and subjectivities with/in the Ivory Tower.* Paper to be presented at the annual conference of the Western States Communication Association, Spokane, WA.

Martin, J., & Nakayama, T. (2009). *Intercultural communication in contexts* (5th ed.). New York, NY: McGraw-Hill Humanities/Social Sciences/Languages.

Martin, J., & Nakayama, T. (2010). *Experiencing intercultural communication: An introduction* (4th ed.). New York, NY: McGraw-Hill Humanities/Social Sciences/Languages.

Masumoto, T. (2004). Learning to 'Do time' in Japan a study of US interns in Japanese organizations. *International Journal of Cross Cultural Management, 4*(1), 19–37.

Mehrabian, A. (2009). *Nonverbal communication.* Piscataway, NJ: Transaction Publishers.

Nagata, L. A. (2004). Promoting self-reflexivity in intercultural education. *Journal of Intercultural Communication, 8,* 139–167.

Norberg-Hodge, H. (2009). *Ancient futures: Lessons from Ladakh for a globalizing world.* San Francisco, CA: Sierra Club Books.

Pearce, W. B. (1989). *Communication and the human condition* (1st ed.). Carbondale, IL: Southern Illinois University Press.

Pearce, W. B. (2005). Coordinated management of meaning (CMM). In W. B. Gudykunst (Ed.), *Theorizing about Intercultural Communication* (1st ed.). Thousand Oaks, CA: Sage.

Pearce, W. B., & Pearce, K. A. (2000). Extending the theory of coordinated management of meaning (CMM) through a community dialogue process. *Communication Theory, 10,* 405–423. doi:10.1111/j.1468-2885.2000.tb00200.x

Philipsen, G. (1975). Speaking "like a man" in Teamsterville: Culture patterns of role enactments in an urban neighborhood. *Quarterly Journal of Speech, 61,* 13–22.

Philipsen, G. (1976). Places for speaking in Teamsterville. *Quarterly Journal of Speech, 62,* 15–25.

Philipsen, G. (1997). A theory of speech codes. In G. Philipsen & T. L. Albrecht (Eds.), *Developing communication theories* (pp. 119–156). Albany, NY: State University of New York Press.

Pierce, C. (1974). Psychiatric problems of the Black minority. In S. Arietie (Ed.), *American handbook of psychiatry* (pp. 512–523). New York, NY: Basic Books.

Robbins, S. R., Smith, S. H., & Santini, F. (Eds.). (2011). *Bridging cultures: International women faculty transforming the US academy.* Lanham, MD: University Press of America, Inc.

Simmons, N. (2012). The tales of *gaijin*: Health privacy perspectives of foreign English teachers in Japan. *Kaleidoscope: A Graduate Journal of Qualitative Communication Research, 11,* 17–38.

Simmons, N. (2014a). My "big" blue health secret: My experience with privacy, or lack thereof, in Japan. *Health Communication, 29*(6), 634–636. doi:10.1080/10410236.2013.786013

Simmons, N. (2014b). Speaking like a queen in RuPaul's Drag Race: Towards a speech code of American drag queens. *Sexuality & Culture, 18*(3), 630–648. doi:10.1007/s12119-013-9213-2

Sorrells, K. S. (2013). *Intercultural communication: Globalization and social justice* (1st ed.). Thousand Oaks, CA: Sage.

15.   Understanding the Relationship Between Culture and Language

Leonard Muaka

The title of this chapter presupposes a relationship between language and culture. The main objective of this chapter is to reflect on this relationship between language and culture and to show how it affects intercultural communication. The language-culture nexus dates back to the days of Otto Jasperson (1955), a linguist who not only declared that language and nation (culture) were synonymous, but he went as far as claiming that the English language was superior to a language like French because of its businesslike and methodical manner. However, the actual debate dates back to the Sapir-Whorf hypothesis in which language was viewed in deterministic terms. In spite of a lengthy period of debate on the subject among scholars, there is still no agreement on the relationship between language and culture and its impact on successful intercultural communication. While one school of thought views language and culture as being independent of each other (e.g., Chomsky, 1965), another school of thought spearheaded by anthropologists views a clear connection between the two concepts.

Using an eclectic sociolinguistic approach, this chapter argues for the centrality of the language-culture nexus in intercultural communication. A careful exploration of important linguistic concepts is presented with examples from different speech communities to elaborate on the issues raised. Specific issues to be explored in this chapter include the role that language and culture play in intercultural communication; the components of language critical in intercultural communication (phonology, semantics, syntax, pragmatics, and morphology); the role of perception in language use; and the Sapir-Whorf hypothesis that is at the center of this discussion. The chapter concludes by arguing that because language and culture are so intertwined, successful intercultural communication can only be achieved if interlocutors from different cultural backgrounds possess both the linguistic competence and the cultural knowledge needed in carrying out a communicative event.

What Is Language?

Defining language is not a simple task. Language is viewed differently based on the different approaches used by scholars. Wardhaugh (1978) defines language as "a system of arbitrary vocal symbols used for human communication" (p. 3). The concept of arbitrariness is due to the association of a word and what it represents. For example, there is no clear connection between the word "table" and the object to which it refers. Yet most speakers, when asked what language is, would probably say it is a tool for communication. Noam Chomsky, the most influential figure in modern linguistics, views language as innate in human beings. For Chomsky and his followers, human beings are predisposed to acquire language irrespective of where they are born. However, Chomsky has also come under attack for disregarding the importance of social aspects of language. Dell Hymes (1974), for instance, argued in defense of **communicative competence** in communication. He noted that communicative competence is the knowledge that a speaker needs in order to be a member of a **speech community**. A speech community may be defined as comprising people who share linguistic norms as well as some of the languages found within that community. They may also interpret the languages they encounter in a similar manner (Mesthrie, Swann, Deumert, & Leap, 2000). Those who take Dell Hymes's approach argue that language is a social product and as such, it is impacted by what happens in the society (see Michael, 2011; Ochs, 1988, among others). Similarly, language impacts what members of that society do and how they do it. Ahearn (2012) adds to this debate by noting that language mediates people's social actions.

Although language is a social product, it is important to view it as a system that entails **semantics** (meaning), **syntax** (sentence structure and the rules that guide them), **sociolinguistics** (language interactions and use in the society), **morphology** (word formation and structure), **pragmatics** (contextualized meaning in language use), and **phonology** (sound distribution and interaction). Knowing a language therefore entails knowing all of these components and how they interact with each other within any given language.

What Is Culture?

Just like language, defining **culture** is not a straightforward task. However, in this chapter, culture entails an entire belief system of a people. It also involves people's attitudes and perceptions about life. When individuals speak, they communicate in a manner that is tied to their cultural identities and beliefs. Yamuna Kachru and Larry Smith (2008) add that even though there are different ways of defining culture, it is not a static or monolithic entity, but rather it is dynamic, evolving, and progressive. This progressive nature of culture is brought about by contact between different cultures and human mobility within an interconnected globalized world (Kramsch, 1988).

The aforementioned attempts at defining culture and language demonstrate that when people judge other speakers or their speech, they do so based on their own cultural criteria. Their opinions come from a subjective perspective that views their own position as the norm

Ammonite/Shutterstock.com

while other people's stand is viewed as nontraditional. Such language judgments are guided by language perceptions and **language attitudes.**

Language and Culture in Intercultural Communication

Human beings are endowed with the phenomenon of language that realistically separates them from other species. Language enables people to talk about their past and their aspirations in a way that not any other species can (Yule, 2010). Human language is built based on what Chomsky (1965) calls a finite set of rules but the rules are very productive and can produce an infinite number of novel sentences. However, as already highlighted above, members of a speech community must not only have **linguistic competence** (which is knowledge of the grammatical rules of their mother tongue acquired prior to adulthood), but they must also have **communicative competence** (the knowledge of what is and what is not appropriate to say in any specific cultural context) (Hymes, 1974). Other scholars such as Goffman (1974) use the concept of framing when referring to communication. To Goffman, communicative events are organized in frames that enable participants to understand what is occurring. When a communicative event is misframed or when used outside its proper contexts, it leads to misunderstandings or a breakdown in communication. The important information needed for the proper framing to take place is shared cultural experiences. Consider the following two examples:

Visitor: I was thinking of cashing in some cheques on Thursday.
Host: Thursday is Thanksgiving.

(Kachru & Smith, 2008, p. 36)

In the foregoing example, although both speakers speak English, the first speaker must have knowledge of the American culture to appreciate the significance of the concept of *Thanksgiving* in American culture and to understand the meaning of the response given. Therefore, it is not linguistic competence that is critical, but rather the sociocultural knowledge that both speakers need in order to understand each other fully.

In many African communities, metaphors and proverbs are a common feature in conversations. Because of the richness of oral literature, speakers embed sayings in their conversations. If a speaker in Swahili were to say *mganga hajigangi* (a doctor does not treat herself or himself), one needs to know what the proverb means culturally beyond the simplistic surface meaning. Given the right context or frame as Goffman (1974) uses the concept, the proverb should inform the addressee that beyond the surface meaning, the contextualized meaning based on Swahili culture is that individualism is not the norm in the Swahili culture. People must collaborate and work together. Another example from the Swahili world is *Nyani haoni kundule* (a monkey does not see its butt). This is a saying that is directed at people who like to blame others without examining themselves first.

Consider another case where a student from Kenya comes to the U.S. to study, and when she sends her boyfriend a letter telling her that she had a good valentine day, the boyfriend is so angry with her for telling him about Valentine whom he considers a real person rivaling him. Although this is a fictional example that John Mugane (1999) creates in his Swahili course book, it is clear that the potential for miscommunication is very high and interlocutors need to be aware of this. Similarly, due to cultural differences, it always surprises people from communal societies when an American child says, "come to my house" rather than "come to our house." Therefore, a full command of intercultural communication hinges on both grammaticality and cultural appropriateness.

Language Attitudes

Language attitudes are the opinions people form about other people and the languages they speak. Language attitudes can be either positive or negative and because of this they can promote or hinder communication (Beinhoff, 2013). A good example is how former colonial masters viewed the people they colonized and their languages as being inferior and inadequate (see Bokamba, 2011; Jaffe, 1999; Muaka, 2011). Linguistically there is no language that is better than another. However, matters about language are sometimes politically motivated and can be viewed from a very subjective point of view. These political views are formulated based on political and **language ideologies**. Language ideologies are the beliefs people hold about other people and the languages they speak. Ideologies do however encompass other beliefs outside language. Such ideologies can be dominant, conservative, or capitalistic. For example, speakers of English may view speakers of Hopi, a language spoken by Native Americans in Arizona as being inferior. When speakers' languages are viewed as being inferior, the affected speakers consider themselves as **marginalized** and they may develop negative attitudes toward their own language. When this happens, they may not speak their own language, leading to **language endangerment**. When a language is endangered it means that people who speak the language continue to decrease and it could end up having no speakers. In Corsica, a French island, many children were reprimanded if they spoke their own language at school. They were told that their language was worthless and they needed to learn and speak French (Jaffe, 1999).

The fear of many minority language activists is the potential loss of the culture of a people for it is within the language that younger generations learn about their people and their belief system. Ngũgĩ wa Thiong'o (1986), a prominent African writer from Kenya also talks about a similar unequal relationship between African languages and former colonial languages such as English, French, Spanish, German, and Portuguese. In most African schools, children would be punished if they were heard speaking their mother tongues. To date former colonial languages are viewed as modern and more marketable in the job market. African languages are viewed as undeveloped, backward, and less marketable for the job market. This kind of view is subjective and does not take into account the role that such languages play culturally in African societies and their economies. In the following section we examine the impact of language attitudes.

The Effect of Language Attitudes and Labeling in Language

Language is more than the tool that people use for communication. It is an intergenerational phenomenon that people identify with and it also connects them with other people who speak a similar language. However, just as it is used to unite people who speak the same variety, it can also be used to discriminate against them. This means that speakers of a given language can be associated with certain negative aspects or their language can be used to undermine them. At the same time, language can be used as a tool to mock its speakers (Bucholtz, 2011; Lippi-Green, 2012). For example, in the examples given above in Corsica, Kenya, and Native American speech communities, speakers were viewed as inferior and their languages were viewed as **illegitimate** (nonstandard or non-official) and irrelevant. This has become so engrained in the speakers' minds that parents tell their students not to speak these languages. This perception leads to **language shift** and may lead to **language death**. Some scholars view it as a mental disease (Bokamba, 2011). Language shift is when speakers shift away from their language and begin speaking a different language—usually a **dominant language** (a language accorded a higher status and power even though it may not be spoken by the majority) in contact with their mother tongue. Language death refers to a situation when there are no more speakers of a given language because of a shift to a different language.

The marginalization of people's language may also be associated with labeling in language—that is, people being referred to derogatively. In most cases, these labels are associated with backwardness, negativity, and even racism or ethnicity. When discussing labels of racial systems, Bucholtz (2011) notes that these labels are ideologically based and it is very difficult for proponents of such ideologies to accept alternative views.

In a documentary titled *Do You Speak American?* (Cran, Buchanan, & MacNeil, 2005), one of the researchers interviewed, John Baugh, a linguist, described how his research on a rental apartment search in American urban cities revealed cases of linguistic profiling based on ethnicity. The responses he received depended on the accent he used in his speech whenever he made a call. For example, whenever he used an African American accent or Hispanic accent, the responses were mixed in upscale neighborhoods, but when he used an educated neutral accent, he got positive responses in the same affluent neighborhoods. In this case, language can define a person just as the color of his or her skin. The minority varieties did not do well in affluent communities. People are viewed through the color of their skin, something that has existed for a long time.

A related stereotyping scenario is provided by Lippi-Green (2012) in her work on people's accents. To reinforce her point on stereotyping based on ethnicity and race she invokes a quote by James Baldwin which states: "It is not the Black child's language which is despised: It is his experience" (as cited in Lippi-Green, 2012, p. 182). However, labeling does not occur at the ethnic level only. For instance, Lippi-Green (2012) provides an example of labeling based on regional variation of dialects. She notes that while growing up in Chicago, her fourth grade teacher told the class that they should not watch programs such as *The Beverly Hillbillies* because of the ungrammatical and ignorant manner of the characters' speech that represented

Yaromir/Shutterstock.com

the Southern speech. She goes on to say that for her, this made her grow up thinking that a Southern accent symbolized a very limited and peculiar set of characters (Lippi-Green, 2012, p. 217) until she was old enough to watch other programs and read different books that enlightened her.

The Sapir-Whorf Hypothesis

The foregoing ideologically charged section leads us to the final question we need to address. It is a question that revisits the Sapir-Whorf Hypothesis. This is a hypothesis that has dominated the language-culture nexus for decades since the middle of the twentieth century. It is usually presented in two forms: the stronger version of it states that language determines or shapes people's worldview (Ahearn, 2012, p. 69). The weak version of the hypothesis, however, states that to a certain extent people think about the world they encounter using the categories provided by their first languages (Ahearn, 2012; Yule, 2010).

Most scholars take the weaker version of the hypothesis because it shows that perception is not absolute but rather very relative. There are, however, arguments that Whorf and Sapir's work has been misreported and misanalysed (see Ahearn, 2012). Most modern linguists and linguistic anthropologists advocate for an appreciation of both language and culture in enabling successful communication. As the examples introduced above demonstrate, a fuller meaning of any linguistic event or situation must create a synergy between language and culture. It is not a matter of overemphasizing one; rather both elements need to be addressed. Language acquires its meaning within a specific cultural setting and the significance of any word, phrase, or linguistic construction is derived based on a shared cultural background between interlocutors.

Concluding Remarks

This chapter has argued that there is indeed a strong relationship that exists between language and culture. In particular, any meaningful definition of language and culture must take into account its speakers and their belief system. As an intergenerational phenomenon, language is both a tool for communication and also a reservoir of the culture of the speakers of that given language. It has also emerged from the discussion in this chapter that culture is not monolithic, but rather it is progressive, and whenever two or more cultures come into contact, new cultural concepts are borrowed and in the process, languages enrich their **lexicon** (an inventory of words in a given language) making intercultural communication possible. Ultimately therefore, a better understanding of the language-culture nexus is to understand that within any given society, its members are guided by a set of norms, beliefs, traditions, imaginations, and views of life among other aspects. These views are current in their daily interactions either through socialization, initiations, or adjudications of cases. During such occasions, members invoke portions of their cultural systems that inform how they can use language appropriately.

Discussion Questions

1. After reading this chapter and based on your prior understanding of the concepts introduced, define the term "culture" in a way that informs your reader of its diverse facets.
2. Everyone has an accent. What accents do you personally dislike or find irritating? Describe a situation in which you reacted this way to a variety (dialect) of English other than your own. After reading this chapter, do you have any insight into your own reactions?
3. The U.S. is a place where people from different countries and cultures come to live. Think of your encounter with a person not born in the U.S. and describe how your conversation with that person was hindered because of your nationality and linguistic differences. If there were any communication difficulties, how were they resolved? In responding to this question, please consider the different elements that were introduced in this chapter such as syntax, phonology, morphology, pragmatics, and cultural differences.
4. If you speak a certain variety (dialect) of English or a different language, what attitudes do others have about your speech? Has someone ever criticized you for the way you speak? How do you view your own variety (dialect) or language vis-à-vis other varieties or languages?
5. As a speaker of English, how do you address different groups of people based on their relationship with you, and what determines your choice? For example, do you address your uncle the same way you address your teacher? Identify at least four different groups and explain what triggers how you address different people.

References

Ahearn, L. M. (2012). *Living language: An introduction to linguistic anthropology.* Chichester, West Sussex: Wiley-Blackwell.

Beinhoff, B. (2013). *Perceiving Identity through Accent: Attitudes towards non-native speakers and their accents in English.* New York, NY: Peter Lang.

Bokamba, E. G. (2011). Ukolonia in African language policies and practices. In E. G. Bokamba, R. K. Shosted, & B. T. Ayalew (Eds.), *Selected Proceedings of the 40th Annual Conference on African Linguistics: African Languages and Linguistics Today* (pp. 146–167). Somerville, MA: Cascadilla Proceedings Project, 2011.

Bucholtz, M. (2011). *White kids: Language, race and styles of youth identity.* Cambridge: Cambridge University Press.

Chomsky, N. (1965). *Aspects of the Theory of Syntax.* Cambridge: MIT Press.

Cran, W., Buchanan, C., & MacNeil, R. (Eds.) (2005). *Do you speak American?* Princeton, NJ: Films for the Humanities & Sciences.

Goffman, E. (1974). *Frame analysis: An essay on the organization of experience.* Cambridge: Harvard University Press.

Hymes, D. H. (1974). *Foundations in sociolinguistics: An ethnographic approach.* Philadelphia: University of Pennsylvania Press.

Jaffe, A. (1999). *Ideologies in action: Language politics on Corsica.* New York, NY: Mouton de Gruyter.

Jasperson, O. (1955). *Growth and structure of English language.* Garden City, NY: Doubleday.

Kachru, Y., & Smith, L. E. (2008). *Cultures, contexts and world Englishes.* New York, NY: Routledge.

Kramsch, C. J. (1988). *Language and culture.* Oxford: Oxford University Press.

Lippi-Green, R. (2012). *English with an accent: Language, ideology and discrimination in the United States* (2nd ed.). London: Routledge.

Mesthrie, R., Swann, J., Deumert, A., & Leap, W. L. (2000). Introducing Sociolinguistics. Philadelphia: John Benjamins Publishing Company.

Michael, L. (2011). Language and culture. In P. Austin & J. Sallabank (Eds.), *Handbook of endangered languages* (pp. 120–140). Cambridge: Cambridge University Press.

Muaka, L. (2011). Language perceptions and identity among Kenyan speakers. In E. G. Bokamba, R. K. Shosted, & B. T. Ayalew (Eds.), *Selected Proceedings of the 40th Annual Conference on African Linguistics: African Languages and Linguistics Today* (pp. 217–230). Somerville, MA: Cascadilla Proceedings Project.

Mugane, J. (1999). *Let's learn Swahili.* Athens; OH: Aramati Digital Publications.

Ochs, E. (1988). *Culture and language development: Language acquisition and language socialization in a Samoan village.* Cambridge: Cambridge University Press.

Thiong'o, N. (1986). *Decolonising the mind: The politics of language in African literature.* London: J. Currey.

Wardhaugh, R. (1978). Introduction to Linguistics (2nd ed.). New York. McGraw–Hill.

Yule, G. (2010). *The study of language* (4th ed.). Cambridge: Cambridge University Press.

Chapter 4

Living the Pop Culture

16. The Multicultural Self:
Negotiating Outsider Identity in South Korea

James Nesmith Anderson

You are standing in front of security at the airport; hugging your mother as she cries into your shoulder. You look into her eyes and all you can read is her competing pride in you and the longing that you will change your mind at the last minute. You hug your father and brother. You see the same emotions reflected in their faces as you did in your mother; but you know they won't know exactly how they feel until they arrive home and see your empty chair at the dinner table. You feel your family's eyes

Muellek Josef/Shutterstock.com

on you as you enter security. You feel their hearts stretching behind you, pulled taut in your wake as you make your way through the checkpoints, until there is an almost palpable snap of separation as you lose sight of each other on the other side of security. It isn't until you are sitting in front of the boarding gate that you let yourself realize that the little piece of your family still trailing behind you is all you will have of them for the foreseeable future.

Then you fly to the other side of the planet. You risk the ire of the other passengers as you crack the window; platinum-white light slicing through the dark cabin. You see Alaska for the first time. You doze fitfully for a few hours and try to watch some tedious Ashton Kutcher movie about him doing who-cares-what before giving up and resigning yourself to an anxious boredom before finally landing at Incheon International Airport in South Korea.

There is nothing in the world quite like your first two hours in South Korea. You are swept by crowds toward the kiosk to buy bus tickets, stuttering and floundering as you make your purchase. You take your seat on the most luxurious bus you've ever seen and stare out the window as the airport fades into the distance and you approach Incheon city, then Seoul. You gape inwardly as the skyscrapers emerge from the horizon, aimed at the sky like spaceships awaiting liftoff, until they swallow you up in the circuitous city streets and bypasses that take you along banks of the mammoth Han River that bifurcates the capital city of South Korea.

You collect your belongings and step off the bus and cannot help but take in with wide-eyed reverie the panorama of your new neighborhood. You watch the kaleidoscopic facades of *noraebang* karaoke bars, *anma* massage parlors, and the neon crosses crowning the buildings. You breathe in the scents of seafood simmering with fiery red pepper mixed with other fragrances that are not in your repertoire. K-pop pulses from shops while young women in kitschy uniforms offer samples of beauty supplies to the passersby. You collect yourself enough to make your way through the throngs of sharply dressed Korean men and women entertaining animated conversations in a language you barely understand. You dip through an alley where teenagers smoke apprehensively as they scroll through their phones and guffaw at the jokes their friends make between gulps of *soju* from paper cups. You enter the lobby of your new apartment building and wait for the elevator while a middle-aged couple regards you not unkindly. They smile broadly as you insist they enter the elevator first and venture a shy "bye-bye!" when you exit on the floor before theirs. You walk to your room and punch in the combination on the door lock. You drop your luggage at the door and collapse on the couch in your furnished studio apartment. After you determine your exhaustion to be the very thing making it impossible to fall asleep, you set up your laptop and begin your obligatory email to the family you left on the opposite side of the globe. They will probably be on their lunch breaks right now. You stare at the screen. You don't know what to write.

You finally manage:

"I made it. I'm ok. I love you."

You hit send and ease back into the couch. You made it. You're ok. You now live in South Korea.

Over the past decade and a half, the Republic of Korea has become a hub in the increasingly global world of teaching English as a foreign language. Attracted by generous financial benefits and relatively lax requirements for experience, native English speakers from around the **Anglophone** world come to South Korea to teach, usually for yearlong contracts at a *hagwon* (private school). The majority of these teachers hail from the United States and Canada, as the "American" accent is generally preferred among school administrators and parents of students. Preference notwithstanding, individuals from the United Kingdom, Ireland, South Africa, Australia, and New Zealand are increasingly represented within the English teacher population in Korea.

Another draw to South Korea, especially in recent years, which should not be understated, is the export of Korean entertainment, especially K-pop music, cinema, and Korean television dramas. The *hallyu* (Korean Wave) is a fairly recent phenomenon. With profits from the Korean music industry alone topping $3.4 billion in 2011, cultural production has become a significant aspect of the South Korean economy. This figure is especially interesting in consideration of the fact that an estimated $180 million was contributed by overseas markets. Korean television dramas have had almost runaway breakout success across the world. With avid viewers from countries as diverse as the Philippines, Indonesia, Japan, and Hong Kong, all the way to Cuba, Chile, and Paraguay, and even further to Iraq, Uzbekistan, and India, Korean dramas have enjoyed a different type of success in foreign living rooms.

It is important to note here that both the import of native English teachers and the export of Korean popular culture are symptoms of globalization. **Globalization** is the process through which the world is increasingly integrated economically, politically, socially, and culturally. It is the force causing families in Bolivia to be unable to afford the crops that sustain them due to rising demand from rich post-industrial nations. Globalization is the reason teenagers in Senegal might be able to recite all the lyrics to a Nicki Minaj track and simultaneously be affected by changes in United Nations foreign policy. It's why the first time I ate Korean food it was with other international students in Brazil. It's why I had the opportunity to teach in Korea in the first place.

I often thought of those first two hours in Korea during my subsequent two years living there. I can conjure traces of the helplessness I felt being unable to read the language, although the feeling is distant now that I read *hangeul* with ease. I remember playing the buffoon when attempting to order at a restaurant and being privately horrified when I realized I had been unintentionally rude. Being immersed in a culture radically different from your own and learning to operate within it can be a challenging procedure for anyone living in an unfamiliar place. Even when these places eventually become familiar, we frequently encounter subtle (and sometimes not-so-subtle) reminders that multiculturalism can be a difficult arena to negotiate. Therefore, examining **cultural relativism** and **ethnocentrism** in the context of **cultural globalization** is an important process in establishing an inclusive theoretical framework for the experience of multiculturalism when living abroad.

One of the most impressive parts of the Seoul metropolitan area is the infrastructure, specifically public transportation. Buses run constantly, the subway system is massive, and both methods are clean, safe, reliable, and cheap. I can think of exactly zero American metropolises that can boast all of these compliments to their respective public transportation systems. Public transportation also provides an excellent case in point for exploring the experience of Korean culture as a foreigner in regard to the previously mentioned theoretical precepts.

For example, as a matter of social etiquette, passengers on trains and buses are expected to be as quiet as possible at all times. Personal conversations are kept to a discrete volume, and all electronic devices are expected to be kept silent. It is not an uncommon experience for recently arrived foreigners to be shushed by older folks on the bus for speaking too loudly, and this creates a scenario that illustrates both cultural relativism and ethnocentrism.

Cultural relativism, a theoretical term used to describe the notion that moral and ethical systems vary across cultures, and that one's own cultural values should not be used to assess other cultures, is particularly useful in assessing this situation. Many foreigners might feel that this older person has just been quite rude, whereas the Korean folk on the bus found their loud voices intrusive and disruptive. Each party is correct according to their respective cultural norms, and the cultural relativist understands the reflexive relationship between two different cultures.

Conversely, ethnocentrism describes the position from which individuals judge the behavior and customs of different cultures based on their own cultural values. The cultural relativist understands that the old man who shushes you on the bus is speaking from his own set of cultural values and that as a guest in his country perhaps you should oblige and have your probably unimportant conversation at a lower decibel. The ethnocentrist, however, becomes incensed that someone they have never met is "butting in" on their conversation. Without attempting to understand the cultural dynamics at play, ethnocentrism establishes one's own culture as absolute truth, and makes negative value judgments about other cultural practices relative to one's own.

I really wish that I could say that most Westerners who choose to live in Korea were less ethnocentric. I really do. However, perhaps due to centuries of imperial and colonial control of much of the world, many Westerners are unable or otherwise unwilling to remove themselves from an ethnocentric mindset. In my experience, the most prevalent example of ethnocentrism among Westerners in Korea is the expectation that Koreans will speak and understand English. Bolstering this ethnocentric expectation is the tendency among these Westerners to flatly refuse to learn Korean. I would run out of fingers and toes before I finished counting the number of times that I saw another Westerner arguing in English with a taxi driver or another service worker who clearly did not understand the vitriol that was being hurled at them. There is a staggering amount of entitlement that informs an expectation that men and women on the opposite side of the planet should speak English, while the outraged individual feels no obligation to attempt to learn the native language of the land in which he or she is currently living. This is a uniquely Western entitlement that must be confronted within the individual before we consider living abroad, especially in non-English speaking cultures. We all must confront the reality that Western civilization is not the center of the world and that there is a considerable amount of deprogramming required in this process.

An important place to start in exploring these precepts is to understand that virtually everything you think, feel, or do is shaped by the culture you grew up in as well as your own identity within that culture. It follows that when I moved to South Korea, I was viewing and processing Korean culture and society through the eyes of a man from the United States of America. More accurately, I was viewing and processing Korean culture and society from the point of view of a straight, white, **cisgender** middle-class male without **disability status** from the American South. Accordingly, my experience is quite different from people of other **marked identity** living in South Korea. Therefore, in reading this essay (and really everything else we read), we should keep in mind the cultural lens through which I, the author, am writing.

Enough of the boring stuff. One of the caveats of overtly theoretical and critical analysis is that it can drown out our actual lived experiences. That is to say, I didn't bide my time in Korea cataloguing everything I felt with a sociological eye. Nope. I taught amazing, brilliant children their second language. I learned the Korean language. I ate succulent grilled meat, stir-fried pork intestine, spicy octopus stew, raw crab, and an array of delicious fermented vegetables. I drank *soju* and watched b-boy battles in parks. I had picnic dates by the river under the cherry blossoms in spring. I danced until daybreak with 7,000 other people at massive clubs. I climbed a mountain and stared in reverie at a land melancholic and beautiful like I had never seen before. I forged incredibly important friendships. I got into fights. I learned that with a whole lot of self examination and acceptance of the unfamiliar there are always bridges between people and cultures. Always.

The world is getting smaller. This is something that people of my generation have come to accept more or less *a priori*. South Korea is a fascinating example of a culture that has planted its own flag deeply within the context of globalization. In many ways, Korea is the place where I learned more about being an American than anywhere else. I was forced to confront my own privilege and the ethnocentrism that was so deeply engrained that I never knew it was there. I am not Korean. I cannot speak for Korean people. I can, however, speak of my experience as a foreigner living there, and how thankful I am for that time. Through the lens of practices such as cultural relativism when living in a foreign country, we learn more respectfully and more thoroughly about another culture. Perhaps just as importantly, we learn who we are and where we come from. As the world becomes increasingly globalized, it is imperative to understand the context in which we became the people we are, and to understand the cultural context in which other people live. And hey, it never hurts to eat some spicy food and dance all night while you do that.

Key Terms

Anglophone: English-speaking

Cisgender: An individual whose experience of gender matches the sex they were assigned at birth.

Cultural Globalization: The increasing integration of, exposure to, and exchange of different cultures across the world.

Cultural Relativism: A theoretical term used to describe the notion that moral and ethical systems vary across cultures, and that one's own cultural values should not be used to assess other cultures.

Disability Status: A term used to describe people who have physical, cognitive, intellectual, or sensory impairment.

Ethnocentrism: Judging other cultures relative to personal cultural values (i.e., religion, diet, language, customs, behavior).

Globalization: The process through which the world is increasingly integrated economically, politically, socially, and culturally.

Marked Identity: Facets of one's identity that are "presented" to the public (i.e., skin color, gender presentation, certain disability statuses).

Discussion Questions

1. What marked identities do you feel pertain to you? How do you think they influence your life?
2. Do you feel like some identity markers could be "unmarked"? Explain.
3. Can you think of a time in your life where you have used cultural relativism to understand a problem you may have had with someone else?
4. Think of a time in your life when you have behaved according to ethnocentric views. How could you have reacted differently?
5. Think of something that can serve as a "bridge" between cultures. How does this facilitate understanding and communication between cultures?

17.   Hip Hop Communitas: Transcendence Through the Beat of the Cypher

Keon Pettiway
North Carolina State University

Introduction

In its current form, it is impossible to place hip hop within one geographic location. Though there are common elements that make up the culture of hip hop, it is a global phenomenon, bursting its way through time and across space and remixed by different cultures. There is no doubt, however, that hip hop possesses distinct forms of Black aesthetics, expressions, and experiences. In particular, three Black cultural repertoires—rhythm, percussiveness, and call-response—coalesce to form a holistic Black cultural product (Nelson, 2011). I consider the hip hop cypher as a holistic product where these three Black cultural repertoires are engaged at once. It is through the cypher, a communitas if you will, where transcendence forms through and is organized by a totalizing beat (rhythm, percussiveness, and call-response).

R. Gino Santa Maria/Shutterstock.com

In a hip hop **cypher**, people gather around in a space and freestyle, an improvised performance of rap. Typically, cyphers are formed around freestyle battles where two people compete in an exchange of improvised rap verses. It is also common for a group of people to freestyle without any battles and simply exchange verses back and forth in a dynamic process of turn-taking. In popular culture, the cypher has taken center stage in mainstream television media, such as *Yo! MTV Raps*, Black Entertainment Television (BET) *Hip Hop Awards*, and *106 & Park Freestyle Fridays*. Cyphers have also gained much attention on social media through digital media outlets such as *Smack/URL*. From watching these mainstream media, it appears that cyphers have the makings of different forms of Black popular culture such as music, hairstyle, dress, etc. However, I would like to reflect on the ways cyphers operate as what Victor Turner (1970) calls **spontaneous communi-tas**, a powerful, creative moment when a community transcends and subverts hierarchies of race, class, and income.

Cyphers were common in my neighborhood. It didn't matter whether we were on the corner, on the bus, in the public bathroom, or on the porch. Cyphers occurred any-where and everywhere (even church). From my early days of cyphers in my neighborhood to freestyling at the *Freestyle Fanatics* cypher event under the "Free Expression Tunnel" during my undergraduate years, cyphers have always been exciting spaces to be a specta-tor or emcee. It is such a dynamic, improvised event where people from different walks of life could participate in a community. Most recently, I watched Rapsody, a female emcee from my home state and alma mater, perform on *The Cypher* during the BET Hip Hop Awards. After watching Rapsody, and having chills experiencing the exchange of flows between the other emcees, I was reminded of the way rhythm, percussiveness, and call-response—the beat—created a moment of spontaneous communitas. It exhibited a kind of group freestyling or battling where you could master the art of expressivity and form community through the transcendence of the beat.

In the 2013 *Cypher*, Rapsody, an African American from North Carolina, is joined by Jon Connor, Emis Killa, Wax, and Rittz. Among the performers, there is a mix of back-grounds. Wax is of Irish/Cuban descent, Emis Killa is Italian, Rittz is a White American from Georgia, and Jon Connor is an African American from Michigan. As each emcee displayed their skill of freestyling, they flowed along with the rhythm of the beat played by the deejay. The **rhythm** organizes the movement of the cypher through musical sounds and flow of music in a way that is ritualistic, a religious experience where meaning is estab-lished not only through words but through the way the beat leads the crowd to be out of control. In this particular cypher, the deejay uses different sonic technologies, hardware, and software, to switch the rhythm through different instrumental beats. But this is not any kind of "beat." The rhythm of the cypher, and thus its ritualistic faculties, is distinctly a **percussive** sound produced through rubbing, shaking, striking, or scraping (Nelson, 2009). It is noticeable that certain actions, such as body movements and vocal shifts, hap-pen around percussive sounds at different moments of the emcees' performance. Here the beat, organized through the rhythm, also manifests through the sonic qualities of percussiveness in a way that dynamically changes how emcees improvise in the moment. In addition to rhythm and percussiveness, **call-response**, the collective participation of the audience (the other emcees in this case) organizes the cypher wherein people attain a unified sense of participation. In most cases, this collective participation is verbal and/or non-verbal as the audience responds to the emcees during their improvised performance. It is during this improvising that an emcee might change vocal patterns, bodily move-ment, or lyrics in order to respond to the audience's verbal and/or non-verbal responses. In *The Cypher*, the other emcees respond verbally and non-verbally through vocal feed-back and body movements in a way that creates a dialogical performance between the audience and speaker.

Put together, these three repertoires, all with historical relation to and expressions of Black culture, creates a dialogic moment of transcendence between the audience and speaker in the cypher. In addition to emcees creating alternative realities through the actual lyrical content during the freestyle, transcendence occurs as social hierarchies are disrupted during the cypher, a space for collective participation and unity organized through the *beat*. More than a space for exchanging rap verses, the hip hop cypher is a product of Black culture that creates a space for potential transformation.

Discussion Questions

1. In what ways is a cypher part of Black popular culture?
2. How does the cypher create what Victor Turner calls a spontaneous communitas?
3. What are some other ways that rhythm might organize the movement of cypher?
4. Can you identify specific verbal or non-verbal forms of call-response in a cypher? Watch a cypher from *Yo! MTV Raps*, Black Entertainment Television (BET) *Hip Hop Awards*, and *106 & Park Freestyle Fridays* to inform your response if you have not experienced a cypher.
5. Though hip hop is global, are there other particular forms of Black expression, Black experiences, or Black counternarratives in hip hop culture?

References

Nelson, A. (2009). The repertoire of black popular culture. *Americana: The Journal of American Popular Culture, 1900 to Present, 8*(1).

Nelson, A. (2011). "Put your hands together": The theological meaning of percussion and percussiveness in rap music. *Americana: The Journal of American Popular Culture, 1900 to Present, 10*(1).

Turner, V. W. (1970). *The ritual process: Structure and antistructure.* Chicago, IL: Aldine Pub. Co.

18.   Popular Culture as a Contested Zone

Andrea Patterson-Masuka, Ph.D.

Neither Allison nor Brandy has ever been to Kenya, Congo, or Nigeria. Yet all of these places inspire daydreams about visiting these countries and cities in Africa. The students look forward to their trips to Oley's African Hair Braiding Salon on West Market Street in Greensboro, North Carolina, near their university. The students enter the salon and posters of colorful head shot pictures of women of African descent with intricate braided hairstyles are displayed on the walls. The images fuel their imaginations and increase their curiosity of what it must be like to live on a different continent. As they settle into the hairstylist's chair, a DVD featuring a drama produced in Nollywood, the entertainment capital in Nigeria, is loaded into the DVD player. The shop is flooded with music and scenes that the students have never encountered.

Sometimes we feel as if we have traveled somewhere when we look at the Travel Channel, a foreign film, or the Discovery Channel. When people actually travel to this land, sometimes what we have viewed in the media confirms our expectations. However, oftentimes the images in popular culture reinforce our misconceptions and stereotypes. Popular culture can impact how we view other cultures, countries, and people; however, these images are also related to what we experience. These intricate relationships emphasize the significance of contemplating the significance of culture when we are thinking about intercultural communication. Culture is focal to intercultural communication, however we often neglect to think about the various meanings of culture in our lives. One type of culture that is significant to intercultural communication is popular culture.

Media and popular culture have significant roles in intercultural communication. Intercultural communication scholar Kathryn Sorrells (2013) argues that the media and popular culture are interconnected. First, media and popular culture facilitate communication across cultural and natural boundaries with the flow of information

Rawpixel/Shutterstock.com

and images. Second, media frames local, global, and national issues and helps shape the way we view the world. Third, the flow of popular culture and media across cultural and natural boundaries can question, disrupt, and break apart cultural ideologies leading to unrest, resistance, and possibly conflict. Finally, media and popular culture can form hybrid transnational cultural identities in the global context by creating new global cultures, trends, and ideologies (Sorrells, 2013).

This chapter will explore the centrality of popular culture in connection with intercultural communication. We begin by defining mass-media, high, low, and folk cultures, and popular culture. We will explore culture as a contested zone and examine three cultural controversies with two popular cultural music icons. We will conclude our discussion with a challenge to critically interrogate and challenge the way we view popular culture images.

Mass-Media

We are so inundated with **mass-media** messages that most of the time we do not even realize it. Vivian (2010) defines mass-media as the means through which messages are delivered to an audience. **Media** is the plural for the word medium, which refers to the channels or means through which these messages are communicated. The term media is also used for industry such as television and book media. Mass-media is also used for businesses delivering mass messages, for example VIACOM and NBC area media companies. Rand (2005) reports that a study conducted by communication scholars Mark Popovich and Mark Holmes cites that the average American spends more time using their iPod, cell phone, television, and radio than any other activity while awake. Rand concludes that we as a society are consumers of media. In fact, we spend more than nine hours a day using some type of media.

Elements of the Media

According to the authors of MediaMaking (Grossberg, Wartella, Whitney, & Wise, 2006) the media is composed of three elements: (a) **technology**—the physical methods of producing cultural products, goods, and services, including television, cell phones, iPads, etc.; (b) **institutions**—social relationships or institutions such as broadcasting organizations; these may include NBC, CBS, or BET; and (c) **cultural forms**—refer to the products' format such as newscasts, sitcoms, action dramas, soap operas, or reality shows.

Defining Popular Culture

The distinction of being "cultured" or not was based on European societal interpretations of "high" culture and "low" culture. Therefore, those in the ruling class who held power and money, were educated at esteemed schools, and viewed as patrons of the arts (literature, ballet, opera, etc.) were considered to possess **"high culture."** Conversely, those in the lower or working classes who liked activities such as folk art, popular theatre, and later, television and popular movies were considered **"low culture."** In today's world, this may be referred to as popular culture. Sorrells (2008) contends that we see the influences of these symbols of high and low culture in film, advertising, television, and commercials to represent not only cultural differences in class but also to reify cultural hierarchy. The increasing desire and consumption of American culture across the globe may partly be influenced by those individuals and societies in general that desire to be perceived as "being cultured." Characteristics of localized culture, known as **folk culture,** which are cultural practices that are completed for the purpose of people within a certain place still remain. However, as these elements begin to be desired by tourists for being genuine and authentic, as folk culture (e.g., hula dances in Hawaii, Halloween, Valentine's Day, Kwanza), the **commodification of culture** occurs, and they become integrated into popular culture. Kathryn Sorrells (2013) argues that "the commodification of cultures often creates barriers for intercultural communication" (p. 191).

AlexAnnaButs/Shutterstock.com

The term media is often confused with the term popular culture. The term popular culture has come to be used in today's society to replace the word "low culture," which carries a negative connotation in today's world. **Popular culture** refers to the systems and artifacts that the general population within a society share or have some understanding of (Brummett, 1994; Sorrells, 2013). Disney characters, reality shows, television evangelists, hip hop artists, Bollywood, Nollywood, and Hollywood movie stars are all forms of popular culture. Three elements that help characterize popular culture include: (a) popular culture is integral and dominant in capitalistic systems, (b) popular culture is manufactured by culture industries, and (c) popular culture serves social functions. In our society, everything from hairstyles, fashion, eyewear, religion, social causes, to health and wellness has been commodified (Sorrells, 2013).

British scholar and cultural critic Stuart Hall (1981) believes that popular culture has at its base the experiences, memories, pleasures, hopes and disappointments, and traditions of ordinary people. The media is a significant area for exploring popular culture. Media studies, cultural studies, English studies, and women's studies have become sites of scholarship for media and popular culture. Hall (1981) contends that the media creates representations of the world and its images. It frames our worldview and helps us understand how the world operates. Hall argues that popular culture does have the potential of changing the disposition and the balance of power.

Popular culture can lead to the question of cultural politics. Popular culture celebrities have been successful in using their status and platform to champion causes and discuss controversial issues. For instance, LIVE AID, a rock concert with popular culture icons, raised money in 1985 for famine victims in Ethiopia (Michaels, 2010). This example depicts how popular culture can be used to generate profit, institute rituals, and facilitate social change and dialogue. Hall (1992) reminds us that although popular culture is "commodified and stereotyped," it represents our desires and is "profoundly mythic" (p. 32).

Most of us will never travel to Nigeria or India. If we do not have direct communication, we may have learned about these cultures through mediated culture. The term **culture industry** refers to industries that produce cultural goods such as the Disney Corporation. Critical theorists Theodor Adorno and Max Horkheimer (1972), who initially developed the term culture industry in the middle of the twentieth century, were apprehensive that these industries would easily manipulate masses of people into becoming passive and docile consumers. Sociologist Dustin Kidd (2007) believes that the primary function of popular culture in "advanced" societies is to produce a profit. However, he also contends that it serves as a way to establish and maintain social norms and social identities, create memories, and develop meanings of shared rituals through consumption.

GoldMyne Media Concept (2013) reports that the film industries known as Nollywood (Nigeria), Bollywood (India), and Hollywood (U.S.) have experienced tremendous growth. In fact, according to the UNESCO Institute for statistics, Bollywood has produced 1,091 full-length films, whereas Nollywood produced 872 productions in video format, in contrast to Hollywood which has produced 485 major film productions. The popularity of these industries alone suggests that mediated forms of communication—film, Internet, television, radio, and YouTube, etc., are important media texts for the study of intercultural communication.

One way to look at the concept of culture is to view it as a contested zone. Moon (2002) contends that when we consider "culture as a contested zone [it] helps us understand the struggles of cultural groups and the complexities of cultural life" (p. 16). The perspective of culture as a contested zone helps us consider the many viewpoints of groups that reside in that cultural space. Hall (1981) believes that we can learn much about culture and cultural struggles from studying media and its texts; it is representations of our world and how we understand the world.

Let's examine how we can look at the concept of culture as a contested zone in relation to the media by discussing a recent cultural controversy over the meanings of cultural icon Katy Perry's performance of her song "Unconditionally" at the 2013 American Music Awards with a Geisha Japanese theme. Perry opened the American Music Awards appearing as a Geisha dressed in an elaborate pink flowered kimono, Japanese style black wig, and white face makeup. Her performance included an elaborate Geisha Japanese style set with dancers dressed as Geisha girls and Japanese men. Perry gracefully sang and danced with a Japanese umbrella on a performance stage set depicting a lush Tokyo garden pond. The performance ended with a breathtaking magic trick at the end whereby Perry disappeared into thin air. Clevver Music (2013) reported that the cultural icon has been reported as saying that she is enamored with Geisha fashion and with Asian culture. The performance triggered opposition from various observers. Groups opposed to the performance contend that the connection to Japanese culture was unnecessary. Newspaper writer Jacob Holley-Kline (2014) stated in his column that there is an extended history of cultural appropriation and commodification in popular culture music. "White pop stars trying on different cultural and racial identities to sell records. It's never been okay" (para. 1).

This same type of cultural appropriation can also be seen in relation to the commodification of Black culture. According to Holley-Kline (2014), Miley Cyrus was reported to have said she wanted her album "Bangerz" to have a "Black" inspired sound. Soon after this reported statement, the artist released the video "We can't stop." The video features Cyrus "twerking" while wearing a gold dental grill as an accessory in the manner of African American males. She is surrounded by five African American friends dancing and "twerking" while she also performs the dance known as "twerking" while gyrating to music like a stripper. Holley-Kline (2014) argues that the Black women who dance in the video are present to give credibility to Cyrus's behavior and actions. "This is the black community as viewed through a white male lens" (Holley-Kline, 2014, para. 8).

Popular culture critic Chris Osterndorf (2014) observes that this cultural appropriation of Black popular culture by White musical artists extends beyond Cyrus and Perry. Osterndorf argues that while Cyrus is the "most blatant culprit" (para. 5), he argues there are other White female popular culture songstresses including Iggy Azalea, for singing rap lyrics written by Black artists and imitating Black singing and culture in her music video "Fancy It." She also uses Black dancers in several of her video scenes including a scene where she is riding in the backseat of a convertible as they are driving down the highway. Popular culture critics Jacob Holley-Kline (2014), Chris Osterndorf (2014), and Derrick Clifton (2014a) have been critical of how female White musical artists such as Katy Perry, Miley Cyrus, Iggy Azalea, and male White song artist Robin Thicke, who use Black male and female dancers in their music videos as human stage props for their cultural escapades and entertainment, while demonstrating their envy of Black popular culture. Hooks (1992c) warns us about the danger of envy in relation to cultural appropriation: "the thing about envy is that it is always ready to destroy, erase, take-over, and consume the desired object" (p. 157).

The cultural appropriation of White female popular culture stars is not a new trend. Osterndorf (2014) discusses that popular culture star Madonna was also guilty of appropriating certain aspects of Black culture. Cultural critic bell hooks (1992c) in her essay "Madonna: Plantation Mistress or Soul Sister" argues that White popular culture stars who culturally appropriate Black culture use their actions as another sign of their "radical chic" (p. 157). She notes that it is only a more recent occurrence for "any white girl to be able to get some mileage out of flaunting her fascination and envy of blackness" (p. 157).

The notion of the cultural appropriation of African American culture is also exhibited by White male pop stars as well. Singer Robin Thicke in his video "Blurred Lines" features an African American woman in one scene. Thicke says softly to the woman, "He tried to domesticate you" (Holley-Kline, 2014). Thicke's performance and video has also sparked controversy. Some critics claim that Thicke sends a clear message that Black women represent animals that need to be domesticated. "She, like all the women in the video, are objectified and made animalistic" (Holley-Kline, 2014, para. 8). The video has been highly criticized for how Black women are portrayed. Holley-Kline (2014) goes further to say that Thicke's performance is an example of a White man having power over African American women. Hooks (1992a) warns us in her essay that if White people, and others who are not Black, who write about or create images such as film or videos do not critically analyze their point of view and the images they produce, the creators then "simply recreate the imperial gaze—the look that seeks to dominate, subjugate, and colonize" (hooks,

Sean Nel/Shutterstock.com

1992a, p. 7). Cultural critic Michael Gonzalez (2013) argues while some believe that the "blue-eyed soul" of Robin Thicke's popular song is more about selling hit records than the race of the singer, there are some songwriters and producers who "argue for authenticity, while also criticizing the audacity of White performers who borrow from the musical well of . . . Blackness" (para. 9).

These examples of popular culture highlight several issues connected to mass-media, popular culture, and intercultural communication. The term "power" can also be viewed as something that is imposed on or held over someone that other people do not have. In this sense, power can be seen as coercion, control, or manipulation through language, thought, or action. In some cases, people are rendered helpless, defenseless, and unable to respond or escape—physically or mentally.

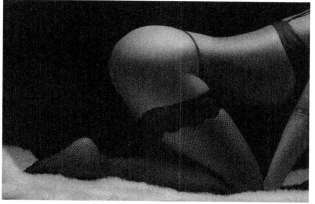

Sergey Mironov/Shutterstock.com

In his writings, philosopher Michel Foucault challenges us to critically examine the relationship between power and the way it is understood, how it develops, its intricacies, how it functions, and how it is formed (Swartz, Campbell, & Pestana, 2009). Foucault (1984) notes that power is not something that is only hierarchical in nature, uniform, or top-down only in its approach; it is something that is pervasive, insidious, and that grows and manifests itself within society. Power not only rests on the elements of repression and ideology, but goes a step further—it can be pleasurable, coercive, and so subtle that we are unaware of its grip on us. Hooks (1992b) in her essay "Eating the Other: Desire and Resistance" refers to White popular cultural artists who package and sell minority groups' culture as "the commodification of otherness" (p. 21). She argues that another culture's identity is delivered to us in a hedonistic and perverse package. The cultural fantasy of dressing in costume as the Other, dancing like the Other, and consuming the Other becomes an aphrodisiac. Hooks' (1992b) essay "Eating the Other" warns us that "within commodity culture, ethnicity becomes spice, seasoning that can liven up the dull dish that is mainstream white culture" (p. 21).

The performances of Perry, Cyrus, and Thicke also bring to question whether or not these performers appropriate or borrow from other cultures for personal gain with very little or no consequences. Unfortunately for many youth, popular culture has become a product to purchase as a consumer, and they are fluent in the language of capitalism. The economic and market forces of capitalism and consumerism have changed the language we use in how we present ourselves and how we assess the behavior of others (Fassett & Warren, 2007; Giroux, 2003; Smith, 2002; Sorrells, 2008; Swartz, 2006; Swartz et al., 2009). Stars such as Michael Jordan, Beyonce, Martha Stewart, Jessica Simpson, LeBron James, and Queen Latifah market themselves as a brand. We are conditioned through advertising and the media to consume the products being sold for self-gratification and to be accepted by society. Giroux (2003) argues that "No longer defined as a form of self-development, individuality is reduced to the endless pursuit of mass-mediated interests and pleasures" (p. 154).

Giroux (2003) cites one such example of individuals marketing themselves as a brand. The case centers around two high school graduates who successfully received corporate sponsorships to finance their college education. Students Chris Barrett and Luke McCabe developed the website ChrisandLuke.com and said they "would put corporate logos on their clothes, wear a company's sunglasses, use their golf clubs, eat their pizza . . ." (Giroux, 2003, p. 154). The students eventually received sponsorship from First USA, a prestigious bank that issues credit cards to students. The students became the first "corporate-sponsored" students and appeared for interviews in several national media outlets, including *The New York Times*.

Intercultural communication scholar Dreama Moon (2002) states that if we agree that media frames our understanding of how we view the world, ourselves, and interact with others, "then current cultural struggles being played out in the media should warrant our attention" (p. 17).

Another issue to consider is that if we believe that it is through communication that cultural realities are created, altered, and sustained, then we begin to consider and understand that Perry, Cyrus, and Thicke represent symbols of a continually debated discussion of what types of social reality that particular communication acts create. Moon (2002) states that the media often mirror and contribute to bigger continual social discussions. Film maker Pratbra Paramor warns us in the essay "Black Feminism: The Politics of Articulation" that images "play a crucial role in defining and controlling the political social power to which individuals and marginalized groups have access" (as cited in hooks, 1992a, p. 5). In recent years, music videos have become very powerful tools in terms of reach and access. These small versions of film have increased their reach through the use of music cable channels such as BET, MTV, and YouTube. Images, particularly in film, are critical. Bell hooks (1992a) reminds us that the images projected on film not only impact how the minority culture view themselves (Blacks, Asians, Hispanics), but also how other groups view and respond to them based upon these images.

The commodification and appropriation of the Black female body continues to be a contested zone. The stereotypical images of hypersexualized Black women are also interwoven into mainstream popular culture through films, advertising, videos, magazines, and popular culture icons. Popular culture icons from Kim Kardashian to Nikki Minaj have further perpetuated the objectification of Black women's body parts (the buttocks). The media's coverage of selected popular culture icons' buttocks have contributed to the distortion of body images to butt-enhanced underwear and surgeries. Several media sources have commented on the popular culture's fascination with the backside during 2014 including Yahoo!, *Vogue* magazine, and *The New York Times Magazine* (Clifton, 2014b).

Derrick Clifton (2014b) reports that reality star Kim Kardashian "broke the internet" (para. 1) with a picture on the cover of *Paper* magazine in November 2014. The cover depicted Kardashian in a slinky black dress displaying her buttocks from a side view. She is holding in front of her a bottle of champagne. A champagne glass is perched on her backside. Champagne flows overhead from the bottle to the champagne glass. Kardashian's photo was taken by renowned photographer Jean-Paul Goude. The *Paper* magazine cover is similar to a 1976 photograph taken by Goude. The photo depicts a dark-skinned naked Black woman in the same pose as the 2014 Kardashian pose. She is holding a bottle of champagne and a champagne glass is placed on her backside. The 1976 photograph is known as the "Carolina Beaumont." Janelle Hobson (2005) discusses how photographer Goude in his photographic book *Jungle Fever* makes a comparison to the back sides of Black women to those of "race horses" (p. 99). Hobson (2012) claims that "with the focus on their infamous behinds, black women's bodies are typically ridiculed, not revered" (p. 100).

The photographic images of Kardashian and the model in the 1976 photo bear a sad and haunting resemblance to the South African woman Saaritjie Baartman of the late eighteenth century (Clifton, 2014b). Baartman, infamously known as "Hottentot Venus," was a Black woman featured in a traveling exhibit that toured though Europe for White audiences. Baartman, a native of Cape South Africa, was separated from her family and coerced into being a servant for a Boer farmer. The farmer's brother persuaded him to enter her into a contract where she would "share in the profit." Baartman began traveling in an exhibition, in a manner similar to a circus sideshow, and displayed for five years nearly nude. Her life was filled with public humiliation and sexual abuse. The 25-year-old Baartman died destitute in Paris. Her body was sold for scientific examination, dissected, and preserved. Sections of her preserved body, especially her genital area and brain, remained displayed in a Paris museum for patrons to view. In 1995, the Grinquas, descendants of the Khosian indigenous groups of South Africa, once labeled the "Hottentots," began a national movement demanding the return of Baartman's remains to South Africa (Hobson, 2005). Baartman did not receive a proper burial until 187 years after her death in her homeland of South Africa.

Hobson (2012) argues that "we now witness, not the decolonization of the black female body, but its commodification and appropriation" (p. 104). She further points out that it is evident in contemporary Black popular culture singers Lil Kim and Foxy Brown. The objectification of a Black woman's body for a commodity is also evident in the career of Black popular culture icon Nikki Minaj. The singer released a single titled "Anaconda" during the summer of 2014. The single's cover depicts her squatting with her backside to the camera. The self-described "Black Barbie" is only wearing a sports bra, Nike shoes, and a scanty thong. There has been controversy surrounding Minaj's decision to display herself in this manner on her single cover. Hobson (2012) believes that the story in today's world is the "story of the media and mediated visions of race and gender in shaping how we view and respond to different bodies" (p. 165).

As a student of intercultural communication and popular culture, consider: What are the ramifications of projecting these popular culture images to worldwide audiences? How do African American women and other women of color, as bell hooks suggests, resist the "oppositional gaze" and engage in "critical black female spectatorship"?

Transforming the Representation of Race and Images

Popular culture is the primary channel through which many individuals learn about other cultural groups and understand who they are. It is important that we reframe the way we view race and representation. Many cultural scholars warn us that we need to critically examine and evaluate how we view these images (Freire & Giroux, 1989; Hall, 1981; hooks, 1992a; Sorrells, 2013). The critical examination of these images begins with what Brazilian educator Paulo Freire (1971) describes as developing a critical consciousness and a moral compass. In the Freirian sense, critical consciousness involves understanding your identity, your world, and obtaining the necessary skills to change your situation. Freire (1971) used the term *conscientizaco*, a Portuguese term, to describe this situation, which he described "as the deepening of the attitude of awareness characteristic of all awareness" (p. 192). Bell hooks (1992a) challenges us to move beyond awareness and create a subversive and radical attitude about race and representation. We must take risks regarding the critical interrogation of popular culture images. Critical theorists Henry Giroux and Freire urge consumers to reflect beyond images and media text. They contend that we must think of the "terrain of popular culture as part of a wider struggle for democracy" (Freire & Giroux, 1989, p. xii). The inability to engage in this critical reflection has negative consequences for our democratic society.

Former U.S. Vice President Al Gore (2007) argues that the increased usage of mass-media and the decreased use of the printed word (newspapers, books, and pamphlets) contributes to the dilemma of our reliance on "electronic images" which can evoke emotional responses, but often without the need for engaged thought or reflection. Gore argues that it was the "emptying out of the marketplace of ideas" (p. 11) that had a negative impact on our nation when we as a country remained silent as former President George W. Bush declared war in Iraq. Gore contends that it was the American people's refusal to question this "'strangeness' that now haunts our efforts to reason together about the choices we make as a nation" (Gore, 2007, p. 11). The strange silence that can impact our society begins with our decision not to question and challenge the popular culture images, music, and sounds that surround us.

This chapter highlighted the significant role that mass-media and popular culture hold in intercultural communication. We discussed the three elements that characterize popular culture: it is integral and dominant in imperialistic capitalistic systems, it is manufactured by cultural industries, and finally, it serves social functions. The links between mass-media, popular culture, and culture as a contested zone were explored. Stereotypical and negative images of women of color in popular culture were examined. The chapter concluded with the importance of critically interrogating popular culture images and media texts.

Discussion Questions

1. What are the social implications of artists from another culture borrowing images and behaviors that may be identified with another cultural group's identity?
2. What are examples of popular culture in television, music videos, and movies today that perpetuate stereotypes of different minority groups? Discuss your responses.
3. How many hours per day do you spend on mediated devices such as cell phones, iPads, computers, etc.? Spend a day "unplugged" from media. How did it make you feel?
4. What impact do you believe interacting with these mass-media devices have on how you communicate with other cultures?

5. How can social media be used as a platform for social change and power? Give a recent example and discuss.

6. What are the larger implications of these popular culture images on African American women and how they are perceived?

References

Adorno, T. W., & Horkheimer, M. (1972). *Dialectic of enlightenment.* New York, NY: Herder and Herder.

Brummett, B. (1994). *Rhetoric in popular culture.* New York, NY: St. Martin.

Clevver Music. (2013, November 13). *Katy Perry Geisha "Unconditionally" performance at American Music Awards 2013.* Retrieved from https://www.youtube.com/watch?v= 0LoI 0oL89U0

Clifton, D. (2014a, July 3). *How to talk to White people about Iggy Azaela.* Retrieved from http://www.dailydot.com/opinion/talking-about-iggy-azalea-white-people

Clifton, D. (2014b, November 13). The big problem with Kim Kardashian's photo that nobody is talking about. Retrieved from http://mic.com/articles/104188/the-big-problem-with-kim-kardashian-s-photos-nobody-is-talking-about

Fassett, D., & Warren, J. (2007). *Critical communication pedagogy.* Thousand Oaks, CA: Sage.

Foucault, M. (1984). Power/knowledge: Selected interviews and other writings, 1972–1977. In P. Rabinow (Ed.), *The Foucault reader* (pp. 51–75). New York. NY: Pantheon Books.

Freire, P. (1971). *Pedagogy of the oppressed.* New York, NY: Harper and Row.

Freire, P., & Giroux, H. A. (1989). Pedagogy, popular culture, and public life: An Introduction. In H. A. Giroux & R. A. Simon (Eds.), *Popular culture schooling and everyday life* (pp. vii–xi). New York, NY: Bergin & Garvey.

Giroux, H. A. (2003). Youth, higher education, and the crisis of public time: Educated hope and the possibility of a democratic future. *Social Identities, 9*(2), 141–168.

GoldMyne Media Concept. (2013, February 3). *Nollywood growth and impact in our economy.* Retrieved from http://goldmyne.tv/nollywood-growth-and-impact-in-our-economy/

Gonzalez, M. (2013, August). The blurred lines of blue-eyed soul. *Ebony Magazine.* Retrieved from http://www.ebony.com/entertainment-culture/the-blurred-lines-of-blue-eyed-soul-111#axzz2cd8zNeHP

Gore, A. (2007). *The assault on reason.* New York, NY: Penguin Group.

Grossberg, L., Wartella, E., Whitney, C. D., & Wise, J. M. (2006). *MediaMaking: Mass media in a popular culture* (2nd ed.). Thousand Oaks, CA: Sage.

Hall, S. (1981). The whites of their eyes. In G. Bridges & R. Brant (Eds.), *Silver linings: Some strategies for the eighties* (pp. 28–52). London: Lawrence and Wishart.

Hall, S. (1992). What is this 'Black' in Black popular culture? In G. Dent (Ed.), *Black popular culture: A Project by Michelle Wallace* (pp. 21–33). Seattle, WA: Bay Press.

Hobson, J. (2005). *Venus in the dark: Blackness and beauty in popular culture.* New York, NY: Routledge.

Hobson, J. (2012). *Body as evidence: mediating race, globalizing gender.* New, York: State University of New York Press.

Holley-Kline, J. (2014). *White pop stars and cultural appropriation.* The Northern Light. Retrieved from http://www.thenorthernlight.org/2014/01/28/white-pop-stars-and-cultural-appropriation/

hooks, b. (1992a). *Black looks: Race and representation.* Boston, MA: South End Press.

hooks, b. (1992b). Eating the Other: Desire and resistance. In b. hooks, *Black looks: Race and representation* (pp. 21–40). Boston, MA: South End Press.

hooks, b. (1992c). Madonna: Plantation mistress or soul sister? In *Black looks: Race and representation* (pp. 157–164). Boston, MA: South End Press.

Kidd, D. (2007). Harry Potter and the functions of popular culture. *The Journal of Popular Culture, 40*(1), 69–89.

Michaels, S. (2010). George Bush: Kenya West Attack was worst day of presidency. *The Guardian.* Retrieved from http://www.theguardian.com/music/2010/nov/04/george-w-bush-kanye-west

Moon, D. (2002). Thinking about "culture" in communication readings. In J. Martin, T. Nakayama, & L. Flores (Eds.), *Intercultural communication.* New York, NY: McGraw-Hill Higher Education.

Osterndorf, C. (2014, August 21). *Why white pop stars can't shake off cultural appropriation.* The Daily Dot. Retrieved from http://www.dailydot.com/opinion/taylor-swift-cant-shake-off-cultural-appropriation/

Rand, M. (2005). *Average person spends more time using media than anything else.* Ball State University News Center. Retrieved from http://www.bsu.edu/up/article/0,1370,32363-2914-36658,00.html

Smith, M. (2002). *Globalization and the incorporation of education.* Retrieved from http://www.infed.org/biblio/globalization_and_education.htm

Sorrells, K. A. (2008). *Linking social justice and intercultural communication in the global context.* Portland, OR: Intercultural Communication Institute.

Sorrells, K. A. (2013). *Intercultural communication: Globalization and social justice.* Washington, DC: Sage.

Swartz, O. (Ed). (2006). *Social justice and communication scholarship.* Mahwah, NJ: Lawrence Erlbaum.

Swartz, O., Campbell, K., & Pestana, C. (2009). *Neo-pragmatism, communication, and the culture of creative democracy.* New York, NY: Peter Lang.

Vivian, J. (2010). *The media of mass communication.* Boston, MA: Allyn & Bacon.

19.   Routes for Transformation: The Repertoires of Black Popular Culture

Keon Pettiway

Introduction

It makes sense to begin a journey of identifying Black popular culture with definitions. **Culture,** in contemporary context, is most commonly understood as a way of life (Williams, 1976) that manifests itself through "a very active world of everyday conversation and exchange" such as everyday dress, having an event to celebrate special occasions, particular forms of hairstyles, a way of speaking, and other distinct exchanges (Heath & Skirrow, 1986, p. 5). This description aligns with rhetorician Barry Brummett's (2010) definition of **popular culture** as systems or artifacts that many people share, know about, identify with, and experience on an everyday basis. These systems or artifacts link group identifications based on the collective experience that binds people together. For example, **Black** is described as a community of people with African/African American descent and refers to their collective experience, memories, and everyday practices of Black culture that are materialized through interrelated systems of artifacts (Hall, 1992; Nelson, 2009). According to Stuart Hall (1992), a British cultural studies scholar, the shape of Blackness is molded by historically-related Black experiences, distinctive Black aesthetics that emerge from Black cultural practices (aesthetics experienced as representations of Blackness in popular culture), and counternarratives that Black people have created to have a means for social action and **agency,** the capacity to have a choice or voice. It is at these crossroads—*Black experiences, Black aesthetics,* and *Black counternarratives*—where Black cultural repertoires are represented in popular culture. Later, I will return to the words *popular* and *culture* to describe how Black cultural repertoires operate in popular culture—a site of struggle over power rather than a space where the most favorable, authentic, ordinary, or desired ways of life are represented.

Reading Black Popular Culture

Black popular culture defies static definitions, although there is a tendency to homogenize the experiences and performances of Blackness. Going beyond simple binary oppositions such as high/low or authentic/inauthentic, Black popular culture can be elusive at times. But how do we get on with answering a critical question necessary to understand the shape of Black popular culture: What are the distinctive artifacts and devices that make up Black culture in popular contexts? In his widely cited essay, "What is This 'Black' in

Black Popular Culture?," Hall (1992) states that there is indeed, a "profound set of distinctive, historically defined black experiences that contribute to those alternative repertoires" (Hall, 1992, p. 11). A system or artifact is "good" Black popular culture if it is an "authentic" representation of the historical experiences of Black people and Black expressions of aesthetics and counter narratives. Angela Nelson describes these "good" forms and products as **Black cultural repertoires**—"specific devices, techniques, figures, black objects, expressive art forms, or products of people of Africana descent" (Nelson, 2009, para. 6). Drawing from Hall's three-part Black repertoire—*style, music*, and the *use of the body as a canvas of representation*, Nelson proposes a seven-part repertoire based on systems or artifacts that materialize the Black experience and Black expressivity: (a) the city [or space and place], (b) food/cuisine, (c) rhythm, (d) percussiveness, (e) call-response, (f) worship service and party, and (g) middle-class ideology. Before describing three of Nelson's seven-part repertoire, I would like to call attention to the way Herman Gray (1995), a cultural theorist, examines Black popular youth style and its associated cultural practices. The case of Black popular youth style provides a pathway to enact a critical sensibility toward reading popular culture, and Black culture in particular.

In "Jammin' on the One! Some Reflections on the Politics of Black Popular Culture," Gray argues that Black youth articulate cultural performances of Blackness through a host of *styles*: body, hair, language, music, and dress. Noting the many hairstyles worn by youth during the 1990s such as dreadlocks, intricate haircuts, braids, and many other textures, colors, and forms, Gray suggests that as a form of Black popular cultural production, youth assert a Black sensibility of identity. While Black youth reinvent, remix, and reassert sensations of Blackness from a constellation of other popular culture systems and artifacts, these distinct forms of Black cultural practices are also connected to a longer stream of Black experience and Black expressivity (e.g., the emergence of Afros in the 1960s during the Black Power movement, box braids, and box haircuts in the 1990s). In addition to hair, Black youth use the body through movement and dance as an expressive statement and re-statement of Black subjectivity. This performance comprises a mix of other products and forms of popular culture, historical traditions of rhythm and movement of Black expressivity, and, at the same time, the body as a site of struggle, transformation, and the collective Black experience. Put another way, Black popular youth style mixes intercultural/transcultural and intergenerational/transgenerational traditions of Black experience and Black expressivity in ways that defy labels of a pure, static form of Black popular culture. For example, while krumping was brought to mainstream media through music videos and the documentary film *Rize* (LaChapelle, 2005), it had long been part of Black popular youth culture during the early 1990s in Los Angeles. Through krumping—free-form, expressive movement of the body in high-energy movements—"black youth make full use of their bodies in convulsive motion to express anger, aggression, and other emotions" (Smith, 2011, p. 393). In this context, Black youth reassert the experiences and an alternative state of the Black condition through movement and dance. While krumping emerged from within Los Angeles, it has also been described as a gesture toward traditions of African/Black dance (Smith, 2011) and a transformative site of Black identity (Todd, 2009).

Kamira/Shutterstock.com

There are a couple of ways of reading these Black popular youth styles. On the one hand, these cultural performances could be read as **nihilistic** behaviors that lead to self-destruction, self-hate, and detachment from community. For Cornel West, philosopher and critic, nihilism, "the lived experience of coping with a life of horrifying meaninglessness, hopelessness, and (most important) lovelessness" leads to self-destructive behavior and outlook on the world (West, 1994, pp. 22–23). For instance, the production and adoption of different systems and artifacts in Black popular youth culture, such as sports logos in hairstyles and hip hop music, could be read as the erosion of self-respect through commercial consumer culture. Oneka LaBennett (2011) makes a similar point in *She's Mad Real: Popular Culture and West Indian Girls in Brooklyn* as she describes how popular representations of Black youth, namely Black teenage girls, "often portray Black adolescents' consumer and leisure culture as corruptive, uncivilized, and pathological" (LaBennett, 2011, p. 3). This nihilistic behavior in Black popular youth culture is read as "threats to civic decorum" (p. 3), which in turn becomes grounds for marginalizing and policing these practices through social protocols and public policies.[1] Here I would like to suggest another reading of Black popular culture youth performance by locating these cultural practices within historical and social discourses of Black experiences and Black expressivity. The behavior exhibited in Black popular youth style, as Gray shows, is more than a psychological state of self-hate, self-disrespect, or detachment; it is a space where the body is used to act out a number of different identities and conditions in ways that also affirm a Black sensibility. Following Kobena Mercer (1990), Gray asserts that these performance are "the continual inventions and articulations of black cultural imaginations played out on the material and symbolic surface of the body" (Gray, 1993, p. 152). In other words, Gray's reading of the body in Black popular youth style echoes other scholars

---

1. This is evident in the laws that have recently emerged that ban sagging pants in states such as Florida and New Jersey. In New York, there was a public campaign to "Stop the Sag" where people were encouraged to "Raise your Pants. Raise your Image."

who suggest that what we see on the surface of Black popular culture is more than what is assumed about collective experiences, identities, and authenticity.[2] Reaching back to Hall (1992), the body *is* the canvas where Black cultural representation is contested and reworked, finding *routes* rather than *roots*,[3] but always historically connected.

Black Cultural Repertoires

I now return to Nelson's concept of "black cultural repertoire" vis-à-vis Gray's analysis of Black popular youth style and Hall's notion that the body is a canvas used as cultural capital. The following repertoires represent an array of canvases of Black popular representations. In Black culture, these canvases are spaces with transformative potential for restoration, reconciliation, regeneration, and recuperation (Nelson, 2009). While each of the seven repertoires Nelson identifies deserve further attention, I will only focus on three components that are perhaps most recognizable in Black popular culture (food/cuisine and worship service), and the less recognizable (middle-class ideology). Later, I will rely on these Black cultural repertoires to answer the following question: What kind of space is popular culture wherein Black culture is represented and reworked?

Food/Cuisine

Typically, African American food and cuisine is referred to as "soul food," but, as Black popular repertoire, it is also a space of Black expressions, counter narratives, and transformation. George Tillman, Jr., producer of the movie *Soul Food* (1997) explains that cooking and having family meals was one of the only spaces where slaves "were able to talk about their souls" (Tillman, 1997, p. 3). The movie *Soul Food* exemplifies this practice as the movie centers on a Sunday dinner to bring a family together torn by multiple crises. From this view, African American food and cuisine is more than bodily sustenance. As Goodie Mob (Barnett et al., 1995) states in the song "Soul Food," "I got a plate of soul food . . . Got some soul on blast in tha cassette/Food for my brain." It provides a means for "upwardly mobile African Americans to affirm their racial authenticity," as well as a form of resisting appropriations of Black culture (Witt, 1999, p. 13).

---

2. For example, see Genova, N. D. (1995). Gangster Rap and Nihilism in Black America: Some Questions of Life and Death. *Social Text, 13*(2), 89; Boyd, T. (1997). Am I Black enough for you?: Popular culture from the 'Hood and beyond. Bloomington, IN: Indiana University Press; Watkins, S.C. (1998). *Representing: Hip hop culture and the production of Black cinema*. Chicago, IL: University of Chicago Press. Also, see Clay, A. (2003). Keepin' it real: Black youth, hip-hop culture, and black identity. *American Behavioral Scientist, 46*(10), 1346–1358.

3. In *Cultural Studies: Theory and Practice*, Chris Barker (2000) uses the term *route* to identify how identities are in motion. This type of motion differs from trying to find *roots*, as pathways for identities are more about response than trying to find the absolutes identity. However, Henry Louis Gates, Jr.'s *Finding Your Roots* television show raises interesting questions about *routes* versus *roots*.

The City [or Space and Place]

The city is also a space from which Black experiences, expressivity, and counter narratives are represented in Black popular culture. In "Toward a Redefinition of the Urban: The Collision of Culture," John Jeffries (1992) extends Hall's three-part repertoires of Black popular culture to include the city as the space where new forms of Black popular culture emerge. Historically, the city has been the "locale of cool," as Jeffries puts it, such as in the narratives and activities of the Harlem Renaissance. In *Black Noise: Rap Music and Black Culture in Contemporary America,* Tricia Rose (1994) comments on the city as a distinctive site where rap emerges as a "black cultural expression that prioritizes black voices from the margins of urban America" (p. 2). In the song "Chi-City," hip hop artist Common states, "They ask me where hip-hop is goin'/it's Chicagoan . . . It's the city, the city y'all, the city." (Lynn, West, & Cornelius, 2005) These lyrics provide a way to describe how Black popular culture, though always in motion like Common's verses, is going and coming from the city. More to the point, it is from the margins of the city that Black popular culture emerges from within the locale of urban America.

Middle-Class Ideology

In Black popular culture, *The Cosby Show*, followed by other recent television shows such as *My Wife and Kids* and *Are We There Yet?*, is one of the most representative examples of middle-class ideology. Some of these characteristics include harmony, equality among races, affluence, nuclear family, mobility (social, economic, educational), and love relationships that are heterosexual. Historically, *The Cosby Show* served as a counter narrative to shows during the 1970s that portrayed "authentic" forms of Black life, such as the television show *Good Times*. *The Cosby Show* is an important example of middle-class ideology as a Black cultural repertoire when it is positioned in dialogue with historical debates and media representations of the Black family, the Black underclass, and morality in the Black community (Gray, 1995). The show featured themes such as family-oriented relationships, upward mobility through education, and racial equality. While this popular form of middle-class Black life offers a different representation of Blackness, it also undercuts the diversity of Black life that do not ascribe to a middle-class ideology. The focus is on Black urban life that satisfies the characteristics of middle-class ideology rather than, for example, the collective experience of Black rural or religious life. This limited view of Black culture in the popular imagination sacrifices opportunities to represent other diverse forms of Black life and culture.

Popular Culture as a Site of Struggle and Contestation

What kind of space is popular culture wherein Black culture is represented and reworked? The three Black cultural repertoires of food/cuisine, the city, and middle-class ideology demonstrate experiences, expressions, and counter narratives of Black cultural practice that subvert any simple definition of *Black*, *popular*, and *culture*. Though culture is understood as a set of values, social practices, and customs that describe the way of life of a particular group, cultural studies scholar Raymond Williams states that culture, as defined in English language, is "one of the two or three most complicated words" (Williams, 1976, p. 76). It is used interchangeably to describe more than one process, and how we define culture frames how we think about and perceive cultural practices of various groups. Here I suggest two other definitions of culture: (a) Culture as **hegemonic** practices and systems whereby one group dictates or dominates the social and political context, and (b) "shifting tensions between the shared and the unshared" (Lee, 2004, p. 5). From these two definitions, *popular* culture is not defined as the arena where truths about different ways of life are found (Hall, 1992). If anything, it is a mythic space rife with many conflicts, yet serves as a site where multiple identities and alternative futures may be formed. Here we may be able to answer the question of what is Black popular culture somewhat differently by redefining common notions of popular culture as an arena of true definitions of experiences.

Discussion Questions

1. What is the relation between "Black cultural repertoires" and Black popular culture?
2. What defines "good" Black popular culture? Do you agree with this rubric?
3. Identify some other examples of the following components of Black cultural repertoires: food/cuisine, the city, and middle-class ideology.
4. What are some challenges of identifying and critiquing Black popular culture?
5. What is meant by the words *Black*, *popular*, and *culture*?

References

Barnett, R., Bennett, B., Benno, M., Boatman, B., Burton, T., & Cameron, W. G. (1995). Soul Food. On *Soul Food* [CD]. Atlanta, GA: LaFace.

Brummett, B. (2010). *Rhetoric in popular culture.* Thousand Oaks, CA: Sage.

Gray, H. (1995). *Watching race: Television and the struggle for "Blackness."* Minneapolis, MN: University of Minnesota.

Hall, S. (1992). What is This 'Black' in Black popular culture? In G. Dent (Ed.), *Black popular culture* (pp. 21–33). Seattle, WA: Bay Press.

Heath, S., & Skirrow, G. (1986). Interview with Raymond Williams. In T. Modleski (Ed.), *Studies in entertainment: Critical approaches to mass culture* (pp. 3–17). Bloomington, IN: Indiana University Press.

Jeffries, J. (1992). Toward a redefinition of the urban: The collision of culture. In G. Dent (Ed.), *Black popular culture* (pp. 153–163). Seattle, WA: Bay Press.

LaBennett, O. (2011). *She's mad real: Popular culture and West Indian girls in Brooklyn.* New York, NY: New York University Press.

LaChapelle, D. (Director). (2005). *Rize* [Documentary]. United States: Lions Gate Entertainment.

Lee, W. (2004). Point of view. In J. N. Martin & T. K. Nakayama (Eds.), *Intercultural communication in contexts* (p. 85). Boston, MA: McGraw-Hill.

Lynn, L., West, K., & Cornelius, E. (2005). Chi-City. On *Be* [Recorded by Common]. New York, NY: GOOD Music.

Mercer, K. (1990). Black hair/style politics. In R. Ferguson, M. Gever, T. T. Minh-ha, & C. West (Eds.), *Out there: Marginalization and contemporary cultures* (pp. 247–264). Cambridge, MA: MIT Press.

Nelson, A. (2009). The repertoire of black popular culture. *Americana: The Journal of American Popular Culture*, 8(1). Retrieved from http://www.americanpopularculture.com/journal/articles/spring_2009/nelson.htm

Rose, T. (1994). *Black noise: Rap music and black culture in contemporary America*. Hanover, NH: University Press of New England.

Smith, J. C. (2011). *Encyclopedia of African American popular culture*. Santa Barbara, CA: Greenwood.

Tillman, G., Jr. (1997). *Soul food cookbook: Recipes of the stars* [pamphlet inserted with video package].

Todd, M. A. (2009). *Getting krump: Reading choreographies of cultural desire through an Afro-diasporic dance* (Doctoral dissertation). Retrieved from ProQuest Dissertations and Theses. (Accession Order No. AAT 3357286.)

West, C. (1994). *Race matters*. Boston, MA: Beacon Press.

Williams, R. (1976). *Keywords: A vocabulary of culture and society*. New York, NY: Oxford University Press.

Witt, D. (1999). *Black hunger: Food and the politics of U.S. identity*. New York: Oxford UP.

Chapter 5

Reviewing the Media

20. Post-Racial Pride and Prejudice: Media Depictions of Racial Conflict in the Networked Public Sphere

Debashis 'Deb' Aikat, Ph.D.

> Nothing in the world is easier in the United States
> than to accuse a black man of crime.

> —American civil rights activist "W. E. B." Du Bois in his 1932 column "Courts and jails"
> in *The Crisis*, (Dubois, 1932, p. 132; Wilson, 1970, p. 126).

The epigraph enunciates the racial conflict of the 1930s, as depicted by American sociologist, historian, and civil rights activist William Edward Burghardt "W. E. B." Du Bois in *The Crisis*, the official organ of the National Association for the Advancement of Colored People (NAACP). First published in November 1910 by Du Bois as "a record of the darker races" and as the premier crusading voice for civil rights, *The Crisis* has empowered, educated, entertained, explicated and, in many instances, enriched the social, political, and economic agenda in the struggle for human rights for people of color in the United States and beyond.

Expressing concern over "disgrace of the American Negro," Du Bois wrote in his 1932 *The Crisis* column that the "emancipated and rising Negro has tried desperately to disassociate himself from his own criminal class" but were repeatedly and unjustifiably "accused and taunted with being criminals" from the early days "since Emancipation and even before" (Dubois, 1932, p. 132).

Du Bois contended that "there is absolutely no scientific proof, statistical, social or physical," that indicate "that the American Negro is any more criminal" when matched or compared to "other elements in the American nation, if indeed as criminal" (Dubois, 1932, p. 132). In the more than eight decades since Du Bois made that contention, his words of wisdom have attained greater significance in the twenty-first century with unabated racial conflict that continues to plague African Americans and other communities of color. The words of Du Bois ring true as post-racial pride and prejudice seem complicated by media depictions of racial conflict in a public sphere replete with racial stereotyping and ethnic discrimination that constitute new lessons for intercultural communication for global engagement.

Research Preamble and Epistemological Objectives

Media representation of **race and ethnic minorities** comprise a critical aspect of the public sphere in our media-saturated world. As Giroux observed, **race and ethnic minorities** are among the "most powerful ideological and institutional factors for deciding how identities are categorized and power, material privileges, and resources distributed" because "race represents an essential political category for examining the relationship between justice and a democratic society" (Giroux, 2003, p. 200). Eric Holder, the first African American U.S. attorney general, has highlighted the need to "to confront our racial past, and our racial present" in these words: "One cannot truly understand America without understanding the historical experience of black people in this nation" (Holder, 2009).

Reiterating that the persistence of "unresolved racial issues," Holder felt that one must examine the "racial soul" of the U.S. "to get to the heart of this country" (Holder, 2009). By situating intercultural communication within a larger context of global understanding and engagement, this chapter presents research that synthesizes multidisciplinary perspectives and examines media depictions of racial conflict in the U.S. in four distinct parts. The first part covers the interplay of race and media in the networked public sphere. The second part chronicles the Civil War legacy of slavery, race, and conflict, and the racial injustice of the Jim Crow era. The third part enunciates media depictions of the 1955 killing of Emmett Till and the power of media images in the 1991–92 Rodney King racial conflict. The fourth and final part analyzes theoretical constructs that explicate prejudice, stereotyping, and discrimination to analyze events that illustrate post-racial pride and prejudice. In addressing the significance of racial issues in fostering intercultural communication for global understanding and engagement, this chapter also delineates the powerful significance of media representation of race and ethnic minorities in the U.S. and beyond.

Race and Media in the Networked Public Sphere

German sociologist and philosopher Jürgen Habermas's *The Structural Transformation of the Public Sphere* (1962/1989) theorized a nineteenth-century bourgeois public sphere with a social space for political dialogue, debate, and dissent. Habermas's public sphere theory spawned related concepts and counter theories that redefined the role of the media in a democracy (Curran, 1991; Dahlgren, 2009; Dahlgren & Sparks, 1991; Kellner, 1990).

As a mirror of the society, newspapers in America did not emerge until the late seventeenth century because colonial officials viewed newspapers as the source of "disobedience and heresy and . . . libels against the best government" (Weeks & Bacon, 1911; Vance, 1917; Wettach, 1925). On September 12, 1686, Sir Edmund Andros, the governor of the Dominion of New England, which included the jurisdiction of all the New England colonies and later of New York and New Jersey, was instructed "not to permit Printing without Licence" because "Great inconvenience may arise by the Liberty of Printing" (Batchellor, 1904, p. 166). In just over four years of that instruction, on September 25, 1690, an English publisher Benjamin Harris surprised the Boston authorities by publishing the first newspaper in the colonies. In sharp contrast to the one-page broadsides printed earlier, Harris's newspaper, *Publick Occurrences Both Forreign and Domestick,* enjoyed the legitimacy of a newspaper, although its influence and circulation was limited (Weeks & Bacon, 1911; Kelly, 1978).

Habermas (1989) recognized media's "ambivalent potential" (p. 303) in the construction of a robust public sphere. A militant Black press began in the 1820s in response to racist media attacks and the refusal of White-owned newspapers to print responses from Black readers. *Freedom's Journal* was the first Black-owned and operated newspaper in the United States. It was founded in 1827 the same year slavery was abolished in the State of New York. In the inaugural March 16, 1827, issue, the *Freedom's Journal* editors, American Presbyterian minister Samuel E. Cornish and American abolitionist John B. Russwurm declared: "We wish to plead our own cause" (p. 1). The *Freedom's Journal* editors enunciated how they wanted to change how "others [have] spoken for us." They criticized the false and misleading representation of race issues in these words, "Too long has the public been deceived by misrepresentations, in things which concern us dearly" (Cornish & Russwurm, 1827). Supported by a group of free Black men in New York City, *Freedom's Journal* served to counter racist commentary published in the mainstream press. The newspaper denounced slavery, advocated for Black people's political rights, campaigned for the right to vote, and criticized lynchings (Bacon, 2007).

More than 1,200 Black-owned newspapers were started in the four decades following the end of the Civil War in 1865. The mid-nineteenth century witnessed the inception of leading U.S. dailies. American journalist and politician Henry Jarvis Raymond collaborated with Albany, New York, banker George Jones to publish on September 18, 1851, the first edition of *The New York Times*, which stated: "We publish today the first issue of the *New-York Daily Times*, and we intend to issue it" every morning (Sundays excepted) "for an indefinite number of years to come." *The Washington Post* published its first issue on December 6, 1877, and *The Wall Street Journal* debuted on July 8, 1889.

While newspaper gained mainstream acceptance in the nineteenth century, the broadcast medium emerged in the twentieth century. The first radio broadcasts began in the early twentieth century. A Detroit station aired on August 31, 1920, what is believed to be the first radio news broadcast. Newspaper publishers were wary of radio because they thought the immediacy of radio might render irrelevant the newspaper's next-day coverage of news events.

Electronic television was first successfully demonstrated in San Francisco on September 7, 1927, but it was not until the 1930s that American television reported news. In 1939, RCA televised the opening of the World's Fair in New York City, including a speech by U.S. President Franklin Delano Roosevelt, who was the first U.S. president to appear on television.

The growth of media forms an important aspect of the public sphere. Habermas (1962/1989) explored both the evolution of the bourgeois public sphere and its decline. This decline, according to Habermas, was caused by several factors including the growing power of the state, corporate expansion, consumerism, and an increasingly privatized society. The twenty-first century digital age has transformed Habermas's concept of public sphere.

One such transformation is the emergence of a **networked public sphere**, which was facilitated by the widespread societal adoption of the Internet and growth of digital technologies. The Internet emerged as a source of news in the 1990s. The White House and the United Nations developed an official Internet presence in 1993. Tim Berners-Lee, a British scientist at CERN in Switzerland, invented the World Wide Web in 1989. The Web facilitated the advent of a fully commercialized Internet in the 1990s and digitally transformed print, video, news, entertainment, and advertising industries. Such media transformations to the traditional media were significant and lasting. Even the mainstays of traditional media in America yielded to the new demands of a changing digital landscape. Renowned newspapers published online versions such as *The New York Times on the Web*, which went online on January 19, 1996, while *The Wall Street Journal Interactive Edition* was launched April 29, 1996. Such media developments heralded a historic shift in the global media industry as the news consumer began reading news online and circulation of paper publications declined.

The twenty-first century has witnessed the growth of the Internet as a medium of news, information, and entertainment. The first decade of the twenty-first century saw the appearance of "born on the World Wide Web" news entities such as Huffington Post (founded May 2005 in New York City), Buzzfeed (founded 2006 in New York City), and Mashable (founded May 2005 in Scotland). They were called "born on the World Wide Web" to distinguish them from the online versions of traditional newspapers. Additionally, the rise of social media in 2004 (when the social media giant Facebook was founded) initiated a dominant engagement of news content on social networks and on mobile devices. As multiple news platforms emerged, news media companies quickly evolved to provide rigorous and accessible news that targeted millions of people as their global audience.

The technological metamorphosis of the media has prompted theorists to posit the **networked public sphere** as an alternative arena for public discourse and political debate because it is decreasingly dominated by large media entities and devoid of government control, and designed for wider participation (Benkler, 2006; Benkler, Roberts, Faris, Solow-Niederman, & Etling, 2013; Bruns, Burgess, Highfield, Kirchhoff, & Nicolai, 2011; Roberts, 2009).

Shirky (2011) pointed out, since the rise of the Internet in the early 1990s, "the world's networked population has grown from the low millions to the low billions" (para. 3). YouTube, the video-sharing website, featured its first video titled, "Me at the zoo," on April 23, 2005. Jack Dorsey, co-founder of the microblogging service, Twitter, sent out the first Twitter message on March 21, 2006, when the service was known as Twttr. While media institutions foster freedom of thought and ideas with their innate ability to enhance public dialogue on important social and political issues, the same media institutions "considerably strengthen the efficacy of social control" through their centralized production of media messages (Habermas, 1962/1989, p. 303).

Research Method

The research reported in this chapter adopted a case study method to analyze media depictions of racial conflict in the networked public sphere. As a robust measure to evaluate the interplay of race and media in the networked public sphere, the case study research method has enabled researchers to address contemporary research issues such as social media strategies based on inspirational case studies from companies (Fine, 2010). This researcher enhanced the case study research method by drawing upon related case study methods in recent studies (George & Pratt, 2012; Jaeger, 2005; Lee, 2014). Lee (2014) analyzed the introduction of NASDAQ by gathering news articles from six publications, George and Pratt (2012) examined socio-cultural issues associated with crisis communication from international perspectives, and Jaeger (2005) traced the conceptual foundations of electronic government in a deliberative democracy. The case study method presented in this chapter draws upon other research works such as Creswell (2014), Yin (2012), and Merriam (2009).

This qualitative case study research method also comprised a detailed review of recent scholarly literature to articulate theories that explicate and enunciate the role of media and race in the networked public sphere (Alexander, 2011; Jarvis, 2007). This research method enabled insightful reviews of the rich historiography of racial conflict and the state of the networked public sphere. It also enabled the author to refine cross disciplinary perspectives, as identified in prior studies of communication (Fischer & Merrill, 1976;

Holledge & Tompkins, 2000; Hooker, 2011; Martin & Wilson, 1997; Prosser, 1973), information and data effects in our society (Aikat & Remund, 2012; boyd & Ellison, 2007) and free speech, Morris & Waisbord, 2001; Rares, Fenger, Rosenmeier, Ehlers, & Carl, 2006; Varennes, 1996).

The Civil War Legacy of Slavery and Racial Conflict

As a historical event, the American Civil War (1861–1865) left a deep imprint on America's collective memory, racial freedom, and ethnic conflict. The Civil War was fought between the "Confederacy" (or the "South") comprising 11 Southern states that seceded from the Union to form the Confederate States of America, and the "Union" (or the "North") encompassing states that did not secede. Although the **Civil War** originated over the fractious issue of slavery, especially the extension of slavery into the western territories, the four-year internecine war was not originally framed to free the slaves. In the initial phase of the Civil War, U.S. President Abraham Lincoln promised not to impose abolitionist goals on the South. But that changed in September 1862 when Lincoln proposed to free the slaves with a provisional proclamation to emancipate slaves in select parts of the South where he lacked authority.

As the Civil War deepened in racial rancor and unabated violence, it became obvious that the South would not cease fighting and rejoin the Union. When the 1862 Battle of Antietam, the bloodiest single day in American military history ended in a draw, the Confederate retreat gave Abraham Lincoln the "victory" he desired to issue the Emancipation Proclamation, which famously ordered slaves freed in all areas of the Confederacy that did not declare by January 1, 1863, loyalty to the Union.

Although the **1862 Proclamation of Emancipation** failed to expressly free slaves in loyal states and exempted Confederacy areas already under Union control, it changed, in fundamental ways, the character of the Civil War with a fervent hope of freedom among Americans. Every advance of Union troops after January 1, 1863, expanded the spirit of freedom and the emancipation proclamation, and therefore captured the hearts and imagination of millions of Americans. Moreover, the 1862 Proclamation of Emancipation enabled the liberated to become liberators by authorizing the acceptance of Black men into the Union Army and Navy. By the end of the war, almost 200,000 Black soldiers and sailors had fought for the Union and freedom.

These developments were significant because slaves had acted to secure their own liberty from the first days of the Civil War. The Emancipation Proclamation confirmed their insistence to consider the war for the Union as a struggle for freedom. Such insistence added moral force to the Union cause and strengthened the Union both in military and political terms. The Emancipation Proclamation was thus a milestone in human freedom toward the final eradication of slavery.

With the end of the Civil War in 1865, the North and South began a slow and painful process of reconciliation in the ravaged American landscape. In the aftermath of the

Civil War, Americans embraced and engaged in the perilous path of remembering and casting off their traumatic past (Blight, 2001). The ensuing decades witnessed triumph of reunion that distinctly emphasized Civil War heroics, and downplayed the tragic consequences of racial inequality and discrimination among other sectional disparities. The national culture in the post-Civil War period seemed conspicuously devoid of the legacy of moral crusades over slavery that ignited the war, the presence and participation of African Americans throughout the war, and the promise of emancipation that emerged from the war (Blight, 2001).

America healed without justice in the decades since the Civil War. By the early twentieth century, the problems of race and reunion were locked in mutual dependence, a painful legacy that lingers to the twenty-first century. More than 150 years after the Civil War, the networked public sphere seems riddled with arguments over the Civil War legacy of slavery and racial conflict.

The Racial Injustice of the Jim Crow Days

Although the July 4, 1776, U.S. Declaration of Independence stated, "All men are created equal," this statement was not grounded in law until after the Civil War and, arguably, not completely fulfilled for many years thereafter due to the **institution of slavery**.

The U.S. Constitution explicated no express reference to federal protection of minority rights until the post-Civil War era of the late-1860s and early-1870s when three amendments to the U.S. Constitution directly addressed and ratified civil rights for all people. These amendments collectively outlawed slavery, provided for equal protection under the law, guaranteed citizenship, and protected the right to vote for all Americans.

The **1865 Thirteenth Amendment to the U.S. Constitution** abolished slavery and involuntary servitude, except as punishment for a crime. Less than three years later, the **1868 Fourteenth Amendment to the U.S. Constitution** strengthened the legal rights of newly-freed slaves by stating, among other things, that no state shall deprive anyone of either "due process of law" or of the "equal protection of the law." Finally, the **1870 Fifteenth Amendment to the U.S. Constitution** further strengthened the legal rights of newly-freed slaves by prohibiting the federal and state governments from denying a citizen the right to vote based on that citizen's "race, color, or previous condition of servitude."

Despite these epochal amendments, African Americans were often racially discriminated and treated differently than Whites in many parts of the U.S., especially in the South. From the 1880s into the 1960s, most American states enforced segregation through **Jim Crow laws** (so-called after a Black character in minstrel shows). From Delaware to California, and from North Dakota to Texas, many states and cities imposed legal punishments on people for consorting with members of another race. The most common types of Jim Crow laws forbade **interracial marriage**, besides stipulating business owners and public institutions to segregate their Black clientele from White people.

This was also a historical period that signified shameful examples of racial injustice in U.S. history. The **1931 Scottsboro Boys case** involved nine Black teens, falsely accused of raping two White women onboard a train near Scottsboro, Alabama. No criminal case in American history, let alone a crime that never occurred, led to so many trials, convictions, reversals, and retrials. Throughout the 1930s and the 1940s, the struggle for justice for the "Scottsboro Boys," as the Black teens were called, made celebrities out of common people, launched and disrupted careers, and unraveled Southern juries to issues of race and class, exacerbated widespread strife, and divided America's political milieu. The sequence of events sparked international demonstrations and succeeded in both highlighting the racism of the American legal system and in overturning the unjust convictions. Cutting across racial divides, courageous newspaper editors, valiant attorneys, fearless judges, and other citizens assiduously strived for justice for the Scottsboro Boys.

In sharp contrast to the racial injustice of the Jim Crow days, the **1954 *Brown v. Board of Education*** ruling marked one of the greatest twentieth-century decisions of the U.S. Supreme Court, which unanimously ruled that the racial segregation of children in public schools violated the Equal Protection Clause of the Fourteenth Amendment. Although the decision did not succeed in fully desegregating public education in the U.S., it put the U.S. Constitution on the side of racial equality and galvanized the nascent civil rights movement into a full revolution.

Media Depictions of the Murder of Emmett Till

In August 1955, one year after *Brown v. Board of Education*, a 14-year-old Black boy from Chicago, **Emmett Till**, was visiting relatives in Money, Mississippi. When Emmett whistled at Carolyn Bryant, a White woman in the local grocery store, he didn't understand that he had broken the unwritten laws of the Jim Crow South until three days later, when two White men dragged Emmett from his bed in the dead of night, beat him brutally, and then shot him in the head. Three days later Emmett's mangled body was pulled from the Tallahatchie River. Although Emmett's killers were arrested and charged with murder, they were both quickly acquitted by an all-White, all-male jury. Shortly afterward, the defendants sold to a journalist their story, including a detailed account of how they murdered Emmett. The murder and the trial horrified the nation and the world. Despite the public outcry and the media coverage, the U.S. federal government failed to intercede in the Emmett Till case. This led Blacks and Whites to realize that they would have to assiduously fight for change.

Emmett's tragic story may have ended with the brutal killing except for an extraordinary decision by his mother, Mamie Till. On the advice of prominent civil rights leaders, Mamie Till decided to leave the casket open at her son's funeral. She instructed the mortician to refrain from cosmetically restoring her son's face because she wanted the people to view for themselves what had been done to Emmett. Thousands of people viewed Emmett's body, which was on display in a Chicago church for four days. The national media and international press published gruesome photos of Emmett's maimed and distorted face. America was shocked out of blissful complacency. The Emmett Till case became international news and sparked a media coverage that led to an international outcry that revived the civil rights movement.

The murder of Emmett Till was a watershed in galvanizing the nascent movement for civil rights. Some historians describe it as the real spark that ignited broad-based support for the movement. Three months after Emmett's body was pulled from the Tallahatchie River, the Montgomery bus boycott began. Sparked by the arrest of activist Rosa Parks in December 1955, the Montgomery bus boycott was a 13-month mass protest that ended with the U.S. Supreme Court ruling that rendered unconstitutional segregation on public buses.

American clergyman, activist, humanitarian, and African American civil rights activist **Martin L. King Jr.** emerged as the leader of the **Montgomery Bus Boycott in 1955**. King thus began a long tenure as the spiritual figurehead and the intellectual strategist for the nonviolent protest in the U.S. civil rights movement. Besides being a Baptist minister, King was a moral leader to the community by dint of his charismatic personality and powerful oratory. As a man of vision and determination, King never stopped dreaming for a better future.

Although the **U.S. civil rights movement** evolved over many decades as a political and legislative issue, the 1960s marked a period of intense activity by the U.S. federal government to protect minority rights. The **1964 U.S. Civil Rights Act** was a significant landmark in legislative attempts to improve the quality of life for African Americans and other minority groups. The Act did not resolve all problems of discrimination, but it opened the door to further progress by lessening racial restrictions on the use of public facilities, providing more job opportunities, strengthening voting laws, and limiting federal funds for discriminatory aid programs. The landmark **U.S. Civil Rights Act of 1964** also prohibited discrimination on the basis of race, color, and national origin in programs and activities receiving federal financial assistance.

Media Images in the Rodney King Racial Conflict

The 1955 murder of Emmett Till gained media prominence due to the power of pictures and news reports. Less than four decades later, the **1991–92 Rodney King racial conflict** illustrated the power of video technology that empowered common citizens with a camera to take moving pictures with sound. The significance of video technology was signified by a video recording that captured the beating of a Black motorist Rodney King, thanks to a common citizen looking through his condo window with a video camera. The now-defunct half-inch video technology thus reflected tremendous empowerment.

As a media depiction, the 1991 Rodney King videotaped beating twice became a symbol of the nation's continuing racial tensions. First, the news coverage of the 1991 brutal beating by the Los Angeles police and, second, the 1992 deadly race riots in Los Angeles that led to more than 50 deaths and $1 billion in property damage.

This racial turbulence began with a traffic violation. In 1991, Rodney King, then a 25-year-old construction worker and convicted robber on parole, admittedly had a few drinks before driving home from a friend's house on the 210 freeway in Los Angeles. King panicked when he spotted a police car following him. Fearing he would be sent back to prison, King led the police on a high-speed chase, eventually reaching speeds of up to 115 miles per hour, according to police records. Realizing he couldn't outrun the police but fearing what the police might do to him when they caught him, King said he looked for a public place to stop. By the time King stopped his car and was ordered to exit his vehicle, several Los Angeles Police Department (LAPD) squad cars arrived on the scene. A struggle ensued and some of the LAPD officers quickly determined that King was resisting arrest. Four police officers, all of them White, struck King more than 50 times with their nightsticks and shocked him with an electric stun gun.

Rodney King's hope of having a witness to his beating was fulfilled in a big way. Not only did several nearby apartment residents see it, one of them recorded it on a video camera, which was still a novelty in 1991, nearly 20 years before people began using mobile phone cameras to take instant pictures and video. The incident was videotaped by a White man named George Holliday, who recorded from his apartment the brutal beating of Rodney King and shared it with the news media. Shot on a dark street in Los Angeles during the wee hours of March 2, 1991, Holliday's video instantly turned King into a worldwide icon of police abuse and racial conflict. The video showed a large lump of a man floundering on the ground, surrounded by a dozen or more police officers, four of whom were relentlessly beating him with nightsticks.

The repeated television broadcast of the Rodney King video provoked widespread anger over what people considered unimpeachable proof of a pattern of aggression and abuse by the Los Angeles police toward Blacks and other racial minorities. The video of the beating generated racially-charged shockwaves around the world and enraged the already frustrated African American community in Los Angeles, which felt that **racial profiling and abuse by the police** had long gone unabated.

After an intense public outcry, four officers were brought to trial. Many people thought the video alone would lead to the conviction of the officers. But on April 29, 1992, a jury of 10 Whites, one Hispanic, and one Filipina in the Los Angeles suburb of Simi Valley acquitted three of the officers, and declared a mistrial for the fourth. The verdict, which cleared the four officers accused in the beating, all of them White, sparked anger and enraged the Black community. It prompted widespread rioting throughout much of Los Angeles. Increasing rage led to the worst single episode of urban unrest in American history. The arson and looting continued for three days, claimed 53 lives, and caused $1 billion in widespread damage. Pleading for calm in the midst of the harrowing violence, King nervously said at a news conference: "Can we all get along?" That utterance has since signified the spirit of the nation's aspirations of racial amity.

Prejudice, Stereotyping, and Discrimination in Media Depictions

American political commentator Walter Lippmann famously referred to stereotypes as "pictures in our heads" (Lippmann, 1922, p. 9) and redefined the modern psychological propensity of stereotyping with these words: "In untrained observation we pick recognizable signs out of the environment. The signs stand for ideas, and these ideas we fill out with our stock of images" (Lippmann, 1922, p. 87). These ideas and images contribute to "stored up images, the preconceptions, and prejudices" that "interpret, . . . and in their turn powerfully direct the play of our attention, and our vision" (Lippmann, 1922, p. 32).

Lippmann's theory of "pictures in our heads" stereotypes was aptly exemplified by noted journalist and renowned educator Charles Sumner "Chuck" Stone, Jr. in his humorous depiction of "24 politically unimpeachable reasons" to explicate "Why Sunday morning is the best time to drive on the Los Angeles Freeway?" (Stone, 2002). "Catholics are at mass. Protestants are still asleep. Jews are playing golf in Palm Springs. Muslims are saying morning prayers" Stone stated in a now famous 2002 letter to Bernie Reeves, the editor and publisher of Metro Magazine in Raleigh, North Carolina (Stone, 2002, para. 17).

In apt celebration of the distinctive diversity of American life, Stone bantered: "Feminists are making protest signs. Gays, Lesbians and Bisexuals are making out in San Francisco" (Stone, 2002, para. 17). In an uncanny way, Stone's words highlight the persistence of **stereotypes**, which by definition, comprise a combination of overgeneralized beliefs, biased impressions, and popular perceptions about a particular ethnic group or class of people.

Such biases may be related to **racial and ethnic stereotypes.** For instance, as Stone joked in his letter "Irish are making milk punch for an all-night hangover. **Greeks** are taking bets over the phone," (Stone, 2002, para. 17). Some of Stone's stereotypical caricatures alluded to offensive connotations such as "Italians are taking wholesale orders in the fish market. Hispanics are picking grapes in fields" (Stone, 2002, para. 17). **Media perpetuate prejudices** that emerge from widespread reporting of cultural depictions in creative works such as films and news media messages among other non-fiction modes that reflect people's **preconceived opinions** that are not based on reason or actual experience.

Way back in 1922, Lippmann theoretically attributed the propensity of **stereotyping** to lack of "time" "opportunity for intimate acquaintance" in contemporary life. As Lippmann observed, in the "hurried and multifarious" state of "modern life" physical distance "separates men who are often in vital contact with each other, such as employer and employee, official and voter" (Lippmann, 1922, p. 88).

As a renowned educator, Stone illustrated Lippmann's propensity of **stereotyping.** As a University of North Carolina at Chapel Hill faculty member, Stone taught a popular class on censorship. In that class, Stone illustrated how the media's spirit of free speech authorizes humorous, but denigrating, observations such as: "Native Americans are beating drums to tribal dances. Koreans are rolling up the iron gates on their convenience store fronts" or target other ethnic segments with gags like "Japanese are stuffing flower arrangements in vases. Chinese are stuffing fortune cookies. Poles think it's Saturday" (Stone, 2002, para. 17). Such racial images, albeit reflected in good humor, are detrimental to a community's aspiring to transcend **prejudice against national origin.**

In a myriad of ways, Stone illustrated how the **media perpetuate stereotypes** with laughter-provoking remarks like: "European-American males are organizing We Don't Get No Respect Day. Hillbillies are watching Pat Robertson on television" (Stone, 2002, para. 17). Through such good-natured witticism, Stone also was humorously ridiculing "everybody, regardless of race, creed, color, religion, gender or sexual orientation" (para. 11) to retaliate the "politically correct straitjacket that smothers free speech in newsrooms" (Stone, 2002, para. 13).

Lippmann pointed out that there was "neither time nor opportunity for intimate acquaintance." Under such circumstances, Lippmann noticed instead a human propensity and "a trait" that generalizes "a well-known type," which "fill in the rest of the picture by means of the stereotypes we carry about in our heads" (Lippmann, 1922, p. 88). Stereotyping occurs from overgeneralizations that simplify complex environments. It enables people to easily categorize new things into comfortable spaces already defined by their experiences. As Lippmann explicated, "There is economy in this" because, as Lippmann, theorized, "the attempt to see all things freshly and in detail, rather than as types and generalities, is exhausting" and "practically out of the question" because of people's "busy affairs" (Lippmann, 1922, p. 87).

Although more than 14 years have elapsed since Stone made his funny quips, news reports have sustained the veracity of his stereotypes. For instance, Stone stated in 2002 that Sunday morning "was the best time to drive" on the Los Angeles Freeway because "Southerners are watching the NASCAR races. College students are reading the comics." With minor post-modern modifications, such observations hold true today. Such is the power of stereotypes when we think of Stone's other funny quips such as "Los Angeles police are reading suspects their rights and taking their money. Lawyers are chasing ambulances" (Stone, 2002, para. 17).

Stone emerged as a leading advocate of social justice by enunciating the journalistic ethos of the U.S. civil rights movement, and served as the first president of the U.S. National Association of Black Journalists. Stone spared no one including his ilk in his bantering badinage that concluded with these words: "Journalists are chasing the lawyers. Blacks are in jail. And Mexicans can't get their cars started" (Stone, 2002, para. 17).

Stone had thus confirmed Lippmann's prognosticative insight that presaged the rampant racial and other stereotypes we see in society today. In many ways, Lippmann's perspicuous theorization of stereotypes has inspired several decades of research on how perceptions of stigmatized social groups are represented in the mind (Gilman, 1985; Hunt, 1997; Kaplan & Bjørgo, 1998; Entman & Rojecki, 2000).

Other researchers have conducted related research that explicate stereotypes. By analyzing the role of racial and ethnic stereotypes based on numerous examples from the workplace, higher education, and police interactions, Carbado and Gulati (2013) demonstrate that, for African Americans, the costs of "acting black" are high, and so are the pressures to "act white." In their book, *Acting White? Rethinking Race in "Post-Racial" America*, Carbado and Gulati theorize this trend with an exemplification. They illustrate how "against the backdrop of stereotypes" such as "blacks are lazy" (p. 38) an employer may be "pleasantly surprised by a black employee whose work ethic is ordinary" (Carbado & Gulati, 2013, p. 38). In other words, this might mean that due to "negative stereotypes of blacks" (p. 38) and, in such situations Black employees who "achieve even minimal success will be hailed as conquering heroes" although "they are only performing at par with or even below their white male co-workers" (Carbado & Gulati, 2013, p. 38). Carbado and Gulati (2013) further observed that racial minorities are judged by how they "perform" (p. 40) their race, the clothes they wear, the way they style their hair, the institutions with which they affiliate, their racial politics, the people they befriend, date or marry, where they live, how they speak, and their outward mannerisms and demeanor (Carbado & Gulati, 2013).

Research indicates that although stereotypes exist of different races, cultures, or ethnic groups, media's stereotypical portrayals of race have obscured reality. For instance, the **media's stereotypical image**s steep into the collective consciences of those who view them and mistakenly believe they've seen the entire truthful picture. In addition, the values, traditions, and practices of media production often unconsciously serve to maintain the alienation of racial groups in society (Campbell, 1995).

Racial images in the news media and entertainment entities filter and manipulate reality in diverse modes. In our globalized world of unlimited access to media content, the media's stereotypical portrayals of race easily manipulate media audiences. As Larson (2006) observed, no matter which minority group is represented, the media in America offer the same bill of fare: first, exclusion; followed by stereotyping that makes a sharp distinction between "good" minority members and "bad" ones; and finally, the telling of stories that justify racial inequality in American society. Such media images perpetuate racism and reinforce stereotyped attitudes on race, thereby leading to underrepresentation within media depictions of minority groups.

Such racial perceptions and prejudices led to racial discrimination or ethnic stereotyping since the late 1980s when police and other law enforcement apparatchiks have resorted to **racial profiling** and **offender profiling**, which connote selection for scrutiny of crime suspects based on race or ethnicity rather than on behavioral or evidentiary criteria.

Such racial and ethnic stereotyping have led to disturbing implications such as "**stop-question-and-frisk**" procedures, which the New York City Police Department (NYPD) intensified after the September 11, 2001, terrorist attacks to stop and question thousands of pedestrians annually, and frisk them for weapons and other contraband. The rules for "**stop-question-and-frisk**" are stipulated in the New York State Criminal Procedure Law section 140.50, and were based on the U.S. Supreme Court's 1968 *Terry v. Ohio* landmark decision. In that historic decision, the U.S. Supreme Court held that the Fourth

Amendment prohibition on unreasonable searches and seizures is not violated when a police officer stops suspects on the street and frisks them without probable cause to arrest, if the police officer has a reasonable suspicion that the suspect has committed, is committing, or is about to commit a crime and has a reasonable belief that the suspect "may be armed and presently dangerous." A significant majority of the people stopped by NYPD were African American or Latino. Some judges found these stops were not based on reasonable suspicion of criminal activity.

Critics claim "stop-question-and-frisk" searches are the result of racial profiling, targeting of Black and other minority groups. Such practices relate closely to **offender profiling**, which is a controversial system of analyzing and recording the probable psychological and behavioral characteristics of the unknown perpetrators of specific crimes so they can be matched with the known habits and personalities of suspects. Since the 1960s, British police have collaborated with psychologists to experimentally profile sex offenders or to help detectives catch them or forecast propensities of sex offenders. The concept, known as **psychological offender profiling**, or POP, originated with the FBI in the U.S. By the late-1990s, offender profiling was widely regarded as a major breakthrough in crime work, but its public reputation has been severely damaged in the privacy-conscious age of the twenty-first century. Security experts maintain that they do not condone or encourage racial profiling.

Post-Racial Pride and Prejudice

From a theoretical perspective, the term **post-racial** designates a time period when racism is no longer institutionalized or is eradicated because people are judged by the content of their character, not the color of their skin.

The post-racial aspirations of modern civilized society began in the mid-twentieth century with the creation of the 1948 Universal Declaration of Human Rights (UDHR), which the United Nations Commission on Human Rights drafted as the foundational document of international human rights law. The UDHR comprise 30 articles that comprehensively list key **civil, political, economic, social, and cultural rights**. For instance, Article 1 of the UDHR states, "All human beings are born free and equal in dignity and rights. They are endowed with reason and conscience and should act towards one another in a spirit of brotherhood" (United Nations, 1948).

The post-racial aspirations of the UDHR have arguably been implemented in U.S. workplace and society. Most U.S. organizations and institutions prohibit **discrimination** based on **race**, color, **national or ethnic origin**, age, religion, disability, gender, **sexual orientation, gender identity** and expression, **veteran status, disabled condition**, or any other characteristic protected under applicable federal or state law. Such pursuit of equity has prompted many people in the U.S. to consider racism as a thing of the past.

The 2008 election victory of U.S. President Barack Obama led political commentators to identify it as a "**post-racial**" moment. The 2009 inauguration of Obama as the first Black U.S. president further prompted public discourse to assert the emergence of a "post-racial" pride (Edge, 2010). However, such post-racial fervor was disrupted with striking events that manifested widespread concerns about **racial prejudice** and **ethnic conflict** being more prevalent in the twenty-first century than in any other period in history.

Within weeks of Obama's inauguration as the first African American president, the "post-racial" enthusiasm was disrupted during Black History Month in February 2009 when Eric Holder, the first African American U.S. attorney general, stirred a controversy by referring to America as "a nation of cowards" when discussing race (Holder, 2009). Holder prefaced his comment with an acknowledgment that ". . . this nation has proudly thought of itself as an ethnic melting pot" but maintained that "in things racial" he felt "we have always been and we, I believe, continue to be in too many ways essentially a nation of cowards," Holder said at the Department of Justice African American History Month Program (Holder, 2009). He said Americans are afraid to talk about race, adding that "certain subjects are off-limits" and, more important, "to explore them risks at best embarrassment and at worst the questioning of one's character" (Holder, 2009).

Holder's impression of race in America set off a firestorm of nationwide discussion on race issues that extended related realms such as racial profiling. During the summer of 2009, an arrest in Cambridge, Massachusetts, generated a national debate about racial profiling by the police. Harvard professor Henry Louis Gates, Jr., who is African American, was mistakenly arrested on July 16, 2009, by a White police officer James Crowley for attempting to break into his own home. The ensuing media firestorm ignited debate across the country (Ogletree, 2010). President Obama's criticism of the arrest and the response by the police raised objections among law enforcement organizations. In his attempt to seek a "teachable moment," Obama invited Gates and Crowley to the White House to discuss the issue over an informal drink of beer. Obama and U.S. Vice-President Joe Biden joined Crowley and Gates in a private and cordial meeting on July 30, 2009, in a White House Rose Garden courtyard.

Racial amity in the U.S. was severely disrupted on February 26, 2012, when **Trayvon Martin**, an unarmed 17-year-old African American teenager was shot dead by 28-year-old George Zimmerman. The shooting occurred as Martin walked home through the gated Sanford, Florida, neighborhood where he was visiting his father's fiancé. The incident revived racial concerns in the U.S. and beyond. Martin's gray hooded sweatshirt and his Skittles—the candy he was carrying—became visual symbols of a public outcry that an unarmed teenage boy was killed, and law enforcement had failed to act. Police authorities initially considered it as a routine homicide but the surging public outcry, as reported in news and social media outlets, catapulted the Trayvon Martin case into a civil rights imbroglio involving the consequences of racial profiling and set off an international discussion of race relations in America.

"If I had a son, he'd look like Trayvon," U.S. President Barack Obama said on March 23, 2012, within weeks of the shooting. He expressed sympathy for Martin's family and called for a thorough investigation. America's struggle with race was further exacerbated by raging concern in the networked public sphere over Obama's impassioned metaphoric comparison of Martin as his son, the sartorial status of hoodies with several popular figures disseminating pictures of themselves in a hoodie to express solidarity, and whether media reports were right to identify Zimmerman as a "white Hispanic" instead of simply a Hispanic.

In July 2013, the mediated messages in the networked public sphere became more significant when Zimmerman was acquitted of murder charges by a jury of six women in the court of the 18th judicial circuit in Seminole, Florida. The jury verdict led to an outcry of shock, anger, frustration, and disbelief that traversed the world through traditional media and social media messages that addressed larger issues of race, racial identity, and cross-racial dialogue in the American public sphere.

Over 300 rallies and vigils were held across the U.S. to protest the Trayvon Martin verdict, and to push for the repeal of so-called "**Stand Your Ground**" laws. The racial significance and impact of the Trayvon Martin case became a rallying point during the summer of 2013 events to commemorate the 50th anniversary of the 1963 March on Washington for Jobs and Freedom. The anniversary events were marked with a wide variety of speeches and performances reflecting upon racial pride and prejudice in the five decades that elapsed since the Martin Luther King's famous "I Have a Dream Speech" that signified the 1963 march.

Other incidents highlighted the futility of post-racial aspirations in America. In June 2013, Indian American Nina Davuluri, a native of Syracuse, New York, was crowned winner of the 2014 Miss America Pageant. In reaction, some sections of social media exploded with **hateful comments** denigrating Davuluri as an Arab, a foreigner, and a terrorist with ties to Al Qaeda. Several counter messages in the networked public sphere were quick to point out that these comments were "disgusting" and made out of "ignorance."

In May 2013, Savannah, Georgia-based celebrity chef and television cooking show host Paula Deen admitted in her deposition for a **racial discrimination** lawsuit that she had used the deeply offensive N-word to describe Black people, made racist jokes, and admitted to having daydreams about recreating a "Southern plantation-style wedding" replete with African American servants playing roles akin to their slave ancestors.

Incidents of protest and violence in **Ferguson, Missouri,** featured as among the most prominent news events of 2014. The networked public sphere emerged as a venue for sustained 24/7 news coverage and social media messages that highlighted the lack of racial amity in some parts of America. Such concerns followed the fatal shooting of 18-year-old unarmed African American man, **Michael Brown**, on August 9, 2014, by local police officer Darren Wilson, who initiated contact with Brown and his friend, Dorian Johnson, for alleged jaywalking. Those allegations resulted in a confrontation that led to the shooting death of Brown. The controversial shooting death resulted in public outrage, peaceful protests, and civil disobedience, and renewed calls for social justice both in the town of Ferguson and across the world. As the public outcry over Ferguson unfolded, peaceful demonstrators clashed with police forces over multiple days and nights in August 2014.

The fallout was immediate and palpable in the networked public sphere. Social media messages and news reports featured insights ranging from images of Brown's body lying for hours in the street to peaceful protests that erupted into violence and vandalism, to local police wearing gas masks and pointing assault weapons as they sat atop armored vehicles. Among the many disturbing words and images from Ferguson were reports of police arresting, confining, and threatening journalists for doing their jobs. The networked public sphere was replete with widespread criticism of how peaceful protesters in Ferguson were silenced with tear gas, numerous officers equipped with body armor and armored vehicles were caught on video spewing hateful invectives at the community, and reporters covering the unrest were arrested without cause.

The U.S. Department of Justice eventually launched a federal civil rights investigation into the Ferguson case as the shooting death of an unarmed Black teenager by a White police officer moved from a crime scene to grand jury adjudications in law courts. In March 2015, a 105-page scathing report, U.S. Department of Justice investigators uncovered a pattern or practice of unlawful conduct within the Ferguson police department that violates the First, Fourth, and Fourteenth Amendments to the United States Constitution, and federal statutory law.

The Ferguson report revealed that the police and courts meted out illegal and unduly harsh treatment, particularly to Black people. It pointed out racial mistreatment, deliberate discrimination, and a primary focus on maximizing city revenue through citations, not to keeping the peace. The investigation determined that Ferguson's policing strategy was built around writing tickets, and assessing fines and fees, to feed the city budget. The resulting practices, it stated, violated people's rights, and was racially discriminatory. Such developments have sown deep mistrust between the affected people and the police department in other parts of the country, thereby undermining law enforcement legitimacy among African Americans in other U.S. communities. Such events have also prompted critics to signify the myth of post-racial America.

The networked public sphere has been replete with widespread concerns about **racial prejudice** and **ethnic conflict** being more prevalent in the twenty-first century than in any other period in history. A rising level of discourse about race, intellectual diversity, religion, identity, and culture have dominated social media messages and news reports. Such public discussion and discourse firmly reiterated the deep-seated determination of U.S. citizens to champion equality for all, regardless of race, religion, gender identity, culture, sexual orientation, or political belief. The networked public sphere thus facilitated an open dialogue that fostered grassroots interaction, greater understanding of diversity, respect for all, among other contemporary issues facing our society.

Conclusion and Discussion

By theorizing the significance of media depictions of racial conflict in the U.S., this chapter reported research that explicates the interplay of race and media in the networked public sphere. Based on intercultural communication perspectives, this chapter constituted four parts. The first part of this chapter addressed the evolution of race and media issues in the networked public sphere. The second part chronicled the racial conflict of the Civil War and the Jim Crow days. The third part enunciated media depictions of the 1955 killing of Emmett Till and the power of media images in news reports about the 1991–92 Rodney King racial conflict. The fourth and final part analyzed theoretical constructs that explicate prejudice, stereotyping, and discrimination to evaluate post-racial aspirations in America. In addressing the significance of racial issues in fostering intercultural communication for global understanding and engagement, this chapter concluded that race continues to matter both in the U.S. and beyond.

As Carbado and Gulati (2013) have observed, in spite of decades of "racial progress" (p. 63) and the pervasiveness of multicultural rhetoric, racial "prejudices" (p. 33) originate not just from skin color, but from how a person conforms to behavior stereotypically associated with a certain race based on comprehensive case study analyses, this chapter delineated issues of freedom, equality, justice, democracy among other components that represent contemporary post-racial aspirations, and the significance of race in sociopolitical and economic justice. The case studies also analyzed racial injustice during the Civil War and the Jim Crow era, the power of media images, racial stereotyping, post-racial aspirations, and other aspects of race and media in the networked public sphere.

This chapter highlights the significance of racial priorities in fostering global understanding and engagement in the U.S. with intercultural communication strategies such as **diversity training and education** to reduce racial prejudice and stereotypes. As studies conducted by Rudman, Ashmore, and Gary (2001) indicate, implicit prejudice and stereotypes are malleable. Automatic biases, therefore, can be "unlearned" and modified through diversity education. In a study conducted by Rudman et al. (2001), research participants enrolled in a prejudice and conflict seminar also showed significantly reduced implicit and explicit anti-Black biases, compared with control participants. Affective processes such as **diversity training and education** can effectively transform implicit prejudice and stereotypes (Rudman et al., 2001). Such research insights may help us develop diversity training and education initiatives that are critical toward nurturing intercultural communication for global understanding and engagement.

As a nation that celebrates the **distinctive diversity of American life,** the U.S. should work toward a post-racial future because population trends estimate that by the year 2050 the U.S. will become **a nation with no clear racial or ethnic majority.** Other nations will experience similar demographic changes. These demographic shifts toward **racial or ethnic diversity** hold important policy implications in a world where racial and ethnic disparities torment society. The research reported in this chapter reflects the compelling need for effective strategies to promote a racially inclusive and progressive society devoid of **racial injustice**. Such strategies may also permeate inspiring opportunities to help America and other nations uphold to their ideals of **equality and justice for all**.

Discussion Questions

Intercultural Communication for Global Understanding

1. Discuss racial bias or ethnic stereotypes in the news content of traditional media (such as newspapers, radio, and television) and emerging media (such as social and mobile media content) in reports about people and cultures across the globe. Cite examples of media representation (and misrepresentation) of race and ethnic minorities to illustrate your point.
2. Intercultural communication for global understanding aspires to address inequities in race, ethnicity, physical ability (such as handicapped status), gender, and sexual orientation. How can social media help or hinder this process? Think of some recent examples and news events.
3. Based on perspectives in intercultural communication for global understanding outlined in this chapter, how do social media help or hinder race relations in the networked public sphere? Illustrate with some real life examples or news events.

Global Engagement Across Cultural Boundaries

1. From a social, political, and economic perspective, how do social media entities adequately acknowledge and/or challenge racial inequities in intercultural communication and global engagement across cultural boundaries? Enunciate your point with some relevant cases and consequences.
2. Based on the research reported in this chapter, how have social media disrupted or contributed to global engagement across cultural boundaries? Discuss with current examples.
3. With the rise of communication technologies such as the Internet, what norms, values, and social hierarchies do social media promote or disrupt in relation to race, gender, and sexual identity in our efforts to foster global engagement across cultural boundaries?

References

Aikat, D. D., & Remund, D. (2012). Of Time magazine, 24/7 media, and data deluge: The evolution of information overload theories and concepts. In J. B. Strother, J. M. Ulijn, & Z. Fazal (Eds.), *Information overload: An international challenge to professional engineers and technical communicators* (pp. 15–38). IEEE Professional Communication Society, Hoboken, NJ: John Wiley & Sons and IEEE Press. doi:10.1002/9781118360491. ch2

Alexander, B. (2011). *The new digital storytelling: Creating narratives with new media.* Santa Barbara, CA: Praeger.

Bacon, J. (2007). *Freedom's journal: The first African-American newspaper.* Lanham, MD: Lexington Books.

Batchellor, A. S. (Ed.) (1904). *Laws of New Hampshire including public and private acts and resolves and the Royal commissions and instructions with historical and descriptive notes, and an appendix.* Volume 1, Province period. Manchester, NH: John B. Clarke Co.

Benkler, Y. (2006). *The wealth of networks: How social production transforms markets and freedom.* New Haven, CT: Yale University Press.

Benkler, Y., Roberts, H., Faris, R., Solow-Niederman, A., & Etling, B. (2013). Social mobilization and the networked public sphere: Mapping the SOPA-PIPA debate. *Berkman Center Research Publication No. 2013–16.* Retrieved from http://ssrn.com/abstract=2295953 and http://dx.doi.org/10.2139/ssrn.2295953

Blight, D. W. (2001). *Race and reunion: The Civil War in American memory.* Cambridge, MA: Belknap Press of Harvard University Press.

boyd, D. M., & Ellison, N. B. (2007). Social network sites: Definition, history and scholarship. *Journal of Computer-Mediated Communication, 13*(1).

Bruns, A., Burgess, J., Highfield, T., Kirchhoff, L., & Nicolai, T. (2011). Mapping the Australian networked public sphere. *Social Science Computer Review, 29*(3), 277–287.

Campbell, C. P. (1995). *Race, myth and the news.* Thousand Oaks, CA: Sage Publications.

Carbado, D. W., & Gulati, M. (2013). *Acting white? Rethinking race in "post-racial" America.* New York, NY: Oxford University Press.

Cornish, S. E., & Russwurm, J. B. (1827, March 16), *Freedom's Journal, 1*(1), p 1. Retrieved from https://web.archive.org/web/20150209163534/http://www.wisconsinhistory.org/pdfs/la/FreedomsJournal/v1n01.pdf

Creswell, J. W. (2014). *Research design: Qualitative, quantitative, and mixed methods approaches.* Thousand Oaks, CA: Sage.

Curran, J. (1991). Mass media and democracy. In J. Curran & M. Gurevitch (Eds.). *Mass Media and Society* (pp. 82–117). London, UK: Edward Arnold.

Dahlgren, P. (2009). *Media and political engagement.* Cambridge, UK: Cambridge University Press.

Dahlgren, P., & Sparks, C. (1991). *Communication and citizenship: Journalism and the public sphere in the new media age.* London, UK: Routledge.

Dubois, W. E. B. (1932, April). Courts and jails. *The Crisis*, April 1932, 39 (4), p. 132.

Edge, T. (2010). Southern Strategy 2.0: Conservatives, White Voters, and the Election of Barack Obama. *Journal of Black Studies, 40*(3), 426–444.

Entman, R. M., & Rojecki, A. (2000). *The black image in the white mind: Media and race in America*. Chicago, IL: University of Chicago Press.

Fine, R. (Ed.). (2010). *The big book of social media: Case studies, stories, perspectives*. Tulsa, OK: Yorkshire.

Fischer, H. D., & Merrill, J. C. (1976). *International and intercultural communication*. New York, NY: Hastings House.

George, A. M., & Pratt, C. B. (2012). *Case studies in crisis communication: International perspectives on hits and misses*. New York, NY: Routledge.

Gilman, S. L. (1985). *Difference and pathology: Stereotypes of sexuality, race, and madness*. Ithaca, NY: Cornell University Press.

Giroux, H. A. (2003). Spectacles of race and pedagogies of denial: Anti-black racist pedagogy under the reign of neoliberalism. *Communication Education, 52*(3–4), 191–211.

Habermas, J. (1962/1989). *The structural transformation of the public sphere: An inquiry into a category of bourgeois society* (T. Burger & F. Lawrence, Trans.). Cambridge, MA: MIT Press. (Original work published 1962)

Habermas, J. (1989). The task of a critical theory of society. In S. Bronner & D. Kellner (Eds.), *Critical Theory and Society: A Reader* (pp. 292–311). New York, NY: Routledge.

Holder, E. (2009, February 18). Attorney General Eric Holder at the Department of Justice African American History Month Program, Department of Justice Office of Public Affairs. Department of Justice. Washington, DC. Retrieved from http://www.justice.gov/opa/speech/attorney-general-eric-holder-department-justice-african-american-history-month-program

Holledge, J., & Tompkins, J. (2000). *Women's intercultural performance*. London, UK: Routledge.

Hooker, R. D. (2011). *First with the truth: Synchronized communications in the counterinsurgency fight*. Arlington, VA: Institute of Land Warfare, Association of the United States Army.

Hunt, D. M. (1997). *Screening the Los Angeles "riots": Race, seeing, and resistance*. Cambridge, England: Cambridge University Press.

Jaeger, P. T. (2005). Deliberative democracy and the conceptual foundations of electronic government. *Government Information Quarterly, 22*, 702–719.

Jarvis, P. (2007). *Globalisation, lifelong learning and the learning society: Sociological perspectives*. London, UK: Routledge.

Kaplan, J., & Bjørgo, T. (1998). *Nation and race: The developing Euro-American racist subculture*. Boston, MA: Northeastern University Press.

Kellner, D. (1990). *Television and the crisis of democracy*. Boulder, CO: Westview Press.

Kelly, C. A. (1978). The Struggle for a Free Press. *Update on Law-Related Education, 2*, 16.

Larson, S. G. (2006). *Media & minorities: The politics of race in news and entertainment*. Lanham, MD: Rowman & Littlefield.

Lee, M. (2014). What can political economists learn from economic sociologists? A case study of NASDAQ. *Communication, Culture & Critique, 7,* 246–263. doi:10.1111/cccr.12043

Lippmann, W. (1922). *Public opinion.* New York, NY: Harcourt, Brace and Co.

Martin, E., & Wilson, G. B. (1997). *Hong Kong speaks: Free expression while becoming China.* Hong Kong: Hong Kong Baptist University.

Merriam, S. B. (2009). *Qualitative research: A guide to design and implementation.* San Francisco, CA: Jossey-Bass.

Morris, N., & Waisbord, S. R. (2001). *Media and globalization: Why the state matters.* Lanham, MD: Rowman & Littlefield.

Ogletree, C. J. (2010). *The presumption of guilt: The arrest of Henry Louis Gates, Jr. and race, class, and crime in America.* New York, NY: Palgrave Macmillan.

Patrut, B., & Patrut, M. (Eds.). (2014). *Social media in politics: Case Studies on the political power of social media.* New York, NY: Springer Verlag.

Prosser, M. H. (1973). *Major books on intercultural communication.* Pittsburgh, PA: Intercultural Communications Network of the Regional Council for International Education.

Rares, E., Fenger, L., Rosenmeier, L., Ehlers, L. N., & Carl, S. M. (2006). *In between freedom and equality.* København, Denmark: Copenhagen Business School Institut for Interkulturel Kommunikation.

Roberts, B. (2009). Beyond the 'networked public sphere': Politics, participation and technics in web 2.0. *Fibreculture, 14.* Retrieved from http://fourteen.fibreculturejournal.org/fcj-093-beyond-the-networked-public-sphere-politics-participation-and-technics-in-web-2-0/

Rudman, L. A., Ashmore, R. D., & Gary, M. L. (2001). "Unlearning" automatic biases: The malleability of implicit prejudice and stereotypes. *Journal of Personality & Social Psychology, 81*(5), 856–868. Retrieved from http://psycnet.apa.org.libproxy.lib.unc.edu/journals/psp/81/5/856/

Shirky, C. (2011). The political power of social media. *Foreign Affairs 90.* Retrieved from http://www.foreignaffairs.com/articles/67038/clay-shirky/the-political-power-of-social-media

Stone, C. (2002, May). The 24 politically unimpeachable reasons answering the question: Why is Sunday morning the best time to drive on the Los Angeles freeway? *Metro Magazine,* "Correspondence" section, May 2002. Retrieved from http://www.metronc.com/article/?id=126

United Nations. (1948). The Universal Declaration of Human Rights. Passed in Resolution 217 A (III) of the General Assembly meeting of December, 10, 1948, Paris, France. Retrieved from http://www.un.org/en/documents/udhr/

Vance, W. R. (1917). Freedom of Speech and of the Press. *Minnesota Law Review, 2,* 239.

Varennes, F. (1996). *Language, minorities and human rights.* The Hague, Netherlands: Martinus Nijhoff.

Weeks, L. H., & Bacon, E. M. (1911). *An historical digest of the provincial press: Being a collation of all items of personal and historic reference relating to American affairs printed in the newspapers of the provincial period beginning with the appearance of The present state of the New-English affairs, 1689, Publick occurrences, 1690, and the first issue of the Boston news-letter, 1704, and ending with the close of the revolution, 1783.* Boston, MA: Society for Americana, Inc.

Wettach, R. H. (1925). Restrictions on a Free Press. *North Carolina Law Review, 4,* 24.

Wilson, W. (Ed.) (1970). *The selected writings of W. E. B. DuBois.* New York, NY: New American Library.

Yin, R. K. (2012). *Applications of case study research.* Los Angeles, CA: Sage.

21. 'Scandalous': Controlling Images of Black Women

Tanya E. Walker, Ph.D.

In my home, Thursday nights are reserved for watching the political drama "Scandal." I admire the strength, intelligence, and boldness of Olivia Pope, a Black television figure who represents various experiences of Black women all rolled into one perfectly coiffed package. While the package appeals to millions of viewers weekly (Olivia's sharp wardrobe, her seemingly impressive bank account, her ability to snag the most powerful man alive), one thing has become apparent to me. The dominant images of Black women on television are disturbing and leave little space for ones that present Black women as whole. Admittedly, more Black women are enjoying their time in the limelight, both as fictional characters and as cast members on reality shows. For example, reality shows such as "Love and Hip Hop Atlanta" and "The Real Housewives of Atlanta" feature several Black women who have reached a high level of success professionally. Yet, traits and acts like jealousy, pettiness, catfights, and marital disputes, which tend to appear in private spaces, are highlighted to overshadow more favorable ones. This fragmented presentation results in skewed perspectives of Black womanhood.

Rena Schild/Shutterstock.com

"Scandal's" Olivia Pope suffers from the same one-dimensional presentation though her character is fictional. Because few aspects of her life are illuminated, her thoughts and behaviors are questionable and will remain so until the superficial layers are peeled back. Why does she remain connected romantically to a married and unavailable man? Given that her familial relationships are dysfunctional, why does she continue to participate in her father's oppressive games? Where are Olivia's girlfriends or, more specifically, sistah-friends? Why does she not seem to have any at all? As viewers, what are we to make of the image put forth through Pope's character? What aspect of Black womanhood is she supposed to represent? These questions speak to Olivia's lack of depth and her appearance as 'damaged goods,' which seems more apparent each season. As such, they reveal an improbability for viewing Olivia as a tool for discussing the historical context and social relevance of Black women. More importantly, they highlight executive producer and writer Shonda Rhimes's failure to expand the narrative of Black womanhood.

Of course, obstacles exist that may explain why Rhimes neglects to take advantage of the opportunity she has been granted, particularly when we think in terms of power. Maybe she is stripped of the power needed to align her creative choices with a more appropriate representation of Black women. In other words, her power may be more perceived than real. If this is the case, it is safe to assume that funding for the show is linked to her controversial character and plot development since they connect directly to the popularity of the show. But should the probability of funding barriers prevent Rhimes from imagining a present and a future in which the controlling images of Black women on television are no longer magnified and without discussion of their existence? I think not.

Now we must ask, why must we acknowledge and critique the prevailing images of Black women? For starters, we must be mindful of the impact on younger, impressionable viewers. According to *The New York Times*, approximately half of "Scandal's" viewers are aged between 18 and 49 (Vega, 2013). Looking at the younger viewers, I question how they "see" a character like Olivia Pope. Do they apply their critical lenses and have "Wait a minute!" moments from time to time? What about viewers who are part of the character's age group? What image do they see and do they find the image relatable? In her groundbreaking study titled "Black Feminist Thought: Knowledge, Consciousness, and the Politics of Empowerment" (2000), Patricia Hill Collins identifies the **controlling images** of Black women littered throughout media and literature. (Controlling images are real or created and dominant perceptions of a particular group.) She argues that "the authority to define societal values is a major instrument of power" (p. 69) and cites the mammy, the matriarch, the welfare mother, and jezebel/whore/hoochie as examples of the images that represent Black womanhood. Hill Collins's critique of these controlling images "reflect[s] the dominant group's interest in maintaining Black women's subordination" (p. 72).

In the case of "Scandal," it appears that another image must be considered: the **trophy mistress**. She is sexually aggressive, shallow, and addicted to unavailable men. Like the jezebel/whore/hoochie, who is described by Hill Collins "as a woman whose sexual [appetite is] at best inappropriate and, at worst, insatiable" (p. 83), the trophy mistress lives a life of promiscuity. Yet, she connects herself to men who cannot commit except for sexual innuendos that require the cooperation of many persons to make the "relationship" possible. In this case, she has little regard for the wives who are not only aware of the trophy mistress's existence but are forced into interaction because the women belong to the same small privileged social circles. Hence, we witness numerous awkward exchanges between Olivia and her lover's wife, First Lady Mellie Fitzgerald. Both women accept their roles in Fitz's life yet struggle with it constantly (Olivia—private lover, Mellie—public mate).

In the consideration of Olivia, it is obvious that her position of trophy mistress is rooted in antebellum sentiments on Black female sexuality. She is Fitz's sex toy who must remain a secret. She is flaunted in front of her lover's wife whose only weapon against Olivia is an anger supported by political power and a wedding ring. Unfortunately, Rhimes does very little to problematize this controlling image that she has created as a dominant and honest depiction of Black women. Week after week, as I watch the strengthening development of this image, I wonder, "Have we reached a time when this type of image is accepted as one of normalcy?"

Again, I ask what we are to think of Olivia Pope and what she represents for the millions of Black women viewers. Statistics indicate that this type of character is not a stereotype in the sense of her unwed status, but a true reflection of a specific population. Numerous studies show that more than 40% of Black women remain unmarried, citing incompatible educational endeavors and economics as the main reasons for this phenomenon. In response, we have seen Black men such as Steve Harvey, Keith Sweat, and Tyrese Gibson (who are entertainers, not experts) solely lay the blame with Black women. According to them, if Black women think, speak, and behave differently, then they would have a better chance at nabbing the man of their choice. Here, you should ask "What is meant by 'different'?" Anyone familiar with the male-authored texts understands that to behave differently is to ignore the myriad of social, historical, and political experiences that shape Black womanhood. Again, in this blame game, achievements are ignored or downplayed while traits and expectations considered problematic to Black women are highlighted and deemed unrealistic. To be honest, I place no stock in the opinions of men like Harvey, Sweat, and Gibson who seek to define Black womanhood on their own terms. Nonetheless, I expect a great deal from a Black woman like Shonda Rhimes who has been granted a platform for influencing present and future cultural conversations surrounding Black womanhood. As mentioned, I see the overwhelming attention given to Kerry Washington's wardrobe but not enough criticism of Olivia's intentional and not very private dismantling of a marriage. As viewers, are we subconsciously ignoring the foolishness in Olivia's life because we can relate to the controversial subjects and depictions that surround her? Or, as I hope is not the case, is the foolishness expected to occur, therefore, unnecessary to address publicly and critically?

Will I continue to engage in conversations about who may be the real fathers of Millie's children, what crime Command may commit next, and who will become Cyrus's new lover? The answer is "yes" because I accept the show "Scandal" for what it is. Entertainment. At the same time, I will continue to be critical of the controlling image of Black women that enters millions of homes every week and hope that the image of the trophy mistress dissipates quickly and quietly. It is my hope that the majority of "Scandal" viewers, regardless of race or gender, will step back and question the intentions of writers and producers who insist on presenting such damaging and narrow images of Black womanhood.

Discussion Questions

1. What definition of culture is most applicable to this essay?
2. Why is it important to identify and confront controlling images of Black women that permeate contemporary media and literature?
3. What should be the expectations of Black producers who feature Black characters in their shows? Black viewers? Non-Black viewers?
4. In your opinion, how does Shonda Rhimes define Black womanhood?

References

Hill Collins, P. (2000). *Black feminist thought: Knowledge, consciousness, and the politics of empowerment* (2nd ed.). New York, NY: Routledge.

Vega, T. (2013, January 16). A show makes friends and history: "Scandal" on ABC is breaking barriers. *The New York Times*. Retrieved from http://www.nytimes.com/2013/01/17/arts/television/scandal-on-abc-is-breaking-barriers.html?pagewanted=all&_r=0

22.   Support the Rights and Privileges of Black Radio

Brian Blount, Ed.D.

Tuning in to Black radio each morning to hear important news and information about the Black communities which they serve is a distinctive right and a privilege. Instead of using your computer browser to turn away from Black radio stations, use the URL address bar to visit websites of online Black radio stations to support the rights and privileges that Black radio provides for current and future Black generations. An important right and privilege that Black radio affords is the unique opportunity it gives to the African American communities of being able to listen to and discuss important social, economical, and political issues.

This right and privilege is a basic consideration which the Federal Communications Commission (FCC) uses when granting Black radio stations their operating licenses. Additionally, this right and privilege primarily serves as motivation for Black radio management whose major objective is to provide relative information and perspectives for minority audiences concerning their social, economic, and political environments.

For the purpose of maintaining a collective meaningful community voice, safeguarding the privilege of Black radio programming is necessary by all of its stakeholders. This privilege essentially guarantees access to knowledge, diversification, and hope for all of the underserved minority citizens who are not represented by the major media organizations. The multitude of famous and unknown influential Black radio talk show hosts existed throughout the prominent history of Black radio nationwide. Black radio has always been a significant medium and agents of change since its first noted broadcast programming by WDIA-AM in Memphis, Tennessee, during late October 1948 (Halper, 2008).

Throughout America's relatively recent history, Black radio programming has delivered to its communities news and information that at times challenged the consciousness of all Americans. The Black radio reporters and talk show hosts, without question, have had a major impact on the overall quality of life of the Black communities that they served. Keen (2004) argues that ". . . black radio stations and disc jockeys often were as important as ministers and politicians . . . of the 1960s" (p. 1). She further adds that these radio personalities instilled a strong sense of ethnic identity, honor, and community pride. The opinions of these Black disc jockeys were more prevalent in the community and their views were more widespread than media personalities on television or in the print media (Keen, 2004). To further review this perspective, as an example, consider the later news events of Ferguson, Missouri, where Michael Brown, an 18-year-old Black youth was fatally shot by Darren Wilson, a policeman on August 9, 2014.

The news about the college-bound African American created a groundswell of attention to the events surrounding the incident, as well as about the personal and public lives of the young Black man and the police officer. Additionally, the historical and present reputation about the town of Ferguson, Missouri, and its integrity about discovering all of the facts of the fatal shooting all became very important information in order to render justice to everyone involved in the tragic international news event.

Itsra Sanprasert/Shutterstock.com

The Ferguson story created a lot of difference of opinions between many individual people and groups of people, along with formal and informal organizations. An enormous amount of discord was generated between the citizens of Ferguson, their law enforcement agency, the clashing supporters, and distractors of both Michael Brown and Darren Wilson at the local and national levels. Also, practicing professionals and scholars of the criminal and social justice fields of study promoted much disagreement about the general and specific circumstances of the case.

Most importantly, in the middle of the intense calamity were the families of Michael Brown and Darren Wilson. Concurrently, on the exterior side of the story were the Black radio talk show hosts and reporters who explored and delivered the story about the unfortunate situation from the perspectives of the people whom they served. Without the Black radio voice of the reporters and talk show hosts, only one side of the story would have been told, omitting the relative perspectives of both sides being explained. This is a reason why all people who are interested in the unknown stories of the struggling class of people should seriously consider supporting the Black radio voices who are messengers of positive change.

As members of the fourth estate, Black reporters and talk show hosts, like all members of the press and media reporters, have a professional responsibility of providing access to essential information for ensuring the existence of democracy for all American citizens. Being informed about the incident in Ferguson, Missouri, for each person who lives in the United States is a fundamental right of citizenship. The Black reporters and talk show hosts who disseminated the story to millions of people across the country basically performed their professional obligations of informing the citizenry. The difference between the Black reporters and talk show hosts is that the Black reporters must be objective in reporting the information.

Conversely, the Black talk show hosts have the flexibility to provide subjective viewpoints about the news stories to which they provide access. In both situations, the Black reporters and talk shows host should be as fair as possible in their delivery of information concerning all news and information. Reporting and presenting news and information in the most objective manner possible via eliminating unsubstantiated reports creates and facilitates fairness for everyone who seeks social justice. The influences of the Black reporters and talk show hosts extend far beyond only providing access to information about the social justice events of the nation. Their influence could be perceived as a voice of the Black community which they serve.

It is worth noting the African American public radio stations because of their commercial-free formats which strongly encourages educational investigations of important information without the concern of comprising the discovery of truths over making a profit.

On the other end of the radio programming spectrum are the commercial African American radio stations that maintain their focus on the bottom line of making a profit. Although the radio stations survive via selling advertisements, the stations' management and talk show hosts thoroughly commit themselves to providing a purposeful venue in exploring the topics that greatly affect the Black communities. It is in their license agreement granted by the FCC to ensure that Black radio serves its people in all areas of community service beyond entertainment. Some of the top commercial Black radio stations that are listed under the Urban format which provide meaningful exchanges of information for their Black communities are:

1. WQHT-FM - Hot 97—New York, NY
2. WBLS-FM - WBLS 107.5—New York, NY
3. KBXX-FM - 97.9 The Box—Houston, TX
4. WVEE-FM - V-103—Atlanta, GA
5. WVAZ-FM - V-103—Chicago, IL
6. WKYS-FM - 93.9 WKYS—Washington, D.C
7. KKDA-FM - K104 FM—Dallas, TX
8. WEDR-FM - 99 JAMZ—Miami, FL
9. KMEL-FM - 106 KMEL—San Francisco, CA
10. KMJQ-FM - Majic 102.1—Houston, TX

As previously indicated, as a right and privilege, Black radio has a professional obligation to investigate and communicate significant information such as the Ferguson case. At the core of that right and privilege of being able to report the news and information is the fact that the FCC controls the airwaves and can determine how long a radio station can continue to operate, if it is unable to appropriately meet its fiscal responsibilities of being responsible broadcasters.

If Black radio is not supported by its target audience, eventually one by one the stations could go silent via alternative programming consuming its operations. Regardless of the viewpoints and perspectives taken about the community issues and ideas by the Black radio local and national audiences, it is very vital that they financially and morally support Black radio if its voice is to prosper and endure the challenges of hostile company takeovers by corporations whose voices may not represent the best interests of America's Black communities.

References

Halper, D. L. (2008). *The first African-American radio station owner: Jesse B. Blayton, Sr.* Retrieved from http://www.lwfaah.net/aaradio/1staa_radio.htm

Keen, C. (2004). *UF researcher: Black radio played a strong role in shaping civil rights.* Retrieved from http://news.ufl.edu/archive/2004/07/uf-researcher-black-radio-played-strong-role-in-shaping-civil-rights.html

23.   Theorizing India's Networked Public Sphere: The Role of Digital Media and Intercultural Communication in the World's Largest Democracy

Debashis 'Deb' Aikat, Ph.D.

Where the mind is without fear and the head is held high
Where knowledge is free
Where the world has not been broken up into fragments
By narrow domestic walls
Where words come out from the depth of truth
Where tireless striving stretches its arms towards perfection.

> — From India's first Nobel laureate Rabindranath Tagore's 1901 poem "Where the mind is without fear" in the *Gitanjali* [English subtitle: *Song Offerings*] (Tagore, 1914, pp. 27–28, poem 35)

This epigraph is excerpted from a classic poem by India's litterateur Rabindranath Tagore, who won the Nobel Prize of Literature in 1913. First published in 1901 when India was under British rule, Tagore's poem has inspired generations to foster a spirit of free-thinking and freedom.

Tagore envisioned that the people of India would thrive "without fear and the head is held high" in a world "not been broken up into fragments" and rising "towards perfection" (Tagore, 1914, p. 28). Tagore's vision was fulfilled in 1947 when India gained freedom from British rule after an arduous freedom movement that culminated in India's re-birth as a modern democracy (Basham, 1975; Narayan & Meherally, 2006; SarDesai, 2008; Thapar, 1966).

In the seven decades since India's independence from British rule, a burgeoning **digital media** have fostered intercultural communication in India's democratic society. By both scope and definition, **digital media** comprise news, information, and entertainment products and platforms that are encoded in a computer-mediated format. India's digital media represent a vibrant mix of traditional and contemporary platforms. While the traditional media comprise newspapers, radio, and television, digital media comprise news blogs, online videos, social media[1] messages, and other media content that can be created, viewed, dis-

---

1. The term "social media" is used as plural in this chapter to be consistent with the American Psychological Association (APA) style guidelines. According to distinguished lexicographers such as the *Merriam-Webster* and the *Oxford English Dictionary*, the term "social media" is a plural noun but may be used singular or plural in construction. In conformance with the APA citation style for conceptual terms, this chapter denotes the term "social media" with lower case letter, as do most published works (*see* Mandiberg, 2012; Mansfield, 2012; Qualman, 2009). It is worth noting that some other publications designate social media with initial capital letters, such as "Social Media."

tributed, modified, and preserved on computers. India has been described as a place where "print is king," but "digital is coming on strong" (Kilman, 2015).

Research Preamble and Epistemological Objectives

India attained the moniker of the **world's largest democracy** based on its surging population of 1.27 billion (Census of India, 2011; Worldometers, 2014), which ranks

LorenzoT/Shutterstock.com

second after China. India's population is projected to exceed China by 2030 to become the **world's most populous country**. India's media cater to this surging population of citizens from a diverse culture in a nation that is at the cusp of a digital media revolution. It is, therefore, important to theorize the role and significance of India's media landscape from an intercultural communication perspective to gain insights on the role of media in a democracy.

Based on extensive case study research, this chapter theorizes India's digital media landscape from intercultural communication perspectives. Drawing upon the theoretical framework of the democratic public sphere, this chapter presents research that theorizes the role and significance of India's digital media in fostering a networked public sphere. By exploring intercultural communication perspectives, this chapter concludes that the networked public sphere fosters India's democratic society.

The Theoretical Framework of Networked Public Sphere

German sociologist and philosopher Jürgen Habermas's 1962 book, *The Structural Transformation of the Public Sphere* (1989a), theorized a nineteenth-century bourgeois **public sphere** with a social space for political dialogue, debate, and dissent. Habermas's public sphere theory spawned related concepts and counter theories that redefined the role of the media in a democracy (Curran, 1991; Dahlgren, 2009; Dahlgren & Sparks, 1991; Kellner, 1990).

Habermas (1989a) explored both the evolution of the bourgeois public sphere and its decline. According to Habermas, this decline was caused by several factors including the growing **power of the state, corporate expansion, consumerism,** and an increasingly **privatized society.** The twenty-first-century digital media have transformed Habermas's concept of public sphere. One such transformation is the emergence of a **networked public sphere** facilitated by the widespread societal adoption of the Internet and growth of digital technologies. As Shirky (2011) pointed out, since the rise of the Internet in the early 1990s, the "world's networked population has grown from the low millions to the low billions" (para. 3). Such growth had led to new structural transformation in our global society where organizations strategically communicate in a networked public sphere (Raupp, 2011). Shirky (2011) observed that over the same period, "social media have become a fact of life for civil society worldwide, involving many actors" (para. 3) such as **regular citizens, social activists, nongovernmental organizations, telecommunications firms,** software providers, governments.

In August 1995, India began full-scale Internet service for public access through the Videsh Sanchar Nigam, India's overseas communications agency. Over the next 20 years, digital communication technologies experienced rapid growth and led to the emergence of India's networked public sphere as an important venue for discussion and debate. Theorists consider the networked public sphere as an alternative arena for **public discourse** and **political debate** because it is decreasingly dominated by large media entities and devoid of **government control**, and designed for wider participation (Benkler, 2006; Benkler, Roberts, Faris, Solow-Niederman, & Etling, 2013; Bruns, Burgess, Highfield, Kirchhoff, & Nicolai, 2011; Roberts, 2009).

Benkler's 2006 book, *The Wealth of Networks: How Social Production Transforms Markets and Freedoms,* theorized the emergence of the "**networked information economy**," as transcending the "**industrial information economy**," which has existed since the late-nineteenth century (Benkler, 2006, p. 3). Benkler et al. (2013) concluded that the media's **fourth estate function** was fulfilled by a network of small-scale commercial tech media, non-media NGOs, and individuals, whose work was then amplified by **traditional media** (Benkler et al., 2013). As Benkler theorized, this shift was also caused by the "increasing freedom individuals enjoy to participate in creating information and knowledge" and related possibilities for a "new public sphere" emerging "alongside the **commercial, mass-media markets**" (Benkler, 2006, p. 10). These changes collectively ushered a more democratic and participative form of **political communication,** which Benkler (2006) designated as the "**networked public sphere.**"

A significant implication of the networked information economy has been the shift it enabled from the mass-mediated public sphere to a networked public sphere. The public sphere has been the space of **communication of ideas and issues** that emerge from society and are addressed to the **decision makers** in the institutions of society. The **global civil society** is the organized expression of the values and interests of society (Castells, 2008).

Case Study Research Method

Five methodological steps enabled us to formulate a **case study research** design to develop an inclusive and detailed analysis of the role of social media in India's networked public sphere.

This qualitative case study constituted rigorous analyses to theorize the role and significance of India's social media in fostering a networked public sphere. The intrinsic value of the case study method relates to how it can be coherently connected to theory (Creswell, 2013; Patton, 2002; Yin, 2013). Eisenhardt (1989) has outlined how case study research can be designed to build theories.

Creswell (2014), Maxwell (2013), and Merriam (2009) have emphasized that qualitative research should incorporate the theoretical and philosophical underpinnings of the research paradigm. This case study is based on qualitative research designed to intricately merge networked public sphere theories with analyses of multiple cases. This study focused on increasing the number of cases that were compared to mitigate risks. The research reported in this chapter reduced these methodological risks by increasing the number of cases in India's digital media landscape for case study analysis. The key elements of the case study research process are explicated in Tables 23.1 and 23.2.

As a robust measure to evaluate the role of social media, the case study research method has facilitated innovative works such as social media strategies based on inspirational case studies from companies (Fine, 2010), assessment of a myriad of social media goals such as improving relationships with customers to generating more sales, product testing to team building (Holloman, 2013), and "theoretical and methodological contributions" from international case studies on the "use of social media in political campaigns, electoral marketing, riots and social revolution" (Patrut & Patrut, 2014, p. viii). This case study enhanced its method by drawing upon current case studies (George & Pratt, 2012; Jaeger 2005; Lee, 2014). Lee (2014) analyzed the introduction of NASDAQ by gathering news articles from six publications, George and Pratt (2012) examined socio-cultural issues associated with crisis communication from international perspectives, and Jaeger, (2005) traced the conceptual foundations of electronic government in a deliberative democracy. The case study method has explored other research issues (Creswell, 2014; Merriam, 2009; Yin, 2012).

The first methodological step in the qualitative case study research involved searches for scholarly works and detailed reports that conceptualized India's digital media and the networked public sphere in India. These searches yielded a substantive body of published texts (see Table 23.2) that delineated scholarly characterizations of India's digital media and the public sphere (Glasser, 2013; Ravi, 2013; St. Amant, 2007).

Research Design for Qualitative Case Study on the Role of Digital Media

Research step	Case study goal	Research approach and/ or information sources analyzed	Type of result	For research question (RQ)
One: Database searches	Establish method framework (Jaeger, 2005)	Find contextual terms through keyword searches in 32 databases (Patton, 2002)	Contextual terms for case study analysis (Maxwell, 2013)	Relates to RQ # 1, 2, 3, & 4
Two: Selecting cases	Examine theoretical perspectives of "public sphere"	Analyze 1752 articles (Creswell, 2014)	Preliminary consideration of research questions (Runyan, 1982)	Addresses RQ # 3 & 4
Three: Case study analysis	Understand theoretical and conceptual underpinnings (Merriam, 2009)	Identify specific cases for analysis based on theoretical perspectives (Yin, 2012)	Criteria for interpreting findings (Yin, 2013)	Theorizes RQ # 3 & 4
Four: Analysis of networked public sphere	Analyze theoretical framework of India's "public sphere"	Study trends through case study analysis (Merriam, 2009)	Analytical generalization (Creswell, 2014)	Connects to RQ # 1 & 2
Five: Comparative case study	Collect and assess other data such as growth figures, demographic and usage statistics	Compare pertinent data to address research questions (Jaeger, 2005)	Posit research results based on comparative perspectives (Merriam, 2009)	Ties in to RQ # 1, 2, 3, & 4

TABLE 23.1   Provides a summary of case study research design and evaluation methods for this study. The case study method was specifically designed to examine trends in networked public sphere for India's media and to theorize the role of the networked public sphere in India's democratic society.

Search Results for 11 Thematic Keywords in Library Databases for Articles Published May 1, 2002, through May 24, 2014, for Qualitative Analysis

Thematic keywords (based on *Library of Congress Subject Headings**) used for searching databases for qualitative analysis of cases, theories, & concepts	Search results in article databases	Items found in library catalogs	Items in Citation databases (such as *Web of Science Core Collection***)	Total items analyzed for 11 keywords for this study
"Digital media" AND India	405	236	53	**85**
"Social media" AND India	890	365	195	**142**
"Online social networks" AND India	126	14	6	**94**
Censorship AND India	23	82	9	**20**
"Free speech" AND India	101	14	11	**56**
"Protest movements" AND India	139	66	105	**83**
Democracy AND India	1570	1166	481	**334**
"Information technology" AND India	2580	761	354	**256**
Internet AND India	1580	768	375	**322**
Corruption AND India	390	488	204	**156**
"Social problems" AND India	1040	840	23	**204**
Search results per database type	8844	4800	1816	
Total scholarly information items analyzed for this study				1752

Table 23.2   Provides cumulative tally of 11 thematic keywords and their respective search results in library databases. The extreme right column lists (in bold type) numbers of articles analyzed for each thematic keyword after eliminating duplicate items and other items irrelevant to this study.

* The Library of Congress Subject Headings (LCSH) is among the most widely adopted subject indexing language in the world. It has been translated into many languages and is used around the world by libraries large and small. LCSH has been actively maintained since 1898 to catalog materials held at the Library of Congress. Most library databases use the LCSH to organize their resources.

** The Thomson Reuters Web of Science Core Collection Citation Indexes provide researchers with quick, powerful access to the world's leading citation databases. This index's authoritative, multidisciplinary content covers over 12,000 of the highest impact journals worldwide, including Open Access journals and over 150,000 conference proceedings, and provides current and retrospective coverage in the sciences, social sciences, arts, and humanities.

This qualitative case study research method also facilitated a review of recent scholarly literature to articulate theories that explicate and enunciate the role of digital media in India's networked public sphere (Alexander, 2011; Jarvis, 2007). This research method enabled insightful reviews of the rich historiography of communication, social media, and the state of the networked public sphere in India. It also enabled the author to refine cross disciplinary perspectives, as identified in prior studies of communication (Fischer & Merrill, 1976; Holledge & Tompkins, 2000; Hooker, 2011; Martin & Wilson, 1997; Prosser, 1973), information and data effects in our society (Aikat & Remund, 2012; boyd & Ellison, 2007), and free speech in India (Fischer & Merrill, 1976; Freedom Forum, 1999; Kaur & Mazzarella, 2009; Morris & Waisbord, 2001; Rares, Fenger, Rosenmeier, Ehlers, & Carl, 2006; Sides, 2006; Thapar, Champakalakshmi, & Gopal, 1996; Varennes, 1996).

Through this qualitative case study research method, we identified related theoretical constructs that advance the role of social media in India's democratic society (Price, Verhulst, & Morgan, 2013) and the transformative power of social media (Fortner & Fackler, 2010; Price et al., 2013). Subsequent analyses of published works helped us broaden the communication perspectives that contribute to communication, digital media, and the networked public sphere in India.

Research Results: Intercultural Communication for Global Engagement in India

We begin our discussion of India's intercultural communication with case study overview relating to India's role in **fostering global engagement.** By situating India's networked public sphere within a larger context of democracy, intercultural communication, and global engagement, this chapter presents results of the qualitative case study that synthesized multidisciplinary perspectives on the role of digital media in India's democratic society. Based on qualitative case study analysis, this research study theorized the role and significance of India's digital media in fostering a networked public sphere.

A land of striking contrasts, India is the world's largest democracy, a nuclear power, and a rising economic giant—but also the world's most ancient surviving civilization, with a rich heritage dating back into prehistory. The Indus Valley civilization, one of the world's oldest, flourished during the third and second millennia B.C. and extended into northwestern India. In the thirteenth century, the Venetian merchant traveler Marco Polo described India as "a land of wonders," and his observation sustains today (Polo, 1958). From the days of Marco Polo, India experienced dominant conquests of several foreign invaders like Arabs, Turks, Mongols, Afghans, and the British. These invaders enriched India with their intercultural influence among other consequences.

The British arrived in India as traders in the early years of the seventeenth century. Until the beginning of the eighteenth century, British presence in India constituted a trade outpost of the East India Company. By the mid-eighteenth century, the Company pursued military dominance that led to **British rule of India** until the mid-twentieth century.

Freedom fighters such as Mahatma Gandhi and Jawaharlal Nehru pursued nonviolent resistance to gain independence from British rule in 1947.

In fewer than seven decades since independence, India has emerged as a major global power. A burgeoning urban middle class, a technology-savvy and skilled workforce, and a somewhat stable political climate are driving India's emergence as a regional and global power. India ranks fourth in military strength after the United States, Russia, and China.

India initiated, albeit haltingly, **market-oriented economic reforms** in 1991 to deepen economic ties with other nations, improve investor confidence, and support economic growth. India has experienced surging growth after economic reforms in 1991, when it transformed into an open-market economy, although remnants of its self-reliance policies and practices endure.

The **economic liberalization** measures facilitated significant reforms such as an increasingly **liberal foreign investment** regime in many sectors, **industrial deregulation**, **privatization of state-owned enterprises**, and **reduced controls** on **foreign trade and investment**. Such reforms accelerated the country's growth, which averaged under 7% per year from 1997 to 2011. India's **economic growth rate** was 7.5% in 2014, faster than China's economy over the same period.

With a fast-growing economy ranked 10th in the world, India estimated in February 2015 that its economic growth would accelerate in 2016 to 8.5%, which could make it the world's fastest-growing large economy.

India's economy combines traditional industries, such as hand weaving and more modern ones like information technology and successful film industry called **Bollywood**. The widely-watched products of India's **Bollywood** and **television entertainment industry**, which are disseminated worldwide by traditional and digital media, comprise a rich kaleidoscope of the country's vibrant intercultural communication and global engagement (Ganti, 2012). In many ways, the **Bollywood** phenomenon has emerged as a potent symbol of India as a rising economic powerhouse.

The neoliberal restructuring of the Indian state in the 1990s has led to tremendous social and economic change in India. The rise of **Bollywood** as a significant entity for intercultural communication and global engagement epitomizes the effects of neoliberalism on cultural production in a postcolonial setting. India's **economic restructuring** has dramatically altered the country's media landscape, which quickly expanded to include multiplex theaters nationwide and entertainment

arindambanerjee/Shutterstock.com

television with a global following among the Indian diaspora worldwide. Scholars contend that the Hindi film industry's metamorphosis into Bollywood would not have been possible without the rise of neoliberal economic ideals in India (Ganti, 2012).

In three decades of economic reforms, India has faced severe **economic problems**, including staggering income inequality and rampant mistreatment of women. India is a land of deep-rooted spirituality and cultural enrichment punctuated by male-dominated traditions, religious violence, social ills, economic woes, and environmental problems. India outlawed discrimination based on caste and introduced various measures to empower disadvantaged groups and give them easier access to opportunities such as education and work.

More than one third of India's citizens still suffer from **widespread poverty** (21.9% live below the poverty line or have income of less than $1.25 a day), unabated illiteracy (32.2% of people age 15 and over cannot read and write), and are deprived of access to basic medical services. India also faces tremendous challenges in unemployment, energy, education, health, water, and sanitation. The vast mass of the rural population remains impoverished. India's Prime Minister, Mr. Narendra Modi, who was elected in May 2014, has promised to bring economic rejuvenation to beleaguered parts of India.

Pertinent to this chapter's research into intercultural communication and global engagement, an important characteristic of the Indian population is the **diversity of religious affiliations**. India is home to people from different religious, social, ethnic, and educational backgrounds. Several religions of foreign origin such as Christianity and Islam coexist and flourish with other religions such as Hinduism, Buddhism, Sikhism, and Jainism, which originated in India. According to the 2011 census, India's **religious segments** comprise 80.5% Hindus, 13.4% Muslims, 2.3% Christians, 1.9% Sikhs, 1.9% Buddhists, 0.4% Jains, and 0.1% did not specify their religion (Census of India, 2011). With its many languages, cultures, and religions, India is highly diverse. This is also reflected in India's federal political system that stipulates sharing of power among the central government, 29 states, and 7 union territories. These regions claim a distinct culture and language of their own.

The significance of India's intercultural communication for global engagement attains greater significance when we analyze India's **language diversity** and **lingua franca**. Often termed as the **bridge language**, **trade language**, or **vehicular language**, lingua franca is a language systematically used, instead of occasionally, or casually, to make communication possible between persons not sharing a native language, in particular when it is a third language, distinct from both **native languages**. The Constitution of India designates a **bilingual approach** of using Hindi and English. Both Hindi and English are used for important official purposes such as parliamentary proceedings, judiciary, business communication, education, and the government.

The 2001 census documented at least 20 other official languages such as Bengali, Telugu, Marathi, Tamil, Urdu, Gujarati, Malayalam, Kannada, Oriya, Punjabi, Assamese, Kashmiri, Sindhi, Sanskrit, and Hindustani, which is a popular variant of Hindi and Urdu spoken widely throughout northern India but is not an **official language** (Census of India, 2011). Faced with such **language diversity**, India adopted English as the dominant language for communication on the Internet and social media.

As one of the legacies of British rule, English is the most important language for **national, political, and commercial communication**. Hindi is the most widely spoken language and primary language of 41% of the people. With more than 121 million English speakers (11% of population), India is the world's second largest English-speaking country after the USA (316 million—nearly 94.2% of the U.S. population).

India's preference for English as the nation's lingua franca makes the nation a significant entity for intercultural communication for global engagement. Prominent newspapers and digital media companies such as the *Wall Street Journal*, Gizmodo, Huffington Post, Quartz, Business Insider, BuzzFeed, and Mashable have launched editions in India to offer localized content and garner advertising revenue. These media entities have reached out to India's surging population of English-speaking, technology-savvy audience members who were eager to read a wide array of content comprising news, information, and entertainment. This has prompted multinational media firms and international entrepreneurs to invest in India's print media. After attaining rapid growth as a twentieth-century phenomenon, India's digital media have engaged and entertained consumers in the networked public sphere of the twenty-first century.

India's Digital Media Complement Traditional Media

India continues to face **democratic challenges** and related **communication problems** (McIntyre-Mills, 2000). Digital media comprise a central role in the nation's **political, socio-economic, and cultural life**, where newspapers continue to thrive as a distinctive part of India's rich heritage. Mahatma Gandhi, the architect of India's freedom from British rule, played a prominent role as editor of three newspapers, *Young India*, *Harijan* (meaning "child of God," coined as a euphemism for Untouchables by Gandhi in 1931) and *Navajivan*, ("new life"), which galvanized the demure people of India to fight against the seemingly invincible British ruler. After India's independence from British rule in 1947, newspapers gained more prominence as the nation's democratic watchdog, especially after the state-imposed press censorship of the mid-'70s (Ramaprasad, 1987). India's social media have conjured Gandhi's vision of freedom in a democratic society.

More people read the newspaper in India every day compared to people in the United States, Europe, and other parts of the developed world, where newspaper circulation has declined. **Print media** in the U.S. and Europe are reeling from vanishing revenues and widespread job cuts as well as the common notion that print media are past their prime. On the other hand, in some developing countries, circulation is surging as these factors are more than canceled out by rising incomes, population, customized content, and rising literacy. In many Asian countries, such as China and India, newspapers are thriving and expanding.

Despite a newspaper downturn worldwide, India's print media remains buoyant and has arguably been experiencing its most successful run in terms of profits, circulation, and journalism. Unabated by the 2009 global economic recession that dwindled advertising revenues and newspaper circulation worldwide, India emerged as the **world's largest newspaper market** by superseding China (WAN-IFRA, 2009, 2010). Six Asian nations dominated the world's top 100 paid newspapers by circulation in 2013. They were China (with 28 dailies), India (24), Japan (17), South Korea (6), Thailand (3), and Indonesia (1), according to 2013 data from the International Federation of Audit Bureaux of Circulations (IFABC, 2015). In these Asian nations, **rising incomes**, **population growth**, **burgeoning advertising revenues**, escalating news readership, and surging literacy have contributed to a rapid rise in newspapers.

In sharp contrast to the rise of Asia in the world's top 100 paid newspapers by circulation, newspaper markets in the U.S. and Europe are reeling under vanishing revenues, job cuts, and the widespread notion that print media are past their prime. The number of the **world's top newspapers** in European countries are down to single digits with the United Kingdom (9 dailies), Germany (1), and France (1). Only four U.S. newspapers, *The Wall Street Journal, The New York Times, USA Today*, and the *Los Angeles Times*, feature in the world's top 100 paid newspapers by circulation (Alliance for Audited Media [AAM], 2015). India, China, and Japan accounted for more than 60% of the world's newspaper sales, with the United States comprising 14%, according to the World Association of Newspapers and News Publishers (WAN-IFRA), the global organization of the world's newspapers and news publishers (WAN-IFRA, 2015).

The WAN-IFRA's list of "World's 100 Largest Newspapers" features 17 Indian newspapers, including three English dailies, seven Hindi publications, and seven regional language publications (WAN-IFRA, 2015). These newspapers publish and maintain an active presence online, including social media (WAN-IFRA, 2010). Most of these newspapers publish color broadsheet editions printed simultaneously in several cities and maintain websites for their domestic and international readers (WAN-IFRA, 2009). Multinational media publishers and private entrepreneurs have increased their investments in India's print media since 2002 when the Indian government eased a 1955 ban on foreign investment in magazines and newspapers.

Low Internet Use Sustains India's Print Media Boom

India's **Internet penetration** is low (15%) and ranks 159 among 228 nations, according to 2013 global statistics from the International Telecommunication Union (ITU), the international body (Acharya, 2014; ITU, 2014). India's **low Internet penetration** has prompted newspapers to enjoy rising circulation (WAN-IFRA, 2015).

With little direct competition from the fledgling Internet media, India's print media revenue and profits have soared. India's print media continues to grow by over 5.95% each year, according to data compiled by India's Ministry of Information and Broadcasting (India MI&B, 2014; RNI, 2014).

India was home to 99,660 **print publications** registered as of March 31, 2014, comprising 13,761 newspapers and 85,899 periodicals publishing more than 451 million copies per publishing day (RNI, 2014, p. xiii), which amounts to nearly one copy per three persons for India's 1.27 billion people, based on estimated population in July 2014 (Census of India, 2011; Worldometers, 2014). Of India's 99,660 print publications, 13,751 were newspapers and 85,899 were periodicals. Of these publications, 13.18% were in English and 40% were in Hindi (RNI, 2014). Such language diversity also contributes to intercultural communication and global engagement.

The prosperous times for India's media may be attributed to several factors, such as the government's liberal reforms inviting foreign investment in media, a traditional print media fare devoid of **free content online** due to low Internet penetration, a rising literacy rate, sophisticated print and broadcast technologies, increased purchasing power of the middle class, rise in advertising and consumerism, growing popularity of infotainment, and round-the-clock media content on television and the Internet.

Even in countries where print newspapers continue to grow, the era of digital is around. The WAN-IFRA quoted one of India's renowned media leaders, **Raghav Bahl,** founder of Network 18 media, predicting a decline in newspapers in these words: "It should take about five years for English newspapers to capitulate before a full scale digital assault." Bahl said it could take a decade before other Indian language newspapers would face "the same reality" (as cited in Kilman, 2015, para. 4). Though print circulation continues to increase in India and in many developing countries, publishers have no choice but to increase their digital presence, Bahl suggested (Kilman, 2015). "In the new order, news publishing cannot continue to be linear, but has to be conversational," he observed (Kilman, 2015, para. 5). Digital media facilitate and drive that conversation.

Bahl's remark about **non-linear** and "**conversational**" digital media was echoed by other experts in addressing **content creation**, **delivery of news**, **revenue models**, and understanding and using **audience data** (Kilman, 2015). In discussing the transformation of the news media industry, the "Digital Media India 2015" conference presented five "takeaways." The five most important lessons learned were: (a) Think at the outset "share-ability and audience of the story," (b) Offer "tailored content" through chat apps, (c) "Sub-segment audience and serve" relevant content, (d) Devise "different revenue strategies for different advertisers," (e) "Embrace programmatic advertising for sale of banner ads, and a direct relationship with advertisers for sale of premium inventory," and news publishers should "come together and build their own ad exchange" (Kilman, 2015, paras. 9–10).

Habermas (1989b) recognized media's "ambivalent potential" (p. 303) in the construction of a robust public sphere. While media institutions foster **freedom of thought and ideas** with their innate ability to enhance public dialogue on important social and political issues, the same media institutions "considerably strengthen the efficacy of social control" through their **centralized production** of media messages (Habermas, 1989b, p. 303).

Digital Media Empower the People of India

In India's emerging **crowdsourced communities**, consumers also submit online reviews that evaluate their experience about a brand's services or products. Market studies indicate that more than two thirds of online consumers read reviews before making their purchase decisions. Better information has led to a simple and obvious trend. Satisfied customers become brand evangelists spreading praise about their products and services, whereas unhappy customers vilify the brand in their social circles.

With the growing number of smartphone and Internet users, India has emerged as a key market for social media activity. As India's media function in a **global 24/7 media environment**, social media have emerged as an important source for companies to promote, to target, and, more importantly, to connect with their consumers.

Influential multinational firms and local companies are learning to appreciate the social media's power of making friends and influencing public opinion. Several Business to Consumer (B2C) companies are strategically developing Customer Relationship Management (CRM) programs to immediately resolve a problem and avoid the possibility of a negative buzz vibrating across social media, which also attract reports in traditional news entities. India's B2C companies have actively engaged CRM programs.

Brands across India's industries are increasing their participation in social media, according to a February 2015 study on India's social media marketing by Ernest and Young, the global business management firm (EY, 2015). The Ernest and Young study concluded that nearly 81% of the brands surveyed considered Facebook to be the most important **platform**. Almost 48% of surveyed brands considered Twitter as the second-most important platform, closely followed by YouTube with nearly 43% surveyed brands ranking the online video site to be the third-most important channel (EY, 2015). The study also concluded that social media were increasingly used for thought leadership and internal communications, recruitment, and CSR in addition to marketing.

India's digital media have empowered the people of India to engage in **democratic redress**. Thanks to burgeoning online access, consumers are increasingly complaining about various brands on Facebook, Twitter, and online consumer fora. India's online consumers monitor discussions of popular brands on social media and vent their grievances online before seeking redress of complaints in India's time-consuming courts of law.

Digital media spurred India's **anti-corruption revolution** that redefined the nation's public sphere. As the theory of the networked public sphere attain multiple and diverse dimensions, the concept of "**counterpublics**" has emerged to connote some publics with explicitly articulated alternatives due to their conflict with the norms and contexts of their socio-cultural, economic, and political environment. Fraser (1990) and other theorists concluded that **marginalized groups** are excluded from a universal public sphere, and thus it was impossible to claim that one group would be inclusive. Such marginalized groups formed their own public spheres, and termed this concept a "subaltern counterpublic" or "counterpublics."

Such theoretical perspectives have succored India's social activist Anna Hazare to demand the setting up of an independent anti-corruption agency in 2010. Hazare's anti-corruption campaigns spread social media with powerful messages that engaged a **global audience** and created a global awareness about India's widespread outrage over political corruption. Enraged over endemic corruption, India's Internet users were united in galvanizing a psyche of freedom in their democratic society.

Relenting to such protests, India's president signed into law on January 2, 2014, an anti-corruption bill that implements an independent anti-corruption agency known as a *lokpal* (Hindi for "caretaker of people"). The lokpal serves as an independent ombudsman with powers to investigate and prosecute **corruption in public office**, the government, and beyond.

India's widespread outrage over **political corruption** signified the efficacy of the networked public sphere to empower counterpublics. Based on analyses of connected cultures of the network society, Tierney (2013) concluded that social media are restructuring urban practices—through ad-hoc experimentation, commercial software development, and communities of participation. Citing how **counterpublics** use diverse digital modes to transmit classified photos, mobilize activists, and challenge the status quo, Tierney argued that online activities do not cease in online conversations but they are physically grounded through mobile GPS coordinates which are then transformed into activities in physical spaces such as the street, the plaza, the places where people have traditionally gathered to demonstrate and express (Tierney, 2013).

Accordingly, the public sphere as the space of debate on public affairs has also shifted from the national to the global and is increasingly constructed around **global communication networks**. As Castells concluded, public diplomacy, as the diplomacy of the public, instead of the government, intervenes in this global public sphere to act beyond the strict negotiation of power relationships by building on shared cultural meaning as the essence of communication and thereby laying the ground for traditional forms of diplomacy (Castells, 2008).

The Power and Influence of India's Social Media

Attributing the decline in citizens' **political engagement**, due to "**socio-cultural changes**" as among the most difficult problems facing Western democracies today, Dahlgren (2009) theorized the role of the media in deflecting and enhancing **political engagement**, as well as in contributing to new forms of **political involvement** and new understandings of what constitutes the political. Public sphere theories have inspired **participatory action research** strategies, which are based on Habermasian theory of system and life-world. Such strategies constitute the **collective** that merges steering media with **cultural reproduction** and **transformation**, social reproduction and transformation, and the formation and **transformation of individual** identities and capabilities (Kemmis & McTaggart, 2005, pp. 595–596; Kemmis, 2006).

In sharp contrast to **Western decline** in **civic engagement**, India's media enjoy considerable influence in shaping the character of civic engagement. Social media enhance communication in India's multicultural society (Mohanty, 2012). India's social media cater to a privileged segment of the Indian population. India's social media users numbered 66 million, which is less than 6% of its population, in June 2013 (IAMAI, 2013). But that has not stopped a small but influential group of users in India from expressing, through social media, their concern about India's many problems.

India's government also initiated social media campaigns for important roles in the Indian democracy. The Election Commission of India's social media campaign drew record levels of voter registration and turnout in India's elections. In the campaign for the nation's 2014 general elections, India's politicians intensified their social media campaigns. Political parties reached voters by embracing innovative social media strategies such as mobile phone messaging.

During the campaign period for the 2014 general elections in India, local comedians gained cult following among some of India's estimated 80 million social media users by starting YouTube channels for their **politically incorrect** shows. As Varma (2014) observed, "long before the Internet, the Indian news media often poked fun at the country's politicians through cartoons and caricatures," local comedians disseminated their spoofs of "political leaders and the media circus to the rapidly growing number of social media users in India" (para. 1). India's social media have **fostered activism** and the **exchange of ideas**.

From the theoretical perspective of a networked public sphere, the Indian elections exemplify the role and significance of India's digital media in fostering **democracy**. Pollsters have correlated election victories of several candidates to digital media presence among other online activities. With an aggressive political strategy that included **vociferous bloggers**, **YouTube videos**, **Facebook campaigns**, and up-to-the minute updates on Twitter and other **digital media activities**, the Bharatiya Janata Party (BJP) won an outright majority in the elections by beating the incumbent party, the Indian National Congress, whose popularity has been damaged by corruption scandals and stalling economic growth.

India's Prime Minister, Mr. Narendra Modi, emerged as a prominent winner of his BJP party and credited digital media entities such as **social media messaging** with helping keep him and his party connected with "local sentiments." He credited social media with these words: "Our party, our campaign and me [*sic*] personally have gained tremendously from social media" (Cadel, 2014, para. 12). Modi felt social media strengthened his election campaign by providing "a direct means of information and gave us the much-needed local pulse on several issues without any bias" and he promised "more power to social media in the days ahead" (Cadel, 2014, para. 12). True to that promise, Modi has effectively used social media as an elected official. Since his May 26, 2014, election victory, Modi is among the elite group of global politicians who are active on social media. With more than 23 million Facebook fans and 7 million Twitter followers, Narendra Modi ranked second only to the U.S. President Barack Obama. Such developments are significant because not everyone in India is an Internet consumer, let alone a social media innovator. Modi has successfully incorporated social media as a pièce de résistance for image building, intercultural communication, and global engagement as an elected official and India's Prime Minister.

Dubbed as India's first "**social media election**," the 2014 general elections involved significant online electioneering and campaigning (Khursheed, 2014a; PTI, 2014). Cadel pointed out that American social media companies were the "more unexpected, winner" in India's 2014 election (Cadel, 2014, para. 2). Media reports credited Facebook, Twitter, and Google with "changing the face of Indian elections" (Khursheed, 2014b; PTI, 2014). New analysts credited three American social media giants, Facebook, Twitter, and Google for emerging as "major players" in the ongoing general elections in India, with political parties and candidates competing with each other to share breaking news on their Facebook pages, spreading Twitter messages, and archiving campaign coverage on Google-owned YouTube, among other outlets, in addition to traditional media message (PTI, 2014).

As Chao observed it was "inevitable" that "social media will become a must in future elections in India" due to "double digit increases in Internet adoption" (Chao, 2014, "Campaigning Style," para. 9). The role and significance of India's social media in the 2014 elections illustrate the rise of India's networked public sphere.

Such developments have enabled us to posit new theoretical paradigms that explicate how social media are redefining civil society amidst the interplay of media and democracy. Acknowledging social media's role in **mobilizing citizen dissent** and upending seemingly invulnerable **authoritarian regimes**, Diamond and Plattner (2012) interpret social media as "liberation technology." This digital space provides an alternative structure for **citizen voices** and **minority viewpoints** as well as highlights stories and sources based on **relevance** and **credibility** (Benkler, 2006; Benkler et al., 2013).

Benkler et al. (2013) conclude that the dynamics of the networked public sphere supports an optimistic view of the potential for networked **democratic participation** enriched by "vibrant, diverse, and decentralized" networked public sphere that exhibited broad participation, leveraged topical expertise, and "focused **public sentiment** to shape **national public policy**" (p. 3).

Discussion and Conclusion: Digital Media Foster India's Networked Public Sphere

In exploring primary theoretical themes and conceptual constructs that foster India's networked public sphere, this chapter delineated the evolution of India's growth in **intercultural communication** and **global engagement**. Drawing upon the theoretical framework of the democratic public sphere, this chapter presented research that enhanced our understanding of the role of digital media in India's democratic society.

By melding **multidisciplinary perspectives** through extensive case study research, this chapter presented research that theorized the role and significance of India's digital media in fostering a networked public sphere. This chapter presents theoretical perspectives that conclude that India's digital media engage, entertain, educate, enrich, empower, and enlighten the networked public sphere in the nation's democratic society.

India is emerging as a prominent global player in economics, politics, media, and intercultural communication. The theory of public sphere powerfully articulates the media's potential role in contributing to the **public dialogue** to foster **democratic norms**. The public sphere framework focuses on mass media as spaces for **public communication** and alerts us to the possibilities and impediments for media systems to facilitate and disseminate wide-ranging public discussion and dissent. For instance, the impact of counterpublics in India's public sphere enunciates how digital media have also raised the ante in **democratic redress**.

India's complex ecosystem of digital media platforms characterizes the nation's networked public sphere. The complex relationship between media and democracy defines key elements of Habermas's theory of the public sphere (Aufderheide, 1991; Friedland, Hove, & Rojas, 2006). Friedland et al. (2006) recommended revisions in the central theoretical assumptions about the structure of the public sphere to accommodate the evolving network since network form is at the core of growing complexity, and centrality of networks in our society's existing economy, political system, **civil society**, and the lifeworld. As an emerging technology integrated into this evolving network, digital media have actively contributed to a democratic public sphere. India's networked public sphere has contributed to fostering a democratic society that is conducive for communication and the creation of **diverse organizational forms**. This chapter presents research that illustrates the **power of digital media** in enriching **intercultural communication** and **global engagement**.

Future Research Directions

The theoretical roots of the public sphere, as propounded in 1962 by Habermas (1984) can be redefined to explicate the vibrant realm of **social discourse** between the state on one hand and the **private sphere** of the market and family on the other. Future research should draw upon key works of Habermas (1984) and other scholars to enunciate the decadence of **traditional public sphere** (Habermas, 1984; Habermas, Lennox, & Lennox, 1974) and its transition to the **networked public sphere**.

Dahlgren (1991) recommended that researchers "render the public sphere as an object of **citizen concern**, **scrutiny** and **intervention**" (p. 9). To that end, a possible future **direction of research** could relate to the role and **significance of digital media** in fostering a networked public sphere in other democratic societies such as Australia, South Africa, Brazil, and Mexico, just to name a few countries. Such studies may provide new insights such as this chapter's research theorizing the powerful role of India's digital media in fostering **intercultural communication for global engagement**.

Acknowledgment

The author gratefully acknowledges his debt to Dr. Andrea Patterson-Masuka and Dr. Regina Williams Davis for leading this book project, appreciates Richard Allen's copy editing suggestions, and thanks three anonymous reviewers for their critiques to earlier versions of this research project. The author also thanks Ms. Divya Aikat and Mr. Vikram Aikat for research help, Dr. Abhijit Sen for research ideas and Dr. Jay Aikat for research feedback to enhance the research presented in this chapter.

Discussion Questions

Intercultural Communication for Global Understanding

1. India is one of the few places in the world where newspapers still thrive. List some possible reasons for the rise or fall of newspapers in India or any other country. For instance, newspaper readership and advertising revenues in some developed nations such as the U.S., UK, and Japan have severely declined. List some possible reasons for this decline. Enunciate your answer with some relevant cases and consequences.

2. In developing nations such as India, how has the recent advent of social media tools and technologies created a myriad of new potentialities and new realities in the creation and dissemination of news, entertainment, and other information, both within and outside communities?

3. If you were invited to develop a code of ethics for social media in India, list some ethical values (such as *transparency, do not harm anyone*) you feel are essential to promote global engagement across cultural boundaries. Illustrate with some real-life examples or news events.

Global Engagement Across Cultural Boundaries

1. Intercultural communicators in developing nations such as India seek to address inequities in race/ethnicity, ability, gender, and sexual orientation. Can you think of some ways to promote intercultural communication for global understanding? Cite some best practices to illustrate your point.

2. In developing nations such as India, how do emerging media (such as social media, mobile applications) supplant traditional media (such as newspapers, radio, and television)? Think of some examples to illustrate your point.

3. In what ways are emerging media revising or deviating from established norms by conceiving, perceiving, or disregarding intercultural boundaries? Discuss with current examples.

References

Acharya, S. (2014, May 5). *2014 information and communication technologies figures.* News release of May 5, 2014. Retrieved from http://www.itu.int/net/pressoffice/press_releases/2014/23.aspx#.VCM9MxY1N8E

Aikat, D. D., & Remund, D. (2012). Of Time magazine, 24/7 media, and data deluge: The evolution of information overload theories and concepts. In J. B. Strother, J. M. Ulijn, & Z. Fazal (Eds.), *Information overload: An international challenge to professional engineers and technical communicators* (pp. 15–38). IEEE Professional Communication Society, Hoboken, NJ: John Wiley & Sons and IEEE Press. doi:10.1002/9781118360491.ch2

Alexander, B. (2011). *The new digital storytelling: Creating narratives with new media.* Santa Barbara, CA: Praeger.

Alliance for Audited Media. (2015). *Media intelligence center.* Retrieved from http://www.auditedmedia.com/data/media-intelligence-center.aspx

Aufderheide, P. (1991). Public television and the public sphere. *Critical Studies in Mass Communication, 8,* 168–183.

Basham, A. L. (Ed.). (1975). *A cultural history of India.* Oxford, UK: Clarendon Press.

Benkler, Y. (2006). *The wealth of networks: How social production transforms markets and freedom.* New Haven, CT: Yale University Press.

Benkler, Y., Roberts, H., Faris, R., Solow-Niederman, A., & Etling, B. (2013). Social mobilization and the networked public sphere: Mapping the SOPA-PIPA debate. *Berkman Center Research Publication No. 2013-16.* Retrieved from ssrn.com/abstract=2295953 and http://dx.doi.org/10.2139/ssrn.2295953

boyd, d. m., & Ellison, N. B. (2007). Social network sites: Definition, history and scholarship. *Journal of Computer-Mediated Communication, 13 (1).*

Bruns, A., Burgess, J., Highfield, T., Kirchhoff, L., & Nicolai, T. (2011). Mapping the Australian networked public sphere. *Social Science Computer Review, 29*(3), 277–287.

Cadel, E. (2014, May 17). Biggest winner in Indian election: American social media. *USA Today.* Retrieved from http://www.usatoday.com/story/news/world/2014/05/17/ozy-india-election-social-media/9200069/

Castells, M. (2008). The new public sphere: Global civil society, communication networks, and global governance. *The Annals of the American Academy of Political and Social Science, 616*(1), 78–93.

Census of India. (2011, August 24). *Population enumeration data (final population).* Retrieved from http://www.censusindia.gov.in/Ad_Campaign/Referance_material.html

Chao, R. (2014, May 21). How much influence did social media have on India's election? *TechPresident.* Retrieved from http://techpresident.com/news/wegov/25062/India-election-social-media-influence

Creswell, J. W. (2013). *Qualitative inquiry and research design: Choosing among five approaches.* Los Angeles, CA: Sage.

Creswell, J. W. (2014). *Research design: Qualitative, quantitative, and mixed methods approaches.* Thousand Oaks, CA: Sage.

Curran, J. (1991). Mass media and democracy. In J. Curran & M. Gurevitch (Eds.), *Mass media and society* (pp. 82–117). London, UK: Edward Arnold.

Dahlgren, P. (1991). Introduction. In P. Dahlgren & C. Sparks (Eds.), *Communication and citizenship: Journalism and the public sphere in the new media age* (pp. 1–26). London, UK: Routledge.

Dahlgren, P. (2009). *Media and political engagement.* Cambridge, UK: Cambridge University Press.

Dahlgren, P., & Sparks, C. (1991). *Communication and citizenship: Journalism and the public sphere in the new media age.* London, UK: Routledge.

Diamond, L. J., & Plattner, M. F. (Eds.). (2012). *Liberation technology: Social media and the struggle for democracy.* Baltimore, MD: Johns Hopkins University Press.

Eisenhardt, K. M. (1989). Building theories from case study research. *Academy of Management Review, 14(4),* 532–550.

EY. (2015, February 19). *Ernest and Young Social Media Marketing: India Trends Study: Insights from social media-savvy brands in India.* Retrieved from http://www.ey.com/Publication/vwLUAssets/EY-social-media-marketing-india-trends-study-2014/$FILE/EY-social-media-marketing-india-trends-study-2014.pdf

Fine, R. (Ed.). (2010). *The big book of social media: Case studies, stories, perspectives.* Tulsa, OK: Yorkshire.

Fischer, H. D., & Merrill, J. C. (1976). *International and intercultural communication.* New York, NY: Hastings House.

Fortner, R. S., & Fackler, M. (Eds.). (2010). *Ethics & evil in the public sphere: Media, universal values and global development: Essays in honor of Clifford G. Christians.* Cresskill, NJ: Hampton Press.

Fraser, N. (1990). Rethinking the public sphere: A contribution to the critique of actually existing democracy. *Social Text, 25/26,* 56–80.

Freedom Forum. (1999). *Media at the millennium: India.* Arlington, VA: Freedom Forum. Retrieved from http://www.freedomforum.org/publications/international/MediaForum/1999/asia/indiaforum.pdf

Freedom House. (2013, May 1). *Freedom of the Press 2013.* Retrieved from: http://www.freedomhouse.org/report/freedom-world/2013/india

Friedland, L. A., Hove, T., & Rojas, H. (2006). The networked public sphere. *Javnost—The Public Journal of the European Institute for Communication and Culture, 13(4),* 5–26.

Ganti, T. (2012). *Producing Bollywood: Inside the contemporary Hindi film industry.* Durham, NC: Duke University Press.

George, A. M., & Pratt, C. B. (2012). *Case studies in crisis communication: International perspectives on hits and misses.* New York, NY: Routledge.

Glasser, C. J. (2013). *International libel and privacy handbook: A global reference for journalists, publishers, webmasters, and lawyers.* Hoboken, NJ: Bloomberg Press.

Habermas, J. (1984). *The theory of communicative action. Volume 1: Reason and the rationalization of society* (T. McCarthy, Trans.). Boston, MA: Beacon Press. (Original work published 1981.)

Habermas, J. (1989a). *The structural transformation of the public sphere: An Inquiry into a Category of Bourgeois Society* (T. Burger & F. Lawrence, Trans.). Cambridge, MA: MIT Press. (Original work published 1962.)

Habermas. J. (1989b). The task of a critical theory of society. In S. Bronner & D. Kellner (Eds.), *Critical Theory and Society: A Reader* (pp. 292–311). New York, NY: Routledge.

Habermas, J., Lennox, S., & Lennox, F. (1974). The public sphere: An encyclopedia article (1964). *New German Critique, 3*(Autumn 1974), 49–55. Durham, NC: Duke University Press. Retrieved from: http://www.jstor.org/stable/487737

Holledge, J., & Tompkins, J. (2000). *Women's intercultural performance.* London, UK: Routledge.

Holloman, C. (2013). *The social media MBA in practice: An essential collection of inspirational case studies to influence your social media strategy.* Chichester, UK: Wiley.

Hooker, R. D. (2011). *First with the truth: Synchronized communications in the counterinsurgency fight.* Arlington, VA: Institute of Land Warfare, Association of the United States Army.

IAMAI. (2013, March 12). *Internet & Mobile Association of India report on social media in India —2012. Retrieved from:* http://www.iamai.in/rsh_pay.aspx?rid=0B2QPqlHSwM=

IFABC. (2015). *The International Federation of Audit Bureaux of Circulations.* Retrieved from http://www.ifabc.org/resources/data-reports%2065/country-specific-circulation-data

India MI&B. (2014, August 28). *Government of India, Ministry of Information & Broadcasting Annual Report 2013-14.* Retrieved from http://mib.nic.in/linksthird.aspx

ITU. (2014). International Telecommunication Union report on percentage of individuals using the Internet. Retrieved from http://www.itu.int/en/ITU-D/Statistics/Pages/stat/default.aspx

Jaeger, P. T. (2005). Deliberative democracy and the conceptual foundations of electronic government. *Government Information Quarterly, 22,* 702–719.

Jarvis, P. (2007). *Globalisation, lifelong learning and the learning society: Sociological perspectives.* London, UK: Routledge.

Kaur, R., & Mazzarella, W. (2009). *Censorship in South Asia: Cultural regulation from sedition to seduction.* Bloomington, IN: Indiana University Press.

Kellner, D. (1990). *Television and the crisis of democracy.* Boulder, CO: Westview Press.

Kemmis, S. (2006). Participatory action research and the public sphere. *Educational Action Research, 14*(4), 459–476.

Kemmis, S., & McTaggart, R. (2005). Participatory action research: Communicative action and the public sphere. In N. K. Denzin, & Y. S Lincoln, (Eds.), *The Sage handbook of qualitative research* (pp. 559–603). Thousand Oaks, CA: Sage.

Khursheed, R. (2014a, April 7). Lok Sabha #Election2014: The view from Twitter. *Twitter India Blog.* Retrieved from https://blog.twitter.com/2014/lok-sabha-election2014-the-view-from-twitter

Khursheed, R. (2014b, May 15). India's 2014 #TwitterElection. *Twitter India Blog.* Retrieved from https://blog.twitter.com/2014/indias-2014-twitterelection

Kilman, L. (2015). *Digital media India: Where print is king, digital is coming on strong.* WAN-IFRA news release. Retrieved from http://www.wan-ifra.org/press-releases/2015/02/12/digital-media-india-where-print-is-king-digital-is-coming-on-strong

Lee, M. (2014). What can political economists learn from economic sociologists? A case study of NASDAQ. *Communication, Culture & Critique, 7,* 246–263. doi:10.1111/cccr.12043

Mandiberg, M. (Ed.). (2012). *The social media reader.* New York, NY: NYU Press.

Mansfield, H. (2012). *Social media for social good: A how-to guide for nonprofits.* New York, NY: McGraw-Hill.

Martin, E., & Wilson, G. B. (1997). *Hong Kong speaks: Free expression while becoming China.* Hong Kong: Hong Kong Baptist University.

Maxwell, J. A. (2013). *Qualitative research design: An interactive approach.* Thousand Oaks, CA: Sage.

McIntyre-Mills, J. J. (2000). *Global citizenship and social movements: Creating transcultural webs of meaning for the new millennium.* Amsterdam, The Netherlands: Harwood Academic.

Merriam, S. B. (2009). *Qualitative research: A guide to design and implementation.* San Francisco, CA: Jossey-Bass.

Mohanty, N. (2012). *Radicalism in Islam: Resurgence and ramifications.* Lanham, MD: University Press of America.

Morris, N., & Waisbord, S. R. (2001). *Media and globalization: Why the state matters.* Lanham, MD: Rowman & Littlefield.

Narayan, J., & Meherally, Y. (2006). *India: Struggle for freedom, political, social and economic.* Gurgaon, India: Hope India Publications.

Patrut, B., & Patrut, M. (Eds.). (2014). *Social media in politics: Case Studies on the political power of social media.* New York, NY: Springer Verlag.

Patton, M. Q. (2002). *Qualitative research and evaluation methods.* Thousand Oaks, CA: Sage Publications.

Polo, M. (1958). *The travels of Marco Polo: With 25 illustrations in full color from a fourteenth-century manuscript in the Bibliothèque Nationale, Paris.* New York, NY: Orion Press; distributed by Crown Publishers.

Price, M. E., Verhulst, S., & Morgan, L. (Eds.). (2013). *Routledge handbook of media law.* Abingdon, UK: Routledge.

Prosser, M. H. (1973). *Major books on intercultural communication.* Pittsburgh, PA: Intercultural Communications Network of the Regional Council for International Education.

PTI. (2014, May 6). Facebook, Twitter, Google change face of Indian elections. *The Times of India.* Retrieved from http://timesofindia.indiatimes.com/home/lok-sabha-elections-2014/news/Facebook-Twitter-Google-change-face-of-Indian-elections/articleshow/34721829.cms

Qualman, E. (2009). *Socialnomics: How social media transforms the way we live and do business.* Hoboken, NJ: Wiley.

Ragin, C. C. (1987). *The comparative method: Moving beyond qualitative and quantitative strategies*. Berkeley, CA: University of California Press.

Ramaprasad, J. (1987). Pre-, during and post-censorship coverage of India by the New York Times. *Newspaper Research Journal, 9*(1), 19–29.

Rares, E., Fenger, L., Rosenmeier, L., Ehlers, L. N., & Carl, S. M. (2006). *In between freedom and equality*. København, Denmark: Copenhagen Business School Institut for Interkulturel Kommunikation.

Raupp, J. (2011). Organizational communication in a networked public sphere. *SC|M Studies in Communication |Media, 1,* 15–36. Retrieved from http://www.scm.nomos.de/aktuelles-heft-und-archiv/2011/heft-1/beitrag-raupp/

Ravi, B. K. (2013). New media order for a safe South Asia. *Academic Research International 4*(2). *March 2013*. Retrieved from http://www.savap.org.pk/journals/ARInt./Vol.4 (2)/2013(4.2-13).pdf

RNI. (2014, November 5). *Ministry of Information & Broadcasting: Press in India: 2013–14 annual report of the office of the Registrar of Newspapers for India*. Retrieved from http://rni.nic.in/pin1314.pdf

Roberts, B. (2009). Beyond the 'networked public sphere': Politics, participation and technics in web 2.0. *Fibreculture, 14*. Retrieved from http://fourteen.fibreculturejournal.org/fcj-093-beyond-the-networked-public-sphere-politics-participation-and-technics-in-web-2-0/

Runyan, W. M. (1982). In defense of the case study method. *American Journal of Orthopsychiatry, 52,* 440–446. doi:10.1111/j.1939-0025.1982.tb01430.x

SarDesai, D. R. (2008). *India: The definitive history*. Boulder, CO: Westview Press.

Shirky, C. (2011). The political power of social media. *Foreign Affairs, 90*. Retrieved from http://www.foreignaffairs.com/articles/67038/clay-shirky/the-political-power-of-social-media

Sides, C. H. (2006). *Freedom of information in a post 9-11 world*. Amityville, NY: Baywood Company.

St. Amant, K. (Ed.). (2007). *Linguistic and cultural online communication issues in the global age*. Hershey, PA: Information Science Reference.

Tagore, R. (1914). *Gitanjali (Song offerings)*. London, UK: Macmillan. Retrieved from http://storage.lib.uchicago.edu.libproxy.lib.unc.edu/pres/2007/pres2007-0239.pdf

Thapar, R. (1966). *A history of India*. Harmondsworth, England: Penguin Books.

Thapar, R., Champakalakshmi, R., & Gopal, S. (1996). *Tradition, dissent and ideology: Essays in honour of Romila Thapar*. Delhi, India: Oxford University Press.

Tierney, T. (2013). *The public space of social media: Connected cultures of the network society*. New York, NY: Routledge.

Varennes, F. (1996). *Language, minorities and human rights*. The Hague, Netherlands: Martinus Nijhoff Publishers.

Varma, V. (2014, May 2). Election-season spoofs thrive in social media. *NYTimes.com* [Web log post] Retrieved from http://india.blogs.nytimes.com/2014/05/02/election-season-spoofs-thrive-in-social-media/?_php=true&_type=blogs&_r=0

Voss, C., Tsikriktsis, N., & Frohlich, M. (2002). Case research in operations management. *International Journal of Operations & Productions Management, 22(2)*, 195–219.

WAN-IFRA. (2009). World Association of Newspapers and News Publishers 2009 and 2010 World Press Trends Database. Retrieved from http://www.wptdatabase.org/

WAN-IFRA. (2010). World Association of Newspapers and News Publishers 2010 World Press Trends Database. Retrieved from http://www.wptdatabase.org/

WAN-IFRA. (2015). The World Association of Newspapers and News Publishers, or WAN-IFRA. Retrieved from http://www.wan-ifra.org/microsites/publications.

Worldometers. (2014). *Population of India.* Retrieved from http://www.worldometers.info/world-population/india-population/

Yin, R. K. (2012). *Applications of case study research.* Los Angeles, CA: Sage.

Yin, R. K. (2013). *Case study research: Design and methods.* Los Angeles, CA: Sage.

Chapter 6

Surviving the Culture Shock

24. Cultural Experiences in Thailand

Sandra L. Crosier

I was a Peace Corps Volunteer in Thailand for 27 months. This essay describes some of the cultural adjustments I experienced there. **Cultural adjustment, or culture shock, is the adjustment one experiences when living in a new culture where things are done differently from the way we are used to doing them.** *It is the frustration of not being able to do even the most trivial things easily. For example, you need to make a telephone call. Where can you find a telephone—it does not look like telephones at home. Then you must figure out how telephones work in this situation. When we experience this frustration again and again,* it can be debilitating unless we know to expect it and have been prepared to deal with it.

I wake up and realize I am in a strange bed—a cot, not my double bed, and there is a mosquito net around it. I look around and the room I am in is different—no ceiling, only rafters. I can hear chickens and it is so hot and humid. Then I remember—my husband and I are Peace Corps Volunteers in Thailand. We arrived at our site last night after three months of training in a very

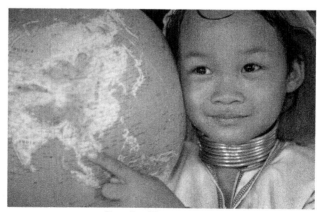

Photodiem/Shutterstock.com

different part of the country. Everything is different—different smells, different food, different climate, and the way everything is done is different. I am a teacher of English as a Second Language and the teaching is different, too. Although my bachelor's degree is in teaching music, I have had only three months of intensive training to teach English as a Second Language. During training, we lived in the south of Thailand with 80 other trainees. We were at a Teacher Training School and ate in a cafeteria. We learned the names of dishes that were served to us.

We ate out occasionally with trainers and other volunteers and learned the names of even more Thai dishes. At the conclusion of our training, we were assigned to a city in the north of Thailand. When we went to a restaurant there, we discovered that we did not recognize any of the dishes served. So, when the waitress asked what we wanted to order,

we resorted to pointing to dishes at tables of other patrons. We asked the waitress for the name of each dish as we ordered and, eventually, were able to order dishes without pointing to them.

I was shocked when I entered the classroom—the students showed respect by holding their hands chest-high and bowing their heads as they all stood up and said, "Good morning, teacher." I learned that teachers are highly respected here because the Buddha was a teacher

Mindscape studio/Shutterstock.com

and Thais are Buddhists. This is a daily ritual. They were not sure what to expect of this new stranger. I was teaching at an all-girls school and they were all in uniform. I had never been in a school where students wore uniforms, so we—the students and myself—had to adjust to each other.

Another cultural difference was that once a month, all of the students lined up in front of the school and the principal talked to them. When she had finished and as the students proceeded into the classrooms, two teachers, one on either side of the line, inspected each girl to check the length of their skirt and their hair. If either did not meet standards, the student was pulled aside. Their hair was cut on the spot. If their skirt was not the correct length, they were sent home. I was shocked and appalled, but I did not say anything as I reminded myself that what was happening was just different—not good or bad. It was another cultural adjustment.

The first time I gave a test, I was surprised that, as I handed each student the test, she bowed her head, folded her hands chest-high, and said, "Thank you, teacher." As I was proctoring the test, I noticed that one student passed her completed page to her friend to copy. I went to the two students, took up their test papers and ripped them in two. I told the students that this was cheating and was not allowed. The next day, I was called into a room with two Thai teachers and the two students. The teachers scolded the students for their misbehavior on the test and then each girl got down on her knees and came to one of the Thai teachers, holding out her hand to receive a slap with a one-inch ruler. Later, I learned that helping a friend on a test is not considered cheating in Thailand. I felt really badly because I had enforced an America cultural value on Thai students. At the time of the incident, it never occurred to me that I was making a judgment based on American values, not Thai. This incident never affected my relationship with the students, but it taught me to be much more careful—to ask questions before I acted and to ask myself if I was being judgmental based on American cultural values or seeing a cultural difference I needed to understand. Over the 24 months at my site, I made many cultural adjustments and slowly adapted to Thai culture. By the end of the first year, I had learned enough about Thai culture and my language skills had improved to a point that I was able to function much better and perform my job much better. I had also been accepted as a part of the community and this enabled me to do my job better.

We lived in a house on the school grounds furnished by the school. Students would often just show up on our door-step on the weekends. We would talk with them about the U.S. and help them practice their English. It was fun and entertaining since we had only a radio and a few books in English to entertain ourselves. We did travel some to other cities, sometimes visiting other Volunteers. We also explored the surrounding area around the city by bicycle.

We spent time in the market, getting to know the foods in our area of Thailand. With no refrigerator in our house, we had to shop every time we prepared meals at home. The first time I bought a pineapple, I asked the seller to peel it for me so that I could learn how to peel a pineapple. By the time she finished, there was a crowd of about 20 people watching the seller show the dumb foreigner how to peel a pineapple—something that every Thai knows how to do.

We became used to being the center of attention. Because we were strangers, we also enjoyed the freedom of not obeying all Thai cultural rules. We could get away with this because we were not Thai. As our 24 months was coming to a close, we considered staying for an additional tour of two years. Although we loved what we were doing and being in Thailand, we became worried that if we stayed for two more years, the adjustment back to life in the U.S. would be very difficult. We decided to leave after our first tour.

We were right about the readjustment to living in the U.S. It took us about a year to readjust. Not only had we changed, things in the U.S. had changed, too. The size of U.S. currency surprised me—U.S. dollars are much smaller than Thai baht. Styles of dress had changed drastically and we found that we really preferred Thai cuisine to that of the U.S. In Thailand, we had only bicycles for transportation in town and depended on bus or train to travel to other cities in Thailand. We found that, although we could get around by bike in the city, it was unusual and not always easy. Traveling out of town was almost impossible without our own car. We were living with my in-laws and used their car for out-of-town travel for about six months. Then, we finally broke down and bought a car. We found that we had not only adjusted to many Thai cultural values, we actually preferred them to those of the U.S. They became a permanent part of our lives.

Peace Corps works with developing countries to evaluate their needs—the kind of expertise they need to further their development. Then Peace Corps recruits American citizens and trains them to perform these jobs. The new volunteers are sent in-country for three months of training in the job they will perform as well as training in language and culture. Then, each volunteer is sent to a site where they will live for 24 months. They are paid the same salary as a host-country national would receive and live on the local economy. The experience is especially important today because the skills one develops are those employers are seeking. In this age of globalization, employers are looking for people with a global perspective which is gained by living in another culture where you learn that not everyone sees things as people in Lubbock, Texas, Winston-Salem, North Carolina, or Sacramento, California. Volunteers also gain proficiency in another language and intimate knowledge of the culture of the country to which they are assigned. There are also programs that involve pursuit of a Master's degree along with service in Peace Corps. If you are interested in finding out more about the Peace Corps, go to http://www.peacecorps.gov

Discussion Questions

1. Have you experienced cultural adjustment in the U.S.?
2. How can one prepare to deal with cultural adjustment?
3. Do you think flexibility is an important trait to have when experiencing cultural adjustment? What are some other important traits?
4. Do you think cultural adjustment for someone going to Europe would be the same as for someone going to Asia or Africa? Why or why not?
5. Why does one have to readjust to U.S. life after living abroad?
6. Most people re-entering the U.S. after living abroad for an extensive time say that readjustment to the U.S. is harder that cultural adjustment abroad. Why do you think that is true? Would you expect to have to readjust to the U.S.—the place where you were born and grew up?
7. Why do you think Peace Corps Volunteers need to live on the local economy? Why would it matter if they had more money than the locals and ate the more expensive Western foods available and prepared American meals at home?
8. Why do you think Peace Corps service is for two years?

25.   Transitions Across Cultural Boundaries: Culture Shock

Joe DeCrosta, Ph.D.

Justine couldn't believe that she had finally arrived. The fact that she had never flown on an airplane before and that her first trip outside of Burundi was going to take 22 hours to get to Pittsburgh did not faze her in the least. She had been offered the opportunity of a lifetime to study at a prominent U.S. university on full scholarship and she wasn't going to pass it up. She was going to take advantage of every opportunity. The fact that her family would be 7,500 miles away in their small country in East Africa was not an issue; there's Skype, Google Hangouts, and every other form of technology at her fingertips to keep in touch. She was ready for everything that would come her way—and why wouldn't she be?

The problem was that after about three weeks in her new home Justine didn't want to get out of bed—for anything. She had slipped into a deep depression and the "go for it" attitude had quickly waned. She couldn't sleep and she couldn't eat. Classes were more difficult than she ever imagined and the other students were just strange and unfriendly. She missed her family, the smells of the air in Burundi, and the warmth of the bright sun on her skin as she walked to school every morning immensely. Mostly, she longed for the taste of her mother's mukéké, a wonderful fish from Lake Tanganika, with piri piri (a spicy sauce) and a side of bananas and beans; this American food was no match. This place was so different and like nothing she ever expected; it was crowded, cold, and chaotic. She couldn't wait to speak to her family every day on video chat, but with the time difference she couldn't quite catch them at a time when they were home—their lives proceeded as normal and they weren't there whenever she wanted (and needed) to talk. To make things worse, she hadn't heard from her best friend, Florence, since she left Burundi and she had just missed Florence's 18th birthday. She really missed her best friend. Mostly, she worried about not being able to ever remember what it was like to live in Burundi and that perhaps she would lose herself in her new culture, never able to retain the familiar Burundian culture she loved so much. Would she lose her own culture forever? Life could not be any worse right now.

Justine remembered a panel of veteran international students presenting at the New International Student Orientation about the effects of something called "culture shock" and how it affected all of them, but she was too excited to even think that that could happen to her. Now she wished she had listened a bit more; she was beginning to think that culture shock was very real, as the students had mentioned, and perhaps their advice could have been useful just about now. Justine literally pulled herself out of bed, took a deep breath, and rubbed her eyes, with the hope that perhaps she'd see a little differently today. Now, where was that Student Handbook they were talking about at Orientation, the one with the information about this thing they called culture shock, and how she might experience this one day? No, that's right, they said that she would most likely experience it sooner rather than later . . .

Understanding Culture Shock

Justine's experience is all too common for someone who chooses to make a major change in her life and deliberately surrounds herself with the unfamiliar, in every sense of the word. Justine was given the unbelievable opportunity to experience another part of the world, receive a high quality education at a reputable university, and meet people that she would have never encountered if she had not left Burundi—ever. The problem was that Justine's situation was clouded by the fact that anything that she had ever known was now in a distant place, both physically and mentally. She could not see the forest through the trees and all she wanted to do was hop on the first plane headed in the same general direction as Burundi. There is no doubt that Justine was experiencing a textbook case of **culture shock.**

As the world becomes increasingly interconnected, or "globalized," individuals have the chance to experience firsthand the world outside of their own idiom more than ever before. Marshall McLuhan (McLuhan & Powers, 1989) first coined this phenomenon as the "global village" to explain the potential of human interconnectedness made possible through modern transportation and communication technologies in particular. More importantly, McLuhan recognized a conceptual shift in the ways people understand the world around them; he explored how this shift would ultimately connect us to each other differently than ever before. The movement toward a global village is wrought with both advantages and challenges, and as people move around within this global village, they are faced with the human problems of **cultural adaptation**, or **acculturation**. Those who communicate through modern technology within the comfort and safety of their own lair may experience intercultural communication challenges, but those who move around the world and physically experience the world around them are faced with a whole other set of phenomena that have come to be known as "culture shock."

In 1955, Canadian anthropologist Kalervo Oberg used the term **"culture shock"** to define the emotional response that "is precipitated by the anxiety that results from losing all our familiar signs and symbols of social intercourse" (Oberg, 1960/2006, p. 142). Although other anthropologists such as Cora Dubois and Ruth Benedict may in fact be the originators of the term in reference to anthropologists researching in the field, Oberg applied the concept to anyone who would travel to another foreign culture for any purpose (LaBrack, n.d.). Such an approach allowed the concept to be applied to business people, students, scholars, and service workers. Culture shock has become synonymous with the struggles that many people face when venturing outside of their own comfort zone.

Of course, the symptoms of culture shock vary, but generally speaking, individuals often feel at their most vulnerable not knowing how to navigate their new environment confidently. The loss of everyday cues, whether through language or common social symbols, has a strong impact on how someone may function in a new culture. Oberg (1960/2006) went so far as to say that someone going through culture shock would become "sick" (p. 144) from the experience. The good news is that culture shock is not fatal or even permanent, but rather a developmental experience where those living through culture shock often emerge transformed and acculturated (Adler, 1975).

Oberg outlined four specific stages that he viewed as indicative of the culture shock experience. The first stage, or the **honeymoon**, is the period of preparation when the impending experience is exciting, new, and full of wonder. Justine could not wait to get on the plane bound for the U.S. and experience everything her new home had to offer. It was only when she arrived and realized how different everything was and how she longed for home that she started to regress, the second stage of the process. **Regression** involves what Oberg (1960/2006) believed to be a "hostile and aggressive attitude" (p. 143) toward others in the host culture. This is perhaps the lowest moment of adjustment for someone who remains in a new culture for any period of time and defines the core of culture shock. This is the moment in which Justine did not want to lift herself out of bed and face the day. Everything she encountered—the people, the smells, the food, the weather, the styles of communication—literally did not agree with her and made her physically and emotionally sick. For this reason, Oberg considered this psychological crisis a "disease" (p. 143).

Eventually, as Justine began to face the day, immerse herself in the local culture and attempt new experiences, and engage in communication with others from her host culture, the process of **recovery** became apparent. In this third stage, Justine could begin to see the forest through the trees, explore the bigger picture, and appreciate her new surroundings with a sense of humor and self-reflection. Slowly, her attitude transformed and her conversations with others started to make more sense within the context of her new environment; it was clear that her worldview had shifted as she lived in this new culture. This process of recovery leads to what Oberg viewed as **cultural adaptation**, or the zenith of one's enculturation. "With a complete adjustment you not only accept the foods, drinks, habits, and customs, but actually begin to enjoy them" (Oberg, 1960/2006). One literally begins to internalize this new environment; new cultural cues become familiar and comfortable and the host culture is the foundation for new ways of thinking and feeling about the world. We might say that Justine was well-adapted when she started to enjoy her new university and experience it for what it actually is—not as an unfamiliar, unenjoyable place that was perhaps the worst decision she had ever made.

This rollercoaster of culture shock was soon schematized and became commonly known as the U-Curve Theory (see Figure 25.1) or what others have adapted as the UCT (Black & Mendenhall, 1991). Sverre Lysgaard (1955), a social psychologist from Norway, was interested in the empirical applicability of Oberg's theory by exploring the experience of prestigious Fulbright scholars from Norway studying in the U.S. Lysgaard's empirical research seemed to validate the U-curve model and gave way to a plethora of psychological, sociological, and communication academic research for many years. Lysgaard's adaptation of culture shock to real life situations is the earliest and most well-established model of cultural adaptation (Hall, 2005). However, the main themes of Lysgaard's work focused on two aspects of culture shock: the fact that the "stages" that Oberg outlined were indeed generalizable to the actual experiences of the Fulbright scholars; and how the amount of time an individual lived in a new culture influenced the extent to which a scholar might be culturally adapted. Various other studies have focused on the idea of cultural adaptation, but many have defined the concept of culture shock and adaptation differently (Black & Mendenhall, 1991; Milstein, 2005).

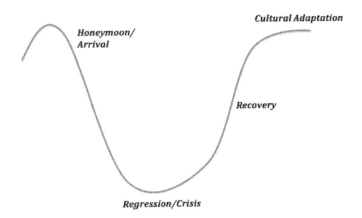

Most importantly, it is necessary to recognize the signs and stages of culture shock because of the ways in which it can affect human communi-

Figure 25.1   The stages of culture shock—the "U Curve" model.

cation and an individual's success in their new host culture (Barna, 1976). One who has never lived through culture shock may find it difficult to recognize and to understand; however, the first step is knowing that those who are new to a culture are perhaps struggling with the aspects of establishing a new life in their new cultural context. You may have experienced this phenomenon if you have ever moved to a new city or even when you moved away from home to a university as a freshman, learning about your new home, the culture of classes, student organizations, etc. The idea is that any shift into unfamiliar cultural territory will most likely affect the ways in which we experience our new world and communicate with those in the new culture. Living in a completely new culture, with an unfamiliar language, customs, and belief systems is perhaps the most dramatic example of what one will experience with culture shock. We often hear about how study abroad is transformative and life-changing for those who have been able to experience it. This is often a result of what they may or may not recognize as the process of cultural adaptation that each individual experiences in their own personal way. This complex phenomenon can often be so profound that the ways in which one sees the world around them is cast in an entirely new light, illuminated from more angles and intensities than they had ever imagined. Justine's experience is very real, but there is also a legitimate reason for the way she was feeling. By confronting this phenomenon of culture shock, Justine will be able to emerge from the experience a strong, adaptable, and flexible person.

Since the emergence of culture shock theory, scholars have approached the issue of cross-cultural transformation, personal development, and adaptation in terms of inter-cultural sensitivity (Bennett, 1993; Bennett & Bennett, 2004) and intercultural trans-formation (Gudykunst & Kim, 1992; Kim & Ruben, 1988). This essay hopes to connect dialogic communication theory to the ideas of culture shock and the process of cultural adaptation.

A Dialogic Approach to Culture Shock

Although culture shock seems to be caused by psychological distress, it seems to be more of a direct result of the inability to communicate effectively with others in our environment; we may not speak the same language, but more importantly, even if we do speak the same language, the cultural context for communicating with others has shifted and affects the ways in which we express ourselves and become effective, productive communicators. Misunderstanding abounds and anxiety is elevated. Because culture shock can have such a strong impact on our relationships and "social intercourse," it makes sense to explore the phenomenon through the lens of dialogic communication.

As we have learned in this text, dialogic communication is not simply a conversation or an exchange of ideas, but it is entering into an authentic communicative experience with the Other—that is, s/he who embodies something quite different from what I already understand in my current cultural context. Justine most likely will ride along the U-curve, but the ways in which she approaches each stage could have an effect on the ways she experiences her new culture and how she communicates her experience to others. Applying the aspects of dialogic communication to culture shock and cultural adaptation can help Justine enter into meaningful conversations not only with her new colleagues, but with the new environment itself. But what does this mean? How can she engage in a conversation with her environment?

Martin Buber (2002) described dialogue as a communicative experience that is fully and authentically human. Words are not always essential, but rather fully attending to the moment at hand can engage us in a dialogic communicative experience unlike any other. Consider this: Have you ever been engaged in a conversation with another person when you have been distracted? Have you found yourself focusing on another part of the room, or on an unrelated thought in your mind and you cannot fully attend to the Other standing right in front of you? This is a form of communication that might be considered "monologic"—the individual is not an active participant in the dialogic act; rather, he is treated as an object that is not fully acknowledged in the communicative act. Buber called this monologic act "I-It" communication (Buber, 1996). On the other hand, you may have been involved in a conversation and an exchange of ideas in which you have felt completely immersed, attending to every detail and nuance and literally felt transformed by the communication experience; the other person, experience, or idea is an active participant and fully acknowledged as an Other that makes communication possible—Buber (1996) called this form of communication "I-Thou" communication, or true dialogic communication. I-Thou relationships are at the core of dialogic communication because you encounter a truly human experience that has affected (and perhaps even transformed) you as a human being. Buber's dialogue offers a philosophy that teaches us *"how to turn toward, address and respect otherness"* (Anderson & Cissna, 1997, p. 110, emphasis in original).

Furthermore, the same can be said about experiences; when we engage an experience fully and authentically, we are engaging that experience dialogically. Buber speaks of this phenomenon when he describes his profound experience of caressing a horse. Although he could not literally engage in an actual conversation with the horse, he had connected so meaningfully and deeply to this horse, that he quite clearly felt as if he were "in communion" with that horse, forever changing his experience as a human being. He had forged a dialogic relationship with the horse (Buber, 2002).

Culture shock is considered to be transformative (Kim & Ruben, 1988); individuals will often describe that emerging from the experience of cultural shock not only transformed their self, but shifted their worldviews and outlook on life. Engaging culture shock dialogically may offer Justine alternative approaches for experiencing this inevitable shock while dealing with it in a healthy way. Journaling may be one approach to processing her culture shock; she may look back at her writing and understand how transformative the experience truly was. Going out of her way to get to know other U.S. students at her new university is only the first step, but diving deep into what it means to live in the U.S., that is, understanding and confronting structures of culture firsthand through whatever is meaningful to her, whether it is food, entertainment, or politics. Justine always loved soccer, so perhaps understanding the popular U.S. sports of baseball or football will help her continue her love of sports within the context of her new host culture. Entering into "dialogue" with her new home will allow her to get past her shock and embrace her new home, all the while knowing that she will always be a Burundian.

Globalization does not necessary mean that the world will quickly flow into an unidentifiable amalgam of cultures (Berry, 2008); perhaps it means that individuals and cultures are connected more than ever to the diverse physical and human world around us. Cultures are maintained, but like individuals, sometimes transform when in dialogue with each other. Justine's experience of culture shock may be the beginning of what Kim (2008) calls "intercultural personhood." This transformation is one that allows Justine to maintain the cultural context through which she has been formed as a human being, but also allows her to authentically immerse herself in the new host culture.

Soon Justine was starting to feel better. Not only had she met some wonderful students at her new university, but she was enjoying the food, the conversations, and even a new love of American baseball that she never thought was possible. Culture shock was much tougher than she ever imagined, but now Justine understood that it was necessary in order for her to break out of her own cultural context and experience the world as it really is—an amazing, colorful bazaar of people and ideas. Perhaps, in the end, Justine had experienced her cultural shock "dialogically."

Conclusion

In this chapter, we explored the meaning of culture shock and the process of cultural adaptation that many individuals experience. We defined culture shock through those scholars such as Oberg and Lysgaard who recognized and tested the phenomenon. We also discussed the idea of culture shock and adaptation in terms of dialogic communication and what it means to engage one's new cultural surroundings dialogically. Justine's story allows us to recognize the experience of culture shock and empathize with others who may be experiencing the process of adaptation while reflecting on situations where we may have gone through cultural shock to a lesser extent. We can see that the phenomenon of cultural shock quite clearly becomes part of one's narrative as well as the larger narrative of intercultural communication. Most importantly, culture shock can affect our emotional state which will have a direct impact on our inability to communicate confidently with others. Ultimately, one's experience of culture shock and the extent to which they believe they have experienced the U-Curve may have a lasting effect on how one approaches the challenges of intercultural communication in their work, their studies, and in their personal relationships. Finally, understanding culture shock could be helpful in the academic, corporate, volunteer, and military communities that require individuals to function in dramatically different cultural contexts.

Discussion Questions

1. Were there moments when you might describe your own experience as culture shock? What makes you think that it was in fact a form of culture shock?
2. Why do you think so many theorists in the humanities and social sciences saw a need for developing hypotheses and theories about culture shock and cultural adaptation?
3. What are some more specific ways Justine could have dealt with her particular culture shock "dialogically," as the article suggests?
4. Do you think that the phenomenon of culture shock has larger implications for other events that emerge not only in one's personal life, but in the life of a community or a nation?
5. What do you think might be perhaps the most challenging example of culture shock?

References

Adler, P. S. (1975). The transitional experience: An alternative view of culture shock. *Humanistic Psychology, 15*(4), 13–24.

Anderson, R., & Cissna, K. N. (Eds.). (1997). *The Martin Buber-Carl Rogers dialogue: A new transcript with commentary*. Albany, NY: State University of New York Press.

Barna, L. (1976). *How culture shock affects communication*. Proceedings from Communication Association of the Pacific Annual Convention: Kobe, Japan.

Bennett, J. M., & Bennett, M. J. (2004). Developing intercultural sensitivity: An integrative approach to global and domestic diversity. In D. Landis, J. M. Bennett, & M. J. Bennett (Eds.), *Handbooks of intercultural training* (pp. 147–165). Thousand Oaks, CA: Sage.

Bennett, M. J. (1993). *Towards ethnorelativism: A developmental model of intercultural sensitivity*. In R. M. Paige (Ed.), Education for the intercultural experience (pp. 21–71). Yarmouth, ME: Intercultural Press.

Berry, J. (2008). Globalisation and acculturation. *International Journal of Intercultural Relations, 32*(4), 328–336.

Black, J., & Mendenhall, M. (1991). The U-Curve adjustment hypothesis revisited: A review and theoretical framework. *Journal of International Business Studies, 22*(2), 225–247.

Buber, M. (1996). *I and thou* (W. Kaufmann, Trans.). New York, NY: Touchstone.

Buber, M. (2002). *Between man and man* (R. Gregor-Smith, Trans.). London, UK: Routledge.

Gudykunst, W. B., & Kim, Y. Y. (1992). *Communicating with strangers: An approach to intercultural communication* (2nd ed.). New York, NY: McGraw-Hill.

Hall, B. (2005). *Among cultures: The challenge of communication*. Belmont, CA: Thomson Wadsworth.

Kim, Y. Y. (2008). Intercultural personhood: Globalisation and a way of being. *International Journal of Intercultural Relations, 32*(4), 359–368.

Kim, Y. Y., & Ruben, B. D. (1988). *Intercultural transformation: A systems theory*. In Y. Y. Kim & W. B. Gudykunst (Eds.), Theories in intercultural communication (pp. 299–321). Newbury Park, CA: Sage.

LaBrack, B. (n.d). *Theory reflections: Cultural adaptations, culture shock and the "Curves of Adjustment."* Retrieved from http://www.nafsa.org/_/File/_/theory_connections_adjustment.pdf

Lysgaard, S. (1955). Adjustment in a foreign society: Norwegian Fulbright grantees. *International Social Science Bulletin, 7*, 45–51.

Milstein, T. (2005). Transformation abroad: Sojourning and the perceived enhancement of self-efficacy. *International Journal of Intercultural Relations, 29*, 217–238.

McLuhan, M., & Powers, B. (1989). *The global village: Transformations in world life and media in the 21st century*. New York, NY: Oxford University Press.

Oberg, K. (2006). Cultural shock: Adjustment to new cultural environments. *Curare: Journal of Medical Anthropology* (Vol. 29, pp. 142–146). (Original work published in 1960.)

Chapter 7

Experiencing Global Engagement

26. The Nexus of Global Engagement, Cultural Boundaries, and the Literal-Visual Cross-Cultural Continuum

James A. Schnell, Ph.D.

Introduction

The impact of digital technologies, regarding changes in education, offers foundation for understanding intercultural challenges that exist based on the disparity in digital backgrounds among U.S. and third world coalition forces in the areas of planning and conduct of military operations. Such challenges exist within the U.S. Army education and training system and operationally around the third world as observed via uneven adaptation of digital technologies in third world countries, such as Afghanistan.

In May 2012 the U.S. Department of Defense disseminated the "Department of Defense Mobile Device Strategy." It includes a **Mobility Vision** that stresses "A highly mobile workforce equipped with secure access to information and computing power anywhere at any time for greater mission effectiveness" (Takai, 2012, p. 1). This document exemplifies the increasing relevance of new communication technologies in contemporary war fighting and builds upon past developments that have led to the present-day emphasis.

Former Secretary of Defense William Perry is quoted in "The Rise of Netpolitik: How the Internet is Changing International Politics and Diplomacy" about the U.S. being anxious for U.S. allies to develop more technological capabilities. "If our allies do not develop these capabilities . . . this could end up being an asymmetrical alliance" (Bollier, 2003, pp. 14–15). Perry's position offers a framework for understanding the uneven use of digital technologies among the U.S. Army and third world allies today.

The significance of the aforementioned can be recognized via the increased emphasis on **visual imagery** over **literal messages**. This is manifested with U.S. Army cultural initiatives in varied contexts. Such speculations are based on fundamental assumptions. As we move

Andrey_Popov/Shutterstock.com

to being a more visually oriented society via web-based and new communication technologies, literal forms of communication that generally have more emphasis on critical thinking are being displaced by the visual domain that stresses more imaginary associations. Thus, the visual dominates at the expense of the literal and the imagination presides over critical thinking.

Visually oriented technologies, as stressed in U.S. Army cultural education, exemplify how the visual dominates at the expense of the literal. Thus, familiarity with this phenomenon will benefit those seeking to enhance Army cultural understanding in that increased emphasis on the visual domain results in dilution of critical thinking about cultural variables when visual images have significant impact upon the development of such cultural awareness.

Dimensions of Culture as Cross-Cultural Landscape

As we come to understand **cross-cultural communication** we need to consider the importance of culture as a foundation for our perspectives, for it is from our perspectives that we communicate. Hecht (1989) describes four dimensions that define culture and affect communication norms within each culture: power distance, individualism, reliance on context, and immediacy. All of these dimensions can be described with a continuum scale featuring the two extremes existing within each dimension.

Power Distance

This dimension deals with how a culture distributes power and how this distribution affects communication. All cultures can be placed on the high-power-distance—low-power-distance continuum scale. Cultures that rank high on the scale (as high-power-distance cultures) will maintain significant separation among social classes, and social classes will differ regarding communicative norms. For instance, the lower classes will be expected to show deference to the higher classes. The U.S. is nearer the low-power-distance position. As such, the American culture leans more toward equality among classes. We have class distinctions but they are not as strong as found in some other countries. This equality is expressed in our form of government (i.e., one person-one vote, equal opportunity provisions in the workplace and equal rights).

High-Power-Distance ———————————————————————— Low-Power-Distance

Individualism

The dimension of individualism varies in each culture. The continuum scale extends from individualist (oriented toward the individual) on one end and collectivist (oriented toward the group) on the other end. Individualist countries, such as the U.S., place considerable importance on individual effort and freedoms. Our economic system rewards the individual who can compete in business and win against others. Individualists are more to the point and don't mind arguing. Collectivist countries value the group and subordinate the individual to the group. Harmony and getting along with others is important in collectivist cultures. When this author first taught in China (a collectivist culture) he observed how his students commented on his "odd habit" of taking daily walks "alone." They tended to function in groups. The Chinese have a saying "It is the nail that stands high and alone that is first to be pounded."

Individualist ———————————————————————— Collectivist

Context Reliance

This author has found awareness of this dimension to be most beneficial in his cross-cultural encounters. The continuum scale for this dimension places high context communication style at one end and low context communication style on the other end. Communicators from low context cultures tend to convey meanings directly and verbally. One does not need to be very sensitive to understand what a low context communicator is trying to convey. If a low context communicator wants to borrow $10.00 to buy lunch he'll/she'll say, "Can I borrow $10.00 for lunch? I'll pay you tomorrow." The U.S. is a low context culture.

Communicators from high context cultures tend to convey meanings indirectly and in nonverbal channels, as well as verbal channels. Much of the message is conveyed in how the message is presented rather than in what is said. Gesture is especially meaningful. Understanding the context or backdrop of the message is important. If a high context communicator wants to borrow $10.00 to buy lunch he/she might say "I haven't eaten in 24 hours. Silly me, to make matters worse, I forgot my lunch money today. Though I am hungry, the uncomfortable hunger pains will teach me not to forget my lunch money in the future. It is a good lesson for me to learn." This being said while he/she holds his/her stomach in an obvious gesture conveying hunger. This exaggerated example illustrates the point of how one can convey a request without explicitly stating it. China is a high context culture.

Cross-cultural communication problems can obviously occur when a high context communicator interacts with a low context communicator. Most striking is that the low context communicator could understandably miss high context messages being presented because he/she is not sensitive to high context messaging (i.e., nonverbal gestures and indirect verbal expressions). Thus, in cross-cultural encounters, it is helpful to consider the role context plays in the other interactants' communication styles.

Low Context Communicator Style ————————— High Context Communicator Style

Immediacy

Immediacy deals with how people convey emotional closeness with regard to physical space. High-Contact culture communicators express emotional closeness by being physically close and touching. Low-Contact culture communicators express emotional closeness in less physical ways. They are far less likely to position themselves physically close to one another or touch another person to convey emotional closeness. However, emotional closeness can be conveyed and perceived through other communication channels.

Low-Contact Culture ————————————— High-Contact Culture

Literal-Visual Communication Style

Hecht conveys the four aforementioned dimensions that define culture. This author is proposing a fifth dimension defining culture and sees it as involving two extremes of literal communication style versus visual communication style. This continuum is understood in relation to information age phenomena and typically arises from how messages are conveyed via mass-mediated channels.

As such, less modern cultures are on the literal end of the continuum. They focus more on literal meanings conveyed in the spoken, and correspondingly written, word. Vivid critical thinking is part of this process. Modern cultures that are more steeped in visually oriented digital technologies focus more on general ideas conveyed via highly nuanced visual images. Critical thinking emphasis is diluted in this process because visual images cannot be readily analyzed as literal word meanings can.

This literal-visual cross-cultural continuum differs from the high context-low context continuum in that the former involves mass-mediated forms of communication and the latter is more commonly associated with face-to-face interpersonal communication. This continuum focuses on how messages differ with regard to usage of highly visual mass-mediated forms or in relation to the absence of such forms.

Literal Communication Style ————————— Visual Communication Style

The Military Context

The previously described thoughts from William Perry regarding asymmetrical alliances were affirmed and developed by Secretary of State Madeleine Albright. "For me, the hardest part of whatever the United States is doing now . . . is the role of nonmilitary action" (Bollier, 2003, p. 15). Biddle and Long (2004) offer insights regarding paralleled considerations for how modern democratic societies, advanced technologically and otherwise, have inherent strengths. "We find that superior human capital, harmonious civil-military relations, and Western cultural background are largely responsible" as reasons for the superior performance of modern democracies in warfare (p. 525).

Sun Tzu, the ancient Chinese warfare theorist, stressed "Know the enemy, know yourself, and you can fight a hundred battles with no danger of defeat" (Zhou & Cui, 2007, p. 77). Though intercultural communication is not a battle it is essential to know both yourself and the target culture because such knowledge perpetuates better understanding. Similarly, one can see benefit in knowing your allies.

We learned that lesson during U.S. involvement in Vietnam in the 1960s. Roger DeCrow attested to this at that time when he wrote that technical advisors are "faced with monumental problems, not the least of which involves effective interpersonal relations with those foreign nationals with whom he deals" (DeCrow, 1969, p. 12). Fast-forward 40 years and one can hear echoes of the advice offered by DeCrow when he stressed the need for "warriors and leaders who know how to communicate with peoples from different cultures, who speak different languages, [and] who practice different customs . . ." (p. 29).

The focus on cultural variables is not limited to foreign cultures. Rather, it also gives consideration to military subcultures. For example, Keats conveys how military culture "may obstruct effective cross-cultural adaptation by promoting a hyper-masculinity that tends to oppose effective management of trauma" (Keats, 2010, p. 290). Similarly, in a Russian context, Poliakov found that military student subcultures "have a powerful influence on their values and behavior, and in some situations are more influential than the official, military culture" (Poliakov, 2011, p. 3).

In a more abstract vein, one can gain insight via reflection on the culture of war and how technology, as one variable, is impacting it. Joelien Pretorius considers this abstraction in "The Technological Culture of War." This phenomenon stresses examination of war as a societal institution. "An important step in this process is to understand the philosophical and cultural bases on which technology is employed as 'tools' of war" (Pretorius, 2008, p. 299).

Consideration of the role of technology within contemporary warfare is relevant, provocative, and timely, especially when one realizes how less technologically enhanced countries are missing out on these developments. Edward Sims discusses the benefits of using virtual humans in military training. "Digital virtual humans are used to represent not only the soldier, and the role-playing actors; but also a mentor . . ." (Sims, 2007, p. 75). The role of the mentor being to provide remediation in relation to language and culture.

It is easy to be lulled into a false sense of security if one sees new communication technologies as offering guarantees of success, however such transitions often result in gains that are made and unexpected problems. The comprehensive development of education could be jeopardized due to "reservations about the decline in reading whole books, in-depth sustained study, the dangers of electronic engagement, and development of character" (Walters & Kop, 2009, p. 284).

A closer look at the impact of new communication technologies reveals potential gains and losses. ICT (Information & Communication Technologies) offer new variables for learning contexts. "We are still exploring and developing the unique characteristics of ICT that enable learners to make and communicate meaning in new modes of expression" (Loveless, 2000, p. 346). It is easy to assume that "new" equates with better, but history is replete with examples of how such an assumption is simply wishful thinking. We may very well find that, although advanced societies often enjoy technological enhancements, there are benefits to being less technologically enhanced. For instance, "participants schooled in constructivist approaches may gain more understanding of the thinking and behaviors of participants from objectivist backgrounds" (Benbunan-Fich & Stoever, 2003, p. 22).

Access to digital technologies can provide observable benefits and have direct effects as has been alluded to thus far. That is, those nations equipped with digital technologies can have marked advantage regarding the employment of weaponry for winning battles. However, such usage can also have subtle effects that are equally compelling, that are not readily observable but make their impact known over time. One such example that will be illustrated has to do with how the increased emphasis on visual imagery over literal messages that is inherent with new communication technologies has implication for how consumers process information. Most relevant in this regard is that critical thinking skills are negatively impacted.

New Communication Technologies and the Increased Emphasis on Visual Imagery over Literal Messages

This illustration offers speculations with regard to the increased emphasis on visual imagery over literal messages as they relate to U.S. Army cultural initiatives in varied contexts. Such speculations are based on fundamental assumptions. Historically, common cultural variables have focused on race (typically linked to physical features) and ethnicity (typically linked to cultural practices). As we move to being a more visually oriented society via web-based and new communication technologies, literal forms of communication (i.e., the spoken and written word), that generally have more emphasis on critical thinking, are being displaced by the visual domain that stresses more imaginary associations. Thus, the visual dominates at the expense of the literal and the imagination presides over critical thinking.

Much Army cultural education is conveyed via visually oriented technologies. For example, this occurs with web-based instruction and, to a lesser degree but still substantial, with materials used in traditional classrooms. Therefore familiarity with this phenomenon will benefit those seeking to enhance Army cultural understanding in that increased emphasis on the visual domain results in dilution of critical thinking about cultural variables when visual images have significant impact upon the development of such cultural awareness.

A central premise with the aforementioned position is that, as we proceed through stages of the information age, there has been an increased emphasis on visual messages at the expense of literal messages. For instance, the Internet technologies are more visual than literal and this has refashioned our rhetorical grammar in subtle ways. These changes do not occur suddenly without warning. Rather, they fade into reality little by little, day by day. One can periodically assess the progression of various phenomena and see commensurate developments related to this increased emphasis on the visual, the decreased relevance of the literal, and a series of side effects related to this evolution.

Access to digital technologies does not happen in a vacuum. That is, soldiers typically use them on the job, off the job, and throughout their daily functioning, so such exposure is often omnipresent. This access results in us needing to consider the whole person and the cultural context within which he/she functions. Thus, we will focus on situations in the U.S. culture overall to illustrate phenomena that are relevant for those working with Army cultural programming. In doing so we will draw from examples in mass-media in general, but are particularly sensitive to Internet-based domains that impact the development of cultural understanding within formal education constructs and in society overall.

In *Digitizing Race: Visual Cultures of the Internet*, Lisa Nakamura (2008) stresses "experiences of the image are now defined by their mediation by machines. The Internet is a visual technology . . ." (p. 202), and she goes on to stress how the distribution of visual capital should be judiciously monitored in that "it must be negotiated and at times actively seized by those to whom it would otherwise not be given" (pp. 206–207). Thus, meanings evolve through a process of negotiation and renegotiation. As such, consumers of mass-mediated messages are active participants with the creation of meanings associated with such messages via interpretive processes. "Meaning is not 'received' in a unidirectional flow from elsewhere: the audience creates and recreates it" (Hansen, 2008, p. 111). Hansen goes on to use advertising as an illustration by stressing "advertisers have to tap the reservoirs of social and cultural knowledge maintained by audiences, and transform this material into the message" (p. 111).

A key premise in this process is that technology is not neutral. In *The Vanishing Word: The Veneration of Visual Imagery in the Postmodern World*, Arthur Hunt (2003) states, "When Johann Gutenberg introduced moveable type in the fifteenth century, a whole new world opened up—liberty, freedom, discovery, democracy" (p. 14). Hunt contrasts the founding days of U.S. culture with the present day and his findings underscore the importance of pictures. "The image has replaced modernism's dependency on the written word" (Hunt, 2003, p. 189). He stresses that this scenario should give us reason to worry. "Images have a way of pushing rational discourse—linear logic—into the background.

. . . Reason is replaced by emotion" (Hunt, 2003, p. 21). The matter of emotion replacing reason is a central idea supporting this illustration.

Similarly, the role of visual images has had a growing impact on the evolution of U.S. foreign policy. In the early 1990s the visual depictions of dead U.S. military personnel, who'd been killed by bands of militants in Somalia, being dragged (practically naked) through the streets among cheering crowds had a vivid impact on the U.S. public

OlegD/Shutterstock.com

mind. The damage was swift, broad, and deep. A reticence regarding U.S. intervention in the region was quickly manifested at numerous levels of U.S. foreign policy goals and objectives.

The revelations exposed in the photographs of the interrogation techniques used in Iraq by U.S. military personnel in 2004 underscores the potent impact of visual images in affecting the direction of U.S. foreign policy. **Rhetorical meanings** are presented on a variety of levels (logical, emotional, spiritual, etc.) that are subject to interpretation, with varying degrees of intensity, by the world community. There are high degrees of political representation in this phenomenon, and corresponding high degrees of relevance, in that the negativity of such visual images can easily be interpreted by all segments of the world community without regard for interpretive sophistication. Again, the damage is swift, broad, and deep.

Matheson and Allan, in *Digital War Reporting* (2009), stress "What distinguishes war imagery in a digital culture is the speed with which such images are transferred" (p. 147). They explain that this type of conveyance results in a unique type of visual genre whereby a single image can evolve through a series of interpretations and meanings. As such, pictures can be "trophies of war one moment, entertainment the next, then pornography and finally evidence of the 'truth' of war. . . ." (p. 147).

The channel through which such images are conveyed is a factor that is gaining more prominence. The Internet makes associations that allow us to grasp "the possibility of a future where there is some degree of liberation from the stranglehold of narrow conglomerate media" (Gross, Katz, & Ruby, 2003, p. 20). This phenomenon points to evolving realities with interactive channels of communication. "The Web allows audiences to explore and react, to interact, in ways that were either infeasible or not easily achieved. . . ." (Gross et al., 2003, p. 21).

One can observe many examples of such images that have lasting negative impressions on the world stage. Reynolds and Barnett (2003), in a book chapter titled "America

Under Attack: CNN's Verbal and Visual Framing of September 11," stress visual images "lack explicit prepositional syntax . . . a viewer's ability to make sense of a series of images is based on other cues" (p. 88). They exemplify other such cues as being how images are edited, framed, and presented contextually for viewing (p. 89).

The aforementioned CNN illustration conveys a negative finding with regard to visual (and verbal) messages. At the same time, there are neutral and positive images that are conveyed as well. For instance, the affluence reflected in the U.S. standard of living is a common "soft" message that is consistently perceived visually around the world. The consumer of such messages may be looking at an advertisement for American toothpaste, but the lifestyle of those Americans (and their station in life) is interpreted as well. These are subtle visual images. Nothing needs to be explained.

The aforementioned phenomena are more common and more vivid as we experience continued growth of the new communication technologies via the growth of the Internet (which is a visual platform for meaning conveyance often at the expense of our literal understanding). The explosive growth of Internet media has further underscored the increased relevance of the visual messages in comparison to literal messages. The Internet, in its present form, is primarily a **visual domain**. It is an advanced illustration of how "the eyes have it" and the overall impact of this shift has yet to be fully understood.

It is from the aforementioned points that those working with Army cultural programming can stand with regard to stressing awareness of the visual versus literal challenge. Derek Gregory (2010), in "American Military Imaginaries and Iraqi Cities: The Visual Economies of Globalizing War," explains how, in 2004, Major General Robert Scales stressed cultural sensitivity should be "given a higher priority than the technical fix of smart bombs, unmanned aircraft and expansive bandwidth" (p. 72). Twelve months later the shift in emphasis resulted in publication of the Army Field Manual on Counterinsurgency (FM 3–24). This new type of doctrine "defined the population as the center of gravity. This required not only cultural knowledge . . . but also immersion in the people" (Gregory, 2010, p. 73). That is, emphasis was stressed on being part of the Iraqi cultural framework rather than being detached observers from separate U.S. military installations.

Conclusion

Our understanding of the common ground that exists among global engagement, cultural boundaries, and the literal-visual cross-cultural continuum is enhanced via Army cultural education practices. They can benefit students by stressing the aforementioned emphasis on critical thinking skills when students are exposed to visual images that impact the cultural understanding/awareness/expertise progression. That is, consumers of such visual images should consistently consider how such exposure impacts the formation of their cultural understanding, and subsequent functioning, and how faulty reasoning and assumptions can be detrimental to that process. Similarly, when critical thinking is applied and valid cultural understanding conclusions are reached, then students can confidently proceed in their work with that awareness.

These processes involve addressing many abstractions and thinking through many assumptions. It is not a clear path and there are many detours. It is an approach that will be distinctly unique for each individual in that each individual builds upon a unique frame of reference. It is from this context that we can seek to chart a way forward via recommendations for steps to assess and adjust teaching methods, and modifications with course content for future cultural education and training. This should include focus on U.S. troops and the allies we will be working with and consideration should be given to how the digital disparity among such nations will impact our working together.

There will be concrete realities and vague nuances within this context. It will not fully resolve the challenges posed but it will help to identify and better understand the challenges. The awareness gained via such identification and enhanced understanding can serve as a framework for more fully working toward resolution of these challenges. This report is intended as a contribution to that fund of enhanced understanding.

Discussion Questions

1. Why is it important for the U.S. Army to be concerned about cross-cultural understanding with our military allies?
2. Some of the allied nations the U.S. works with have militaries that do not have access to the new communication technologies that the U.S. military does. How does this affect the ability of the U.S. to work closely with such third world allies?
3. How does the literal-visual cross-cultural continuum pose a challenge for the U.S. military in their work with third world allies who have less communication technology capability?
4. What steps can the U.S. military take to improve functional working relationships with third world allies?
5. In what ways might third world allies, who have far fewer communication technology innovations at their disposal, be superior in relation to their U.S. counterparts?

References

Benbunan-Fich, R. P., & Stoever, W. H. (2003). Using information technology to promote multi-cultural case teaching: A pedagogical framework. *Journal of Teaching in International Business, 14*(2/3), 13–27.

Biddle, S. C., & Long, S. T. (2004). Democracy and military effectiveness: A deeper look. *Journal of Conflict Resolution, 48*(4), 525–546.

Bollier, D. R. (2003). *The rise of Netpolitik: How the Internet is changing international politics and diplomacy*. Washington, DC: The Aspen Institute.

DeCrow, R. (1969). *Cross cultural interaction skills: A digest of recent training literature.* Syracuse, NY: ERIC Clearinghouse on Adult Education.

Gregory, D. O. (2010). American military imaginaries and Iraqi cities: The visual economies of globalizing war. In C. D. Lindner (Ed.), *Globalization, violence and the visual culture of cities.* New York, NY: Routledge Press.

Gross, L. E., Katz, J. T., & Ruby, J. S. (2003). *Image ethics in the digital age.* Minneapolis, MN: University of Minnesota Press.

Hansen, A. W. (2008). *Mass communication research methods.* Thousand Oaks, CA: Sage.

Hecht, M. A. (1989). The Cultural Dimensions of Nonverbal Communication. In M. U. Asante & W. N. Gudykunst (Eds.), *Handbook of International and Intercultural Communication.* Newbury Park, CA: Sage.

Hunt, A. K. (2003). *The vanishing word: The veneration of visual imagery in the postmodern world.* Wheaton, IL: Crossway Books.

Keats, P. A. (2010). "Soldiers working internationally: Impacts of masculinity, military culture, and operational stress on cross-cultural adaptation," *International Journal of Advanced Counseling, 32,* 290–303.

Loveless, A. K. (2000). Where do you stand to get a good view of pedagogy? *Journal of Technology and Teacher Education, 8*(4), 337–349.

Matheson, D., & Allan, S. (2009). *Digital war reporting.* Malden, MA: Polity Press.

Nakamura, L. N. (2008). *Digitizing race: Visual cultures of the Internet.* Minneapolis, MN: University of Minnesota Press.

Poliakov, R. I. (2011). The barracks subculture of military school students. *Russian Education and Society, 53*(2), 3–11.

Pretorius, J. N. (2008). The technological culture of war. *Technology & Society, 28*(4), 299–305.

Reynolds, A. T., & Barnett, B. J. (2003). America under attack: CNN's verbal and visual framing of September 11. In S. V. Chermak, F. G. Bailey, & M. C. Brown (Eds.), *Media Representations of September 11.* Westport, CT: Praeger Press.

Sims, E. S. (2007). Reusable, lifelike virtual humans for mentoring and role-playing. *Computers and Education, 49,* 75–92.

Takai, T. Q. (2012). Department of Defense Mobile Device Strategy. Washington, DC: Department of Defense.

Walters, P. D., & Kop, R. K. (2009). Heidegger, digital technology, and postmodern education: From being in cyberspace to meeting on MySpace. *Bulletin of Science, Technology & Society, 29*(4), 278–286.

Zhou, B. Y., & Cui, F. L. (2007). On the promotion of intercultural communication competence. *Sino-US English Teaching, 4*(9), Serial No. 45, 75–87.

27.   Global Engagement for the Greater Good?

Christine L. North, Ph.D., MPH

Kellan and Peter Go Abroad

Kellan and Peter, stuffed backpacks pulling on their shoulders, lugged their suitcases loaded with their own clothing and donations up to the check-in counter at the airlines. They had worked hard to save the money and gather the donations to participate in this volunteer trip to Nicaragua to work with children in an impoverished community. They were working with an organization that provided a number of services to communities that had little financial means and few resources available to them. This organization would come into a community and provide medical clinics, basic health education, and assist with some necessary infrastructure or construction aid that the community might need. The individuals who came to help were often from universities or church groups who wanted an opportunity to travel and to give back to the world in some way—to make a difference in the lives of others. Kellan and Peter were Spanish majors at the same Midwestern American university and felt like this two-week trip would be an excellent way to improve their language skills while giving to those who were less fortunate than they were. They decided that they would enjoy working with the children in this particular village.

Kellan and Peter learned about this aid organization at a study abroad fair at their local university. The representative at the table had a number of materials, photos, and videos of past groups of travelers showing the work that was being done in the communities and explaining how the program worked. Kellan and Peter would each pay $2,800 for their two-week excursion. This cost would cover airfare, lodging, and food. There were ample translators available to help the team with the work that they were doing, and the tour representative assured Kellan and Peter that without the generous help of volunteers like the university students at their school, the people in these communities would continue to suffer. The pictures looked inviting. The children were smiling and having a great time with the aid workers in the villages. Aid workers were being hosted in the homes of the local villagers sharing coffee and meals. The meals looked amazingly delicious. The rainforest was beautiful, with exotic flowers, parrots, and beautiful Caribbean blue seas and sandy shores. Kellan and Peter were convinced that this was what they wanted to do—to make such a difference for people who had so little in a place that was so beautiful.

Filled with excitement, they boarded the plane and finally arrived in Nicaragua. After a four-hour bus ride on an old school bus on dirt roads, they finally arrived in the village where they would be working, the students piled off the bus with 22 other North Americans from all over the United States and Canada. Kellan and Peter had already started making friends with the 10 other American college students from other universities who were also spending part of their summers in Nicaragua. The team was nowhere near the beach, but the scenery in the mountains was gorgeous, nonetheless. They were ready for their first day and anxious to see what kind of difference they could make.

The first day was a bit chaotic as they made their way from the hostel-like accommodations where they were staying into the community where they would be working. They arrived in town, and began to set up the medical clinic in the local school. There was already a line of people waiting to see a doctor or dentist as soon as the clinic was ready. Part of the group was working to build additional classrooms for the two-room school building that was dramatically too small for the 85+ students who attended school there. And another part of the team was working with the children on basic elementary skills and team-building skills. Kellan and Peter were excited to start working with the children and using the Spanish skills they had been acquiring for the past three years at their university. The children swarmed around the "Americanos," excited to see what they had brought. Kellan and Peter tried talking to them, but much to their frustration, the children did not seem to understand what they were saying. And Kellan and Peter could not understand the students, either. The whole day had left the two college students frustrated, but they chalked it up to it just being the first day.

Day after day passed with many of the same frustrations. Before long, the two weeks had passed and it was time to head back to the U.S. As they sat next to each other in the airport waiting to board the plane and then on the flight home, Kellan and Peter were reflecting on their trip and their time in Nicaragua.

"Y'know, this trip really wasn't quite what I expected," said Kellan. "I mean I learned a lot and got to see some cool things, but I don't think I really made much of a difference here in this community. I thought

Anton_Ivanov/Shutterstock.com

my Spanish was pretty good, but heck, I couldn't even hardly talk to the people, let alone understand them! I was better at the end of two weeks, but by the time I was beginning to get the hang of talking to them, it was time to pack up and head home."

"I know what you mean," Peter answered. "I know that the day I got to help build the school rooms, I wondered what we were all doing here. There were three locals here who kept following along with us fixing the mistakes and helping us lay block. None of us are block layers. We really weren't prepared to come down here and do this kind of work. I think we actually slowed down the guys who knew what they were doing—as if we were in their way more than being a help to them. I guess our money helps to buy supplies and all, but think how much further our money would have gone if it hadn't bought our plane tickets and paid for our food and lodging."

Kellan continued, "But I did get to experience things that made a huge impression on me. I just don't know. The kids were great, and all the village people seemed really happy that we were there. But we didn't get the school finished. And the lady who had the broken arm—who will follow up with her now that our little clinic is gone? I just have such mixed feelings. Who knew that this trip could be so complicated? I have *a lot* of thinking to do about what I experienced this summer."

Volunteer Tourism

Trips such as the one taken by Kellan and Peter involve global engagement, and one type of global engagement that is becoming increasingly popular is volunteer tourism or **voluntourism.** Voluntourism is a combination of travel for the purposes of both pleasure and volunteering (Seymour, Benzian, & Kalendarian, 2013). Having the opportunity to volunteer and provide service in some other part of the world began as part of the gap year phenomena in Great Britain, Australia, and Europe, where young adults take a year off between high school and college to travel. During that year of travel, many choose to engage in some type of volunteer service, such as working in a biological reserve, volunteering in an orphanage, or volunteering in a school in another country, perhaps teaching English (Alexander, 2012; Ouma & Dimaras, 2013; Wearing & McGehee, 2013). One 2008 study estimated that 1.6 million people were participating in volunteer tourism projects on an annual basis and that these volunteer tourists were spending more than £ 832m ($1.35 billion U.S.) annually (Wearing & McGehee, 2013). Clearly, this industry is far more than a mere "fad" or "trend" among recently graduated high school and college students today.

As a form of global engagement, volunteer tourism seems like a win-win situation for both the volunteer and for the individuals being helped. However, the situation is not quite so simple. As Kellan and Peter noticed in their volunteer experiences, the best intentions do not always yield the best outcomes.

There has been a fair amount of research examining the impact of volunteer travel on both the vol-

Lakeview Images/Shutterstock.com

unteers as well as on the communities being visited. For the volunteers, the experiences are often mixed, as they were for the student travelers in the story above. Most volunteer travelers engage in these activities because they genuinely hope to make a substantive difference in the world in some way. Other motivations for these trips include self-development, giving back to the host community, participating in community development activities, and increasing cultural understanding and relationships with those from other countries (McLennan, 2014; Palacios, 2010; Pluim & Jorgenson, 2012; Seymour et al., 2013; Watson, Siska, & Wolfel, 2013; Wearing & McGehee, 2013). While on the surface these motivations seem positive, Seymour et al. (2013) note that "these motivations are extremely short-sighted, are mostly fulfilling self-interests, and are violating principles of professionalism" (p. 1253).

Palacios (2010) also cites additional potential pitfalls of voluntourism when he writes that many times volunteer opportunities "do not seem to encourage critical reflections about poverty, where foreign interests are prioritized over local ones" (p. 861). He also is concerned that the tourists receive more benefits than the people who are receiving the volunteers. One area of significant concern has to do with sending unskilled and unprepared volunteers to places to do skilled work. As Peter noted in the above story, he was not at all skilled to be laying block while volunteering in Nicaragua. Such experiences are common among volunteers. This experience is especially notable among those volunteers who travel to assist in orphanages or residential childcare facilities. Often seen as some of the most desirable types of volunteer placement experiences, these volunteering experiences can be some of the most damaging of all.

As so poignantly articulated by Reas (2013), children in orphanages and residential care facilities are often "objectified as adorable innocents, waiting to be loved by enthusiastic westerners" (p. 121). Volunteers rarely understand fully how those children came to be at the facility or what the backgrounds of the children really are. Volunteers often cite the most important needs of the children as being "love and affection," while teaching and education are viewed as important ways for children to be able to move forward and succeed in life. Most volunteers who go to orphanages talk about how cute the children are and how the children are living in such difficult circumstances, and yet are so happy and upbeat.

The problem is that what volunteers report and see is not the reality of life for these children. According to Punaks (2014) from Next Generation Nepal (NGN), Nepal has over 800 registered children's homes—and many more that are unregistered. Of these registered homes, over 90% are located in the top three tourist areas of Nepal, yet there are probably not statistically more orphans in tourist regions than other regions! At least two out of three of the children residing in these facilities has at least one living parent and is not truly an orphan. Some children are sent to these homes because parents are promised that their children will receive an education. Other children are simply taken from their families to fill the homes.

Volunteering in an orphanage is easy in Nepal. Flyers hang in cafes throughout the region advertising fulfilling experiences working with these children. The volunteers who do go to these facilities have had no background checks, are not trained in education or teaching, and cannot speak the language. What skills and abilities have prepared them to work in these facilities with these children? In some cases, children are being taken from their families and placed in "for profit" facilities that make these children look destitute and desperate so that tourists will feel pity and donate even more money or to fill orphanages to satisfy the demand for tourists seeking volunteer opportunities (NGN, 2014).

In recent years, there have been a number of publications, social media movements, and media publications trying to publicize the issues associated with voluntourism in orphanages, as well as the issues associated with voluntourism in general. One such effort has been launched by SafeChildnc.org, an effort by Friends International with the backing of UNICEF, to stop orphanage tourism in Cambodia (Safechildnc.org, n.d.). SafeChild has a Facebook page with over 3,500 Likes and continues to grow. NGN is also working to educate tourists about orphanage tourism and issues involved to stop the exploitation of these children. This organization's goal is to reconnect children and families that have been separated because of war or child trafficking (NGN, 2014). Other sites focused on academics and universities have echoed these concerns (see Globalsl.org, 2014) as a way to educate and help create awareness among well-meaning travelers.

The issues for children in these facilities are many. First, separation from the family of origin is a cause of great distress for children, especially when their parents are still living (Punaks, 2014; SafeChildnc.org, n.d.). Such stress has been shown to have lasting effects on brain function as well as psychosocial effects on the children (Cohen et al., 2013). When children are spending time with volunteers, they often get very attached to these individuals and then are left with feelings of abandonment when the volunteer leaves, never to return, after a week or a month, creating additional stress in their lives (Hartman, 2014). Children in orphanages suffer from developmental issues, adjustment issues after leaving the orphanage, and do not achieve as well in school (The St. Petersburg-USA Orphanage Research Team, 2008). All of these issues have come to the attention of many national governments, and as a result, countries are actually trying to move away from the residential care model for children. However, the demand placed by volunteers who want to work with orphans has created pressure to maintain orphanages and for unregistered orphanages to begin operations (UNAIDS, UNICEF, & USAID, 2004).

Global Engagement

While voluntourism clearly has ethical and other challenges associated with it, global engagement is still beneficial for students. As Graf (2004) states, "[e]xplosive growth in globalization has led to a growing number of individual with international assignments" (p. 1124). As a result, she concludes, "the concept of inter-cultural competence has become increasingly important . . ." (p. 1124). Engaging in cross-cultural experiences can be done in responsible, ethical, and sustainable ways that provide students with an opportunity to engage in the critical thinking and inter-cultural experiences necessary to gain inter-cultural or **cross-cultural competence.**

Cultural competence has been defined in a number of different ways. Hammer (2004) defines it as "the capacity to generate perceptions and adapt behavior to cultural context" (p. 2). Others provide similar definitions that emphasize both perception and appropriate behavior as part of cultural competence. One model taken from the realm of public health is the process of cultural competence developed by Campinha (1999). This model states that cultural competence is comprised of five parts: cultural awareness, cultural knowledge, cultural skill, cultural encounters, and cultural desire. When taken together, the individual has the opportunity to demonstrate the greatest degree of cultural competence.

Let's examine each of these five components separately and see how they work together to create cultural competence. **Cultural awareness** is a person's ability to look at another culture and be sensitive to the beliefs, values, mode of life, and problem solving methods of that other culture, while at the same time acknowledging one's own prejudices and stereotypes about another culture. Since most people tend to be **ethnocentric** (judging another culture using one's own as the basis against which we measure and judge), we often view other cultures as being strange or "wrong" in the way they do things. Being culturally aware is noticing the differences and recognizing that the values, beliefs, and behaviors of another culture are not "wrong," but just different.

Cultural knowledge is the active learning about another culture and the way that culture operates. When gaining cultural knowledge, we look at how the other culture's **worldview**—the way the culture views human nature, what happens after death, the meaning of life, good and evil, whether there is one truth or multiple truths, etc. Cultural knowledge also involves learning about the foods, government, economies, family lifestyles, religions, and leisure activities of a culture.

Cultural skill involves using cultural awareness and cultural knowledge to craft communication messages that are appropriate for the cultural context. Culturally competent individuals are able to adjust their skills for the different cultures with which they interact. Sometimes a person encounters a new culture before having a chance to obtain much cultural knowledge. At this point, the individual may struggle because of a lack of cultural skill.

Cultural encounters are the experiences that we have with people who are not from our own cultures. These individuals may be from another country or simply from another **co-culture** (a co-existing culture within our own country) like the inner city, another racial group, or a different religious group. Cultural encounters allow us to examine our own cultural awareness, gain cultural knowledge, and practice cultural skills. Without these cultural encounters, becoming culturally competent is virtually impossible.

Cultural desire is just what it says—a desire to engage with others culturally and to truly know and understand their cultural lives and how they differ from one's own. Individuals who possess cultural desire have the motivation to seek out cultural encounters so that they are able to engage in the process of gaining cultural competence. Cultural competence takes work. Without that motivation, becoming truly culturally competent rarely occurs.

Individuals living in today's world will increasingly be working and interacting with people from different cultures and backgrounds. According to the U.S. Census (2010), minority populations will increase to 48% of the total U.S. population by 2050 and the Hispanic population will comprise 24.4% of the total population. Additionally, today's workers have a greater chance than ever before of being assigned to a work position outside the borders of their native countries, and that trend continues to grow as globalization grows (Graf, 2004). Being culturally competent is now an essential skill for individuals engaging in today's society.

As Kellan and Peter learned on their trip to Nicaragua, there is a great deal involved in becoming culturally competent and prepared to engage with others from another culture. Language and location are only two factors involved in learning to engage and interact with other cultures. Much more is necessary. Kellan and Peter certainly had the right idea in trying to expand their horizons and gaining intercultural experiences that would help provide cultural education and sensitivity that is more difficult to come by in one's own home country. While their experience was not as beneficial as they had hoped, there are plenty of ways to become globally engaged and grow one's own cultural sensitivity.

A study of employers done by the Association of American Colleges and Universities (AAC&U) reports that 45% of employers believe that recent graduates are "not well prepared" as global citizens, and 76% believe that promoting intercultural competence as a learning outcome is critical (AAC&U, 2006). Study abroad opportunities and cultural exchange opportunities focused on educating visitors about another culture rather than placing individuals as aid workers can be excellent ways to expose people to different cultures in the world. Having international experiences and cultural encounters have been shown to positively correlate with cultural awareness and cultural knowledge, but cultural skill and cultural desire are not always directly impacted by the study abroad or travel experience (Feast, Collyer-Braham, & Bretag, 2011; Varela & Gatlin-Watts, 2014). Having opportunities to interact with locals to learn the cultural behaviors and skills is an important part of becoming culturally competent. Spending more than a few days and venturing outside of one's comfort zone to experience a culture from the native's perspective helps one to learn the skills. One's desire is an internal motivation to achieve competence. Engaging in internships, living with host families, and taking classes at foreign universities can be excellent ways to immerse oneself to learn how to become more culturally sensitive. The more culturally competent we are, the better equipped we are to be global citizens who engage across cultures within our own national boundaries and across countries.

Discussion Questions

1. In what ways is international volunteering potentially damaging to those being served?
2. Why is cultural competence crucial for engaging in any kind of international service or aid?
3. Is voluntourism an economically viable business model to benefit those in the countries being visited?
4. What alternatives might exist in place of short-term volunteer missions abroad?
5. How can cross-cultural communication help prevent unintended consequences associated with voluntourism or short-term missions?
6. Why is cultural competence important to be an effective global citizen?

References

Alexander, Z. (2012). International volunteer tourism experience in South Africa: An investigation into the impact on the tourist. *Journal of Hospitality Marketing & Management, 21*, 779–799.

Association of American Colleges and Universities (AAC&U). (2006, December 28). *How should colleges prepare students to succeed in today's global economy?* Retrieved from http://www.aacu.org/sites/default/files/files/LEAP/2007_full_report_leap.pdf

Campinha-Bocate, J. (1999). A model and instrument for addressing cultural competence in health care. *Journal of Nursing Education, 38*(5), 203–207.

ChildSafe.Org. (n.d.). *About.* Retrieved from www.Safechildnc.org

Cohen, M. M., Jing, D., Yang, R. R., Tottenham, N., Lee, F. S., & Casey, B. S. (2013). Early-life stress has persistent effects on amygdala function and development in mice and humans. *Proceedings of the National Academy of Sciences of the United States of America, 110*, 18274–18278. doi:10.1073/pnas.1310163110

Feast, V., Collyer-Braham, S., & Bretag, T. (2011). Global experience: The development and preliminary evaluation of a programme designed to enhance students' global engagement. *Innovations in Education and Teaching International, 48*, 239–250. doi:10.1080/14703297.2011.593701

Graf, A. (2004). Screening and training inter-cultural competencies: Evaluating the impact of national culture on inter-cultural competencies. *International Journal of Human Resource Management, 15*, 1124–1148. doi:10.1080/09585190410001677340

Globalsl.org (2014).

Hammer, M. R. (2004). Assessment of the impact of the AFS study abroad experience. Retrieved from https://idiinventory.com/wpcontent/uploads/2014/02/afs_study.pdf

Hartman, Eric. (2014, September 5). *RE: Why UNICEF and Save the Children are against you caring for orphans.* [Web log post]. Retrieved from http://globalsl.org/why-unicef-and-save-the-children-are-against-you-caring-for-orphans/

McLennan, S. (2014). Medical voluntourism in Honduras: 'Helping' the poor? *Progress in Development Studies, 14,* 163–179. doi:10.1177/1464993413517789

Next Generation Nepal. (2014). *Orphanage trafficking and orphanage tourism: Frequently asked questions.* Retrieved from https://www.google.com/l?sa=t&rct=j&q=&esrc=s&source=web&cd=1&ved=0CB4QFjAA&url=http%3A%2F%2Fwww.nextgenerationnepalorg%2FFile%2FNext-Generation-Nepal_FAQs-on-Orphanage-Trafficking-and-Orphanage-Voluntourism.pdf&ei=ThYXVKLxPIWpyATh3oLACg&usg=AFQjCNFHjYSSp1uxL7V7UKzAa_LKhU1EOQ&sig2= AVNKlracYE1vkVgdLzPKnQ&cad=rja

Ouma, B. D. O., & Dimaras, H. (2013). Views from the global south: Exploring how student volunteers from the global north can achieve sustainable impact in global health. *Globalization and Health, 9.* Retrieved from http://www.globalizationandhealth.com/content/9/1/32

Palacios, C. M. (2010). Volunteer tourism, development and education in a postcolonial world: Conceiving global connections beyond aid. *Journal of Sustainable Tourism, 18,* 861–878. doi:10.1080/09669581003782739

Pluim, G. W. J., & Jorgenson, S. R. (2012). A reflection on the broader, systemic impacts of youth volunteer programmes: A Canadian perspective. *Intercultural Education, 23,* 25–38. doi:10.1080/14675986.2012664751

Punaks, M. (2014, June). Presentation at Better Care Better Volunteering Workshop. London, England. June 17–18, 2014.

Reas, P. J. (2013). 'Boy, have we got a vacation for you': Orphanage tourism in Cambodia and the commodification and objectification of the orphaned child. *Thammasat Review, 16.*

Seymour, B., Benzian, H., & Kalendarian E. (2013). Voluntourism and global health: Preparing dental students for responsible engagement in international programs. *Journal of Dental Education, 77*(10), 1252–1257.

The St. Petersburg-USA Research Team. (2008). The effects of early social-emotional and relational development of young orphanage children. *Monographs of the Society for Research in Child Development, 73*(3), 1–264.

UNAIDS, UNICEF, & USAID. (2004). Children on the brink 2004: A joint report of new orphan estimates and a framework for action. Washington, DC: Population, health and nutrition information project for United States Agency for International Development.

U.S. Census Bureau. (2010, November 30). *Quick facts.* Retrieved from http://www.census.gov/quickfacts/table/PST045214/00 Varela, O. E., & Gatlin-Watts, R. (2014). The development of the global manager: An empirical study on the role of academic international sojourns. *Academy of Management Learning and Education, 13,* 187–207. doi:10.5465/amle.2012.0289

Watson, J. R., Siska, P., & Wolfel, R. L. (2013). Assessing gains in language proficiency, cross-cultural competence, and regional awareness during study abroad: A preliminary study. *Foreign Language Annals, 46,* 62–79. doi:10.1111/fla.1216

Wearing, S., & McGehee, N. G. (2013). Volunteer tourism: A review. *Tourism Management, 38,* 120–130. doi:10.1016/j.tourman.2013.03.002

28. Understanding Cultures: Bridging the Communication Gap

Abhijit Sen, Ph.D.

In this chapter we will try to understand the process of intercultural communication and how communication between cultures can be facilitated. What is culture? Many scholars have tried to define the term, but it is one of those elusive concepts about society and the arts that have been variously defined by scholars from different fields. From an anthropological perspective, culture refers to the patterns of beliefs and values found in artifacts, objects, and institutions that are passed down through the generations (Berger, 1995). From a sociological perspective, culture is to be found in patterns embodied in the social traditions related to the knowledge, ideas, beliefs, values, standards, and sentiments of the group (Fairchild, 1967). Kottak (1987), on the other hand, says that culture is shaped by sharing of symbols and language, and learned behavior and beliefs that are transmitted across the generations. Every society has a culture, but there are considerable differences in cultures found in nations and societies all over the world. Human culture often involves the creation, transmission, and use of symbols. Humans are able to do this because we create and use symbols that convey to the rest of the society shared ideas developed and built by humans. These shared ideas are symbolically mediated or expressed orally that contain intrinsic meanings, and it is these meanings that make up a culture. When we talk about a culture we may talk about the meaning of a dress style, code of behavior, a scenic place, language, a system of belief, architectural style, etc. So, symbols take on infinite forms, and language, written and spoken, is full of symbols (Longhurst, Smith, Bagnall, & Crawford, 2008).

Intercultural communication becomes easier if there are common signs and symbols to which people can relate. The soccer ball appears to be a global symbol which a large percentage of the world's population seems to understand. The recent World Cup soccer championship in Brazil (2014) showed conclusively that the world can come together over a round leather ball and enjoy the competition as one without any malice or causing harm to the opponents. The leather ball becomes the global symbol for a global competition of the sport we call soccer. All nations in the world are allowed to take part in this championship, but only 32 teams make it to the final

Don Mammoser/Shutterstock.com

rounds through a process of elimination. The World Cup event takes place every four years, and any cultural and national differences between the competing nations are laid aside while the games are taking place.

Code Switching

Every culture or subculture has its own set of codes. A culture can be viewed as a "collection or system of codes," and codes vary from the universal to the local. Cultural codes are hidden in the sense that we are usually not aware of them, but they shape our behavior and mannerisms, and they typically deal with morals, cuisines, etiquettes, aesthetic sense, and so on. As Berger (1995) noted, we tend to be blind to the codes that we have learned from our family, schools, church, and other institutions because they seem obvious to us (Berger, 1995). As humans, we constantly "encode" and "decode" signs and symbols to get and create meanings. Codes differ from culture to culture and if we can move from one set of codes to the other, we are really "code switching," and as "code switchers," we become effective communicators in both or many cultures. The key phrase here is "code switching." If one can understand the nuances in communication it is possible to adjust to a new culture. Many people can "switch" from one cultural mode to another cultural mode within a matter of hours or even minutes. They can switch from talking to a person from their own culture to another person from a different culture or a subculture very swiftly. The people who can "code-switch" from one culture to another are most efficient and effective in their professional and personal interactions in any culture. So if a person knows, understands, and can translate codes of both the cultures, he/she can become an effective communicator, disseminator of information, and an impressive persuader.

Model of Intercultural Communication

To understand intercultural communication we may have to create a communication model to see the process. The "structural model of intercultural communication" does just that (Barnett & Rosen, 2007). There are individuals, groups, and institutions that serve as intermediaries between two cultures. They act as a liaison between cultures. They may be sojourners, tourists, educators, businessmen, diplomats, students, or military personnel who sometimes facilitate interactions between these disparate cultures. These individuals bring back information, ideas, anecdotes, mannerisms, language, and cultural artifacts from other cultures and share them with members of their own culture. Intercultural communication is about creating linkages between two or more cultures. Mass media, telecommunications, and the Internet provide the necessary linkages and connection for information and symbols that facilitate the mutual understanding between the cultures, to be transmitted efficiently and effectively. Also connecting people across different cultures are international governmental agencies like the United Nations (UN), International Monetary Fund (IMF), and the World Bank; non-governmental agencies (NGOs) like

Amnesty International, Oxfam, Greenpeace, etc.; and trans-national corporations like IBM, General Electric, etc. The connections between these institutions, corporations, and "multicultural individuals" have increased in number and frequency in recent years, resulting in a rapid globalization of communities, communication, and economy.

The new communications technology has aided in transmission and diffusion of values, ideas, opinions, and information amongst cultures. The new technology, including the Internet, compresses time and space, thus becoming a catalyst of globalization (Giddens, 1990; Robertson, 1990). According to some scholars, transborder communication has opened up cultural boundaries and initiated the process of "cultural convergence." This is also known as "cultural homogenization," where all cultures come to resemble each other in form, lifestyle, consumption, and ideology. Global communication is creating a global community with an increased homogenous culture, especially when it relates to political, economic, educational, and scientific activities, but less so for moral, religious, and philosophical ideas (Beyer, 1994; Robertson, 1992). Scholars say that information flow via the Internet may eventually facilitate the convergence of national cultures with a universal set of beliefs and values including their global identity (Barnett & Rosen, 2007). As for production of images, the United States holds the number one spot in terms of reach and penetration into cultures of the world. Many scholars conjecture that the Americanization of the global village has already resulted in the breakdown of traditional values and ways of life in many countries (Kamalipour, 1999, p. xxiii). We can strongly argue that the global village is indeed being Americanized. A popular sentiment among the Third World developing nations and also in a few developed nations like France and Canada is that the U.S. media conglomerates and their content have diluted the indigenous traditional cultures. Scholars indicate that the relentless process of cultural homogenization is now almost here making the world more Westernized and culturally uniform. As Kamalipour notes, "We now live in a world in which the physical boundaries between nations are becoming increasingly blurred" (Kamalipour, 1999, p. xxvii). The other side of "cultural homogenization" is a hybrid culture.

Hybrid Cultures

Ideas and cultural products from the dominant culture, mostly Western, sometimes get modified and translated, interpreted, and consumed in a local way, and in the process become something other than the original. Sometimes the dominant culture takes on the characteristics and traditions from the migrant cultures. This kind of "fusion" of styles and forms tends to create a hybridized culture and cultural forms. Musical genres become mainstream because of their widespread acceptance such as reggae from Jamaica; Shakespearean plays get interpreted differently in other cultures; Bollywood movies incorporate Western styles of dance choreography and music—all these exemplify hybrid cultural artifacts (Ogan, 2007).

When people belonging to a culture adapt cultural items or artifacts from another, they make these cultural forms and artifacts part of their own culture. This process of adaptation is called "hybridization" and even termed "glocalization" by some, since the finished cultural product may have lost its original attributes by fusion and incorporation of the other element. This fusion has been occurring in music for a long time, but with the international exchange of ideas and cultural products, hybrid forms are appearing in visual arts, films, culinary and food products, fashion, and festivals. Music has strong cultural ties and it evokes a strong emotional response from the listeners. "Hip Hop" and "Tejano" music conjures up specific ethnic groups but the music is not limited to any specific racial group. Hip Hop is increasingly popular worldwide and there are singers and musicians in China and Mongolia, hugely popular in their own countries, who try to emulate the style and mannerisms of famous American rappers. Music retains its cultural connotations, but because of digitization and the Internet this cultural exclusivity seems to be declining and more indicative of specific age groups than cultures around the world (Newsom, 2007). Now let's look at other ways of communicating with another culture.

Communication and Culture

Learning the language of foreign cultures helps in the communication process when one visits different countries. Language facilitates communication and there is nothing better than knowing language of that culture in order to build relationships, ask for directions, get more information, or even transact business deals. But there's more to communication than just language—your gestures, mannerisms, behavior, facial expressions, and all forms of non-verbal expressions and signs help to convey meanings to the people from other cultures. Sometimes the clothes that you wear and the color of your clothing can convey different meanings to the audiences of other cultures. In Italy, almost all churches require visitors to cover up the upper body and wear longer dresses to avoid exposing the limbs as a mark of respect to a place of worship. Short skirts and tank tops mostly worn by women are frowned upon. It's a religious norm, but a cultural one as well. Some cultures require women to be covered from head to toe, especially when going outside the house, as in most Islamic societies.

Non-verbal communication between people carries distinct cultural overtones. Customs, etiquettes, and behavior are often culturally defined and practiced. For example, in Hong Kong (China) people always hand over their business cards with both hands and it is considered disrespectful and rude to slide the card across the table to another person (Galloway, 2014). Touching a person when you don't personally know them is taboo in many Southeast Asian countries, especially in Thailand and Malaysia. One should not touch anyone's head, especially a child's, or pass things or food over the heads of people sitting at the dining table. The "head" is considered to be a sacred part of the body and the "seat of the soul," according to the Buddhist tradition. Touching is inappropriate even in informal settings, and this also applies to children. In London, there are unwritten rules followed by the subway riders: one is to avoid eye contact with fellow passengers, and the other is not to strike up a conversation with strangers in the train. As one Londoner points out, ". . . avoiding eye contact is the only way to preserve your sense of personal space" (Galloway, 2014, p. 1).

Colors have different meanings in different cultures. Cultures decode the meaning of a color in their own unique ways. We know that people wear black clothes during funerals here in the U.S., but it's the color white for funerals in India and China, the color purple in Brazil and Latin America, and red in Africa (Newsom, 2007). But what about numbers? An even number of flowers in a bouquet in Russia is for the dead. An odd number of flowers are given on happy occasions. In Russia, a bouquet should have one, three, five, or seven flowers to be deemed lucky. In China, the word "four" sounds very close to the word for death, so it is highly recommended that one should not give anything to anyone in China in fours. In Japan, the traditional wedding gift of cash should not be given in an amount which is divisible by two, because that signifies a marriage could end up in a divorce (Galloway, 2014).

Clothing and food also convey meanings to various audiences. There are fewer differences in clothes and dress nowadays because of the widespread use of Western styles, but there are still regional variations around the world especially in African, Arab, and some Asian regions. Clothing with head coverings are more prevalent mainly in Muslim societies, but orthodox Jewish men also cover their heads with traditional caps and hats; Indian women wear mostly saris (a 3-yard long piece of cloth), but young, modern Indian women prefer to wear Western style clothing than traditional styles. The universal dress code for the global young ones appears to be jeans and t-shirts (Newsom, 2007). As mentioned before, a few traditional societies and religious institutions require women to dress modestly and to "cover up" the exposed parts—these norms are enforced mostly for religious and moral reasons.

In bigger, cosmopolitan American cities food choices have grown exponentially. You can get Mexican, Jamaican, Lebanese, Brazilian, Italian, South Indian, Japanese, Chinese, Thai; you name it, you can get it. Food items are typical of a culture but even they undergo some modification—call it "hybridization"—to suit the taste of the local population. It is well known that Chinese food that we eat in American cities have undergone some alteration to the point that they taste different from Chinese food available on mainland China or even in the China Towns of various U.S. metropolitan cities. You can make out the authenticity of a Chinese restaurant by the number of Chinese customers who frequent those restaurants. This goes for all other ethnic restaurants. The "hybridized" Chinese food is now being exported back to China because of a large influx of Westerners, foreign tourists, and business people in China. On the reverse side, when Americans travel abroad, they see familiar brand names and logos on the main streets—KFC, McDonalds, Pizza Hut, Subway, Starbucks, etc. The menus, however, are not exactly the same as their American counterpart. A KFC in Bangalore or in Singapore may have some items that are different from those on the American menu. A manager at a McDonalds in Caracas,

Venezuela, said, "We can say that we always have clean restrooms and good coffee, wherever" (Newsom, 2007, p. 51). Food preparations and the dining experience in a restaurant serving food from another culture actually give some insight into that culture. But the question is how authentic will the experience be—is it 100% authentic or is it a "hybrid" experience?

Spatial Configurations in Cultures

Understanding the use of "space" and spatial distances also facilitates intercultural communication. The use of space differs from culture to culture. Proxemic patterns in cultures differ, and perceiving the world through different lenses leads to multiple definitions of what constitutes crowded living, interpersonal relationships, local and international politics, global business, and so on. There are significant differences in the way space is constructed around people, objects, and buildings in the German, English, French, Japanese, and Arab societies. The orderliness and hierarchical quality of German culture are communicated through the use of space. The English are differentiated by the social class into which they are born, while in the U.S. we use space as a way of classifying people and activities. The French, however, are accustomed to compact space as in crowded trains, buses, cafes, and also in their homes, and crowded living normally means high sensory involvement. In Japan, space and social organization are interrelated. The concept of a center that can be approached from any direction is a major factor in Japanese culture. Thus, the Japanese name the intersection of roads rather than the streets themselves. The entire experience of space in Japan is different from that of the Western culture. In the West, we perceive and react to the arrangements of objects and think of space as "empty." When we talk about space, we mean the distance between objects. The Japanese give meaning to spaces and arrangement of spaces, which they call "ma." The "ma" is a basic building block in all Japanese spatial experiences (Hall, 1969). Arabs, on the other hand, like to deal with people at close proximity. They seem to come very close when talking to other people and "smell" the persons with whom they are communicating. To the Arabs,

chungking/Shutterstock.com

good smells are very appealing and congenial, so smelling nice presents a good image of the person. Arabs apparently look at each other in a manner that often seems hostile or challenging to Americans (Hall, 1969).

Advertising and Culture

Cultural products often are embedded with ideological values. Ideology, as Berger explains, is a systematic and comprehensive set of ideas that explain to people why and how things happen in social and political life justifying the status quo (Berger, 1995). Ideology is a belief system that explains the power structure of the political reality. Signs and symbols represent things, objects, ideas, concepts, and beliefs, and the systematic study of signs and symbols is known as semiotics. The signs and symbols used in creating promotion, advertising, and marketing messages are "loaded" with ideological and cultural meanings, so when a symbol used in the message is a common one in the home culture, it may turn out to be inappropriate in another culture because it carries a different meaning to the audience. Thus, capitalism and free market system signs and symbols are part and parcel of commercial messages and advertising. Since advertising incorporates signs and symbols that project those values and the belief system, it is important to read and analyze signs and symbols carefully.

The spread of advertising throughout the world had a major impact on global culture. Advertising that is mostly visual can overcome illiteracy and communicate messages about products and services effectively. Advertising also carries secondary messages about lifestyle, values, and consumption; thus, they have a powerful impact on creating a worldwide, global consumption culture. There are universal values and appeals that cut across national boundaries and across cultures. Globalization tends to bring homogeneity to cultures around the world. Yet, there are cultural differences which communicators need to take into account in order to get the message across. In most developing nations—Third World countries—with unique cultures, "validating local and national culture and identity" is far more important than promoting the Western, liberal, consumer lifestyle, and values around the world as found in most advertising. Some countries explicitly warn against using foreign cultural values or symbols in advertisements, or projection of foreign culture and lifestyle not acceptable to the communities, or even overt symbol of Westernization that could offend religious or social sensibilities, as in Malaysia (Frith, 2003). The need for advertisers and communicators who understand the subtleties of communicating with other cultures is great and growing.

Advertising campaigns often go global with some modifications. The signs and symbols, words, pictures, and images used in the commercials are tweaked to make sense to the audience of a specific culture. Advertisers have to be very careful which images to use in the ad. Taboos regarding nudity and sexual matters should be carefully evaluated. Most Islamic societies are sensitive about representation of the human body, especially of partially or completely exposed human bodies. Nudity or semi-exposed bodies in commercials, however, do not cause a furor in some Western countries. In the majority of countries, Western-style clothes is the norm for men but the head coverings for both genders have to be culturally correct, along with feet and hand positioning (Newsom, 2007).

Problems arise due to inaccurate translations and inappropriate visuals in multicultural advertising. The "Got Milk?" campaign, when exported to Mexico, was translated as "Are you lactating?"; a Toyota ad showing a Toyota 4-wheel auto towing a Chinese truck was not well received by Chinese audiences; Colonel Sanders Kentucky Fried Chicken created a problem in Germany because the "colonel" was associated with the U.S. military stationed in Germany (Newsom, 2007).

Ads and commercials are often tailored to indigenous tastes and perspectives; some ads would be questionable or disastrous if used elsewhere. Examples of such advertisements would be: Swedish furniture company IKEA (UK) featuring IKEA employees sniffing a colleague's armpits; a Coca Cola ad in Germany showing women donning frozen panties; a British ad using Holocaust images to promote an Imperial War Museum exhibit; a John Hancock Financial services commercial featuring two Caucasian women at an airport holding an Asian baby, turned down by adoption agencies knowing that the Chinese government would strongly object; Unilever launching a skin lotion for Black women in Brazil that has the second largest Black population after Nigeria, and to Unilever's chagrin, it finds that the Brazilian women do not identify themselves as Blacks (Kruckerberg & Vujnovic, 2007). The point here is that effective advertising must operate in a multicultural world that penalizes marketers and advertisers who lack understanding of other cultures, and who are insensitive to the needs and desires of the audiences of other cultures. Multicultural awareness sometimes goes beyond advertising. Microsoft learned this the hard way when their products were banned in some of the biggest markets because of careless mistakes. The products were banned in India, Saudi Arabia, Korea, Kurdistan, Uruguay, and China because of wrongly-colored pixels in creating maps, bad choice of music, and a bad English to Spanish translation of sensitive words (Newsom, 2007).

Media and Culture

Media in foreign countries, and even in one's own county, recreates perceptions and images of other cultures and societies. The images, sometimes stereotypical, cause what is known as "cultural myopia" or short-sightedness in evaluating a foreign culture based on assumptions of one's own culture. A study done in France with American students studying abroad showed that the stereotypical image of America as a "spoilt and rich" country was perhaps promoted and sustained by the exported U.S. media content and cultural products available around the world. In short, much of the imagery of being "rich and spoilt" was created by the American media (Mckenzie, 1999). Studying U.S. imagery in media content in a global context is necessary to overcome our "cultural myopia" because images are ubiquitous at the global level, and as humans we must find a common platform to conduct information exchanges and transactions for a mutual understanding of each other's culture. Cultural artifacts and media texts and content can and do influence people's perception of other cultures. Cultural factors have an impact on the U.S.

image abroad. These images could either hinder or facilitate intercultural communications amongst people, societies, and nations of the world.

Since their invention in the early twentieth century, movies have been an integral part of a culture. Film and film-making are major elements of the twenty-first century culture. Films tell stories of happenings and of people within a culture and also about the culture. The narrative of films made by the people mirrors the history and the social milieu of a specific culture. Thus, Hollywood reflects, portrays, and represents the American society in the minds of perhaps billions of people around the world. But Hollywood is not the only film-making center creating narratives for its own people and society. Bollywood and Nollywood have also become huge film production hubs in their respective countries and regions. The Bollywood film industry is based in Mumbai (formerly known as Bombay), India, and churns out more than a thousand movies per year with annual revenue of approximately $1.3 billion and selling about 3.6 billion tickets worldwide. Hollywood in comparison produces about 740 movies per year with revenue of approximately $51 billion per annum (Motion Pictures Association of America, 2001–2002). Earlier movies had nationalistic and indigenous themes, but recently Bollywood has started targeting the global audience by incorporating more Western and Latin elements in the narrative featuring various musical and dance styles, and romantic and sexual relationships. To that are added high-speed action, random violence, car chases, song and dance routines, and some mayhem to make the movie more entertaining for the masses.

The Nollywood film industry, based in Lagos, Nigeria, has barely been around for 20 years, yet it is already raking in about $5 billion and producing over 2,000 movies per year, according to the latest estimates (YouTube.com, 2013). Nollywood's early film narratives had more traditional themes but currently it has picked up Western film elements making Nollywood films more violence-prone, action-packed, and sexed-up. Contemporary Bollywood and Nollywood movies, combining both traditional and Western textual motifs, are creating a new genre in films that could be categorized as "hybrid." The audience's perception of a culture is often shaped by the movies but whether the movies represent and reflect the true nature of the culture is open to questioning.

In summary, in this chapter we noted how we communicate with each other within a cultural context and how cultures evolve over a period of time to converge toward one dominant culture or become hybridized. To better understand the communication process with other cultures, we studied the structural model of intercultural communication. We also looked at how spatial arrangements affect our intercultural communication, and the efficiency by which we move from one culture to another depends on our capacity to switch codes to suit the cultural environment. In this age of globalization, global trade and business depend to a large degree on marketing. So we see how effective advertising tuned to the local culture can increase market share and improve business outcomes. Lastly, we looked at the role of the media in creating perceptions of different cultures that ultimately have an impact on intercultural communication.

Discussion Questions

1. What is "code switching"? Discuss.
2. Explain the "Structural Model of Intercultural Communication." Give some examples of a multicultural person.
3. What is a "hybrid culture"? Discuss how a culture could evolve into a "hybrid" culture and how a "hybrid" culture could develop through fusion of cultures. Give examples.
4. Discuss how movies could affect our perception of different cultures. Use Hollywood, Bollywood, and Nollywood film industries and their film narratives as examples.
5. Why do advertisers in a global market have to be sensitive to the local culture? What could happen if marketers and advertisers use the Western model to promote products in African, Asian, or Middle-Eastern markets? Discuss.

References

Barnett, G. A., & Rosen, D. (2007). The global implications of the Internet: Challenges and prospects. In Y. R. Kamalipour (Ed.), *Global communication* (2nd ed.). New York, NY: Wadsworth.

Berger, A. A. (1995). *Cultural criticism: A primer of key concepts.* Thousand Oaks, CA: Sage.

Beyer, P. (1994). *Religion and globalization.* London: Sage.

Fairchild, H. P. (Ed.). (1967*). Dictionary of sociology and related terms.* Totowa, NJ: Littlefield, Adams.

Frith, K. (2003). International advertising and global culture. In W. Anokwa, C. Lin, & M. Salwen (Eds.), *International communication: Concepts & Cases.* New York, NY: Wadsworth.

Galloway, L. (2014, June 15). *What should I absolutely not do when visiting your country?* BBC Travel, The Quora Column. Retrieved from www.bbc.com/travel/

Giddens, A. (1990). *The consequences of modernity.* CA: Stanford University Press.

Hall, E. T. (1969). *The hidden dimension.* New York, NY: Doubleday Anchor.

Kamalipour, Y. R. (Ed.). (1999). *Images of the U.S. around the world: A multicultural perspective.* Albany, NY: SUNY Press.

Kamalipour, Y. R. (Ed.). (2007). *Global communication* (2nd ed.). New York, NY: Wadsworth.

Kottak, C. P. (1987*). Cultural anthropology* (4th ed.). New York, NY: Random House.

Kruckeberg, D., & Vujnovic, M. (2007). Global advertising & PR. In Y. R. Kamalipour (Ed.), *Global communication* (2nd ed.). New York, NY: Wadsworth.

Longhurst, B., Smith, G., Bagnall, G., & Crawford, M. (Eds.). (2008). *Introducing cultural studies* (2nd ed.). New York, NY: Longman.

Mckenzie, R. M. (1999). Images of the U.S. as perceived by U.S. students in France. In Y. R. Kamalipour (Ed.), *Images of the U.S. around the world: A multicultural perspective.* Albany, NY: SUNY Press.

Motion Pictures Association of America. (2001–2002*). Hollywood vs. Bollywood.* Retrieved from www.businessweek.com

Newsom, D. (2007). *Bridging the gaps in global communication.* New York, NY: Blackwell.

Ogan, C. (2007). Communication and Culture. In Y. R. Kamalipour (Ed.), *Global communication* (2nd ed.). New York, NY: Wadsworth.

Robertson, R. (1990). Mapping the global condition: Globalization as the central concept. *Theory, Culture & Society,* 7, 15–30.

Robertson, R. (1992). *Globalization: Social theory and global culture.* London: Sage.

YouTube.com. (2013). *Nollywood: The economics behind Nigeria's film industry.* Retrieved from http://www.youtube.com

29.   Understanding Communication for Education Abroad From Chinese International Students in the United States

Qinghua Yang
Lan Jin

The number of international students in the U.S. has increased tenfold over the past two decades, reaching 820 million in the 2012–2013 academic year, according to the statistics from the Institute of International Education (IIE, 2013). International students are attracted by advanced technology, newest information, a strong educational system, and scholarship policy in the U.S., which remains the world's leading economic power. Studying abroad is also a trend influenced by globalization thanks to the advances in transportation and communication technologies.

Transition to the university, however, is by no means an easy process and could be a tremendous change for international students. Besides the academic challenges that are confronted by both domestic and international students, international students have to cope with cultural relocation and therefore tend to experience more stress than do American students (Cheng, Leong, & Geist, 1993). One stringent stress, for instance, is caused by the difficulty of communicating in a foreign language. Because English is not their first language, a large proportion of international students have difficulties in understanding lectures, participating in group discussions, delivering presentations, and completing assignments. The language and other psychological stresses (e.g., loneliness, homesickness, perception of discrimination) are likely to exert a negative influence on international students' overall performance and their satisfaction with academic programs.

The current review focuses specifically on Chinese international students for two reasons. First, Chinese students, numbering 194,029, comprise 29% of the total international students, and make China the top sending country of international students (IIE, 2013). Such a large number warrants specific attention to this group. Second, Chinese international students are likely to face more stress in the transition process than students from Western countries due to cultural differences. According to Hofstede (1980), the U.S. emphasizes an *individualistic* culture, whereas China shows a strong *collectivistic* orientation. A collectivistic orientation means that Chinese international students tend to strive for group honor and belonging, such as to family, friends, community, or country. They are assumed to suppress their individual needs for the sake of the group, while the U.S. culture basically pursues individual goals and interests (Liu, 2009). Therefore, Chinese international students with collectivistic orientation may feel confused and find it difficult to engage into the new environment when talking with Western students.

Chinese International Students' Acculturation

In order to adjust to the culture of the United States, Chinese international students generally undergo an ***acculturation*** process as they move from their own ***ethnic/home community*** to the ***host community*** (Rogler, Cortes, & Malgadi, 1991). Ethnic/home community here refers to the country where they were born and nurtured, while a host society is the country where they have moved to—the U.S. in this case. Acculturation is a process that occurs when individuals come into contact with groups or environment from distinct cultures, which may cause psychological and behavioral changes (Berry, 2002). For example, international students undergo fundamental changes in many aspects, such as language, routines, values, relationships and customs, to adapt their ***home culture*** to the ***host culture***. Home and host cultures are referred to the mainstream cultures in their home or host communities, respectively. For instance, China is the ethnic community for a Chinese international student studying in the U.S., which is his/her host community. In the acculturation process, the Chinese international students have to modify their ethnic Chinese culture, and adopt the host U.S. culture. In this accultura-tion process, they may feel excessive physical and psychological demands of adaptation, which cause a unique type of distress called ***acculturative stress*** (Allen, Amason, & Holmes, 1998). Acculturative stress takes place as individuals face pressure and problems during acculturation process (Liu, 2009).

ipag/Shutterstock.com

Due to the challenges of cultural adjustment to a new social and school environments, Chinese international students have been found to struggle with a number of difficulties, such as language barriers, cultural shock, homesickness, racial discrimination, academics stress, lack of social supports, and financial problems (Berry, 2006; Liu, 2009). Despite these difficulties, healthy socialization with professors and peers could be of help in overcoming these difficulties. However, since communication plays a pivotal role in college students' socialization, the huge cultural differences between the two countries acts as an obstacle for Chinese international students to be able to effectively communicate. For instance, having been cultivated in an educational system valuing collectivism, many Chinese students feel uncomfortable asking questions or expressing their viewpoints in the classroom. Likewise, they are inclined to keep silent when the professor asks a question to the whole class, even though they know the answers. In this case, unlike their American classmates who are used to self-expression in the individualistic society, Chinese international students usually receive low grades in class participation.

Besides their hesitance of speaking in the public, Chinese international students are also fearful and anxious about communicating with their American professors and peers outside of class. Such fear or anxiety associated with either actual or anticipated interaction with people from different cultural or ethnic groups is referred to as ***intercultural communication apprehension*** (ICA) (Neuliep & McCroskey, 1997). Chinese international students' ICA is attributed to their language barrier and acculturative stress. Due to the huge difference between English and Chinese, the language barrier not only impedes Chinese international students' academic performance, but also prevents them from consuming media from the host country. For instance, a Chinese college student in the U.S. seldom uses American media but prefers Chinese media simply because he gets information more efficiently through Chinese media than through U.S. media. In his words, he would spend ten minutes on a news story in English, which would take two minutes to read if it were written in Chinese.

Acculturative stress, on the other hand, places Chinese international students at a high risk for mental health problems, which are related to depression, anxiety, substance abuse, poor academic performance, and even suicide (Hysenbegasi, Hass, & Rowland, 2005; Hyun, Quinn, Madon, & Lustig, 2007; Jeon, 2011; Mori, 2000; Whitton & Whisman, 2010). Chinese students usually socialize among themselves and have limited interaction with American students. In this case, Chinese students are under the risk of being isolated from the majority at school and can receive little support when facing academic, social, professional, and financial difficulties. What is worse, because of the long distance between China and the U.S., Chinese international students have limited support from their strong bonds, who are their close friends and family members in China. As a consequence of lack of social support, the hardship in Chinese international students' daily lives may have an excessive negative impact.

Protective Factors in Acculturation

Despite the acculturative stress experienced, intercultural communication competence (ICC) was found to be a protective factor. General ***communication competence*** describes a person's ability to demonstrate skills or to conduct effective behaviors to achieve communicative goals during an interaction. In other words, an individual who is able to effectively and appropriately communicate with others to realize their purposes is assumed to be having communication competence. Such ability is specifically referred to as ***intercultural communication competence (ICC)*** when communication occurs "between people from different national cultures" (Gudykunst, 2002, p. 179). A person who is competent in intercultural communication is more capable of accomplishing his or her communicative objective(s) appropriately when interacting with others of different ethnic groups or cultures. Intercultural communication competence is important in addressing acculturative stress, since Chinese international students with a high level of intercultural communication competence are able to find ways to receive social support, exchange helpful information, and cooperate with others to address acculturative stress. For instance, there were students who were extensively exposed to American media before coming to the United States, including newspapers, radio, TV shows, films, and websites. Such exposure to host country media (a) protects them from experiencing a high level of *cultural shock*, the effects associated with the tension and anxiety of entering a new culture; and (b) enables them to be competent in intercultural communication, and easily make new friends in the U.S. As a consequence, Chinese international students competent in intercultural communication are more likely to feel at home in the U.S. culture, and experience less distress during the acculturation.

Compared to the amount of literature reporting the challenges, the empirical interventions and programs that aim to address acculturative stress of Chinese international students are still lacking. Previous research has highlighted the importance of *group level intervention* (Smith & Khawaja, 2011). It refers to the program that provides social support or assistance to the adaptation of international students. For example, many universities have attempted to increase coping skills and enhance the acculturation of international students through support services, tackling acculturative stressors, and providing culturally sensitive counseling for practical and academic issues (Andrade, 2006; Arkoudis, 2006; Hawthorne, Minas, & Singh, 2004). Besides, a healthy *mentoring relationship* was found to be effective in facilitating international students' socialization (Myers, 1998; Myers & Martin, 2008), and ultimately improving their satisfaction with their programs (Lyons & Scroggins, 1990). A mentoring relationship is a "personal relationship between a more sophisticated mentor and a less advanced protégé" (Kalbfleisch, 2002, p. 63). A mentor in universities or colleges is usually a faculty member within the student's academic department. Mentoring relationships are built with the goal of establishing a rapport for the international students. Given the potential positive effects brought by mentorship, administrators in higher education are suggested to have mandatory mentoring relationships for international students, and provide related trainings to faculty members as mentors for international students.

By reviewing the challenges confronted by Chinese international students and potential protective factors, our work can be applied to helping Chinese international students adapt to the American environment with more competence. Also, implications can be provided to American university administrators and policy-makers to better address the needs of Chinese international students, and offer effective support to cope with acculturative stress. Given the multiple challenges faced by Chinese students pursuing a degree in the U.S., future research is encouraged to take variety and individual differences into consideration when addressing their learning experiences.

Discussion Questions

1. In the globalization context, why is intercultural communication competence important?
2. How will you improve your intercultural communication competence in the multi-cultural classroom in the United States?
3. Suppose you are designing a mentoring program for international students, what aspects in your opinion should be covered in the faculty training?
4. What elements should be considered when we design an intervention targeting Chinese international students to address their acculturative stress?
5. Before entering into a new culture, what preparation do you think can be helpful to reduce acculturative stress in that culture?

References

Allen, M., Amason, P., & Holmes, S. (1998). Social support, Hispanic emotional acculturative stress and gender. *Communication Studies, 49,* 139–157. doi:10.1080/10510979809368525

Andrade, M. S. (2006). International students in English-speaking universities. *Journal of Research in International Education, 5,* 131–154. doi:10.1177/1475240906065589

Arkoudis, S. (2006). *Teaching international students: Strategies to enhance learning.* Retrieved from http://www.cshe.unimelb.edu.au/pdfs/international.pdf

Berry, J. W. (Ed.). (2002). *Cross-cultural psychology: Research and applications.* Cambridge University Press.

Berry, J. W. (2006). Stress perspectives on acculturation. In D. L. Sam & J. W. Berry (Eds.), *The Cambridge handbook of acculturation psychology* (pp. 43–57). Cambridge: Cambridge University Press.

Cheng, D., Leong, F. T. L., & Geist, R. (1993). Cultural differences in psychological distress between Asian and American college students. *Journal of Multicultural Counseling & Development, 21*(3), 182–189.

Gudykunst, W. B. (2002). Intercultural communication. In W. B. Gudykunst & B. Mody (Eds.), *Handbook of international and intercultural communication* (pp. 179–182). Thousand Oaks, CA: Sage.

Hawthorne, L., Minas, I. H., & Singh, B. (2004). A case study in the globalization of medical education: Assisting overseas-born students at the University of Melbourne. *Medical Teacher, 26,* 150–159. doi:10.1080/0142159032000150539

Hofstede, G. (1980). Motivation, Leadership, and Organization: Do American Theories Apply Abroad? *Organizational Dynamics, 9*(1), 42–63. doi:10.1016/0090-2616(80)90013-3

Hysenbegasi, A., Hass, S., & Rowland, C. (2005). The impact of depression on the academic productivity of university students. *Journal of Mental Health Policy and Economics, 8,* 145–151.

Hyun, J., Quinn, B., Madon, T., & Lustig, S. (2007). Mental health need, awareness, and use of counseling services among international graduate students. *The Journal of American College Health, 56,* 109–118. doi:10.3200/JACH.56.2.109-118

Institute of International Education. (2013). *Top 25 Places of Origin of International Students, 2011/12–2012/13.* Open Doors Report on International Educational Exchange. Retrieved from http://www.iie.org/opendoors

Jeon, H. (2011). Depression and suicide. *Journal of the Korean Medical Association, 54,* 370–375. doi:10.5124/jkma.2011.54.4.370

Kalbfleisch, P. J. (2002). Communicating in mentoring relationships: A theory for enactment. *Communication Theory, 12*(1), 63–69. doi:10.1111/j.1468-2885.2006.00280.x

Liu, M. (2009). Addressing the mental health problems of Chinese international college students in the United States. *Advances in Social Work, 10,* 69–86.

Lyons, W., & Scroggins, D. (1990). The mentor in graduate education. *Studies in Higher Education, 3,* 277–285. doi:10.1080/03075079012331377400

Mori, S. (2000). Addressing the mental health concerns of international students. *Journal of Counseling & Development, 78,* 137–144. doi:10.1002/j.1556-6676.2000.tb02571.x

Myers, S. A. (1998). GTAs as organizational newcomers: The association between supportive communication relationships and information seeking. *Western Journal of Communication, 60,* 54–73. doi:10.1080/10570319809374597

Myers, S. A., & Martin, M. M. (2008). Socializing yourself into graduate study and the communication discipline. In S. Morreale & P. A. Arneson (Eds.), *Getting the most from your graduate education in communication: A graduate student's handbook* (pp. 29–42). Washington, DC: National Communication Association.

Neuliep, J. W., & McCroskey, J. C. (1997). The development of intercultural and interethnic communication apprehension scales. *Communication Research Reports, 14*(2), 145–156. doi:10.1080/08824099709388656

Rogler, L. H., Cortes, R. S., & Malgadi, R. G. (1991). Acculturation and mental health status among Hispanics. *American Psychologist, 46,* 585–597. doi:10.1037/0003-066X.34.10.906

Smith, R. A., & Khawaja, N. G. (2011). A review of the acculturation experiences of international students. *International Journal of Intercultural Relations, 35*(6), 699–713. doi:10.1016/j.ijintrel.2011.08.004

Whitton, S., & Whisman, M. (2010). Relationship satisfaction instability and depression. *Journal of Family Psychology, 24,* 791–794. doi:10.1037/a0021734

Chapter 8

Making the Intercultural Connection in the Workplace

30. Interpersonal Interactions Across Cultural Boundaries: Communication, Diversity, and Cultural Awareness in the Age of Globalization

Chrys Egan, Ph.D.

Introduction

You likely are reading this book as a university student somewhere around the globe. With the privilege of access to higher education and promising career comes an expectation and responsibility to apply your knowledge wisely as a future global citizen and professional in an increasingly diverse, interconnected world. Perhaps you are a student in Norway, which currently has the highest percentage of college graduates of any nation (Organization for Economic Cooperation and Development [OECD], 2012), or studying in China, witnessing a rising economy and middle-class (Barton, Chen, & Jin, 2013), or a college student in the U.S. where "American" companies are moving their headquarters to other nations for tax benefits and have franchises located all over the world. Wherever you live now, you are already experiencing globalization in at least three major ways in your daily life: media content, personal relationships, and professional career opportunities.

First, **international media conglomerates**, a few world-wide corporations that own many smaller companies and shape the mass media content, are now the standard. This means that the artist you are listening to on your iPod may not be from your country, might be strategically marketed to another culture, and that international stakeholders are profiting from your music selection. Second, you have diverse **interpersonal relationships**, meaningful connections with other people in varying degrees of closeness and different contexts. These relationships are becoming more **intercultural**, crossing boundaries between nations, heritages, languages, beliefs, and customs. Within your own culture there are numerous co-cultures with unique traditions. You probably have friends or relatives who live in other parts of the world with whom you communicate through social media, video conferencing, phone calls, texts, or other technology. You may have traveled to or lived in other places in world. Third, your professional career will rely on enhanced global **organizational communication**, the complex ways that individuals inside and outside of organizations, agencies, and companies interact to accomplish goals. Your career will rely upon increasing interdependence among other countries and sensitivity toward different cultures. This interconnected world will expand throughout your lifetime as technology, politics, global economies, and shared resources continue to develop. How will you prepare to live, work, play, serve, and lead with diverse others in this age of globalization? To succeed you must increase your intercultural communication skills and appreciation of cultural diversity.

Interpersonal and Intercultural Theories

Successful intercultural communication and leadership with diverse people in our growing international network of interpersonal and mediated contexts starts at the individual level. An individual's self-identity, how we view and accept who we are, and ability to interact with others arises from a complex interplay among unique psychology, life experiences, social expectations, and biology. Similarly, one's **leadership identity**, the ability to conceive of oneself as an agent of change in various contexts and to project that image to others, stems from the culmination of this lifetime of influences. This essay focuses on two significant, interdependent, global leadership identity factors that are vital to success: relationships and communication.

To illustrate how your relational skills and communication skills are essential for success in a diverse cross-cultural world, consider these established relational and intercultural communication theories that demonstrate how an individual's sense of self, community, and leadership are heavily influenced by each other. **Social Penetration Theory**, nicknamed the "onion theory," proposes that relationship stages and **self-disclosure**, strategically revealing personal information, are peeled back in layers toward the core, like an onion (Altman & Taylor, 1973, 1987). When you meet someone from a culture that is unfamiliar to you, you will be naturally curious yet socially appropriate, asking initial questions and interacting with the person to learn more about both the person and the culture. Once you know the person better, you will see more of that person's true identity and be more comfortable asking deeper questions. Also looking at stages, the **Knapp and Vangelisti Model** applies a staircase metaphor with people moving together up the staircase from initiating relationships to bonding in them, but possibly coming down the staircase separately by differentiating themselves from the other person to terminating the relationship (Knapp, 1984; Knapp & Vangelisti, 2008). This theory appreciates the positive and negative interpersonal and cultural factors influencing communicators both in their private and professional interactions. Sometimes cultural differences can cause stress on relationships, but other times they enhance the experience so people can learn about and experience other cultures. Rather than anticipate predictable stages, the relational trajectory model **Turning Point Theory** states that major pivotal moments in life change everything, as when an individual is first immersed in a completely new culture (Baxter & Bullis, 1986). If you have traveled to or lived in another society, consider the initial shock you may have experienced and how you needed to adapt. Similarly, **Relational Dialectics Theory** explores the daily "tug-of-war" of opposing personal and social needs like how much "alone time" you need versus how much connection you want with other people. People must continuously negotiate and balance cross-cultural relationships and differences (Baxter, 1988). These are just a few of the many useful interpersonal relationship theories that explain how people interact and how they can improve their connections to other people.

In addition, there are many applicable intercultural communication theories that demonstrate how we can succeed in personal and professional interactions with diverse people. **Communication Accommodation Theory** notes how our **verbal** (spoken and written word) and **nonverbal** (physical) expressions change or adapt based on the communication style of the other person. In the workplace, ability to accommodate to cultural communication styles improves a person's success and satisfaction (Giles, Coupland, & Coupland, 1991). Further, **Face Negotiation Theory** examines cultural expressions of conflict, winning/losing, and respect. Some cultures tend to be more **collectivist**, emphasizing the group over the individual, while other cultures are more **individualistic**, valuing the individual over the group. Knowing about a culture's assumptions can assist you in your business relationships and negotiations, while respecting the people involved (Ting-Toomey, 2005). These interpersonal and intercultural communication theories offer insights on **intercultural relational leadership**, how an individual is influenced by, utilizes, and appreciates the importance of diverse interpersonal communication, networking, relational support, and work-life enrichment.

Intercultural Relational Leadership

As an educated global citizen and intercultural working professional, you will be called upon to serve many leadership roles in various contexts: family, community, politics, media, business, education, and other areas. Understanding this interconnection of cultural communication, relationships, and leadership has evolved to conceptualize intercultural "leadership identity as moving from a leader-centric view to one that embraced leadership as a collaborative, relational process" (Komives, Owen, Longerbeam, Mainella, & Osteen, 2005, p. 593). Culturally sensitive relational leadership acknowledges and values trust, shared vision, reciprocity, collaboration, ethics, and authenticity (Allen & Cherrey, 2000; Avolio & Gardner, 2005; Chrislip & Larson, 1994; Ciulla, 1998; Komives, Lucas, & McMahon, 1998; Kouzes & Posner, 2003; Pearce & Conger, 2003; Rost, 1993; Terry, 1993). In action, this global relational leadership combines self, other, and expression to motivate people toward a common goal by believing in one's potential and nurturing the same in others. Successful individuals remain flexible by being consciously aware of essential factors influencing themselves and others: diverse interpersonal skills, networking, relational support, and work-life enrichment.

"People skills," "reading people," or more academically referred to as diverse **interpersonal skills** describe a person's verbal and nonverbal interactions, listening aptitude, and interpretation of feedback. As fundamental and essential as these concepts are to personal and professional success, neither do all individuals have sharp skills nor are they open to learning new interpersonal skills. For example, research indicates that women and cultural minorities have enhanced **nonverbal interpretation skills**, ability to read and interpret the physical cues of others, compared to men and dominant cultural groups because underrepresented individuals *must* understand the nonverbal expressions of those in power, while the reciprocal is not necessarily true (Leathers & Eaves, 2008). Individuals who appreciate the usefulness of interacting clearly and effectively with all types of people have developed a diverse relational leadership identity.

Similarly, having strategic **networks**, connected webs of people who can rely on each other, impacts a person's formation of cultural leadership identity. Networks also strengthen a leader's likelihood of accomplishing tasks in a variety of settings. While the expression, "It's not what you know, it's who you know" is only partially correct, the adage testifies to the importance of maintaining connections to other people with diverse skills and backgrounds. For example, some gender and cultural differences may be seen in leadership styles, in part due to obstacles that some leaders might face in certain fields. As such, skilled leaders need to know when it is best to utilize their personal network connections to accomplish a task and when it is best to use their positional power over others. Managing diverse group dynamics and applying useful connections helps relational leaders accomplish goals, which further enhances a successful leadership identity (Eagly & Carli, 2003; Eagly & Karau, 2002).

Beyond your skills, you also need support and balance to succeed in globalization. **Relational support** is the empathy and encouragement from others that allows people to realize their full potential and fulfill it. Evidence indicates that disenfranchised individuals may need stronger relational support from people at work and/or home to break through historical and institutional barriers to leadership. Research on leadership limitations in higher education reveal that women need more verbal and personal encouragement than men before pursuing promotion, but that women are more successful at achieving promotion once they finally apply (Murray, Tremaine, & Fountaine, 2012). These relational supports may be formalized organizational programs such as assigned mentors or human resource policies, or informal practices such as work-based friendships or a strong sense of accountability to the team. Contemporary and future leaders need to actively support the relational leadership identity of colleagues to ensure diversification.

The final factor considers the whole person within the scope of relationships and life. Also referred to as "work-life balance," **"work-life enrichment"** is the integration of labor, leisure, family, community, culture, and health for the well-being of the individual and the community. The concept initially was viewed in negative terms as concern over employees' ability to manage their private lives while making work the priority (Marks, 1977). However, this newer **"enrichment model"** examines both negative and positive crossover from work and home, in each direction, with questions like: How can work positively and negatively impact home life? and How can home positively and negatively impact work life? (Greenhaus & Powell, 2006; Grzywacz & Carlson, 2007; Grzywacz & Marks, 2000; Rothbard, 2001). The enrichment model is an expansive rather than a deficit view of people's energy, time, and productivity. To illustrate, an extensive analysis of job flexibility and personal life balance concluded that job flexibility benefits employers and employees. Not only do people with flexible work schedules complete assigned tasks while keeping a healthy balance with their personal live, but they also are able to work longer hours before workload negatively impacts their work-family balance (Hill, Hawkins, Ferris, & Weitzman, 2001). Diverse relational leadership flows appreciates the value of home, community, and workplace to allow whole people to interact together for mutual benefit.

Conclusion

In essence, people's global communication strategy should help them envision themselves as culturally-sensitive change agents in the numerous roles they fulfill in their lives, while sharing this vision with the people in their personal and professional relationships. This skill involves our ability to relate and communicate, sometimes in predictable stages with layers or steps, but other times with turning points or tensions. It considers how to accommodate and protect the dignity of diverse communicators. Cultivating intercultural identity in ourselves and other people involves diverse interpersonal communication, networking, support, and work-life enrichment. Technology, travel, media, education, politics, and commerce are making the world feel smaller and more connected. Your task is to not only navigate this new world, but to take a leadership role in shaping it.

Discussion Questions

1. Give examples of how you are already a global citizen. In what areas do you see globalization increasing even more in your future?
2. Our understanding of leadership has expanded to consider all contexts in which a person can influence others to enact change or accomplish tasks. Using this definition, list the areas of your personal, academic, and professional life in which you are a leader. How does your cultural background shape your ability to lead in these areas?
3. What are the benefits of an intercultural relational leadership model where individuals use personal and communication skills to support diversity among groups of people? What are the challenges of trying to live and lead by this model?
4. Rank the global relational skills in order of importance from most to least: diverse interpersonal communication, networking, relational support, and work-life enrichment? What does that exercise teach you about the value of these skills in a global world?
5. What recommendations would you give your academic institution to prepare students for personal and professional leadership across cultural boundaries? How well does your institution currently meet these needs?

References

Allen, K. E., & Cherrey, C. (2000). Systemic leadership: Enriching the meaning of our work. Lanham, MD: University Press.

Altman, I., & Taylor, D. (1973). *Social penetration: The development of interpersonal relationships.* New York, NY: Holt.

Altman, I., & Taylor, D. (1987). Communication in interpersonal relationships: Social Penetration Theory. In M. E. Roloff & G. R. Miller (Eds.), *Interpersonal processes: New directions in communication research* (pp. 257–277). Newbury Park, CA: Sage.

Avolio, B. J., & Gardner, W. L. (2005). Authentic leadership development: Getting to the root of positive forms of leadership. *Leadership Quarterly, 16,* 315–338.

Barton, D., Chen, Y., & and Jin, A. (2013, June). *Mapping China's middle class.* McKinsey Quarterly. Chicago, IL: McKinsey Global Institute.

Baxter, L. A. (1988). A dialectical perspective of communication strategies in relationship development. In S. Duck (Ed.), *Handbook of personal relationships* (pp. 257–273). New York, NY: Wiley.

Baxter, L. A., & Bullis, C. (1986). Turning points in developing romantic relationships. *Human Communication Research, 12*(4), 469–493.

Chrislip, D. D., & Larson, C. E. (1994). Collaborative leadership: How citizens and civic leaders can make a difference. San Francisco, CA: Jossey-Bass.

Ciulla, J. B. (1998). Leadership ethics: Mapping the territory. In J. Ciulla (Ed.), *Ethics: The heart of leadership* (pp. 3–25). Westport, CT: Praeger.

Eagly, A. H., & Carli, L. L. (2003). The female leadership advantage: An evaluation of the evidence. *Leadership Quarterly, 13,* 807–834.

Eagly, A. H., & Karau, S. J. (2002). Role congruity theory of prejudice toward female leaders. *Psychological Review, 109*(3), 573.

Giles, H., Coupland, J., & Coupland, N. (1991). *Contexts of accommodation.* New York, NY: Cambridge University Press.

Greenhaus, J., & Powell, G. (2006). When work and family are allies: A theory of work-family enrichment. *Academy of Management Review, 31*(1), 72–92.

Grzywacz, J. G., & Carlson, D. S. (2007). Conceptualizing work-family balance: Implications for practice and research. *Advances in Developing Human Resources, 9,* 455–471.

Grzywacz, J. G., & Marks, N. F. (2000). Reconceptualising the work-family interface: An ecological perspective on the correlates of positive and negative spillover between work and family. *Journal of Occupational Health Psychology, 5*(1), 111–126.

Hill, E. J., Hawkins, A. J., Ferris, M., & Weitzman, M. (2001). Finding an extra day a week: The positive influence of perceived job flexibility, on work and family life balance. *Family Relations, 50*(1), 49–58.

Knapp, M. L. (1984). *Interpersonal communication and human relationships.* Boston, MA: Allyn & Bacon.

Knapp, M. L., & Vangelisti, A. L. (2008). *Interpersonal communication and human relationships* (6th ed.). Upper Saddle River, NJ: Pearson.

Komives, S. R., Lucas, N., & McMahon, T. R. (1998). *Exploring leadership: For college students who want to make a difference.* San Francisco: Jossey-Bass.

Komives, S. R., Owen, J. E., Longerbeam, S. D., Mainella, F. C., & Osteen, L. (2005). Developing a leadership identity: A grounded theory. *Journal of College Student Development, 46*(6), 593–611.

Kouzes, J., & Posner, B. (2003). *The leadership challenge* (3rd ed.). San Francisco, CA: Jossey-Bass.

Leathers, D., & Eaves, M. H. (2008). *Successful nonverbal communication: Principles and applications* (4th ed.). Upper Saddle River, NJ: Pearson.

Marks, S. R. (1977). Multiple roles and role strain: Some notes on human energy, time and commitment. *American Sociological Review, 42,* 921–936.

Murray, N., Tremaine, M., & Fountaine, S. (2012, May). Breaking through the glass ceiling in the ivory tower: Using a case study to gain new understandings of old gender issues. *Advances in Developing Human Resources, 14*(2), 221–236.

Organization for Economic Cooperation and Development. (2012). *Education at a glance 2012: OECD report finds U.S. lags behind other countries in higher education attainment rate.* Retrieved from http://www.huffingtonpost.com/2012/09/11/oecd-education-at-a-glanc_n_1874190.html

Pearce, C. L., & Conger, J. A. (Eds.). (2003). *Shared leadership: Reframing the hows and whys of leadership.* Thousand Oaks, CA: Sage.

Rothbard, N. P. (2001). Enriching or depleting? The dynamics of engagement in work and family roles. *Administrative Science Quarterly, 46,* 655–684.

Rost, J. (1993). *Leadership for the twenty-first century.* Westport, CT: Praeger.

Terry, R. (1993). *Authentic leadership.* San Francisco, CA: Jossey Bass.

Ting-Toomey, S. (2005). The matrix of face: An updated Face-Negotiation Theory. In W. B. Gudykunst (Ed.), *Theorizing about intercultural communication* (pp. 71–92). Thousand Oaks, CA: Sage.

31.   Cultural Influences on Communication: An International Business Perspective

Suresh Gopalan, Ph.D.

In this chapter, we focus on the relationship between cultural influences on communication in the context of international business. By the end of this chapter, you will have gained a better understanding of national cultures and their impact on language and other forms of communication. While reading the pages that follow, please keep the following questions in mind, which you will be asked to answer at the conclusion of this chapter: Why do Japanese prefer bowing even if they are familiar with shaking hands? Why do Thais avoid direct criticism of their subordinates? Why do Indians (from India) say yes when they mean no? Why are Americans so candid when giving feedback? What is your cultural profile based on the dimensions discussed in this chapter and what does this imply for how you should interact with those from cultures substantially different from your own?

What Is Culture?

Scholars have defined culture in a variety of ways based on their field (or occupation). Hofstede (1980) defines **culture** as "the collective pattern of the mind which distinguishes the members of one human group from another" (p. 25). He considers values as the core of culture. **Values** are normative preferences (desired end-states) that can be rank-ordered to denote priority.

The easiest way to conceptualize culture is to think of an onion (see Figure 31.1). As each layer is peeled off, another emerges, and one can continue to peel until the core is reached. At the outermost cultural layer, there are the superficial traits, such as dress, food, rituals, symbols, objects, and other stimuli that are readily visible and observable. This is what most people consider culture, but there is far more to culture than initially meets the eye. Beliefs and norms constitute the next layer—they are harder to infer but they shape the way that individuals communicate with and relate to one another. The innermost layer consists of values. These are the most difficult to ascertain but the behavioral patterns of individuals from various cultures are directly impacted by values.

For example, let us consider how the American culture appears to outsiders. American culture appears to the uninitiated to consist of McDonald's, Nike, and Hollywood. Americans uniquely celebrate the Fourth of July and American Thanksgiving as remembrances of their common history and politics. Going further, we find that Americans are perceived to love their country, are fond of owning guns, but prefer less government control over their individual lives. Americans value their independence, their religious diversity, and their ability to vocalize unpopular opinions in the public space. The love of country, fondness for guns, and desire for less government are direct manifestations of these values, while the celebration of the Fourth of July and American Thanksgiving follow directly from the nationalistic individualism that is at the core of their beliefs. Now that we have discussed the American culture, we can move on to understand how cultural misunderstandings lead to conflict and negative stereotyping.

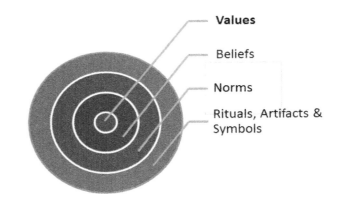

Figure 31.1   Cultural Layers.

Let us clarify a couple of points before proceeding further. First, when referencing *national* culture, we are referring to the *dominant* culture, whose values are followed by the majority of people in a country. While we readily acknowledge the presence of multiple subcultures that are present in a country, they are not the foci of our discussion, although when dealing with an individual from a subculture, it is important to utilize that subculture rather than the dominant one when engaging in communication. Second, this chapter does not treat culture as an entity unto itself. Instead, it recognizes that culture impacts communication patterns and it is these communication patterns, rather than culture itself, that we will be addressing (see Figure 31.2).

Cross-cultural communication occurs when two or more individuals from different countries or cultures interact with one another in business or social settings and encompasses all manner of communication, both obvious (written and oral communication) and subtle (body language, intonation). Cross-cultural scholars have

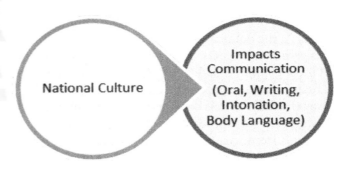

Figure 31.2   Culture and Communication.

observed that cultural knowledge and empathy enhances trust, cooperation, and mutual understanding. Lack of cultural empathy and insight contributes to loss of trust, misunderstanding, and conflict, and can have disastrous consequences (Hofstede, 1991; Trompenaars & Hampden-Turner, 1997).

Flatter World = More Cross-Cultural Communication

The widespread use of the Internet and mobile phone technology, as well as the deepening of free trade, has resulted in a flatter world (Friedman, 2006). This means that there are greater commercial opportunities to engage with individuals from other cultures and countries. As the volume of global business transactions continues to grow, national borders have become porous and interaction between various nationals has become more frequent. The North American Free Trade Agreement (NAFTA) resulted in greater economic integration and contact between Canadians, Americans, and Mexicans. The formation of the European Union's common market has increased the frequency of contact between Western Europe (France, Germany, U.K., etc.) and Eastern Europe (Romania, Bulgaria, Poland, etc.). Free trade agreements like MERCOSUR and ASEAN have broken down trade barriers in South America and South-East Asia, respectively. We are living in an increasingly interlinked and intertwined world.

Closer to home in the U.S., many companies have off-shored business functions to other countries (Gopalan & Madjd-Sadjadi, 2012). Tax forms are processed in the Philippines, information technology maintenance and related issues are handled in remote sites in India, and reservations are taken by staff working in Chile. When interacting with individuals from all these countries, there is no need to leave the U.S. to encounter cross-cultural communication. It can happen over the telephone, over the Internet (through Skype), and even seemingly one-way communication such as television. Increasingly, our lives are touched by others who think, act, and speak differently from us. Cultural insights enhance cross-cultural communication skills in a global setting. Effective communication is a key to success in all these global relationships.

Cultural Variables That Impact Communication

In this section, we discuss important cultural variables impacting cross-cultural communication (Hofstede, 1991; Triandis, 1994; Trompenaars & Hampden-Turner, 1997). This discussion is intended to enable you to gain greater insight about *yourself* and *others* in a cross-cultural communication setting. In the following table, we list, describe, and offer a brief narrative of how these variables impact communication.

Cultural Variable	Description	Impact on Communication
Power Distance	The extent to which a culture emphasizes equality in relationships and purports to either minimize or maintain the distance. High power distance cultures reinforce inequality while low power distance cultures minimize their impact.	Use of titles, different forms of addressing individuals based on age and social strata, politeness toward superiors, abruptness toward subordinates, keeping a physical distance, avoidance of touch, etc.
High Context versus Low Context	High context cultures infer meaning based on the context in which the communication takes place, attach importance to long-term relationships, and value trust. The need to maintain harmony and not embarrass others is paramount in these cultures. Low context cultures prefer precision and directness in oral and written communication, use contracts, and do not attach importance to external cues.	Preference for relationship building, paying attention to external cues, message medium, source, degree of gentleness and ambiguity, etc.
Individualism and Collectivism	Cultures that emphasize individualism consider individuals to be autonomous and free to decide on which groups they join or leave. Cultures that emphasize collectivism consider groups to be primary and individuals derive their identity from their group membership.	Individualist cultures use more "I" words when referencing activities or projects. These cultures tend to be progressive, and allow a great deal of freedom for both men and women. Collective cultures use more "we" terms and group/team references when discussing work related items and projects. They are more conservative and prescribe the level and degree of interaction between men and women, the rituals of greeting, dress, etc.

Affective versus Neutral	Affective cultures are demonstrative, expressive, and emotional. Love, anger, disgust, etc., will be freely expressed. Neutral cultures socialize their people to keep a poker face and adopt an even tone even under difficult circumstances.	Volume, pitch, emotion, facial countenance, and body posture.

Power Distance (Low/High)

Power Distance can be defined as the extent to which individuals in a culture are socialized to accept equality or inequality in relationships across social and professional settings (Hofstede, 1980). High power distance cultures (from Asian and Latin American countries like India, Pakistan, and Mexico) socialize their people to be cognizant of whom they communicate with and act accordingly. When addressing elders and superiors, they are encouraged to use titles, behave in a formal and deferential manner, avoid direct eye-contact, and maintain a physical distance. Low power distance cultures (Anglo-Saxon cultures with a history of large-scale immigration, such as the U.S., Canada, and Australia) raise their nationals to be informal, egalitarian, and avoid deference to any form of class system. In these countries, people tend to quickly progress to a first-name basis and readily maintain eye contact when talking to superiors. Consider the following hypothetical scenario:

> Thomas Jones had just returned from visiting his company's R&D plant in Chennai, India. Tom was debriefing his colleagues in the U.S. about the Indian colleagues and this is what he said. "Well, the Indian subordinates are hardworking. But I don't understand their reluctance to freely participate in meetings and offer ideas for improvement. They are more interested in knowing what I think and are quick to agree with anything I say! I have tried several times to break the ice by asking them to call me Tom, but they insist on calling me Mr. Thomas or Sir! I am beginning to wonder if they (Indians) are independent and can think outside the box."

In front of their boss (their superior), the Indians were displaying culturally appropriate behavior from the context of a high power distance culture. They addressed him in a formal and deferential manner, asked him for ideas, and avoided calling him by his first name even when requested to do so. Thomas, who is from a low power distance culture (USA), equated their behavior and communication as obsequious, servile, and devoid of creativity. If Thomas had understood the impact of power distance on superior-subordinate relationships, he could have conducted his meetings with his Indian colleagues in a different manner and achieved desired results. Instead, he left the country with an inaccurate view of his Indian colleagues. What Thomas could have done was provide a more structured meeting and given his subordinates clear instructions to provide candid feedback without fear of reprisal.

So, in a cross-cultural encounter, predetermine the degree of similarity or difference in power distance between yourself and the other party. Next, write down a list of what is considered "appropriate" and "inappropriate" styles and behaviors for both parties. This will heighten your sense of awareness and empathy and help you avoid making hasty judgments about the other party. It is important that the person in the relationship who is perceived to hold power over another take the lead in making the other person feel comfortable in voicing his or her opinion.

High Context—Low Context

According to anthropologists Hall and Hall (1990), **high context cultures** socialize individuals to pay attention to the context in which the communication takes place. Meaning is inferred from the source, timing, location, choice of words used, body language, etc. In high context cultures (encompassing Asian countries like Thailand, Japan, India, and China), it is common to encounter phrases that seem to suggest an affirmative (yes) when it is actually reinforcing a negative (no). Replying with a blunt "no" can break a relationship and cause one to embarrass others. This is especially important when individuals are not on the same level. Subordinates who are embarrassed by their superiors will tend to shut down and this will lead to a breakdown in employee-employer relations. At the same time, subordinates, ever mindful of their place in society, are loath to embarrass their superiors by refusing a request that they cannot deliver. Therefore, ambiguity in language is viewed as politeness (and a desirable trait) across all settings. **Low context** cultures place emphasis on logic, clarity, precision, directness, and accuracy of both verbal and written forms of communication. If something is important, it has to be explicitly spoken or written—it cannot be left unsaid or implied. Much of North America and Western Europe are considered to be low context cultural regions.

Consider the following hypothetical conversation between a Chinese supplier and a British manufacturer:

Wang: I am sure we should be able to meet the deadline of March 15, but I hope you can be flexible.

Maxmillan: Well, a deadline is a deadline. We must have the merchandise in our factories by March 15, so we can meet our customers' deadlines. Can you meet it or not? Yes or No?

Wang: Of course, we will try hard to accommodate your request. You are a valuable customer and we do not wish to lose your business.

Maxmillan: So, it is settled. March 15 is our deadline.

Wang: (Shakes his head and smiles—does not say anything)

Maxmillan: (leaves the room thinking the merchandise will arrive on March 15)

What actually happened in this scenario? The British manufacturer was pressing hard for a firm commitment for a March 15 deadline and felt that the Chinese supplier had agreed to his request. The Chinese supplier was trying to save face and provided many hints (at least three to be precise) that he was unable to meet the deadline. The high context Chinese subtlety was lost on the British manager who was oriented to be direct and blunt, which is typical of a low context culture. Obviously, both managers could have communicated differently and, in this case, since both are equals, both are responsible for this communication failure. The Chinese supplier could have been more candid and expressed his inability to meet the stipulated deadline. Conversely, the British manager could have phrased his request in more indirect and circumspect ways and paid attention to the body language to accurately gauge the Chinese supplier's timeliness.

Individualism and Collectivism

Renowned Dutch scholar Hofstede (1991) defined **individualism** as "a preference for a loosely-knit social framework" focused on individual rights and freedoms, and one in which individuals are expected to take care of only themselves and their in-group. In an individualistic culture (most of Western Europe, Australia, and North America excluding Mexico), self-expression, freedom, and autonomy are encouraged. **Collectivism** represents "a preference for a tightly-knit framework in society" in which individuals can expect their relatives or members of a particular in-group to watch out for each other's well-being in a spirit of mutual loyalty and reciprocity. In a collective society (Asia, Africa, and South America), individuals draw their identity from an in-group (family, caste, tribe, etc.) and interdependence and cooperation are fostered from a young age.

A logical conclusion from this discussion would be that a high frequency of "I" usage in individualist cultures and "We" usage in collectivist cultures. Additionally, collectivist cultures are more conservative in their dress codes, greeting protocols, social interactions, and desired behaviors of men and women. Individualistic cultures tend to be progressive, allowing a wide range of freedom to men and women in both business and social situations. They tend to be less prescriptive and allow more room for individual judgment and preferences.

Let us read the following hypothetical conversation between an American executive and her Japanese partner:

Olivia: Thank you for arranging the party for our customers, Tanaka. I am looking forward to the evening and unwinding with a few beers.

Tanaka: Olivia, you must be tired after the long flight. Perhaps you should stay at the hotel tonight. It's a bunch of guys who will be at the party and you will be bored.

Olivia: Not at all! I wouldn't miss it for the world. I was selected by my company to be here as I am the best sales executive. Being here is an achievement and I intend to be at the party.

Tanaka: (coughing) Olivia . . . but

Olivia: But what?

Tanaka: In Japan, women do not attend an after-hours party with all men. Perhaps you could stay for a short while and leave. The customers would like that.

Olivia: (looking visibly annoyed) I am a big girl and I know how to take care of myself. Japanese rules are for Japanese. I am an American!

The reader does not have to do an in-depth analysis of this conversation to infer that cultural preferences were placing a strain on the relationship between Olivia and Tanaka. Olivia is clearly from an individualist culture and considered her attendance at the party as a sign of *her* achievements and self-expression. She was clearly raised in a culture where men and women interacted quite freely in a social setting and consumption of alcohol was clearly not an issue. Tanaka, who is Japanese, was clearly a collectivist and was conveying his cultural preferences which stressed modesty, importance for group preferences, and a clear delineation of roles for women and men. Another important distinction between these two cultures is how decisions are made. In an individualist culture, one person makes the decision—it can be done quickly. In a collectivist culture, many participate and consensus is sought, which takes time.

What should also be taken from this vignette is that even while Tanaka has done everything correctly in this conversation by recognizing the cultural conflict and attempting to bridge the gap, it is Olivia's insistence on the maintenance of her individualist behavior without considering these differences that leads to the breakdown in the communication. Such errors in judgment will often lead to failures in international business relations.

Affective or Neutral

Affective cultures encourage the free and spontaneous expression of verbal and non-al thoughts and actions in all societal settings. Emotions expressing love, anger, hate, happiness, dismay, etc., are all expressed openly using animated language and expressions. **Neutral** cultures stress control over overt emotional expressions and to be stoic across all situations. Speakers are encouraged to use a steady monotone with minimal use of gestures. Across Europe, most of the Scandinavian and Western European countries fall under the neutral category. Southern Europe (especially the Mediterranean area countries) like Greece, Italy, and Cyprus would be considered as affective cultures. In Asia, India would be considered as affective while Japan would be considered as neutral.

The following scenario, based on a real-life situation with minor changes made to preserve anonymity, illustrates a situation involving individuals from affective and neutral cultures.

> One evening a Chapel Hill, North Carolian, police officer was dispatched to investigate loud and raucous noises coming from an apartment that was part of a larger complex. Neighbors who filed the complaint said they heard loud voices, screams, and shouts. They felt a major fight was occurring. The policeman knocked on the door and it was opened by Grimaldi, an international student from Italy.
>
> Grimaldi: Hello officer, can I help you?
>
> Officer: Good evening! We are investigating complaints from some of your neighbors that a big fight is going on in your apartment. There appeared to be shouting and screams coming from inside.
>
> Grimaldi: (looking surprised) There is no fight, officer. We were discussing the results of the Italian parliamentary elections and we got into a heated discussion. We were just expressing our opinions and having a good time.
>
> Officer: (poking his head inside and seeing half-a-dozen surprised faces) You mean you were yelling at one another and having a good time? There was no fighting? No one was hurt?
>
> Grimaldi: Absolutely not!
>
> Officer: (shaking his head in disbelief and noting the information in his pad) Guys, just keep it quiet and don't make too much of a racket. (Leaves)

In neutral cultures, loud voices, screaming, and shouting equal conflict and dysfunctional behavior. In affective cultures, they are manifestations of constructive arguments accompanied by free expressions of thoughts and ideas. The Italians' neighbors, presumably Americans, mistook the loudness to reflect a fight. The Italian students, on the other hand, were enjoying an evening of camaraderie with expressive and vivacious conversations. In this vignette, the officer was able to grasp the situation and addressed it in an appropriate manner. It is important to note that since the officer is the perceived authority figure in this conversation, it is up to him to address any cross-cultural misunderstandings. This vignette underscores the importance of teaching cross-cultural skills to law-enforcement officials who are increasingly coming into contact with people from a variety of non-American cultures.

The chapter started by stating that culture impacts communication, and that it was important to understand culture to have effective cross-cultural communication skills. Hopefully, by the end of this chapter, you have gained additional insights about key cultural variables and their impact on communication. While it was not possible to cover all the cultural variables, the ones that are included should shed some light on what is important.

Discussion

1. Why do Japanese prefer bowing even if they are familiar with shaking hands?
2. Why do Thais avoid direct criticism of their subordinates?
3. Why do Indians (from India) say *yes* when they mean *no*?
4. Why are Americans so candid when giving feedback?
5. What is your cultural profile based on the dimensions discussed in this chapter and what does this imply for how you should interact with those from cultures substantially different from your own?

References

Friedman, T. (2006). *The world is flat: A brief history of the twenty-first century.* New York, NY: Farrar, Straus, and Giroux.

Gopalan, S., & Madjd-Sadjadi, Z. (2012). Trends impacting global services offshoring: Will India remain the world leader? *International Journal of Innovation, Management and Technology, 3*(1), 71–75.

Hall, E. T., & Hall, M. R. (1990). *Understanding cultural differences: [Germans, French and Americans]* (Vol. 9). Yarmouth, ME: Intercultural Press.

Hofstede, G. (1980). *Culture's consequences: International differences in work-related values.* Beverly Hills, CA: Sage.

Hofstede, G. (1991). *Cultures and organizations: Software of the mind.* London: McGraw-Hill.

Triandis, H. C. (1994). *Culture and social behavior.* New York, NY: McGraw-Hill.

Trompenaars, F., & Hampden-Turner, C. (1997). *Riding the waves of culture: Understanding cultural diversity in business.* London: Nicholas-Brealey.

32.   Across the Divide: Intercultural Communication in the Global Workplace

Elizabeth H. Jeter

Our experience of the world is no longer tethered to local geographies and isolated cultures. We are connected through **globalization**—the process of global integration that is creating an expanding network of governments, economies, and media—which is made possible by swift advances in technology. From interpersonal conversation to public discourse, communication is instrumental in the spread of globalization (Guo, Cockburn-Wootten, & Munshi, 2014). Diverse communication media allow individuals and groups to act, interact, and clash across the global network with an immediacy that blurs the boundaries between traditionally disparate communities (Barker & Gower, 2010). Increased migration, within and across borders, further blends these communities causing new and unexpected communication challenges (Cruickshank, 2007; Gunnarsson, 2014). Despite our differences, global crises—such as economic disparity, climate change, wars, terrorism, and epidemics—require coordination between local, national, and global organizations to mobilize efforts and accomplish goals (Keyton, Ford, & Smith, 2008).

Nowhere are the effects of globalization, technology, and migration more evident than in the modern workplace. As Zoels and Silbermayr (2010) argue, globalization is "completely changing working habits and conditions" (p. 215) that demand organizational and individual flexibility in adapting to "dynamic and rapidly changing environments" (p. 215). In response, organizations are balancing the benefits and challenges of diversity by implementing new communication strategies and programming (Oliveira, 2013). While the majority of research focuses on for-profit companies competing in global markets (Scott, 2007), workplace diversity research is expanding to address the needs of non-profit, government, and community organizations. This attention to diverse organizations also brings attention to non-traditional forms of employment such as contract, internship, and volunteer relationships. Scholars and professionals are contributing more applied research for navigating intercultural and international challenges and conflicts in the workplace because, as Zoels and Silbermayr (2010) observe, employees entering any type of organization are "confronted with attitudes, values and beliefs diverging from their own" (p. 207).

Conventional approaches to workplace diversity research focus on managing intercultural and international communication through leadership and planned initiatives (Feng, Byram, & Fleming, 2009; Lieberman, Simons, & Berardo, 2004). These approaches often focus on **socialization** or **assimilation**—"the processes by which individuals become integrated into the culture of an organization" (Jablin, 2001, p. 755)—as the primary methods for achieving effective and productive communication. These approaches assume that employees want thorough assimilation into organizational culture "in order to get along and succeed in the business world" (Barker & Gower, 2010, p. 297). This approach can ignore or lessen the benefits of differing points of view and voices in employee collaborations and teamwork. Thus, it is imperative to strike a balance between socialization and valuing individuality (Myers & Oetzel, 2003).

In the U.S., workplace research traditionally studies the categories of gender, race, ethnicity, language, and/or nationality when addressing the needs and concerns of organizations (see Turner & Shuter, 2004). To expand on existing knowledge, recent studies have embraced a more nuanced approach that account for complex intersections and combinations in cultural characteristics and categorizations such as "hybrid identities and fluid points of view" (Guo et al., 2014, p. 171; see Martin & Nakayama, 2010). The following essay embraces all these perspectives. The aim is to introduce the diverse literature and research on workplace diversity by defining cultural diversity, discussing challenges organizations encounter, and identifying communication strategies to overcome these challenges.

Defining Cultural Diversity

The modern workplace is one of the few locations where every day "a wide cross-section of society convene, explicitly collaborate, follow the same policies and guidelines, and work toward the same goals" (Muir, 2007, p. 81). Unfortunately, cultural diversity has become a buzzword that leads to more talk than change (Guo et al., 2014). Workplace diversity has many meanings across countries and cultures, which complicates the process of defining and addressing this broad concept, but clarifying the meaning of culture and workplace diversity for our purpose is essential to understanding the benefits of diversity as well as the challenges organizations face.

Culture is defined as a system of attitudes, values, and beliefs that provide the framework for interpreting context and meaning in social interactions, which Pearce (1989) argues is a social reality constituted through communication. Building on this definition of culture, **workplace diversity** "refers to policies and practices that seek to include people who are considered, in some way, different from traditional members" (Herring, 2009, p. 209). Thus, organizations embracing workplace diversity should "create an inclusive culture that values and uses the talents of all would-be members" (Herring, 2009, p. 209). Some workplace scholars emphasize language as the foundation of cultural diversity in the workplace, which is important for domestic and international organizations that pull from an increasingly international and multicultural workforce. Governments and organizations can be threatened by diversity and respond with systemic controls such as laws and policies (Gunnarsson, 2014; Lønsmann, 2014). Mandating a **lingua franca**—a common, or bridge language among a group whose members speak different native languages—policy can standardize communication with both positive and negative consequences (Dietz & Pugh, 2004). In contrast, other organizations embrace a multilingual workplace to attract and maintain diverse employees and clients (Gunnarsson, 2014), but diversity can lead to more communication challenges and conflicts.

Whether given freedom or restrictions, culture develops gradually through social interactions. This development is affected equally or asymmetrically by spontaneous change and planned interventions that meet groups' short-term and long-term needs. It is important to view cultures as complex systems with internal logic and contradictions to fully understand the relationships between different cultures. For example, in response to globalization, governments have authorized agencies to regulate and preserve national culture by weed-

zelijkodan/Shutterstock.com

ing out undesired cultural elements (Cheney, Christensen, Zorn, & Ganesh, 2004), while implementing laws to protect employees from workplace discrimination based on similar "undesirable" cultural characteristics (Muir, 2007).

Organizations also develop distinct cultures on a foundation of structure, purpose, and goals. As a result, communication scholars are drawn to organizational sites as unique systems of policy and practice under the metaphor of culture (Eisenberg & Riley, 2001). Over time, organizations can evaluate their culture to identify these unique assumptions and norms (Martin, 2000) for the purpose of improving productivity and profits. Heterogeneous organizational cultures can emerge when a variety of voices and perspectives are represented (Barker & Gower, 2010). This type of open multicultural workplace can inspire "ethical awareness and independent thinking that are essential for [employees'] ability to transverse a diverse business world" (Guo et al., 2014, p. 180). Thus, it is important to see cultural diversity as more than dominant independent categories (Turner & Shuter, 2004) and examine the interplay between cultures and creation of hybrid cultures. A more inclusive accounting of culture considers the complex relationships between characteristics—such as gender, race, ethnicity, language, nationality, age, religion, disability, labor organization affiliation, sexual orientation, and education level, among many others—as contributing to the development of organizational culture. Embracing this complex view on organizational culture can bring new insight into work processes, successes, and quality of communication. This more holistic approach views individuals as complete, embodied participants in relation to group affiliations (Kramer, 2011). As a result, organizations should value employees' lives in and outside of the workplace, including the cultural influences from family, friends, extracurricular activities, and community affiliations that can further enrich workplace diversity. For example, police departments often encourage law enforcement officers to participate in community groups to manage job stress, build social capital, and understand the communities they serve.

Valuing cultural diversity is not just a theoretical practice or ideal. It is connected directly to findings from empirical studies demonstrating the benefits to organizations of all types. Cox (2001) outlined five benefits of workplace diversity, including "improved problem solving," "greater creativity and innovation," "increased organizational flexibility," "better quality personnel," and "improved marketing strategies" (p. 6). In addition, Herring (2009) found dedicating resources to developing diversity "offers a direct return on investment," "has a net positive impact on organizational functioning," and yields "greater corporate profits and earnings" (p. 220). While these findings are persuasive, organizations must identify and overcome the unique challenges and barriers that prevent them from capitalizing on these benefits.

Challenges to Workplace Diversity

Despite barriers and conflicts, organizational "growth and innovation depend on people from various backgrounds working together and capitalizing on their differences" (Herring, 2009, p. 220). When increasing diversity among their employees, organizations can take an "achieving competitive advantage and a 'quick-fix' orientation" (Kirby & Harter, 2002, p. 28) without preparing management and employees for possible challenges. Organizations need to identify and overcome intercultural challenges to maximize the benefits of a diverse workforce, but identification and strategy implementation can be a difficult process (Holmes & Riddiford, 2010). A review of academic literature finds resources, privilege, and biased evaluation standards as the primary types of challenges organizations face when managing workplace diversity. Each is described below with examples from the literature.

Resources. Adapting to a more diverse workplace requires resource investment in short-term and long-term initiatives (Scott, 2007). Time and funding can be scarce resources that limit the types of evaluation needed to identify organizations' unique challenges. Structural changes in systems, policies, and procedures are especially time-consuming (Martin, 2000). Even after structural changes are enacted, the implementation of these changes can vary and result in uncertain long-term outcomes. This uncertainty can affect confidence levels between and among leadership and employees, which can increase anxiety. For example, researchers have found discrepancies between management and employee interpretations of diversity when implementing change initiatives, which have led to conflicts and disengagement (Al-Jenaibi, 2011; Irizarry & Gallant; 2006; Oliveira, 2013). In a health care setting, Irizarry and Gallant (2006) found that diversity was discussed as an uncomfortable and sensitive topic, leading participants to require further information and direction from leadership, which delayed policy implementation and change. These problems demonstrate the long-term commitment needed to enact this type of systemic and cultural changes. This type of management and employee uncertainty can increase when diversity initiatives include communities with longstanding conflicts. For example, in Dickson, Hargie, and Wilson's (2008) research in North Ireland the workplace blended people with "deep ethno-politico-religious differences . . . [that caused] murder and mayhem over several decades" (p. 129; also see Jackson & Mostin, 2010). In this study, avoidance and stereotyping limited coworker communication, which decreased the "flow and distribution of functional information within the organization" (p. 128).

Organizational members may also have overly simplistic conceptions of diversity that limit the implementation of diversity initiatives, especially when diversity differs in meaning across cultures (Usluata & Bal, 2007). Oliveira (2013) found crisis management professionals worked on narrow perceptions of diversity—such as participants "equating cultural diversity with communicating with Latinos" (p. 253)—that limit their ability to reach broader audiences. This limited awareness of diversity as a broad spectrum combined with limited resources for change can decrease employee satisfaction. While investment in diversity demands many resources, the resources lost can be greater when employees leave the organization. The losses include the employees' talents and the resources expended in hiring, training, and fostering those talents during employment.

Privilege. Challenges also occur when one or more groups are privileged over others, which result in "greater difficulty communicating and coordinating" in the workplace (Pitts & Jarry, 2009, p. 507). The privileging of groups can have adverse effects on employee satisfaction and quality of coworker relationships (Turner & Shuter, 2004). Some privilege-based barriers to intercultural and international communication were found to be more common in the literature than others. Workplace privilege begins with the organization's culture, which can incorporate attitudes, values, beliefs, and language(s) found in broader societal cultures. Miscommunication and misunderstandings are inevitable when employees represent different cultures and languages (Al-Jenaibi, 2011) with varying outcomes. Differences in language, culture, and mutable and immutable characteristics cause coworkers to change and adapt their behavior and communication to fit the social situations that they encounter. For example, in both the United States and Thailand, McCann and Giles (2007) found that younger employees, who were new to the organization, are more likely to accommodate and avoid older coworkers in conversation, which limited knowledge sharing and activity coordination across generations. Despite the benefits of diversity, Holmes and Riddiford (2010) observe that some organizations avoid the challenges of miscommunication and intercultural and/or international cultural competence by maintaining a more homogeneous workplace—what their participants identified as the "disincentive to hiring migrants" with "inadequate communication skills" (para. 1).

Stereotyping was discovered in multiple studies (Dickson et al., 2008; Gunnarsson, 2014; Guo et al., 2014; Pitts & Jarry, 2009; Singh & Point, 2006). As a consequence of performance evaluation processes, stereotyping can diminish groups' earning potential, which in turn hinders socio-economic mobility (Hopkins, 2009; Turner & Shuter, 2004).

Stereotypical beliefs can break down over time as coworkers are provided with or initiate opportunities to build relationships and successfully collaborate toward goals. Researchers call this the **model effect**—when coworkers "get a better idea of what other employees are like, beyond surface-level features, and form more complex opinions" (Pitts & Jarry, 2009, p. 507). But, discrimination can still occur after stereotypes are weakened.

Discrimination happens at any status level within organizations and works to exert power and control over others (Ogbonna & Harris, 2006). Through systemic policies and coworker interactions, discrimination can diminish employee participation in workplace communication and activities (Kirby & Harter, 2002; Ogbonna & Harris, 2006). Research has found that employees can experience social isolation—characterized by feeling lonely, undervalued, powerless, and/or hopeless—(Gunnarsson, 2014; Lønsmann, 2014; Turner & Shuter, 2004; Urban & Orbe, 2007), which can decrease employees' job satisfaction and increase their willingness to leave an organization (Allen & Judd, 2007, p. 163). Persistent discrimination can result in the **silencing or muting** of diverse voices, as people are censored and/or self-censor in social interactions (Guo et al., 2014; Meares, Oetzel, Torres, Derkacs, & Ginossar, 2004). Voice is key in these situations. When diverse voices are valued, underrepresented groups can contribute to organizational decision-making and development, gain and exert power, and create space for diverse voices in organizations (Basu & Dutta, 2011; Pal & Buzzanell, 2013).

Evaluation standards. Professionalism is the mastery and performance of standards, including skill and behaviors, required for professional status in a particular field (Cheney & Ashcraft, 2007). These standards are culturally specific to an organization and can vary across industry. The evaluation of one's professionalism occurs through formal measurement systems, including policies and rules, and informal, daily social interactions. For example, two programmers dressed in Polo shirts and khaki pants playing Ping-Pong beside cubicles might be a normal sight for a tech startup in a Silicon Valley, but this behavior would be unprofessional in a corporate law firm in New York. In everyday interactions, these standards are often ambiguous, varied, unspoken, and/or taken for granted among the majority population. Often, it takes breaking a rule or standard before it becomes apparent to outsiders, which can cause uncertainty and anxiety for new employees (Holmes & Riddiford, 2010; Irizarry & Gallant, 2006). When formalized in policies and evaluation processes, standards will privilege some individuals and/or groups over others. In multicultural international workplaces, standards for "appropriate" communication and behaviors can have different interpretations, which can lead to miscommunication, misunderstandings, and conflict (Cheney & Ashcraft, 2007). Employees and management often cite intercultural communication competency as necessary skills for avoiding these professional mistakes (Cruickshank, 2007). These standards of professionalism can have lasting negative consequences for employees whose merits and contributions are not included in measurement tools. Holmes and Riddiford (2010) found stigmatized employees struggled to negotiate or change coworkers' negative perceptions of their professional behavior and competency after miscommunication or misunderstandings occurs. These negative perceptions can limit individuals' access to social capital, professional networks, and career advancement (Lønsmann, 2014; Turner & Shuter, 2004).

The question of communication and language competency can be a great source of frustration for international employees, especially as one attempts to express expertise in skills through a new culture and language that are not yet mastered (Holmes & Riddiford, 2010). Miscommunication and misunderstandings interpreted as "unprofessional" behavior can mask the unique skills that originally led to the individual's hiring because individuals may not have the social observation and adaptation skills needed for success in the new workplace (Guilherme, Glaser, & Mendez-Garcia, 2010). These types of professionalism-based barrier require new and creative strategies for navigating intercultural and international communication in the modern workplace.

Communication Strategies

Organizations need effective communication strategies to minimize challenges and barriers to benefit from a diverse workforce. As a first step, Grimes and Richard (2003) suggest, "we must consciously examine our ways of communicating" (p. 11). Organizations need to evaluate the effects of their policies and practices to evaluate the outcomes of privileging groups and characteristics over others (Muir, 2007; Velo, 2012). Tailoring these evaluations and solutions to each organization is important because "uniform diversity management practices cannot be applicable . . . irrespective to [organizations'] diverse cultural characteristics" (Usluata & Bal, 2007, p. 102). Thus, solutions need to address the complex contexts of each organization and embrace the differences between and similarities among cultural groups. Organizations should ask difficult questions about the policies and practices within their system and among their employees. For example, "how can people from different groups work well together" (Grimes & Richard, 2003, p. 11); "how [do] particular historical and cultural contexts [affect our] understanding [of] differences in the workplace" (Guo et al., 2014, p. 170); how do organizations communicate across cultural boundaries to combat global issues on the local level (Jeter, 2014); how do we change organizational policies to maintain diverse members after incidents of discrimination and conflict? (Kellett, Matyok, Blizzard, Avent, & Jeter, 2011); "how [do] communication processes and structures shape employee relationships, practices, and understandings about diversity in the workplace" (Guo et al., 2014, p. 169); how does technology affect the flow and use of communication among diverse employees to complete tasks and achieve goals (Dickson et al., 2008)? The answers to these questions can empower all voices to contribute their talents and insight toward organizational and personal goals (Turner & Shuter, 2004).

Some scholars direct organizations toward forms of communication, such as dialogue and storytelling, as strategies for bridging the cultural divide among their members (Barker & Gower, 2010; Kellett et al., 2011). These communication tools can "quickly disseminating information, frame organizational events through their value-laden features, and promote organizational culture identification by establishing a social context" (Barker & Gower, 2010, p. 304). Narrative and dialogue can be effective communication tools for implementing the knowledge sharing and organizational learning necessary to adapt to a diverse, global workplace (Boje, 1991; Lämsä & Sintonen, 2006). Scholars also offer applied intercultural theories that examine how cultures function in relation to others. For example, Barge, Lee, Maddux, Nabring, and Townsend (2008) and Martin and Nakayama (2010) create evaluative matrixes by comparing pairs of cultural characteristics and communication features as "tensions" between dualities for application in organizational settings. Scholars have also designed communication models for examining culture while employees engage in specific collaborative tasks and process. For example, Dunphy (2004) offers the "Wuzzle puzzle" game for improving team-based collaborations, while Myers and Oetzel (2003) offer the Organizational Assimilation Index (OAI) that accounts for complex relationships between culture and socialization processes for use with new employees. No matter the communication strategies used, every tool needs to be matched with sufficient investments in evaluation and implementation to have real success in our global workplace (Cruickshank, 2007; Martin, 2000).

Discussion Questions

1. In the U.S., English is a lingua franca and not an official language. What language policies or practices should American organizations adopt in the workplace?
2. What role do broader historical and cultural contexts play in the global workplace?
3. How can technology increase the representation of minority voices in a diverse workplace?
4. How have you balanced cultural similarities and differences with coworkers to accomplish tasks or goals?
5. If you were a leader of an American organization, what types of communication strategies would you implement in a diverse workplace?

References

Al-Jenaibi, B. (2011). The scope and impact of workplace diversity in the United Arab Emirates—An initial study. *Journal for Communication and Culture, 1*(2), 49–81.

Allen, J. L., & Judd, B. B. (2007). Participation in decision-making and job satisfaction: Ideal and reality for male and female university faculty in the United States. *Human Communication, 10*(3), 157–180.

Barge, J. K, Lee, M., Maddux, K., Nabring, R., & Townsend, B. (2008). Managing dualities in planned change initiatives. *Journal of Applied Communication Research, 36*(4), 364–390. doi:10.1080/00909880802129996

Barker, R. T., & Gower, K. (2010). Strategic application of storytelling in organizations: Toward effective communication in a diverse world. *Journal of Business Communication, 47*(3), 295–312. doi:10.1177/0021943610369782

Basu, A., & Dutta, M. J. (2011). 'We are mothers first': Localocentric articulation of sex worker identity as a key in HIV/AIDS communication. *Women & Health, 51*(2), 106–123. doi:10.1080/03630242.2010.550992

Boje, D. M. (1991). The storytelling organization: A study of story performance. *Administrative Science Quarterly, 36,* 106–126.

Cheney, G., & Ashcraft, K. (2007). Considering "the professional" in communication studies: Implications for theory and research within and beyond the boundaries of organizational communication. *Communication Theory, 17,* 146–175.

Cheney, G., Christensen, L. T., Zorn, T. E., Jr., & Ganesh, S. (2004). *Organizational communication in an age of globalization: Issues, reflections, practices.* Prospect Heights, IL: Waveland.

Cox, T. (2001). *Creating the multicultural organization: A strategy for capturing the power of diversity.* San Francisco, CA: Jossey-Bass.

Cruickshank, P. (2007). Immigrant diversity and communication practices in the New Zealand business sector. *Business Communication Quarterly, 70*(1), 87–92.

Dickson, D., Hargie, O., & Wilson, N. (2008). Communication, relationships, and religious difference in the Northern Ireland workplace: A study of private and public sector organizations. *Journal of Applied Communication Research, 36*(2), 128–160. doi:10.1080/00909880801922847

Dietz, J., & Pugh, S. D. (2004). I say tomato, you say domate: Differential reactions to English-only workplace policies by persons from immigrant and non-immigrant families. *Journal of Business Ethics, 52,* 365–379.

Dunphy, S. M. (2004). Demonstrating the value of diversity for improved decision making: The "Wuzzle-Puzzle" exercise. *Journal of Business Ethics, 53,* 325–331.

Eisenberg, E. M., & Riley, P. (2001). Organizational culture. In F. M. Jablin & L. L. Putman (Eds.), *The new handbook of organizational communication: Advances in theory, research, and methods* (pp. 291–322). Thousand Oaks, CA: Sage.

Feng, A., Byram, M., & Fleming, M. (2009). *Becoming interculturally competent through education and training.* Bristol, UK: Multilingual Matters.

Grimes, D. S., & Richard, O. C. (2003). Could communication form impact organizations' experience with diversity? *The Journal of Business Communication 40*(1), 7–27. doi:10.1177/002194360304000102

Guilherme, M., Glaser, E., & Mendez-Garcia, M. (2010). Conclusion: Intercultural competence for professional mobility. In M. Guilherme, E. Glaser, & M. Mendez-Garcia (Eds.), *The intercultural dynamics of multicultural working* (pp. 241–245). Bristol, UK: Multilingual Matters.

Gunnarsson, B. (2014). Multilingualism in European workplaces. *Multilingua, 33*(1–2), 11–33.

Guo, S., Cockburn-Wootten, C., & Munshi, D. (2014). Negotiating diversity: Fostering collaborative interpretations of case studies. *Business and Professional Communication Quarterly, 77*(2), 169–182. doi:10.1177/2329490614530464

Herring, C. (2009). Does diversity pay? Race, gender, and the business case for diversity. *American Sociological Review, 74*, 208–224.

Holmes, J., & Riddiford, N. (2010). Professional and personal identity at work: Achieving a synthesis through intercultural workplace talk. *Journal of Intercultural Communication, 22*. Retrieved from http://www.immi.se/intercultural/nr22/holmes.htm

Hopkins, B. (2009). *Cultural differences and improving performance: How values and beliefs influence organizational performance.* Farnham, England: Gower.

Irizarry, C., & Gallant, L. (2006). Managing diversity: Interpretation and enactment in a health care setting. *Qualitative Research Reports in Communication, 7*(1), 43–50. doi:10.1080/17459430600964901

Jablin, F. M. (2001). Organizational entry, assimilation, and disengagement/exit. In F. M. Jablin & L. L. Putnam (Eds.), *The new handbook of organizational communication: Advances in theory, research, and methods* (pp. 732–819). Thousand Oaks, CA: SAGE. doi:http://dx.doi.org/10.4135/9781412986243.n19

Jackson, R. L., & Mostin, J. (2010). Identity and difference: race and the necessity of the discriminating subject. In T. K. Nakayama & R. T. Halualani (Eds.), *The handbook of critical intercultural communication* (pp. 348–363). Malden, MA: Blackwell.

Jeter, E. H. (2014). *Human trafficking: Fighting the hidden crime of modern-day slavery. Through a gender lens: Issue brief.* Winston-Salem, NC: Winston Salem Foundation, Women's Fund. Retrieved from http://issuu.com/wfws/docs/human_trafficking_brief_final

Kellett, P., Matyok, T., Blizzard, S., Avent, C., & Jeter, E. (2011). Interracial conflict and campus hate speech: The case for dialogic engagement in college settings. In D. Brunson & L. Lampl (Eds.), *Interracial communication: Contexts, communities, and choices* (pp. 254–275). Dubuque, IA: Kendall Hunt.

Keyton, J., Ford, D. J., & Smith, F. L. (2008). A mesolevel communicative model of collaboration. *Communication Theory, 18*, 376–406. doi:10.1111/j.1468-2885.2008.00327.x

Kirby, E., & Harter, L. (2002). Speaking the language of the bottom-line: The metaphor of "managing diversity." *The Journal of Business Communication, 40*(1), 28–49.

Kramer, M. W. (2011). Toward a communication model for socialization of voluntary members. *Communication Monographs, 78*(2), 233–255. doi:10.1080/03637751.2011.564640

Lämsä, A.-M., & Sintonen, T. (2006). A narrative approach for organizational learning in a diverse organisation. *Journal of Workplace Learning, 18*, 106–120.

Lieberman, S., Simons, G. F., & Berardo, K. (2004). *Putting diversity to work: How to successfully lead a diverse workforce.* Menlo Park, CA: Crisp Learning.

Lønsmann, D. (2014). Linguistic diversity in the international workplace: Language ideologies and processes of exclusion. *Multilingua, 33*(1–2), 89–116.

Martin, D. M. (2000). Re-examining diversity paradigms: The role of management communication. *Journal of the Northwest Communication Association, 29*, 12–31.

Martin, J., & Nakayama, T. (2010). *Intercultural communication in contexts* (5th ed.). New York, NY: McGraw-Hill.

McCann, R. M., & Giles, H. (2007). Age-differentiated communication in organizations: Perspectives from Thailand and the United States. *Communication Research Reports, 24*(1), 1–12. doi:10.1080/08824090601120841

Meares, M. M., Oetzel, J. G., Torres, A., Derkacs, D., & Ginossar, T. (2004). Employee mistreatment and muted voices in the culturally diverse workplace. *Journal of Applied Communication Research, 32*(1), 4–27. doi:10.1080/0090988042000178121

Muir, C. (2007). Communicating diversity at work. *Business Communication Quarterly, 70*(1), 80–82.

Myers, K. K., & Oetzel, J. G. (2003). Exploring the dimensions of organizational assimilation: Creating and validating a measure. *Communication Quarterly, 51*(4), 438–457.

Ogbonna, E., & Harris, L. C. (2006). The dynamics of employee relationships in an ethnically diverse workforce. *Human Relations, 59,* 379–407.

Oliveira, M. F. (2013). Multicultural environments and their challenges to crisis communication. *Journal of Business Communication, 50*(3), 253–277. doi:10.1177/0021943613487070

Pal, M., & Buzzanell, P. M. (2013). Breaking the myth of Indian call centers. A post-colonial analysis of resistance. *Communication Monographs, 80,* 199–219. doi:10.1080/03637751.2013.776172

Pearce, W. B. (1989). *Communication and the human condition.* Carbondale, IL: Southern Illinois University.

Pitts, D. W., & Jarry, E. M. (2009). Getting to know you: Ethnic diversity, time and performance in public organizations. *Public Administration, 87*(3), 503–518. doi:10.1111/j.1467-9299.2009.01776.x

Scott, O. L. (2007). Diversity issues and practices at work in San Antonio. *Business Communication Quarterly, 70*(1), 82–87.

Singh, V., & Point, S. (2006). (Re)presentations of gender and ethnicity in diversity statements on European company websites. *Journal of Business Ethics, 68,* 363–379. doi:10.1007/s10551-006-9028-2

Turner, L. H., & Shuter, R. (2004). African American and European American women's visions of workplace conflict: A metaphorical analysis. *The Howard Journal of Communications, 15,* 169–183. doi:10.1080/10646170490479787

Urban, E., & Orbe, M. P. (2007). "The syndrome of the boiled frog:" Exploring international students on US campuses as co-culture group members. *Journal of Intercultural Communication Research, 36*(2), 117–138.

Usluata, A., & Bal, E. A. (2007). The meaning of diversity in a Turkish company: An interview with Mehmet Oner. *Business Communication Quarterly, 70*(1), 98–102.

Velo, V. (2012). *Cross-cultural management.* New York, NY: Business Expert Press.

Zoels, G., & Silbermayr, T. (2010). Intercultural relations at the workplace. In M. Guilherme, E. Glaser, & M. Mendez-Garcia (Eds.), *The intercultural dynamics of multicultural working* (pp. 207–215). Bristol, UK: Multilingual Matters.

33.   Communicating a Socially Acceptable Identity in the Workplace: Lesbian Passing

Amanda M. Gunn, Ph.D.

Sally leaves each morning for work following the same ritual day after day. She kisses her lover, Karen, good-bye, grabs her coffee, walks outside, gets in her Honda Accord, and leaves for an eight- to nine-hour workday as an executive at one of the top soft drink companies in the southeast. As she drives down the freeway, she begins her mental transformation into what she assumes is the only identity that is safe to possess in her position: she begins to pretend that she is heterosexual. When Sally arrives at work, Karen will become Keith. Her weekend with women will have the addition of men's names, and she will call her friend Mark to see if he will once again be her fill-in boyfriend Keith for the upcoming company golf tournament. Sally is just one of countless homosexuals who lives a professional life engaged in the phenomenon of "passing."

Passing relies on the social-construction and self-construction of identities that are deemed, or perceived to be, desirable by society. It is dependent on the norms of a society and the subjective interpretations of those norms. With an increase in diversity awareness and the implementation of programs designed to bridge diversity gaps in the workplace, one might assume that passing—as an alternative for homosexuals—would become obsolete. The current emphasis in organizational scholarship on worker satisfaction, inclusion, and involvement would suggest that organizational leaders would attempt to eradicate behaviors within the organization—such as passing—that inhibit those outcomes (Cheney, 1995); yet, as Carnevale and Stone (1995) point out, "gay men, lesbians, and bisexual individuals are one of the 'new minorities' in the workplace and among the least understood" (p. 415). The inclusion of sexual orientation in the discussion of organizational diversity is rare, and when it is included it is often mentioned in the listing of diverse groups with an absence of elaboration (Allen, 1995; Chemers, Oskamp, & Costanzo, 1995). The issues that homosexuals face at work are couched in the "erroneous stereotypes" that perpetuates a desire to remain silent and "invisible in the workplace" (Carnevale & Stone, 1995, p. 416). This is a silence that works in direct opposition to ideologies that promote diversity and voice in the organization.

For many homosexuals, passing at work is certainly motivated by the desire to possess an acceptable identity; however, it is driven by more than that. Homosexual passing is about social strategies that are deemed necessary to survive in a heterosexually dominated society. It is affected by the expectations of a work environment that exist in a society that often discriminates against differences. Woods and Harbeck (1992) contend that the "workplace is heterosexist in the sense that it structurally and ideologically promotes a particular model of heterosexuality while penalizing, hiding, or otherwise symbolically annihilating its alternatives" (p. 9). Taken together, these perspectives indicate that the only option for Sally and others like her is to pass to, as DPhil (1994) suggests, "homosexuals daily engage in an elaborate ruse about their private life" (p. 188). This "ruse" is accomplished through conscious communicative practices. Figure 33.1 is a summation of how five lesbians that pass in the workplace carry out that ruse through communicative behaviors.

This is a summation of the findings. It is not all-inclusive; these examples are representative of the descriptive accounts (Gunn, 1998). Sally spends her days at work in fear

Gollwitzer's Methods of Strategic Self-Presentation	The Methods Employed by Five Lesbians That Pass as Heterosexual at Work
"Displaying material symbols"	▶ Placing pictures of male friends on an office desk ▶ Wearing a ring that indicates marriage or an engagement ▶ Wearing feminine clothing that would not be worn otherwise ▶ Maintaining a longer hairstyle to adhere to perceived gender norms ▶ Wearing more makeup than usual to adhere to perceived gender norms
"Performing daily duties associated with a particular identity"	▶ The addition or substitution of male names and pronouns in conversations ▶ Bringing male dates to company functions ▶ Utilizing traditionally feminine mannerisms such as smiling and crossing legs while sitting ▶ Participating in office flirtations
"Verbal claim to possession of a particular identity"	▶ Replacing the name of a girlfriend with a male name ▶ Creating stories about nonexistent heterosexual relationships ▶ Discussing intimate relationships with men ▶ Verbalizing attractions for men

Figure 33.1   Strategic self-presentation by lesbians that pass in the workplace.

of being found out. She then returns home to a love that she has denied just one more day out of many. Employee protection based on sexual orientation exists in very few companies and is almost nonexistent at the state and federal levels. Sally can be fired in most employment situations because she loves someone of the same sex. These behaviors of passing take a great deal of energy—both emotional and psychological. The time that it takes to create a heterosexual person is at once demeaning to the individuals engaged in passing, the partners at home that they are denying, and unproductive for the task and maintenance agendas of the workplace.

Toranico/Shutterstock.com

Sally and countless others continue to leave their voice at home. Organizational leaders must be made to see that this practice of passing undermines the goals of an organization. Once a foundational understanding is established of how all the factions of an organization are affected by homosexual passing, we can begin to work toward a true "democratic workplace." Perhaps then Sally will no longer have to lie. She will not live in a reality of continuous stress, and perhaps she can begin to feel the connection with her coworkers that she is missing. Ultimately, Sally will be able to answer "yes" when she is asked if there is someone important in her life.

Key Terms

Acculturated, Cultural Capital, Dialect, Discourse, Elocution, Hegemony, Heterogeneous, Strategic Self Preservation, Vernacular

Chapter 9

Meeting the Challenges and Barriers

34. Emotions in Race Talk in the Post-Obama Era: Unpacking a Dialogic Pedagogy of Talking Back

Nathaniel Simmons

Yea-Wen Chen

Dongjing Kang

Haunted by the killings of Michael Brown, Trayvon Martin, and countless racial others, this essay addresses difficult classroom conversations on race, racism, and racial justice in a "Post-Obama Era." As an example, in 2013, Professor Shannon Gibney received administrative reprimanding because of White student complaints about feeling "uncomfortable" during her lecture on structural racism (McMillan Cottom, 2013). We currently do not live in a post-racial society; however, popular discourses of post-racialism, colorblindness, or racelessness after the Civil Rights Movement have led many to believe that racism is a thing of the past. Halualani (2011) described the **post-racial era** as the late 1990s to modern day where the United States "invoked a neoliberal stance through which race, in all social and political matters, was to be avoided, shunned, and discarded" (p. 248). Discourses of "post-racialism" from Obama's administration signal new narratives, politics, and racial terrains (Kaplan, 2011; Logan, 2011; Orbe, 2011; Temple, 2010). In this case, we reflect upon and discuss—both independently and collaboratively—challenges we have experienced when teaching about race within an intercultural classroom.

We have all separately and jointly taught an introductory course to intercultural communication.

Situated within a historically White institution in the Midwestern United States, we, the teachers/authors, begin as students of the students as we first seek to learn from our students as we reflect upon themes that emerged throughout courses. For example, in a past writing assignment from our classes, one White, heterosexual student commented, "My family isn't racist, however they believe that leaders of America should be Caucasian." Such comments suggest racial discomfort, and perhaps fear of dealing with the first Black American president, which speaks to the persistence of racism in our "post-racial" society. On the other hand, an upper/middle-class Black woman argued for the provocative idea of "*Black privilege.*" She said, "President Barack Obama awarded my identity group with an undermining 'black privilege.'" She explained, "His presidency grants us the ability to elect another black president and increase the presence of minority politicians." Examining privilege as a systemic issue and practice, the term "Black privilege" problematically assumes a new racial order that benefits Blacks, neglects racial histories, and ignores ongoing systematic racism against people of color. DeVoss, Jasken, and Hayden (2002) argued most students' unawareness of their dominant, or privileged, group position is the primary challenge in teaching intercultural communication.

Paulo Freire (2000), wrote that the key to uncover dominance and oppression is to rename the world. Dialogue is the activity that enables and co-creates the possibility of becoming human (Buber, 1987; DeTurk, 2006; Hoover, 2011; Keaten & Soukup, 2009; LaFever, 2011; Simpson, 2008; Xu, 2013). As Freire (2000) defined, dialogue is the "encounter between men [and women], mediated by the world, in order to name the world" (p. 88). Such an authentic encounter cannot exist without engaging in critical thinking besides sharing, loving, and trusting. Freire (2000) argued that dialogue cannot occur without critical thinking that involves fear and risk, interconnects with our actions, and challenges dichotomies and static realities. Critical thinking laid up the basis for praxis, which refers to reflection and action in a dialogical process. To create meaningful dialogue of race in the classroom, instructors, and students must engage in an active co-learning process that generates critical thinking.

In this essay, we first describe who we are and then discuss challenges we've experienced in teaching and facilitating dialogues about race in the "post-racial" era. When individuals such as Michael Brown and Trayvon Martin are killed as a result of prejudice, misunderstanding, and racism, such instances not only influence and reflect post-racial ideologies present within the U.S., but translate into our daily discussions of race. Such discussions may be seen through **micro-aggressions**, or brief verbal, nonverbal, and emotional prejudice and/or discrimination that is often rendered invisible by perpetrators (Sue, 2010) and classroom conduct.

In the sections below, we feature praxis-oriented critical reflections. In order to situate our reflections, we first discuss our salient cultural identities. The process we follow in our individual and collaborative reflections is self-reflexive and dialogic in nature in order to raise consciousness about issues that we might not be aware of otherwise. First, we each reflect and write about a particularly memorable moment in discussing race with students in an intercultural communication course. Then, we read one another's responses, discuss our reactions, and formulate our next guiding question. Our discussions of a particularly memorable moment highlight the critical role that emotions play in such moments, yet we seldom address emotions in conversations about race. So, we agree to focus on the emotional undercurrents of race talk. Finally, we process our reflections through two hours of conversations.

Who Are We?

As a global team committed to social and racial justice, we situate our individual **standpoints,** or the position from which we view the world (Dainton & Zelley, 2013), to contextualize our conversations. We feature our individual reflections below based on the order of authorship.

Nathaniel Simmons: As a white, gay, southern, American-born, native-English speaking man, I grapple with my own privileged, yet marginalized, positionality. On one hand, being white often puts me into positions, often unknowingly, in which I receive beneficial treatment, known as **white privilege,** but on the other hand, as a gay man, I am constantly fighting **heteronormativity,** or the belief that heterosexuality and its affiliated norms are superior and appropriate modes for communicating, organizing, and acting (Yep, 2003). As a professor, I feel my own experiences with privilege and marginalization put me in a unique situation. Having taught within several historically white institutions, I find myself often toggling between lines where I am both "similar to" and "different from" my students.

Yea-Wen Chen: As a racial other, a non-U.S. citizen, and a new immigrant, the moments of trying to locate myself in conversations about race have been particularly challenging. I continue to grapple with what it might mean for me to be "Asian" in the classroom and how student perceptions of my racial identity might affect conversations about race. I don't know if my students always remember that I am from Taiwan but I think that they recognize me as "Asian." As much as I have experienced being racialized as an Asian other, what being "Asian" means for me has evolved over time and is still evolving. In my first conversations about race with students, I felt more Taiwanese than Asian. I was constantly challenged to think about what it might mean to be from Taiwan, a country in Asia. For example, my lack of familiarity with many U.S. cultural references that my students brought up in class (e.g., regional difference in the use of pop vs. soda) marked me as Taiwanese. Later, as I learned more about the histories of raced relations in the United States (e.g., the Chinese Exclusion Act of 1882, the Japanese concentration camps during WWII, the Civil Rights movement), I came to know myself more as Asian. Every time I was mistaken, whether as Thai, Korean, or Japanese, I experienced myself more strongly as Asian. Now that I have been granted permanent residency in the U.S. after more than a decade, I feel yet another shift in my racial identity. For one thing, having permanent residency means that I can travel more freely in and out of the U.S. and also that there are fewer immigration-related restrictions on employment opportunities. Pedagogically, it is important that I incorporate both conversations about race and immigration into discussions with my students.

Dongjing Kang: I self-identify as Chinese, which consists of two layers of meaning. First, I am a Chinese national (a citizen). Second, my ethnicity is Han Chinese, the largest ethnic group in China. In the past seven years in the United States, my "Chinese identity" has been challenged, created, and recreated in and outside of the classroom. Being an international teaching assistant, what I have been challenged about most often in the classroom is my Chinese accent. When I first started teaching as an independent instructor in 2011, I introduced myself to students that I was Chinese and that I had a Master's degree from the University of Nebraska-Lincoln. I told my students to ask questions if they could not understand my accent. One student immediately spoke up, "That is the Chinese Nebraskan accent!" I immediately dramatized my response, "I hope that is what a Chinese Nebraskan accent looks like and I hope it is clear to you!" Everybody in the classroom nodded and laughed.

Particularly Memorable Moments When Discussing Race

We individually reflected upon the following question prior to speaking: *What has been a particularly memorable, challenging, or difficult moment when discussing race for you in your intercultural communication classroom?*

Nathaniel Simmons: These last few years, rather than gloss over critical conversations regarding race that the "post-racial" society merit such as race relations, power, and privilege, I decided to confront these topics and my own fears of disrespecting a person of color or being misunderstood through discussions with my students. Yet, within these conversations, I often feel "stuck" as students default and refer to my white identity as a way in which to stop the conversation. For instance, I frequently hear, ". . . you know what I mean, right?" In a discussion of how we might become more **mindful,** the process of becoming self-aware by seeking information, one self-identified white student said that she was "lucky" because her family was "open-minded," but stated that other white families she knows are "stuck in the 'white bread of America,' you know what I mean, right?" The reality is, I had no idea what this "white bread" was—privilege? Power? Lack of diversity? I asked for clarification, but she responded "Well, you know."

It isn't just white students who speak this way in class. Just the other day when discussing the killing of Michael Brown, an unarmed 19-year-old African American teenager who was killed by a white cop in Ferguson, Missouri, in light of how perceptions and attributes influence stereotypes and prejudice, one self-identified black student said, "Perception is definitely important. There is definitely a lot of racism in the United States . . . white people . . . I don't want to offend anybody (glanced around the room and laughed), but yeah . . . never mind, I feel like you get it. It's a problem." I encouraged the student to continue, after all, students' examples and experiences, particularly students of color, are able to offer a perspective I might not quite articulate and/or understand. Yet, the student declined expanding by saying, "I think you know what I'm trying to say."

These two instances give me pause. What am I doing wrong? How can I better guide conversations about race, culture, and relationships in this "post-racial" era? Is "post-racialism" the reason my students don't want to discuss race? Although I have certainly had students express their opinion that "racism is dead," the majority of my students acknowledge the existence of racism.

Since "you know?" is a recurring theme I encounter when discussing "difficult topics," I often feel as if my own white racial identity hinders conversations of race by maintaining whiteness in a position of dominance that my students are too timid to touch. As a white person, I find it difficult to ensure that whiteness is not the dominant lens from which to explore conversations about race and ethnicity—especially when students stop short of speaking and default to "You know what I mean, right?" Although challenging, I believe such conversations are vital for intercultural communication. Past students have told me that they have never "thought about" or "talked about" this "stuff." The challenge, for me, is how to use my own identities as a tool with which to ignite conversations, and to ultimately bring change.

Yea-Wen Chen: Talking about race and racism with an Asian immigrant woman is not something that many of my students have experienced before. The invisibility of Asians and Asian immigrants in the master narrative about race in the United States poses particular challenges for me. Early in my career, such invisibility used to make me pause: What if the students perceived me as a "reverse racist" because I challenged them on the taboo topic of race? Was it relationally too risky to push my students hard to examine their racial identities? What if I could not get the conversation going? What if my end-of-semester evaluation suffered? Now I consider it a core learning objective in my intercultural communication course to make the invisible visible. Not talking about race in my intercultural communication classes would be like leaving a picture unfinished. The challenge is to lead such conversations in ways that are relevant, meaningful, and hopeful for my students and myself alike.

Dongjing Kang: I had 29 Caucasian students and one African American student in the class of intercultural communication. Around the fifth week of the semester, my students had built up good climate by commenting on each other freely on issues related to language, realities, and power. Soon it came to a chapter that focused on race. I decided to use the most current scenarios to generate questions and/or pose the case as a question to students on the topic of race. The plan at the end of the class was focused **on race in the Post-Obama Era**. I prepared the case of Indian American Nina Davuluri, Miss America 2014, and showed the students the xenophobic comments about her being a terrorist or a Muslim extremist in social media. "What do you all think?" I stated the case and asked a question. I was expecting some "discussions" between students or at least a response from students about this social injustice. What stoned me again was another long silence—no one wanted to talk about it. My students' eyes were neither on the slides nor on me. I felt the need to wait and remained silent for two or three minutes. Eventually, a voice from the corner broke the ice, "These are just crazy people's comments somewhere! I don't think they are among us! Just some crazy people think that way! I never thought she wasn't American." I thanked her for her comments and asked her one question, "Do you think racism is going away now?" She responded, "I don't think it exists here. Just exists in some crazy heads. We are pretty liberal, and we are all equal human beings." I thanked her again and raised a question to the whole class, "Is this racism, Miss America case? Are you all with me?" No one responded. I can hear the fan of the air conditioner and the cicadas outside of the window but no sound from my classroom. Some students were looking down on their phones and books. Some were staring at corners of the classroom.

At the moments of silence, I interrogated myself as to why it was so difficult to even start a conversation about race in the classroom. Is it something about my identity as a Chinese instructor/teaching assistant who is not able to create the space for the discussion about race in America? Or is it my Chinese accent that makes me such a distinct and visible "social other" that prevents the dialogue to occur? I kept questioning myself as to why silence repeatedly occurred in my classroom in the discussion of race, but I still do not have an answer.

***

As we reflected upon our experiences, we noted a common theme of silence. Freire (2000) explained, "The theme of silence suggests a structure of mutism in face of the overwhelming force of the limit-situation" (p. 106). In our experiences, students perceived race in the Post-Obama Era as a silent, absence of racial presence, which created obstacles for initiating an authentic dialogue in the classroom.

Particularly Emotional Interactions

We read and discussed each of our reflections and noticed that our experiences were quite emotional for us, as instructors, and for our students. This led us to reflect upon emotions within our classroom. Although topics of race and racism trigger and involve great emotions, we recognize that we rarely attend to the emotional undercurrents of classroom discussions about racial privilege, domination, and oppression. Therefore, we posed the following question: *What is a particular interaction with students (via assignments or discussion) that was the most emotional for us about race? What made this an emotional moment? What emotions were triggered? How were such emotions managed?* Below are our individual reflections.

Nathaniel Simmons: Teaching about **cultural identity,** or perceived acceptance and/or identifying with a group that shares a particular culture (Collier & Thomas, 1988) in a historically white institution has been a particularly challenging and emotional process for my students. Students have been frustrated and angered that cultural identity was a topic of the class. Such students believed such conversations "fueled racism" and should not be discussed. The majority of white students in my courses claimed a "lack of culture." In fact, one white, female student from the mid-western U.S. said, "I'm just a boring white girl, I don't have any culture."

To address the challenge students, particularly white students, face when attempting to acknowledge their unique cultural identities, I used six-word memoirs as a tool and outlet for emotional expression. In their six-word memoirs, students had to identify at least one cultural identity and then tell a story about their cultural identity in six words (Simmons & Chen, 2014). For example, one white, male, heterosexual, Christian wrote, "Lots to say, but nobody asks." In class discussion he explained that because he is white and a member of dominant groups that he feels muted and that his perspective is often overlooked and discounted. This particular student expressed the opinion that racism exists "only because concepts, such as whiteness and white privilege, are discussed in class." He believed that "it [racism] would go away if we stopped talking about it." This assignment provided an outlet for students frustrated with course material that conflicted with their post-racial mindset. A self-identified minority student proudly shared her memoir: "Better to be seen than overlooked." She explained that as a minority, she gains a lot of attention, but is glad to be visible amongst the majority instead of ignored. As my students shared their six-word memoirs, they began to see how their unique perspectives influenced their interactions. Several students commented afterwards that they "never thought about everyone's unique cultural identity before." This assignment changed the tone of my class. There were still those frustrated and uneasy with racial discussions, but it provided them a space to share who they are as unique individuals. It was as if students who felt threatened by conversations of race needed an emotional outlet to "weigh in" on the conversation. In other words, white students, in particular, needed to feel included in conversations of race.

Yea-Wen Chen: I have rarely talked with my students about the emotions involved in how we communicate about race. However, I now see a need to consider the emotional hold that racism has on each and every one of us. My rethinking is prompted by my encounter with a white student tearing up behind closed doors inside my office. This encounter rested on complex three-way interactions between two students and myself. Out of ethical concerns, I will unpack my emotional experience with minimum circumstantial information about the students. Since race, gender, and power are at the crux of the interactions, it is necessary to identify them as a white woman and a black man. Historically, (white) fear of black men is rooted in Western imperialism, colonization, and enslavement. Inevitably, I experienced the complex interactions from my intersecting position as an Asian immigration woman faculty. At the heart of the tear shedding incident lies the conflicting interplays of (a) fear of black masculinity, (b) anger at white privilege, and (c) unspoken racial ambivalence. The intricate interactions involved both micro and macro issues about race (e.g., interracial relating, colonial histories, etc.). In my eye, it boils down to this—straddling between a white woman and a black man, I as an Asian immigrant woman faculty was pulled between contradictory expectations. The white female student expected me to intervene whenever comments about racism might threaten or intimidate whites like her, which I think she perceived to be causing classroom "incivility." The black male student expected whites to be aware of their levels of white privilege. I, as a critical race scholar, have always privileged counter-storytelling that exposes the inner working of race as a social system. Personally, I had to confront my own fear of black masculinity in becoming an anti-racist teacher-scholar. However, my mistake is that I underestimated the depth of fear that a white person could feel in witnessing a black man's angry accounts of black enslavement. I was alarmed when she told me that she felt sick to the stomach before coming to my class for fear of his intimidation. Her fear was real. I could not guarantee her emotional safety but I knew that he would never intentionally intimidate her. Also, the myth of a post-racial society under Obama made it disorienting to talk about racism today. Should I have attended more to her fear? Would she feel less resentment toward me if I had? What could I have done differently to raise consciousness about racial and intersecting identity positions? How could I better facilitate productive conversations about racism and whiteness? I realize that all three of us were caught between fear, anger, and other emotions.

There are at least two lessons that I have gained from reflecting on this emotional counter. First, without confronting fear and anger, whites and people of color remain stuck in their racial positions and remain unable to listen to each other's stories and perspectives. On the road to healing from racism, crying, feeling angry, and other emotional responses might be productive ways of discharging hurt feelings. Racism hurts both whites and people of color. Second, as a racialized Asian straddled in-between whites and blacks, I realize that I am in a unique position to better understand both sides. My charge to myself is to challenge myself to be a better ally to both whites and other people of color so that I can better facilitate productive dialogues about race, racism, and whiteness. Ultimately, understanding racism as a deeply emotional topic means that emotional responses play a critical role in shaping, directing, or enabling/constraining conversations about race.

Dongjing Kang: Hesitant and frustrated about my students' silence from teaching the "Race Matters" chapter last week, I walked back and forth in my office, trying to find out what to teach for the next class about the "Race Matters" chapter. I had spent a whole week seeking solutions by asking other instructors about class activity and researching visual materials.

Thursday morning, I walked in the classroom with my PBS documentary "Matters of Race" in hand as if I was carrying the magic candy because I did not have to talk about "race" with my mouth. I felt that the PBS documentary would appeal more to the students who were born in this information age and also ease the class climate in some way. I was very pleased with my plan and secretly imagining that my students might have a wholehearted reflection on race. Soon I introduced this PBS documentary series on race with my dancing eyebrows. My students seemed cheered up a little bit. When the room gets dark, the PBS documentary on the screen was telling a story of King-Drew County Medical Center in South Central Los Angeles. King-Drew hospital was the black and Latina/Latino hospital and it was where diversity was celebrated. The documentary showed the daily activity of hospital staff and patients. In one scenario, children of color from immigrants or low income families saw black and Latina/Latino doctors and nurses in the hospital, which opened up possibilities for them to think differently about their future: "people who look like me can even become doctors and nurses," because they rarely saw that people of their race can become "someone like that." King-Drew hospital soon became black and Latina/Latino only, and was charged with public discrimination against "whites," so it was facing the risk of being shut down. But it eventually reopened with many struggles.

While students were working on their worksheet, I started to celebrate the fruitfulness in my imagination—my students would be more likely to exercise their critical thinking and reflect on their privileges. Students finished up the worksheet and quickly passed them to me, walking out with joy on their faces—they said "Goodbye and happy weekend" to me! That is very different from last class! Holding the stack of worksheets, excited and expecting, I immediately seated and started with grading. My pupils were dilated on the first response on the first worksheet: "I couldn't imagine this. 'Black only' is terrible!!! King-Drew should just shut down . . . This is **reverse racism**." I could not believe my eyes—the second one, third, and the twenty-third page, shared the same anger against King-Drew. Ironically, sitting in my office, I wanted to laugh and weep at once when I read through my students' answers—the charge against King-Drew with public discrimination was convicted. Guilt arises immediately after my exhaustion of grading all the responses. I wished the whole class on race had not occurred or at least I would have shown another section of the documentary. All night I had been tossing and turning, racking my brain to think what could have been done to create the space for reflecting on race in America. I also felt embarrassed of myself—my students' responses must be a result of the way I teach.

"This is racism!!!" another answer from a student's worksheet kept appearing in my brain. My world was completely flipped over.

***

Our individual and collaborative reflections highlight what we coin, or term, the "**emotional labor of race talk**." In other words, talking about race is not only emotional, but requires emotionally-laden work. Emotions must be dealt with for us, as global citizens, to heal (Smith, 2005), but also to engage in true dialogue about how systems of oppression harm our intercultural communication competence. We believe that, as citizens, we have an ethical obligation to engage in the emotional labor of race talk. This process involves not only sharing your own story, but listening to another's. People are sharing their story, but unfortunately, not enough people are listening. Globally, we need such **counter-storytelling**—featuring personal and communal experiences of people of color as legitimate sources of knowledge (Delgado Bernal & Villalpando, 2002; Love, 2004)—and listening ears. This is not just an American, Black, or White issue. Such dialogue should include reflections and discussions of micro-aggressions, identity politics, power, privilege, histories, and discrimination with attention to context and emotions. Each individual is needed and vital for the collective emotional labor of race talk in order to usher in social and racial justice through dialogue.

Primarily, story-telling between instructors and students can open up spaces for learning from experiences, solidarity, and trust. This dialogue of stories is a praxis-oriented activity that generates meaningful themes of the classroom in a larger social/political sphere. As Freire (2000) noted, thematic investigation thrives toward awareness of reality and serves as the starting point for educational process or for cultural action of a liberating character. Sharing emotional stories on race are reflective truthful recollected human experience that renders action.

As a global team, we found this process empowering to discuss our shared experiences as we reflected together about our emotional labor. Further, this process allowed us to engage in building an **intercultural alliance**. Collier (2003) defined an intercultural alliance as "a relationship in which parties are interdependent and responsible for and to each other" (p. 2). Collier (1998) explained that three key issues must be addressed in order to form partnerships in this context: (a) unearned privilege and power, (b) historical influences, and (c) maintaining an orientation of affirmation where partners affirm the others' cultural identity. In fact, the first step toward transforming relationships is a "critical analysis of how dominance is being enacted and reinforced, and how those processes preclude intercultural alliance connections" (Collier, 2003, p. 14). Your current classroom offers an excellent opportunity to start your emotional race talk labor through the following discussion questions. Such dialogue enables one to build intercultural empathy, which DeTurk (2001) defined as "a foundation on which intergroup relationships and alliances may be built" (p. 383). Race talk is not always easy. It requires sincere effort and managing multiple, sometimes conflicting, emotions and histories. However, the benefits are worth it. We are hopeful that productive dialogue may bring our global society closer to racial justice, one conversation at a time. Consider the following words of wisdom from Freire (2000) as you join us in the emotional labor of race talk, dialogue requires faith, faith in humankind who is able to create and recreate (beings, things, and structures in the world as well as themselves); and a dialogical person is critical and reflexive about the power of humans to transform realities in interdependence with other persons.

Discussion Questions

1. In what ways are cultural identity differences (e.g., race, nationality, gender, sexuality, and class, etc.) communicated and/or not communicated?
2. How might the emotional labor of race talk inhibit and enhance discussions of race?
3. How has having the first Black president in the U.S. history affected the ways in which you relate to, think about, and talk about issues of race?
4. What do you see as a citizen's responsibility regarding conversations on race/ difference/diversity in an increasingly globalized world? What do you think about the author's call for us all to partake of the emotional labor of race talk?
5. Discuss the dangers of micro-aggressions. What are some examples of micro-aggressions that you are aware of? What are some ways of handling these examples differently in order to promote racial justice?
6. What actions are you willing to take as a result of this conversation?

References

Buber, M. (1987). *I and thou* (2nd ed.; R. G. Smith, Trans.). New York, NY: Scribners. (Original work published 1923.)

Collier, M. J. (1998). Intercultural friendships as interpersonal alliances. In J. N. Martin, T. K. Nakayama, & L. A. Flores (Eds.), *Readings in cultural contexts* (pp. 370–378). Mountain View, CA: Mayfield.

Collier, M. J. (2003). Negotiating intercultural alliance relationships: Toward transformation. In M. J. Collier (Ed.), *Intercultural alliances: Critical transformation* (pp. 49–80). Thousand Oaks, CA: Sage.

Collier, M. J., & Thomas, M. (1988). Cultural identity: An interpretive perspective. In Y. Y. Kim & W. B. Gudykunst (Eds.), *Theories in intercultural communication* (pp. 99–120). Newbury Park, CA: Sage.

Dainton, M., & Zelley, E. (2013). *Applying communication theory for professional life: A practical introduction* (2nd ed.). Newbury Park, CA: Sage.

Delgado Bernal, D., & Villalpando, O. (2002). An apartheid of knowledge in academia: The struggle over the "legitimate" knowledge of faculty of color. *Equality & Excellent in Education, 35*(2), 169–180.

DeTurk, S. (2001). Intercultural empathy: Myth, competency, or possibility for alliance building? *Communication Education, 50*(4), 374–384. doi:10.1080/03634520109379262

DeTurk, S. (2006). The power of dialogue: Consequences of intergroup dialogue and their implications for agency and alliance building. *Communication Quarterly, 54*(1), 33–51. doi:10.1080/01463370500270355

DeVoss, D., Jasken, J., & Hayden, D. (2002). Teaching intracultural and intercultural communication: A critique and suggested method. *Journal of Business and Technical Communication, 16*, 69–94. doi:10.1177/1050651902016001003

Freire, P. (2000). *Pedagogy of the oppressed.* New York: NY: Continuum.

Halualani, R. T. (2011). Abstracting and de-radicalizing diversity: The articulation of diversity in the post-race era. In M. Lacy & K. A. Ono (Eds.), *Critical rhetorics of race* (pp. 247–264). New York, NY: New York University Press.

Hoover, J. D. (2011). Dialogue: Our past, our present, our future. *Journal of Intercultural Communication Research, 40*(3), 203–218. doi:10.1080/17475759.2011.617771

Kaplan, H. R. (2011). *The myth of post-racial America: Searching for equality in the age of materialism.* Lanham, MD: Rowman & Littlefield.

Keaten, J. A., & Soukup, C. (2009). Dialogue and religious otherness: Toward a model of pluralistic interfaith dialogue. *Journal of International & Intercultural Communication, 2*(2), 168–187. doi:10.1080/17513050902759504

LaFever, M. (2011). Empowering Native Americans: Communication, planning, and dialogue for eco-tourism in Gallup, New Mexico. *Journal of International & Intercultural Communication, 4*(2), 127–145. doi:10.1080/17513057.2011.556829

Logan, E. (2011). *"At this defining movement": Barack Obama's presidential candidacy and the new politics of race.* New York, NY: New York University Press.

Love, B. (2004). *Brown* plus 50 counter-storytelling: A critical race theory analysis of the "majoritarian achievement gap" story. *Equality & Excellent in Education, 37*, 227–246.

McMillan Cottom, T. (2013, December). Want to teach your students about structural racism? Prepare for a formal reprimand. *Slate.* Retrieved from http://www.slate.com/articles/life/counter_narrative/2013/12/minneapolis_professor_shannon_gibney_reprimanded_for_talking_about_racism.html

Orbe, M. P. (2011). *Communication realities in a "post-racial" society: What the U.S. public really thinks about Barack Obama.* Lanham, MD: Lexington Books.

Simmons, N., & Chen, Y.-W. (2014). Using six-word memoirs to increase cultural identity awareness. *Communication Teacher, 28*, 20–25. doi:10.1080/17404622.2013.839050

Simpson, J. S. (2008). "What do they think of us?": The pedagogical practices of cross-cultural communication, misrecognition, and hope. *Journal of International & Intercultural Communication, 1*(3), 181–201. doi:10.1080/17513050802101807

Smith, A. (2005). *Conquest: Sexual violence and American Indian genocide.* Cambridge, MA: South End Press.

Sue, D. W. (2010). *Microaggressions in everyday life: Race, gender, and sexual orientation.* Hoboken, NJ: John Wiley & Sons.

Temple, C. N. (2010). Communicating race and culture in the twenty-first century: Discourse and the post-racial/post-cultural challenge. *Journal of Multicultural Discourses, 5*(1), 45–63.

Xu, K. (2013). Theorizing difference in Intercultural Communication: A critical dialogic perspective. *Communication Monographs, 80*(3), 379–397. doi:10.1080/03637751.2013.788250

Yep, G. A. (2003). The violence of heteronormativity in communication studies: Notes on injury, healing, and queer world-making. *Journal of Homosexuality, 45*(2–4), 11–59. doi:10.1300/J082v45n02_02

35.   Community Frustration Plus a Culture of Fear Equals Ferguson, Missouri

Winsora Blanford, Ph.D.

When rioting began in response to a police officer shooting of an unarmed African American adolescent, my well-educated family who lives in the St. Louis area cried out. How do we understand rioting as a response to violence? I research the intersection of education, violence, and trauma. As a professional academic advisor, I resorted to my experience as a sworn law enforcement and probation parole officer. I remained calm while critical information emerged slowly and strategically. This information neither proved nor disproved the provocation or the response. However, I did start to suspect that different understandings and approaches in American education could have prevented this traumatic incident.

A critical thinker has both a right and duty to judge opinions based on **evidence**, "supporting material . . . sufficient in both quality and quantity to remove all reasonable doubt and establish certainty" (Ruggiero, 2009, pp. 69–70). To gather critical and relevant evidence it is best to employ an intersectional lens. **Intersectionality** refers to the way our lives flow across the boundaries of disciplines. Imagine every aspect of your life tied to a rubber band. Anything that alters the tension on one aspect will cause the other aspects to shift. Through this perspective, we can examine the effectiveness of American education.[1]

In a social media video, a young man in a downtown St. Louis parking lot exclaims that race is a social construct. His clean-cut, serious, and somber demeanor led me to guess that he was coming from or headed to work. The video seemed impromptu as the man recording prompted him to repeat what he just said. His exclamation seemed to explain something for them. However, "social constructions must be understood through *intersections*" (Garcia & McManimon, 2011, p. 13). **Social construction** is a process of giving meaning to interactions, behaviors, and conditions to facilitate communication. Cultural norms are social constructs and by deciding the norm for the culture, we assign everyone a position in the hierarchy. For instance, male, White, wealthy, adult, and Christian compose the American norm. So intersectionality becomes significant in understanding that variation in any of these labels one as lesser and weaker as we differ in gender, race, class, age, religion, and/or nationality.

---

1. To read an illustration of the power of intersectionality on America's promise of democracy see Stephen M. Caliendo (2015). He argues that housing determines education, education determines employment, and education as a contributor to incarceration.

Social constructs have powerful consequences and are difficult to exterminate (Garcia & McManimon, 2011). The assertion that "Black and Hispanic males tend to be viewed as deviant in criminal and economic institutions" (p. 10) has far-reaching influence on their encounters with employers, educators, politicians, counselors, advocates, judges, aides, and administrators, as well as with the media and community members. The problem is the tendency for the reactions to be negative.

Rena Schild/Shutterstock.com

The American Dream

In a foundation course for preservice teachers, we exchanged our personal interpretations of an article about the American Dream. Until the class discussion, I had given little thought since elementary school about the American Dream. I developed a habit of encouraging young people to search within themselves by asking in the hours that we spent together when they were taken into custody what they would do if they could do anything. Amazingly, not once would I have ever guessed the things that mattered to them. But I did note that their demeanor shifted as they shared their dreams. Some even said that no one had ever asked them that before.

During our meetings, our empathy emerged and students expressed their values, their visions, their hopes. Listening to one young woman describe in tears what her mother's attainment of citizenship would mean to her family, others started to share how some of their beliefs were being challenged. A young man told us how wronged he felt when a high school Spanish teacher chose work by Hispanic authors. He came to accept that White male authors were not the only authors with opinions worth studying. We could see that even thinking about the American Dream was relevant to social status and that those who are poor and those who are wealthy in America have different dreams. The difference may underlie the interpretation of Messner and Rosenfeld (2007). They suggest that those who are disenfranchised take Malcolm X's comment on the attainment of civil rights "by any means necessary" as an invitation to criminal behavior.

Poverty researcher Dail (2012) sums up her questions related to the American Dream: "As long as the desire to increase material wealth supersedes any desire to build moral wealth, inequity will endure" (p. 228). She stresses the problem of having dominant culture legislators who have no experience with poverty making "decisions, based upon the wrong premises" (p. 228). The themes poor women worry about or fear the most include the intersectional needs that determine quality of life. For example, they struggle with "feeding their kids, violence in their neighborhoods, drugs and alcohol issues, school problems, and paying the rent" (Dail, 2012, pp. 226–227).

Consider the ways that the struggling poor are exploited through check cashing and payday loans, subprime lending, beauty supply stores, lack of affordable child care, and overpricing or absence of big box stores (Dail, 2012). These are all "issues compassionate and effective policy can significantly impact, when the political will to do it is forceful enough" (p. 227). Themes that may preclude thinking about the American Dream include "fractured families; racial inequalities; entanglements with men; sexual abuse; and histories of personal and familial drug and alcohol abuse" (p. 227).

In a study of **sundown towns**, towns that did not allow African Americans, Loewen (2011) explains how two American Dreams exist. He asserts that while Obama's election and reelection are progress, residential segregation continues. While we may live integrated lives "on the job, on most college campuses, on American Idol, in the armed forces, in the White House" (p. 73), White supremacist thinking influences where we live and how we vote.

When Dail (2012) asked an informant what she dreams about doing (if she could do anything), she answers that ". . . me or nobody else I know gonna have any chance to do what other folks who got more money can do" (p. 226). This supports my experiences with juveniles.

Community

Community somehow feels like the extreme opposite of individualism. Black community members supported the segregated school and the schools supported the community. The sense of community developed while "parents, teachers and community members provided high expectations, financial contributions, advocacy, and leadership" (Horsford 2011, p. 47). Without interrogating race and racism, desegregation policies succeeded at "[treating] the symptoms of racism but never the disease" (Horsford, 2011, p. 84). Horsford asserts that if all children are to be educated, educators need "to understand what race is, why it is, and how it is used to reproduce inequality and oppression" (p. 96). This understanding is "an instrument of social, geographic, and economic control of both whites and blacks" (Guinier & Torres, 2002, as cited in Horsford, 2011, pp. 95–96). Intersectional thinking helps us to see that a symbiotic relationship existed between the community and schools.

Teachers, parents, and community members serve as community elders who are integral as leaders and guardians. Elders share values, exercise agency responsibly, and respond to respect by lighting the way for community's youth. Through elders can flow growth and healing. There is balance between elders' contribution to the community and the respect they experience.[2]

Criminal Justice

I visited Ferguson, where the shooting occurred. It felt like déjà vu, but I wasn't prepared. As a police officer, my arrival was never unannounced. It was usually preceded by a call for service, announced by my patrol vehicle, a uniform, and a partner.

Despite my somber mood, people appeared to move on as usual. About 15 to 20 feet of withering flowers and toys, tributes to the loss of a life, populated the median of the roadway. Under a tree north of the roadway wreaths, cards, and candles littered the landscape.

I wondered when the grounds crew last cleaned in the complex. I did not find even a gum wrapper on the ground. Vehicles were scarce (it was mid-afternoon). A few people walked, a few were at the bus stop.

I should not have been, but was surprised by the activity at the corner store. Ironically, I have always delineated between the corner store and a convenience store. The latter is a chain store that offers high prices wherever they are to account for the extended hours, security, risks, etc. The corner store is the individual- or partner-owned store that sells candy, sodas, and often illegal single cigarettes. A tremendous difference is the lack of respect some corner store owners exercise toward customers. At the corner store of the video, the lot overflowed with cars. While officers were imported to restore control, there was no sign of boycott of the store.

As a police officer, I learned quickly that law enforcement was a new culture for me. I was surprised to learn that many people were out and about at night while I thought everyone was at home asleep in preparation for work the next day. In fact, asking what police officers do is actually how I found myself swearing to serve and protect the laws of the country and the state. Soon after, I began to learn that I was not alone in lack of knowledge about law enforcement. Even many of the people I arrested were not knowledgeable about the proceedings of the criminal justice system.

Not long after my father's death, I came to realize how proud and hurt he was that I became a police officer. My father worked hard, paid his taxes, and once he was allowed to vote, he not only voted in every election, but reminded each of us of our privilege and responsibility to vote. He never experienced the protection or service of the police. Now his only daughter was one of them.

---

2. To read more about culture, community, identity, and education try Daniel Black's (2005, 2011) novels. He pens a compelling story with beautifully detailed creations of elders, a cultural space, and education. You actually follow the protagonist as he makes life-defining decisions related to bidirectional membership in community. See Black (2005, 2011).

What he never knew was what it is like to be accepted based on performance. He protected me from the horrors of Jim Crow. I never saw a sign that signaled that I could not use a fountain, bathroom, or front door of a restaurant. The five of us in my eighth-grade graduation class had sufficient personal attention from teachers. We knew everyone in the school as well as each other's families. Each of us went to church with public school teachers and principals who knew us.

Few of the officers I know consider that many citizens know little about the law. The face and gatekeepers of the criminal justice system and among the first responders in a crisis (Garcia & McManimon, 2011), police officers are people; their behavior is not subject to generalization. This means that we must search for qualitatively and quantitatively sufficient evidence to evaluate their behavior. Less than two years ago, an off-duty sheriff's deputy shot and killed a young man who I babysat as a toddler. A part of the information that surfaced was that the deputy had been charged but not yet convicted of several questionable behaviors. I also heard that when challenged, my young friend refused to relinquish the weapon in his hand. I was relieved that it had not been my decision to make, but I realized how much I dreaded ever experiencing a similar life or death encounter. While I have been successful in disarming people by talking to them, I have had to make the hard decision that I would fire.

We believe our eyes and think that videos present the evidence and probable cause that authorize police officers' actions. However, many videos do not document what precipitated the events in question. In Ferguson, the video broadcast of the store video is reportedly unrelated to the victim's encounter with the officer. By accounts on both sides, the encounter began when the officer told the two men to get out of the middle of the street. Fear can easily overwhelm the pressure of making a legally appropriate decision. In the same classroom where some students learn to fear based on myths of meritocracy, race neutrality, and colorblindness, others learn that they and others like them have no value. Psychological abuse in classrooms is described later.

The point of contention here is authority. We expect parents to discipline their children if they misbehave. Societies need rules, boundaries, and people empowered to enforce them (Law, 2006). Police officers have the legitimate authority to wield certain power based on their expertise and training. They exercise power over the rest of us. They have the power to lock us up or punish us for the violation of society's rules or boundaries. Very specific to this power is **Police Use of Force**.[3]

Police use of force refers to the very important limitations of how far an officer goes in the discharge of her duty. It concerns the "force necessary to control an incident, effect an arrest, or protect themselves or others from harm or death" (National Institute of Justice, 2012, para. 2). Emphasis on the use of force continuum was part of my training as an offi-

---

3. For detailed information about Police Use of Force, I suggest two websites:
http://www.nij.gov/topics/law-enforcement/officer-safety/use-of-force/pages/welcome.aspx
http://www.nij.gov/topics/law-enforcement/officer-safety/use-of-force/Pages/continuum.aspx

cer and it was frequently part of professional development. Arguably, training that fails to emphasize this aspect of the job would be of little value to officers or the citizens they swore to protect.

Essentially, it holds officers to the understanding that from officer presence through lethal force, responsible evaluation of the circumstances is serious.

Ideas of deserving and undeserving victims mushroom within

simez78/Shutterstock.com

media presentation (Garcia & McManimon, 2011). Victims, who are regarded as ideal victims, are provided all the help available by the justice system and the community. An obvious problem arises when a victim is determined to be other than ideal. Some victims are "blamed for the crimes committed against them . . ." (p. 60). Authorities treat victims they view as undeserving as suspects who contribute to their attack through demeanor, dress, their presence, or even their failure to realize vulnerability. When unfamiliar with the victim's culture, blaming the victim becomes "apparent in the criminal justice and community response" (p. 63). In Ferguson, the store video insinuated urgency in the officer's approach.

Education

Education is often referred to as *the great equalizer*. As such it was believed to be the major tool to change the direction of American history. For a comprehensive and intersectional study of America's persistent inequality of educational opportunity I suggest Caliendo's (2015) *Inequality in America: Race, Poverty, and Fulfilling Democracy's Promise*. It defines the "systemic disadvantage perpetuated by and within the American institution (education) that was designed to interrupt it" (p. 84). He explains the powerful links among housing, education, employment, and crime in inner-city and rural areas which are inhabited disproportionately by African Americans and Hispanics.

In postsecondary education, Jenkins (2013) proposes that we provide a more culturally sensitive environment. I concur that education extends beyond "knowing and testing, it is about striving, achieving uplifting, and understanding"—self, community, culture, and the world" (p. 21). The principles that constitute the reality of economic justice, as described by Dail (2012) are unenforceable because America is governed by the rule of law. To this end, she suggests including more minority faculty and staff. But when she suggests that family be invited to campus to participate as lecturers or group facilitators, I wonder if she has considered that this period, while it should be about more than job training, is a period in which students separate and work toward individuality. My experience is that often, campus administrators develop cultural programs that mandate participation. Mandatory participation equals time that nonminority students might spend socializing, exploring the library, or attending lectures. I wonder if they might by harmed by these restrictions. At the least, I believe that students must be treated responsibly so that lack of understanding of the existence of these extra limitations can be factored into a student's understanding of the stress they experience.

Of the many definitions that I have read, I closely identify with Roberts's (2010) description that one who is educated can "discern with clarity the gross difference between wisdom and folly . . . to live lives of substance, integrity, and forthrightness" (p. 157). He continues that rather than meaning that one knows everything, education means that one recognizes how much there is that one does not know. He holds that attaining an education is not passive; it requires effort. I would add that the returns of education are proportional to the effort expended. So much of what one learns is in addition to what is offered in class and on campus. Campus libraries put the world of literature at a student's disposal.

A few points help me associate the crisis at Ferguson with the devaluation of American education. Education is best examined through a lens of intersectionality. Legal integration has had limited success in correcting America's shameful period of slavery and the Jim Crow Era. Writing about bankruptcy's impact on the middle class, Warren (2014) points out the devaluation of education. She suggests that "over the past generation, America's determination to give every kid access to affordable college or technical trading has faded" (p. 2). She explains that America's infrastructure and shrinking research funding have beaten and broken American optimism. How many times have we heard about how different people have greatly improved their chances by working their way through school and hard work?

Christian's (2014) analysis of *The Black Flame Trilogy* illustrates how definitions and valuation of education was fundamental to the segregated Black community during Reconstruction. We can see that the relationship between the schools and the community were symbiotic. But after desegregation, the schools and the communities no longer enjoyed the sense of community that "systemizes and imparts the sum total of the psychological, cultural, biological dimensions of society" (p. 18). Black children were experiencing hardship not only in the journeys to school but by being ignored and excluded in school. So even though they were attending as mandated, closing the achievement gap meant and continues to mean learning to "acquiesce to their socially constructed inhumanity or to dehumanize themselves and others" (p. 18) like themselves.

Christian (2014) asserts that the dominant culture legislators who have no experience with poverty are making "decisions based upon the wrong premises" (p. 228). This is part of the awareness that when it comes to the material nature of the American Dream, "inequity will endure as the social norm" (p. 228) until Americans value the desire for moral wealth more than the desire for material wealth.

McKenzie (2009) analyzed dialogues with seven White middle-class teachers investigating these women's "perceptions of being white female educators working in schools serving students of color" (p. 131). She reports her surprise at the released "hostility and racism toward their students and the students' families" (p. 131). I wonder whether these participants would have felt free to comment similarly if the group was not homogenous, for example, in a diverse Educational Leadership classroom.

McKenzie (2009) drew from her childhood abuse to hear the psychological and emotional abuse the teachers unleashed against the children they are charged to teach. She noted that the teachers harmed children's psyches by shaming children in three ways. First, the teachers "saw them as diminutive 'gangsters' or freaks" (p. 133). Second, they hollered at them and "blamed the students for making them . . . act in uncaring and disrespectful ways" (p. 133). Third, "the teachers humiliated and excluded students" (p. 133), mocked them, and often put them out of the classrooms.

Even if the teachers do not verbally communicate their hostility to the students, students often know how teachers feel about them. Interestingly, but not surprisingly, the teachers who complain of students' lack of response are also the teachers who students report do not like them. "Many students know on some level, whether it is intuitive, somatic or otherwise, how their teachers feel about them" (p. 135). These interactions cause "real and negative psychological effects on the students" (p. 135).

The teachers shamed the students—treated them in ways that devalued them. What is worse, they justified their hateful treatment by claiming students seemed to need or want to be treated in unkind ways, "ways they are accustomed to being treated and they understand" (p. 136). The teachers **blamed the victims**, shifting "the blame to the abused" (p. 136).

McKenzie (2009) describes how teachers' humiliation and exclusion of students was not atypical. Putting students on display, taunting them, and encouraging other students to taunt them caused the students to experience shame.

We all pay, albeit not necessarily monetarily, for education. We may sacrifice or postpone love (Clarke, 2011). Or maybe we leave a career. Do you plan to return to your community? Is there a position there for you? These are some of the costs of education. What are your expectations?

Profoundly Disappointed

I am profoundly disappointed. As I watched the televised district attorney's announcement, I wondered how the world felt about the events as presented. Each comment from citizens of ally nations or otherwise were negatively critical of the manner in which this was handled. I will leave it to the reader to check the comments from our allies, Germany and France. Also look at comments out of Kenya and Brazil. They do not reflect a flattering opinion of the situation.

The training that was attributed to the officer's conduct was spared a trial through a scarcely used legal process. He did not have to face his peers or the citizens who he was purported to serve. So my hope is centered in the federal investigation. But I am concerned with the timing of Eric Holder's visit to Ferguson followed closely by his announcement of resignation.

Why were guardsmen called in, if the announcement was a fair carriage of justice? Would not an announcement of justice have quelled the concerns of protestors? The community offended was not represented in the system as officers, jurors, or attorneys. I believe in a system that seeks to justly serve and protect citizens. Where was even an attempt at justice?

I watched the officer's interview after being absolved of any wrongdoing. I listened intently to hear what he had to say. I was startled that he was ready to not only return to work in the same area, but thought that he would make an excellent instructor. He not only had the audacity to return to face people who still believed he unjustly took a human life, but he now imagined he was qualified to instruct others. He wasn't remorseful for the loss of life.

Discussion Questions

1. The media often speaks of the Black community. What is the Black community? Discuss the "give and take" of becoming a responsible member of a community.
2. A child feels shame as a consequence of being abused. As a survivor of childhood abuse, how might McKenzie's experience of abuse differ from the abuse the students experience at the hands of teachers? Discuss whether McKenzie honored her ethical responsibility to protect students from abuse.
3. Discuss what your education is costing you, how hard you are willing to work, and what you expect from your education.
4. Many of the stories that we hear of people "working their way through school" are from previous generations. Pell Grants started in 1972 and loans available now were not available to them. Discuss some other differences in paying for education.
5. How did the media contribute to blaming the victim in the wake of Ferguson's crisis? Who is the victim? What institutions interrupt his victim status?
6. What are the origins of victim blaming in issues of arrest and prosecution?

References

Black, D. O. (2005). *They tell me of a home.* New York, NY: St. Martin's Press.

Black, D. O. (2011). *Twelve gates to the city.* New York, NY: St. Martin's Press.

Caliendo, S. M. (2015). *Inequality in America: Race, poverty, and fulfilling democracy's promise.* Boulder, CO: Westview Press.

Christian, J. C. (2014). *Understanding the Black Flame and multigenerational education trauma.* Lanham, MD: Lexington Books.

Clarke, A. Y. (2011). *Inequalities of love: College-educated Black women and the barriers to romance and family.* Durham, NC: Duke University Press.

Dail, P. W. (2012). *Women and poverty in 21st century America.* Jefferson, NC: McFarland & Co.

Garcia, V., & McManimon, P. M. (2011). *Gendered justice: Intimate partner violence and the criminal justice system.* Lanham, MD: Rowman and Littlefield.

Horsford, S. D. (2011). *Learning in a burning house: Educational inequality, ideology, and (dis) integration.* New York, NY: Teachers College Press.

Jenkins, T. S. (2013). *My culture, my color, my self: Heritage, resilience, and community in the lives of young adults.* Philadelphia, PA: Temple University Press

Law, S. (2006). *The war for children's minds.* New York, NY: Routlege.

Loewen, J. W. (2011). Dreaming in Black and White. In S. L. Hanson & J. K. White (Eds.), *The American dream in the 21st century* (pp. 59–76). Philadelphia, PA: Temple University Press.

McKenzie, K. B. (2009). Emotional abuse of students of color: The hidden inhumanity in our schools. *International Journal of Qualitative Studies in Education, 22*(2), 129–143.

Messner, S. F., & Rosenfeld, R. (2007). *Crime and the American dream* (4th ed.). Belmont, CA: Thomson.

National Institute of Justice. (2012). http://www.nij.gov/topics/law-enforcement/officer-safety/use-of-force/pages/welcome.aspx

Roberts, T. (2010). *Simple, not easy: Reflections on community, social responsibility and tolerance.* Little Rock, AR: Parkhurst Brothers.

Ruggiero, V. R. (2009). *The art of critical thinking: A guide to critical and creative thought* (9th ed.). New York, NY: Longman.

Warren, E. (2014). *A fighting chance.* New York, NY: Metropolitan Books.

36. Life of Racism

Jennifer Evens

If we speak about religion, we can say that God has created man to be equal. We all share common anatomical structures that makes us who we are. We all have two arms for labor, two legs for walking, two ears for hearing, and a mouth for speaking. Yet, there are differences in the outer appearance, skin color, eyesight, medical conditions, and so much more. With the differences in our outer appearance, such as skin color, it is very common for some people to feel superior and discriminate. At the young age of seven, I experienced discrimination for the first time.

Diversity is the recognition and valuing in difference (Gregory, 2010). In Jacksonville, Florida, diversity isn't something that is out of the norm. Everyone was friendly with everyone, no matter if they were African American, Caucasian, Asian, etc. Since my dad is an engineer for the company BE Aerospace and since engineering wasn't big at the time in Florida, we were forced to relocate. My family had the chance to choose between three places: Miami, Tampa, or North Carolina. After visiting the three locations, my parents decided that the cozy country life that North Carolina had to offer was going to be a nice change for us all. I seemed to adjust faster than my brother because I was much younger than he and didn't spend much time in Florida like he had. Unfortunately for me, my parents never really discussed that people might be prejudiced toward me. The term prejudice means how we feel toward people who are different (Gregory, 2010). On my first day of school, I was the only minority in my class. As I walked in, all eyes were on me and I could feel myself being silently judged. At the time, I was very tenderhearted and every little thing that I heard someone say about me would break my heart. My mother could see the hurt in my eyes each day and would tell me to brush ignorant comments away.

As I said before, it didn't take too long for me to get settled. I was able to make new friends and I soon thought that the bad comments that were being made about me were finally diminishing. Or so I thought. During recess one afternoon, a boy that I recognized from the neighboring classes had approached us. My friend apparently was very good friends with the boy due to the fact that she had engaged in conversation with him rather quickly. After she introduced me to him and tried to include me in the conversation, he ignored me completely and only spoke to my friend. When he finally noticed me, he gave me a look as if I was something repulsive. When I had asked him what was wrong, he only asked, "What *are* you?" I was so young and I didn't understand that he was asking me what my race was. After a few moments of silence, he told me that I was not White. I remember telling the little boy that my dad was White and my mother was Black. I had also included that my parents were both from Europe and spoke French. His expression changed from disgust to outrage. I can remember him telling me that God didn't love me and that I was going to Hell for having interracial parents.

I had been strong up to that point, but being told that God didn't love me was my breaking point. My parents would always tell me how much God loved me and how much of a good child I was. They had spoken to me about Heaven and Hell, but would always end the conversation with, "But don't worry, baby. You will go to Heaven because Jesus loves you." They never told me I was different in race; they never thought that it was important. In Florida, there was always someone of a different race in my classes and in my neighborhood.

As I got older, I taught myself to ignore comments being made to and about me and learned that not everyone will like me. I am who I am and I love who I am becoming.

References

Gregory, H. (2010). *Public speaking for college & career* (9th ed.). Boston, MA: McGraw Hill.

37.   Is That How They Sing in Your Church?

Gladys Exum Huggins, Ed.D.

After Barack Obama was elected for a second term as America's leader, here and there I heard comments that suggested some African Americans might be persecuted, verbally and otherwise, in retaliation of his second term victory. Of course, being the "give most people the benefit of the doubt" person that I am, I did not respond or react to such comments. Life is already much too brief with too many distractions to be concerned about unsubstantiated ideas and worries. Besides, in America, a nation of opportunity and equality for everyone, and in this dispensation, who could be so mean-spirited as to plague another human without provocation? With so many races and cultures in the U.S., understanding, acceptance, and tolerance of a multitude of races and diverse cultures must now be the norm.

Laying aside an aspect of my trusting nature and viewing race relations as they sometimes are, from observation and personal experiences it is apparent that persecution of races remains an issue. Persecution can come by the process of stereotyping, an evil that plagues and destroys in diverse ways, even to the point of severing long-standing relationships. In brief, stereotyping can be viewed as the process of harboring unsubstantiated, unwarranted, and/or unhealthy beliefs (as in the case of negative stereotypes) and ideas about individuals or groups of individuals. Often, stereotyping occurs because individuals are uninformed; they lack familiarity with other individuals and groups. Blum (2002) pointed out that "all stereotyping discourages recognizing the individuality of members of the group" (p. 212).

There is a difference between racism and stereotyping, but the two can clearly be connected. Racism is deemed to be illegal by most law abiding citizens; stereotyping is deemed to be more harmful than illegal. In his article, "Racism: Negative and Positive?," Gracia (2010) discussed negative and positive racism. He proposed that "*Racism* is an attitude toward individual members of a racial group or toward the racial group as a whole . . ." (p. 210). I am in agreement with Gracia (2010) when he cautioned that racism is often based on stereotypes. It is my belief that in the minds of some perpetrators, racist ideas are birthed after such perpetrators dwell or focus on stereotypical beliefs about others.

Although I am sure I have been a victim of stereotyping in the past, my sensitivity to the act was increased a few months ago when I visited my dentist office on a typical Monday morning. Perhaps I was experiencing a higher than usual level of dental anxiety, or perhaps I had a high level of expectancy to be reassured and comforted during such a stressful time. In either case, it was one of my vulnerable moments, and I was reminded that no human will always be spared from the effects of negative stereotyping.

Guiding my black Jetta into the narrow driveway situated next to a second slender driveway that led to another medical office complex was not unfamiliar to me. For more than a quarter of a century, I had pulled up in the same parking lot, and eyeballed the same physical structure that housed the office where trusting patients, like myself, showed up periodically for the maintenance and treatment of dental affairs. Until a few years ago my husband of more than 36 years and my three children, now young adults, frequented the same office and entrusted their dental affairs to the professionals located at 630 Harryland Drive. Then as most young adults do, my three moved on to establish themselves in various ways. This included establishing new personal and professional relationships. As for my husband, he decided nearly three years prior that there was just something that made him quite uncomfortable at our dentist office. He left after a dental cleaning one day and never returned. I could tell from his comments that he felt I should follow suit.

In retrospect, my husband and I both knew that our former, mature, highly trained, tall, blue-eyed dentist had allowed a younger, black haired, in-training dentist to work with him for a couple of years before the younger doctor purchased the practice. Both my husband and I missed the sincerity and commitment that the older dentist seemed to have. We trusted our aesthetic well-being to him, as it related to dental affairs, and we were disappointed that a transition of such magnitude would occur. After the transition, it took a while to get used to the change. The younger doctor was friendly enough, I suppose, but his conversation usually was the same. He remembered that I am an English teacher so he made comments about when he was in high school or college and his experiences in studying English.

There was little to nothing extraordinary about the design of the buildings in the entire office complex. Buildings looked like red, brick triplets, but they were useful and economical. Pulling up less than ten minutes before my appointment, I parked as quickly as I could position my Jetta in an available parking space, and I hurriedly moved toward the office's entrance. As early as it was in the day, the heat was beginning to make me uncomfortable. At the moment, I was glad to find refuge in a cool, refreshing environment, albeit it was the dentist's office.

The smell in the lobby was not a medicinal one; it was neutral and clean. I had been counseled a few weeks earlier, so I knew what to expect. The plan was to extract my dental bridge that had been a stable part of my existence for more than 20 years, to possibly do a root canal, and ultimately to replace the flawed bridge with a new one. Since I knew what to expect, initially there was little dental anxiety in my heart and in my spirit. In a few hours, I was told, the procedure would be over; I could leave pretty much the way I came, I surmised.

Shortly after I entered the lobby and checked in with the receptionist, an unfamiliar voice called my name and greeted me with a moderate amount of enthusiasm. "Good morning Mrs. Huggins, how are you this morning? My name is Ana." The dental assistant, who would be a part of my life for the next few hours, had come through the door connecting the lobby to the rest of the facility. She led me to our destination, a room near the back of the facility. It was not the room where I was usually attended to, neither was the dental assistant my usual person, but the décor appeared to be similar to the other room.

There was, however, no massaging chair as was used during regular dental cleanings or no flat screen television in the ceiling to watch. This dental procedure would require more concentration and less entertainment. I knew that things would be different that day.

I felt a change in the environment from the very beginning. Ana's first task was to take an x-ray of my mouth. After three unsuccessful attempts to get the x-ray machine in the surgical room to comply, she guided me to an adjoining room where the machine was more agreeable. This surely was confirmation that things would be different, yet determined to maintain a healthy attitude, I strove to remain calm.

Ana asked, "Would you like to listen to some music? What kind of music do you like?"

I replied, "Gospel music is good." Taking my response as her cue, she selected contemporary gospel artist Kirk Franklin. Although at times I don't mind listening to Kirk Franklin, his upbeat lyrics and music were a little less than comforting in my hour of need. "Are you enjoying the music?" In response, I commented that it was okay but that I really like old school gospel music or worship songs. Rance Allen's selections were more comforting, followed by other artists. Overall, the music kept my mind off of what was to soon take place, and when the dentist sedated me, all was well. He left the room to attend to the needs of someone else as the numbing process took place.

The doctor came back to begin step one of the surgical procedure. As he and Ana worked, they conversed with each other. It was hard for me to determine what they were doing or all that they were saying. Even though I was anxious to know, my mouth was in no position to form words. Neither Ana nor the doctor felt the need to share with me. After a period of time, my dentist left the room again to attend to the needs of someone else in his office. When he returned to continue my procedure, he administered more medicine to numb my mouth. (The process of leaving me to attend to someone else and numbing my mouth occurred one more time during my procedure.) At last, my dentist was ready to finish what he had started with me. I thought to myself, "Surely, this three hour procedure will be over soon." He walked back into the operating room with a goal in mind, and I was ready. Ana was the first to initiate conversation. This time I was included, to a certain degree.

Again, Ana asked if I enjoyed the music, and I responded that overall I did enjoy it. "I am glad you enjoyed the music," Ana declared. By this time, I could hear sounds made by the doctor's instrument. I knew he must be getting close to the end of whatever he was doing. I could also hear bits and pieces of their conversation. "We won't be able to save this one," the dentist stated to Ana. I don't know what type of expression might have come on my face before Ana repeated to me what he said. I felt dental anxiety trying to enter my body when I internalized what his statement meant: I would not only lose a bridge, I would lose a tooth. This would mean more procedures, more costs, and most importantly, the loss of an important part of me.

The doctor finally addressed me by reiterating that fact that I would lose my tooth. Pausing for a moment, he declared "Well, we won't be able to save your tooth—unless Jesus grows you another one." My mouth was still in no position to form words freely, but

I felt an urgent need to respond. "Hey, he did walk on water," I tried to come back at him. Ana entered the conversation with a somewhat familiar phrase, "At least you enjoyed the music." The doctor asked, "Is that how they sing in your church?" By this time, the fast, somewhat loud tempo of more contemporary music filled the room, causing my dental anxiety to heighten. I simply responded, "Ah-no." "I think I will visit an African American church," my dentist announced. Ana agreed; she would visit one also. "It will be a good experience, but I will have to eat first," my doctor added. He justified his statement by saying, "I heard a comedian talk about how Sunday services end at 3:00 p.m." With some discomfort, yet calmly I said, "I don't stay in church until three o'clock." The conversation (at least the one that included me) ended as quickly as it had started.

My dentist resumed doing whatever he was doing in my mouth. He finished soon after our conversation, and ended our time together by suggesting I return within a few weeks to start the process for a dental implant. The surgical procedure was over, and I felt violated in more ways than one. I was left with a hollow and a bad taste in my mouth. The hollow was there because of the extractions; the bad taste was there because of insensitive medical professionals who chose an inappropriate time and place to carry on an inappropriate conversation. Perhaps without knowing it, or perhaps intentionally, their remarks and reactions were deemed by me as stereotypical and demeaning.

Some common stereotypical beliefs about African Americans include ideas that Blacks are usually very religious, they love loud music, and they are superstitious. The dentist probably considered it religious and superstitious to believe that Jesus could grow a replacement tooth, and certainly it is an inappropriate, stereotypical remark to suggest that all African American churches have extremely lengthy Sunday services. Finally, as I reflect on my doctor's visit, and my former doctor-patient relationship, that "give most people the benefit of the doubt" person I am looks at some things in a different light.

Discussion Questions

1. What is racism?
2. What is stereotyping?
3. What is the difference between racism and stereotyping?
4. Does positive racism exist? If so, what is meant by positive racism?
5. What is the difference between positive and negative racism?

References

Blum, L. (2002). Racism: What it is and what it isn't. *Studies in Psychology & Education, 21*(3), 203–218.

Gracia, J. J. E. (2010). Racism: Negative and positive? *Monist, 93*(2), 208–227.

38. Overcoming Intercultural Barriers in the Workplace: The Experiences of "Una Estadounidense" in Buenos Aires, Argentina

Elizabeth H. Jeter

In our era of globalization, the world continues to connect governments, economies, and cultures across borders. Organizations provide distinctive sites for studying intercultural and international relations, as these are places where every day "a wide cross-section of society convene, explicitly collaborate, follow the same policies and guidelines, and work toward the same goals" (Muir, 2007, p. 81). As we work within and across geographic and cultural boundaries, organizations of all types are confronted with the basic questions, "how can people from different groups work well together" (Grimes & Richard, 2003, p. 11) and "how [do people] communicate among and between these groups" (Barker & Gower, 2010, p. 296). Communication studies is particularly suited to address these questions and concerns by offering unique insight into the ways we negotiate complexity and meaning through contextualized social interactions (Eisenberg & Riley, 2001; Guo, Cockburn-Wootten, & Munshi, 2014; see also Martin & Nakayama, 2010; Pearce, 1989). Within organizational communication, scholars studying socialization theories can contribute to intercultural and international workplace collaborations by identifying the processes through which challenges arise. If challenges and their contributing factors are ignored, organizations risk effectiveness and competitiveness in a global marketplace (Herring, 2009; Zoels & Silbermayr, 2010). The following essay looks to capture the complexity and context involved in workplace intercultural and international communication that lead to conflict and misunderstanding through a narrative ethnography methodology, or autoethnography (Goodall, 2000, 2004) and socialization literature. This approach assists in understanding how interpersonal and structural dynamics affect social interactions in diverse workplaces as well as how to overcome cultural and language barriers.

Narratives of Socialization

Narrative is a powerful communication tool for conveying the context and complexities involved in intercultural and international settings. The sharing of narratives across cultures can both reveal and challenge the norms, values, and beliefs embedded within those cultures (Barker & Gower, 2010; Guo et al., 2014). When adapting to workplace diversity, narratives are essential communication tools for organizational learning and change (Barker & Gower, 2010; Boje, 1991; Lämsä & Sintonen, 2006) because "stories help us to make sense of what we are, where we come from, and what we want to be" (Soin & Scheytt, 2006, p. 55). These narrative sense-making processes also "help participants and their groups derive a stronger self and organizational identity" (Barker & Gower, 2010,

p. 306; see also Holmes & Riddiford, 2010). In other words, narratives provide an accessible framework for understanding how individuals and groups identify and position themselves in relation to organizational structure and culture (see McPhee & Zaug, 2000/2009). The ways in which individuals and groups are socialized into an organization can provide an influential frame for new members' interpretation of appropriate communication and behavior in social interactions. **Organizational socialization**, or assimilation, is defined as "the processes by which individuals become integrated into the culture of an organization" (Jablin, 2001, p. 755), which benefits new employees by reducing uncertainty as they learn the organization and find their place within it (Sollitto, Johnson, & Myers, 2013).

Recent socialization models are designed to be more culturally and circumstantially inclusive by comparing and contrasting relationship building, job performance, and organizational knowledge acquisition over time (Sollitto et al., 2013). Narratives about socialization processes can capture the cultural and contextual influences on these variables at different points in an individual's or group's career(s), especially with the clarity of hindsight to draw connections between events and create meaning to inform future behavior (see Freeman, 2009). Memorable messages and turning points are two forms of communication hindsight that function within socialization processes that contribute to narrative construction and sharing. Stohl (1986) introduced the concept of memorable messages as a method of understanding how communication has lasting value within the workplace and beyond. A **memorable message** is defined as "a message that individuals remember for a long period of time that had a major influence on their life" (Barge & Schlueter, 2004, p. 238; see also Knapp, Stohl, & Reardon, 1981). Memorable messages are informally shared between coworkers or leadership and are not a "formal socializing technique used by the organization" (Stohl, 1986, p. 234). Memorable messages are valuable because they provide "the social knowledge and skills necessary to maintain the system and behave as competent members of the organization" (Stohl, 1986, p. 231). When using memorable moments in narrative construction, it is also important to consider the turning points experienced by individuals that help make these communicated messages have a lasting effect. Bullis and Bach (1989) defined **turning points** as "specific messages that had long-term impact on [participants'] relationships . . . [and their] acceptance within the organization" (Myers & Oetzel, 2003, p. 440; see also Bullis & Bach, 1989). Building on the concepts of memorable moments and turning points, Myers and Oetzel (2003) develop a tool for measuring socialization called the Organizational Assimilation Index (OAI). The index identifies six areas of development through which successful socialization occurs, including "familiarity with others," "acculturation," "recognition," "involvement," "job competency," and "adaptation and role negotiation" (Myers & Oetzel, 2003, p. 444).

Using such tools, researchers trained in ethnography can offer unique insights into socialization processes by examining their own socialization experiences, especially when comparing the relationships between self, group/s, and organization. Goodall (2004) defines this personal methodology approach as **narrative ethnography** or autoethnography—linking "the literature in a field or on a subject with the actual telling of a life story," which creates "a new embodiment of applied communication research" (p. 187). This emphasis on applied research is fundamental because "it creates a legitimate place for telling stories about the usefulness of our theories in everyday life" (Goodall, 2004, p. 185; see also Bochner, 1994) and unites "the personal and its relationship to culture" (Ellis, 2004, p. 37; see also Peterson & Langellier, 1997). Using narrative ethnography, the researcher's observations and analysis can highlight the intimate ways socialization functions from an insider perspective, but this insight requires an awareness of and deep reflection on one's self and others in the organization (Blinne, 2012). This everyday awareness is called **reflexivity**—the process through which "people monitor their behaviors and attempt to make behavioral choices on the basis of past actions," which "enables them to modify goals, plans, and future action" (Scott & Myers, 2010, p. 80). Organizational scholars cite reflexivity as key to improving management-employee relationships and effectiveness of organizational policies and procedures (Martin, 2000). These improvements are also attributed to increases in employee satisfaction with job performance and coworker relationships (Turner & Shuter, 2004). Writing from a reflexive position requires thick description to convey the significant connection between ethnographic observations and the literature (Cheney, Christensen, Zorn, & Ganesh, 2004; see also Geertz, 1973). As an analysis of the personal and cultural, narrative ethnography can be an effective tool for interrogating power and privilege within international and intercultural organizations and institutions, especially the voices of underrepresented groups (Dutta & Basu, 2013; Meares, Oetzel, Torres, Derkacs, & Ginossar, 2004; Pal & Buzzanell, 2013; Peterson & Langellier, 1997). The following socialization narrative was constructed using Myers and Oetzel's (2003) OAI index with a focus on memorable moments and turning points (see Appendix A). Reflexivity and thick description were practiced throughout the writing process to connect academic literature, lived experience, and culture. While not all connections are explicit, the narrative demonstrates two creative socialization methods—the sharing of tea and photographs—as ways to inspire creative socialization techniques in overcoming miscommunication and conflict within an intercultural and international workplace setting.

Tea, Photos, and . . .

The interview. I sat at the small conference table in my only suit. I arrived in Argentina the week before. With the stress of moving into my apartment and starting Spanish classes, I had little time to be nervous about this interview. My Spanish teacher, Marco, was my translator, filling in the gaps between the manag-

Filipe Frazao/Shutterstock.com

ing director Maria's limited English and my nonexistent Spanish. Back in the United States, I wanted an adventure and to travel abroad, so I sent my resume in English out to 30 NGOs across Buenos Aires. This women's rights organization was the only organization that wrote back with an interview offer. Maria reviewed my credentials again, and then explained the position and her expectations. I was to come to the office four days a week from 3–7 p.m. for the next four months. During that time, she needed me to help with ongoing grants and evaluation with the grant writing team and independently complete a new grant-writing project. Their goal was to raise funds for a new program providing job training and legal assistance to unemployed or underemployed women in the city. They wanted new connections and funding from international organizations to increase their overall funding pool and expand their reputation domestically and internationally. My solo project was to build profiles on three to four organizations, and then apply for a grant with at least one. More than anything, she needed my English skills. Many international grant organizations only accept grant applications in English. Their organization had lost previous grants to miscommunication or mistakes in the application process, and they wanted at least one grant application by a native English speaker to serve as a template for future proposals. I had grant research and writing experience, so I was confident in my abilities. Marco voiced concern that my limited Spanish would cause problems, but Maria stressed the importance of my English and grant writing experience.

Marco asked me, "Eli, what do you think?"

I responded, "The project and responsibility is more like a job than an internship. Maria mentioned possible pay in our emails. Is there any money for the position?"

Marco said, "No. It is an internship, but a paid position may open in January."

"It is an opportunity worth taking."

"Perfect. You can start Monday," Maria said with a smile.

Mate and meetings. The organization had three full-time employees, four part-time employees, and community volunteers working on various projects, including community programming, grant writing, advocacy, and organizing political events. I felt a connection to my coworkers because we were all women under 27 years of age, unmarried, and college educated. My Argentine coworkers had either graduated or were currently attending the University of Buenos Aires (UBA)—the top national university that sponsored many of our events and programming. We were socially conscious with progressive political views. The organization was a steppingstone for jobs across the public and political sectors in Buenos Aires, so my coworkers were focused on doing quality work and building a strong professional network through our organizational partners. We partnered with powerful organizations and people from the public and government sectors, including federal agencies and politicians. Unfortunately, low salaries and long hours meant high employee turnover and burnout—most employees stayed three to four years—with the director, Maria, and the four members of the board of directors offering consistency.

Everyone wanted my Spanish to improve as soon as possible. I started Internet research on international grant opportunities, but I needed to collaborate with my coworkers to complete work assignments. Maria gave me the job of serving mate tea at our weekly staff meetings. I followed all her instructions—don't let the water boil, put the loose tea in the gourd, tip the gourd to get rid of the smallest tea leaves, pour the water down the side, hand the tea to a coworker, take back the empty gourd, and repeat for the next coworker around the table. In the process of serving the tea, I interacted with coworkers and practiced Spanish. Mate was symbolic for many reasons in Argentinean culture. Argentines drink mate every day. Mate is shared among friends and family, a sign of respect and camaraderie. By serving the tea, I was a part of the group. I listened to the conversation, which was a mix of professional and personal life. With help from Maria, I learned the personalities, job responsibilities, relationships, programs, projects, and hierarchy. I wasn't going to drinks or lunch with my coworkers, but I was asked to assist with professional events—such as political rallies, marches, and meetings with partnering organizations. My confidence was building.

Just keep serving the tea. I sat down at the table with mate and began serving the tea. Daniela, the grant team leader, asked me questions about deadlines and grant applications. My coworkers were talking across the table about politics and upcoming events. I still didn't share my thoughts with the entire group. It was easier to express myself in dialogue with one or two people because every conversation was a mini-lesson with language corrections and suggestions from coworkers. Give me two more weeks, and then I will be ready. I hated the puzzling looks I received from some of my coworkers as if they were questioning my presence. Sometimes, my coworkers' looks and lack of patience made me feel stupid, but I was excited about my project. My research was complete. I built a notebook filled with organizations' profiles, sample applications, and notes about the training and legal aid program. I had only shared my progress with Maria. During this meeting, I was so preoccupied with the mate that I didn't notice the group's conversation switch to foreign policy. One of the full-time employees, named Lucia, looked at me from across the table. She has a charismatic personality. I was moved by a beautiful and passionate speech she gave at a recent rally for legal reform and voter empowerment. We didn't talk much. She usually ignored me.

"Did you vote for Bush?" Lucia asked. "Do you support your country's wars?" I didn't know what to say. Political conversations were commonplace at work, but I didn't feel comfortable sharing my thoughts because of my limited Spanish. These political conversations were fiery debates, usually about Argentinean politics and history. I only knew the basics on these national topics from listening to office conversations and reading the newspapers. Now, everyone at the table was silent and looking at me.

"No," I responded. Thoughts were racing through my head, but all were too complex for me to explain. "I like diplomacy better. I don't know. I don't have an opinion." Everyone started talking. My coworkers agreed the wars were unjust. The words imperialism, capitalism, and criminal flew across the room. Lucia looked at me again.

"Do you know your history?" Lucia asked. I didn't understand the question. I didn't understand her meaning. "Do you know that your government supported the Dirt War? Tens of thousands of Argentineans disappeared, who were killed with the support of your country." I was embarrassed. We had attended rallies for and worked with the Mothers of Plaza de Mayo, but I only knew the basics of historical events. I had been a political science major and U.S. history minor in college, but Argentina was never mentioned. Many countries were just ignored in favor of countries like England, France, Germany, Russia, and China. I just stared at my coworkers. "Don't worry. Just keep serving tea," Lucia said. I didn't talk again during staff meetings.

Through the camera lens. I had a problem. Other than my boss, Maria, my conversations with coworkers were limited. I finished assisting the grant committee with updates and evaluations, but I needed more information about the training and legal aid program to finish my solo grant project. I felt incompetent. To help, Maria invited me to more political rallies and marches, but I needed a new way for connecting with others. I was on the sidelines at one street march, so I starting taking photos. My camera was a new Canon digital-SLR that produced high quality prints. Despite my improving language skills, I couldn't be myself in Spanish. My photos let me communicate without words. I gave photos of our events to Sofia for the website and newsletter, and shared photos with coworkers through email. My coworkers' phones didn't have quality cameras and many were too busy during events to take pictures. They appreciated the gesture. Coworkers started inviting me to lunches or coffee. These meetings were friendly, but professional. I didn't make close friends, but at least I got the information I needed to complete the grant application.

Moving on. On my last day at the organization, I gave a presentation for Maria and Daniela. I walked them through the notebook and grant application. They looked through the research, application, and recommendations.

"I submitted that application to the foundation last week. Daniela's email is the contact, so they should contact you for a phone interview in two months. This is the first phase of the application, so additional information and interviews will be needed. The foundation will provide translators for interviews, but most contact will be in English. Feel free to contact me by email for translation. I've also included a template for future grant applications. The information is ready to cut and paste where needed." Maria and Daniela smiled.

"This is great. We really appreciate your hard work," Maria said.

"Yes, wonderful, and your Spanish has really improved," Daniela added.

"Thank you. I appreciate how patient and helpful everyone was with me."

Maria added, "I am sorry we can't offer you a paid position with the organization. If you want to continue your internship, then we would love to see you after the holiday."

"I'm actually going to do some traveling. I'm planning trips with friends from England and Germany."

"I hope you enjoy your trips. I haven't traveled in years," Daniela said.

"Me either. Eli, you will have to send us pictures. If we need any further information about your grant project, then we will contact you. You will have access to Internet over the next six months, yes?"

"Of course, feel free to contact me anytime. I appreciated this opportunity. I learned a lot."

Discussion Questions

1. What role can narratives play in studying workplace diversity?
2. How does socialization function in bringing new members into an organization?
3. What experiences of socialization have you had in an organization?
4. Who or what is privileged in the story?
5. Can you think of creative methods for overcoming communication conflicts?

References

Barge, J. K., & Schlueter, D. W. (2004). Memorable messages and newcomer socialization. *Western Journal of Communication, 68*(3), 233–256. doi:10.1080/10570310409374800

Barker, R. T., & Gower, K. (2010). Strategic application of storytelling in organizations: Toward effective communication in a diverse world. *Journal of Business Communication, 47*(3), 295-312. doi:10.1177/0021943610369782

Blinne, K. C. (2012). (Re)storying illness identity: A five-element perspective. *Health Communication, 27*(3), 314–317. doi:10.1080/10410236.2011.618437

Bochner, A. P. (1994). Perspective on inquiry II: Theories and stories. In M. Knapp & G. Miller (Eds.), *Handbook of Interpersonal Communication* (2nd ed., pp. 21–41). Thousand Oaks, CA: Sage.

Boje, D. M. (1991). The storytelling organization: A study of story performance. *Administrative Science Quarterly, 36*, 106–126.

Bullis, C., & Bach, B. W. (1989). Socialization turning points: An examination of change in organizational identification. *Western Journal of Speech Communication, 53*, 273–293.

Cheney, G., Christensen, L. T., Zorn, T. E., Jr., & Ganesh, S. (2004). *Organizational communication in an age of globalization: Issues, reflections, practices.* Prospect Heights, IL: Waveland.

Dutta, M., & Basu, A. (2013). Negotiating our postcolonial selves: From the ground to the ivory tower. In S. Holman-Jones, T. Adams, & C. E. Ellis (Eds.), *Handbook of autoethnography* (pp. 143–161). Left Coast.

Eisenberg, E. M., & Riley, P. (2001). Organizational culture. In F. M. Jablin & L. L. Putman (Eds.), *The new handbook of organizational communication: Advances in theory, research, and methods* (pp. 291–322). Thousand Oaks, CA: Sage.

Ellis, C. (2004). *The ethnographic I: A methodological novel about autoethnography.* Walnut Creek, CA: AltaMira Press.

Freeman, M. P. (2009). *Hindsight: The promise and peril of looking backward.* Oxford, UK: Oxford University.

Geertz, C. (1973). *The interpretation of cultures: Selected essays.* New York, NY: Basic Books.

Goodall, H. L. (2000). *Writing the new ethnography.* Walnut Creek, CA: AltaMira.

Goodall, H. L. (2004). Narrative ethnography as applied communication research. *Journal of Applied Communication Research, 32*(3), 185–194. doi:10.1080/0090988042000240130

Grimes, D. S., & Richard, O. C. (2003). Could communication form impact organizations' experience with diversity? *The Journal of Business Communication 40*(1), 7–27. doi:10.1177/002194360304000102

Guo, S., Cockburn-Wootten, C., & Munshi, D. (2014). Negotiating diversity: Fostering collaborative interpretations of case studies. *Business and Professional Communication Quarterly, 77*(2), 169–182. doi:10.1177/2329490614530464

Herring, C. (2009). Does diversity pay? Race, gender, and the business case for diversity. *American Sociological Review, 74,* 208–224.

Holmes, J., & Riddiford, N. (2010). Professional and personal identity at work: Achieving a synthesis through intercultural workplace talk. *Journal of Intercultural Communication, 22.*

Jablin, F. M. (2001). Organizational entry, assimilation, and disengagement/exit. In F. M. Jablin & L. L. Putnam (Eds.), *The new handbook of organizational communication: Advances in theory, research, and methods* (pp. 732–819). Thousand Oaks, CA: Sage. doi:http://dx.doi.org/10.4135/9781412986243.n19

Knapp, M. L., Stohl, C., & Reardon, K. (1981). Memorable messages. *Journal of Communication, 32,* 27–42.

Lämsä, A.-M., & Sintonen, T. (2006). A narrative approach for organizational learning in a diverse organisation. *Journal of Workplace Learning, 18,* 106–120.

Martin, D. M. (2000). Re-examining diversity paradigms: The role of management communication. *Journal of the Northwest Communication Association, 29,* 12–31.

Martin, J., & Nakayama, T. (2010). *Intercultural communication in contexts* (5th ed.). New York, NY: McGraw-Hill.

McPhee, R. D., & Zaug, P. (2000/2009). The communicative constitution of organizations: A framework for explanation. In L. L. Putnam & A. M. Nicotera (Eds.), *Building theories of organization: The constitutive role of communication* (pp. 21–47). New York, NY: Routledge. (Reprinted from *Electronic Journal of Communication, 10*(1–2), 2000)

Meares, M. M., Oetzel, J. G., Torres, A., Derkacs, D., & Ginossar, T. (2004). Employee mistreatment and muted voices in the culturally diverse workplace. *Journal of Applied Communication Research, 32*(1), 4–27. doi:10.1080/0090988042000178121

Muir, C. (2007). Communicating diversity at work. *Business Communication Quarterly, 70*(1), 80–82.

Myers, K. K., & Oetzel, J. G. (2003). Exploring the dimensions of organizational assimilation: Creating and validating a measure. *Communication Quarterly, 51*(4), 438–457.

Pal, M., & Buzzanell, P. M. (2013). Breaking the myth of Indian call centers. A post-colonial analysis of resistance. *Communication Monographs, 80,* 199–219. doi:10.1080/03637751.2013.776172

Pearce, W. B. (1989). *Communication and the human condition.* Carbondale, IL: Southern Illinois University.

Peterson, E. E., & Langellier, K. M. (1997). The politics of personal narrative methodology. *Text and Performance Quarterly, 17*(2), 135–152.

Scott, C., & Myers, K. (2010). Toward an integrative theoretical perspective on organizational membership negotiations: Socialization, assimilation, and the duality of structure. *Communication Theory, 20,* 79–105. doi:10.1111/j.1468-2885.2009.01355.x

Soin, K., & Scheytt, T. (2006). Making the case for narrative methods in cross-cultural organizational research. *Organizational Research Methods, 9,* 55–77.

Sollitto, M., Johnson, Z. D., & Myers, S. A. (2013). Students' perceptions of college classroom connectedness, assimilation, and peer relationships. *Communication Education, 62*(3), 318–331. doi:10.1080/03634523.2013.788726

Stohl, C. (1986). The role of memorable messages in the process of organizational socialization. *Communication Quarterly, 34*(3), 231–249.

Turner, L. H., & Shuter, R. (2004). African American and European American women's visions of workplace conflict: A metaphorical analysis. *The Howard Journal of Communications, 15,* 169–183. doi:10.1080/10646170490479787

Zoels, G., & Silbermayr, T. (2010). Intercultural relations at the workplace. In M. Guilherme, E. Glaser, & M. Mendez-Garcia (Eds.), *The intercultural dynamics of multicultural working* (pp. 207–215). Bristol, UK: Multilingual Matters.

39.   The Day My Bubble Burst

Eric Magruder Price II

I grew up in a bubble. Not literally, but issues of racial tension were something that I often heard of from a secondary source. I spoke with my great grand and grandparents about their experiences dealing with racial tension, as well as learned the experiences of my mother and father who were born during the height of the Civil Rights Era. Still . . . Anything involving racial tensions was something that I knew was real, but an experience that I was lucky to not be faced with. Even through seeing gentrification affecting my hometown, or being called "nigger" while working as a camp counselor in Blacksburg, VA, racial prejudice was real to me, yet also felt like it barely touched me. I always felt like even in those situations, I was somewhat confident, felt at ease. I felt that I still had power over myself and my situation.

Then the summer of 2014 happened.

Starting with Sean Bell in 2006, it started to feel closer and closer to home hearing stories of police treatment of Black men. The ability to relate on one level or another to the killings of Bell, Trayvon Martin, Michael Brown, Ezell Ford, John Crawford, and Lennon Lacy were affecting me on a higher level than any similar news had affected me previously. What changed? Location. I was no longer in my bubble of being in Chocolate City, as Washington, DC, has been affectionately been called for decades. I moved to Winston-Salem, NC, to continue my education. Little did I know how my mental bubble was about to burst.

I started to notice some things that were different about what it meant to operate as a Black man in America, mostly because for the first time I was not a member of the immediate majority. Interactions between Black men and the police officers in Washington, DC, were bad, but there was not a thought of racial prejudice. The majority of the city's population was Black, the Mayor has been Black for as long as I can remember, the majority of the city council members were Black, the fire chief was Black, and most of my school-teachers were Black. My "I'm not home anymore" moment came to me around 10:30 a.m., on October 24.

I live in an area of Winston-Salem known as Ardmore, near Wake Forest Baptist Hospital. I've never been one to actively get out and meet my neighbors, but I have learned to wave and be cordial when walking by and seeing them. I am aware that I have to be one of the few Black people living in this area of Winston-Salem, but I didn't think it would be a big deal. On the morning of October 24th, I left out of my home to make my way toward the bus station to head to school. I had a presentation to present for my class, and I was dressed accordingly. It was nice out, bright, with a slight breeze letting you know that it was still autumn. I was wearing black loafers, Deep Royal Purple linen dress pants, a black dress shirt, a black and purple bow tie, and a Dolce and Gabbana Motorcycle-style jacket. Over my right shoulder I was carrying my grey book bag. I walked up the steep street my home is located on and made a left turn to head down another hill going toward Peter's Creek Parkway, where I needed to catch a bus to make my class on time.

When I reached the top of the hill I noticed a police car cruising down the street at a slow pace. The officer and I saw each other, I nodded to acknowledge him, and continued on my way. As I made my way down the hill, I came upon the local Hispanic-owned mini-grocery store. To my left I noticed an older black couple sitting along a wall by the store enjoying a good conversation. On my right, I noticed the same police car and officer turning in front of me just in time. I stopped so that he could enter the parking lot, and after he pulled ahead I continued to walk forward toward the bus stop.

"Excuse me, sir."

I heard in a voice behind me and I turned around. The officer had gotten out of his car and asked me if he could talk to me for a moment. I obliged and walked back toward the officer's car. He asked me what my name was and where I was going.

"My name is Eric Price, I'm heading to the bus stop to head to my campus."

"Where are you coming from?"

I told him where my house was located. He asked me for some identification and as I prepared to hand it to him, he interrupted me and asked *"Wait, first, do you have any weapons on you at all, in your bag, anywhere?"* At this moment I began to feel worried, for I was confused at the situation.

"Officer, I carry a knife with me for protection as I walk from my job to my house in the evenings."

"Well Mr. Price, let me just place your book bag over here while I ask you some questions."

Again, I obliged, at this point reacting literally to everything from a relaxed state of panic. I handed him my book bag, which he placed beside his car away from my reach, my DC ID, and my WSSU Student ID, and told him I was a student. At this point I become nervous and wanted to place my hands in my pockets.

"Take and keep your hands out of your pockets, sir!" he said not by yelling, but with sternness in his voice. I removed them quickly.

"Okay, Mr. Price, this is what's going on. There was a burglary reported earlier today on Academy and Lockland. Do you know where that is?"

"Yes I do, sir."

"Okay, we received a call about a black man wearing dark clothing and a hat carrying a bag out of a home in the area. Were you anywhere in the area of Academy and Lockland this morning?"

"Sir, I just left out of my house, which is a couple blocks from Academy and Lockland and . . ."

"And where do you live again?" I responded with my address again.

"Did you walk through anyone's yard or anything while you were heading here?"

"No, I live in a duplex and the front of the house isn't facing the street, it's facing my next door neighbor's house. I have my lease agreement in my book bag if you want to see it." He ignored my offer.

At this point, I notice out of my right periphery two other WS Police cars pulling into the same parking lot where I was being questioned. Two officers left out of their respective cars, and the officer questioning me walked over to speak with them. I turned my body to the right while he went to check my "information" with the other officers and noticed my bus pulling off from the stop I should have been standing at . . . and another police car pulling up and parking across the street.

At this point, my confusion and sense of being powerless became accompanied by subdued anger. I looked at the Black couple that was watching everything that took place along that wall and shared a laugh with them—one of those moments where both parties understood the other's sentiment, yet the words didn't need to be spoken because of shared experiences.

Nisarg Lakhmani/Shutterstock.com

Another five to 10 minutes of deliberating went by and the officer returned to where I was standing, and took out a note pad and a pen. At this point he asked me my full name, height, weight, if I had a home phone number, what was the best number to reach me at, what do I do for a living, where I work, and did I have a number for my place of employment. I answered all of his questions, hiding my fear, anger, and irritation with politeness.

"Wait, Mr. Price . . . What's your address again?"

I told him, for the third time, as he handed me my book bag which was placed out of my reach beside his car. I turned down the street in the direction I was heading to wait for another bus. I called my girlfriend just to vent, and took pictures of the police cars behind me. I was late for class and wouldn't be there to make my presentation.

Part of the Black experience in America is being in a state of fear when confronted by the police, even when you have done nothing wrong. This was extremely apparent to me in this situation, and the more I thought about it, the angrier I became—not only at the situation, but how the situation made me react. I know my rights, I didn't have to answer those questions, I didn't deserve to feel that powerless and be in a positon where four police officers needed to be present for something that I may not have done. I literally felt stuck, both vocally and physically. I know I should have asked for names and badge numbers, but everything is easier to know except when being confronted with a situation where you feel powerless. I feared for what could happen and knowing that the odds were completely stacked against me. I don't know all legal police procedures, but I do think back to one situation and wonder what if.

What if instead of 10:30 a.m., it was 10:30 p.m.? When putting my hands in my pocket would there have been enough light to show I wasn't brandishing a weapon? And at what point will me being a Black male not be considered a threat to an officer's life? When will I not be a suspect? Would I even be able to tell this story? And even though those are all what-ifs, I honestly fear for the day this can possibly happen again.

Discussion Questions

1. Why is it important to understand the role of the social and historical contexts in intercultural conflict?
2. Why do you think the author was concerned about this incident happening at night? Do you think his concern is justified? Explain.
3. How does the context of the larger society contribute to the formation of identity?
4. What stereotypes are reinforced in television shows and movies about African American males and the criminal justice system?
5. Reflect upon your own identity and how they relate to intercultural communication. In what contexts and in which relationships do you feel most comfortable? Which aspects of your identity are most confirmed?

40.   Ni Latino, Ni Hispano: A Journal of Resiliency and Social Justice

Juan A. Rios Vega, PhD

Childhood

I was born on January 1, 1971, in a province located in the western part of Panama City. Although my birth name is David, my mother decided to baptize me as Juan since that was her father's name. Her father passed away three days before my mother gave birth to me. I am the youngest of three children. My parents split up when I was four years old, so I never really had a chance to live with my father. As a result, my childhood was not easy. I do not remember having a conversation with my father as two friends would. I only knew he was my father and that I needed to respect him. I used to see him on Saturdays when he gave us money to buy food and pay some household bills. My father owned a welding and car repair shop, and my mother was an elementary school home economics teacher. I did not have a lot of luxuries as I was growing up since my mother lived on a very tight budget; however, I had the opportunity to attend a neighborhood school where I was able to learn how to read and write.

Education

When I was four years old, my mother did not want me to know that she and my father were no longer together. My mother decided to register me in a local school since there was no one who could take care of me at home. I still recall my *maestra* (teacher) Margarita and my first field trip in the city downtown dressed in a clown costume. When the end of the school year was approaching, my mother decided to take me out of class since she did not want me to get excited about graduation; however, my teacher suggested to my mother that the school psychologist would be testing students' IQ to make sure everyone was ready for first grade and that she should let me be tested as well, so my mother agreed. After I was tested, the teacher told my mother that I was ready for the first grade. Since then, I have not stopped studying. When I was in the fourth grade, I first experienced having a teacher whose ethnicity was different from my ethnic group. Since she was a tall Black teacher, all of my classmates considered her a tough woman. It was not common to see a Black woman working in the countryside, especially as a teacher. Most Black Panamanians used to live in the city or nearby regions. I wondered how she felt being the only Black woman in the school. Even though she was a good friend of my mom's, I failed her class. I guess it was traumatic since it was the only bad grade I've received in my transcripts since then. I studied in the same school building for over nine years during my elementary and middle school years until I attended high school in the city.

For that, I had to use public transportation, and then walk over 30 minutes to my school. I have always liked to study and to learn; however, I never thought I had the patience to become a teacher. I recall reading my mother's schoolbooks. I had wonderful role models in my life. First, my mother who always worked so hard to raise my siblings and me became our best friend and confidant. Second, my grandmother, my mother's mom, who while in a wheelchair taught us how read, write, recite poems, and enchanted us with her storytelling from her childhood. Third, my *Tio Roger* (Uncle Roger), who I considered the most intellectual man in the family, became my biggest inspiration. He knew almost every single word in the dictionary. His love for reading and his stories of hard work and success gave me the foundations to become as good as he was; however, through my uncle, his wife, and children, I first understood about socioeconomic class. My cousins were not very close to us even though my mother was their only aunt. They usually attended better schools, received a lot of presents for Christmas, participated in sports, and traveled to Disneyland in the summer. Later on, I discovered that their attitudes were influenced by their mother, a White middle-class woman, who used to live in one of the best areas in the country. Later on, I also learned that she was very prejudiced against Blacks and indigenous Panamanians. Her attitude of superiority toward others was always obvious but she and I got along fairly well. She used to invite me to her house around Christmastime so I could help her decorate her house. She used to pay me for doing that. Maybe it was just another way to show me that she belonged to a higher social class, or maybe she was trying to help me with some extra money. My lack of knowledge about my country's societal structure along **White privilege** made me internalize that my relatives' lifestyle was the norm. Peggy McIntosh (1989) defines White privilege as "an invisible package of unearned assets" (p. 216) which White people use on a daily basis but are not consciously aware about it. For Bonilla-Silva (2010), that White privilege is analyzed as White supremacy in Latin American countries, along with a color-blind racism, which are understood as the norm, silencing those who decide to challenge it. Unfortunately, once you talk about *"rabiblancos"* (White rears), as we call them in Panamá, people either remind you there is nothing you can do about it or that you have an inferiority complex. In other words, people internalize a hidden racism and classism as the norm. Pease (2010) claims that most White people have little awareness about their racial identity since they do not have to think about themselves as White; however, they still benefit from White privilege.

I have always considered myself as an extroverted person. During my school years, I liked to meet new people, get involved in different school projects, and volunteer in the community, especially at church. When I was in my junior year, I happened to hear of some scholarships given by the American Embassy to high academically achieving students in Panama to pursue an undergraduate education in the U.S. I always wanted to receive one of those scholarships, and for that I studied very hard during my last two years of high school; however, I never got it, so I gave up. When I finished high school, I was only 15 years old, but I wanted to leave my mother's house so bad because I felt frustrated because of the lack of economic resources my mother could offer me to pursue a higher education. By that time, I used to have a girlfriend named Graciela. We made many plans of going to college and becoming successful people. We dated for almost two years until I decided to move to Panama City to make my dream of pursuing a higher education, and more opportunities, come true. By that time my cousin Iris came to visit us during the summer of 1989, and she encouraged me to move to the city to live with her parents, my mother's half-sister and her husband.

It was not until I decided to leave my mother's house when I first truly experienced race, racism, and White privilege. Historically in Panama most Blacks speak Caribbean English, even when their English has been stereotyped as bad for many years; as a result, I was not expected to know much English since I did not represent that ethnic group. On the contrary, I came from an area that had been famous for raising cattle and farming, so my classmates and professors' expectations were not very high. Since I had a different accent while speaking Spanish, my cousins in the city used to make fun of me. I could never find a job during my first years of college. It was very hard for me to live on a limited budget. There were many times when I felt miserable, but I always found my comfort zone while reading my books or using the libraries as my biggest hiding places. Being an avid reader allowed me to win a writing contest, which then helped me to find my first job. My writing professor, Melva Goodin (a Black Panamanian woman), asked the class to watch a video of the construction of the Panama Canal by the West Indians. After that, we were asked to write a critical paper about the video. Since I had already watched that video at the U.S. Embassy library, it was easy for me to brainstorm my ideas about the topic. To my surprise, I won the contest, and it was also the first time that I had written about a different ethnic group other than my own. This experience helped me to value other people's contributions in my country, but most importantly it helped me to stop being prejudiced again Black Panamanians. Takimoto Amos (2003) suggests the marginalization of a minority group within a country by making them feel invisible and insignificant in mind, values, beliefs, and behaviors. This contest also allowed me to get my first job as a part-time secretary for a nonprofit organization that promoted the Afro-Panamanian culture. My willingness to work and loyalty to my first boss, Ms. Goodin, led me to first become a museum guide for the Afro-Panamanian Museum; then I became its executive director for three years. This job helped me to meet people from different parts of the world. My experiences of living and studying in Panama City, as well as working at the Afro-Panamanian Museum of Panama helped me to understand and value an ethnic group different than my own. My college professors, most of them Black women, instilled in me that hard work will always pay off. Now I am a current member of the nonprofit organization that supports the Afro-Panamanian Museum of Panama.

While still in my last semester of college, I was called to apply for a scholarship contest the U.S. Embassy was offering. I reluctantly applied to this contest since I had had negative experiences during my high school years. To my surprise, I became one of the winners. This scholarship took me to Delaware for two months. During that time, I was placed in an English Language Institute, where I improved my English language. I also had the opportunity to do some research on my graduation paper. Three months after I came back from Delaware, I graduated from the University of Panama with a Bachelor of Arts in English.

After working three years in the Panamanian public school system and six months in a private school, I decided to apply for an international job as a teacher in America. Again, to my surprise, I was chosen to come to North Carolina on August 1, 1999.

My American Dream

Living and working in the U.S. as a teacher, community leader, cultural broker, and graduate student have been the most challenging and rewarding experiences of my life journey thus far. Through part of this journey, I first experienced racism, xenophobia, segregation, and prejudice. When I first came to work in a rural area in North Carolina, I never thought that a country that I had considered as the best role model for democracy and equality was still living issues that I had previously learned through history books back home. My first **culture shock** was to witness racially segregated churches. It was hard for me to believe that there were separate services for Blacks, Whites, and Latinos. I realized that there were more churches than schools. Suárez-Orozco and Suárez-Orozco (2001) claim that immigrants shape their identities based on how they are viewed and welcomed by the dominant culture. They agree that discrimination and society structure add to the stressful experience of immigration. Pedersen (1995) claims that culture shock is an individual's immersion in an unknown place where he does not have a clear picture about his and others' expectations. This state of uncertainty pushed me to move to a city close by (45 minutes away from my workplace), so I could witness more diversity and tolerance.

Living my dream of coming to the U.S. to work never made me think that my Spanish language, skin color, and ethnicity would label me as a Mexican. Later on and through my students and their parents, I learned that being Mexican was also a **micro-aggression.** A micro-aggression is the representation of a complex and understated form of racism (verbal, nonverbal, and/or visual) toward people of color, often automatically or unconsciously. Microaggressions are rarely analyzed. Instead, they are taken as normalcy (Delgado & Stefancic, 1992; Johnson, 1988; Lawrence, 1987; Solórzano, 1998; Solórzano, Ceja, & Yosso, 2000). In my experience as a Latin American immigrant, my presence as a brown-skinned man with a Spanish accent in English made me illegal, a drug dealer, a cheap laborer, unintelligent, ignorant, a gang member, drunk, violent, and a risk for teen pregnancy. I also learned that being Mexican meant being an individual who did not pay taxes or who came to this country to take Americans' jobs. Takimoto Amos (2003) agrees that people in America make distinctions according to language skills. After I came to realize that all of these things were also part of living my American dream, I decided to become an advocate for my students' parents and their voice in the community at large. This leadership role led me to become a freelance writer for a Latino newspaper, a guest columnist for a local paper, a community liaison, cultural broker, cross-cultural leader, interpreter, translator, and community leader. After five years of hard work and commitment, a group of loyal community members and I founded the Latino Coalition of Randolph County, a nonprofit organization that promotes and educates Latino/Hispanics on how to navigate the American system, and also helps people who are set in their old ways to better understand their new neighbors.

Since schools are a reflection of everyday society, I also experienced a lot of racism and xenophobia from teachers, colleagues, and American students. I felt marginalized many times by colleagues who never included me as another staff member, but who made me feel as an outsider. I felt that they never appreciated my culture and language and how both things could also enrich their own lives. There were times when I attended some school events and no one talked to me. Maybe because no one ever talked to me about the "culture of power" (Delpit, 2006), it was totally new for me to understand that the school had different codes and rules that I needed to learn in order to participate in the culture of power. I used to volunteer at the school games in order to fit in, but I always felt ignored, especially by my own colleagues.

I always share two micro-aggression examples I faced while working as an ESL teacher. On a weekend night on May 5, I ran into one of the school administrators who greeted me so nicely (maybe he was already tipsy or drunk). When he saw me, he started shaking his hands, pretending he had two maracas, and said, "Mr. Rios, Cinco de Mayo, Ricky Martin." I wondered if he knew Cinco de Mayo is related to Mexico's Battle of Puebla, which has become commercialized in the U.S. I wondered if he realized that Ricky Martin was Puerto Rican. I still do not know the meaning of the maracas. The second micro-aggression took place in another school. After summer break, a school secretary asked me, "Mr. Rios, were you the one waving a flag on the highway? I saw somebody who looked just like you." I looked at her and other secretaries and responded, "You know, well all Mexicans look alike." My colleagues and other secretaries were in shock with my comments. I was really upset about carrying all those labels that do not define me at all. Even though I have to acknowledge prior Latino/a studies in academia, I still claim that the Latin American immigrants' experiences before and after coming to this country should be analyzed through a qualitative lens. I argue that lumping Latin American immigrants or U.S.-born Latinos/as into the category of Latino or Hispanic perpetuates majoritarian and dominant assumptions that understand the Latino/Hispanic group as homogeneous, static, and passive. As a result, most of us become victims of stereotypes, biases, and low expectations.

After 15 years in this country, I learned how to navigate the margins of the odd. My firsthand experiences with issues of race, ethnicity, language, class, and gender caused me to wonder how these things shaped my identity and my students' identities. This constant questioning pushed me to pursue graduate education after almost four years of waiting since I could not attend graduate school unless I paid out-of-state tuition. Once I changed my immigration status, I was accepted as an in-state-tuition student. I not only learned about the history of English language programs in the U.S., but also I found answers to my questions on how living in a culture of Whiteness influenced Communities of Color in the U.S., especially in education.

Unfortunately, by the end of 2012 I decided to quit my job as a high school ESL teacher. My critical analysis on the education system and its disservice toward students of color, as well as feeling disrespected and frustrated for becoming a teacher assistant, which administrators called co-teaching, pushed me to leave the public school arena to become a full-time doctoral student. I have to confess that it was a big stretch, financially and personally, but it was the time I needed to focus on my dissertation work to gain some experience teaching pre-service teachers.

Even though I find myself at a different level on my educational journey, my former students, their families, and new families are still my friends and they are the reason why I keep advocating and teaching for and about Latino/a students in this country. I know that I am not alone on this journey since there are other scholars like me who advocate for social justice in education.

Discussion Questions

1. What is White privilege and how does it travel beyond the U.S. borders?
2. Why do the labels Latino or Hispanic affect Latin American immigrants in this country?
3. How do microaggressions affect Communities of Color? Can you give some examples of microaggressions found in children's books, magazines, songs, movies, etc.?
4. Have you ever met a person of color whose experiences with racism, gender discrimination, skin color, English language accent, immigration status, or sexual orientation have shaped his/her identity in this country? How?
5. Based on the author's narrative, how can schools better prepare teachers and school administrators to support the educational experiences of Latin American students and their families?

References

Bonilla-Silva, E. (2010). *Racism without racists: Color-blind racism and racial inequality in contemporary America* (3rd ed.). Lanham, MD: Rowman & Littlefield.

Delgado, R., & Stefancic, J. (1992). Images of the outsider in American law and culture: Can free expression remedy systemic social ills? *Cornell Law Review, 77,* 1258–1297.

Delpit, L. (2006). *Other people's children: Cultural conflict in the classroom.* New York, NY: Norton & Company, Inc.

Johnson, S. (1988). Unconscious racism and the criminal law. *Cornell Law Review, 73,* 1016–1037.

Lawrence, C. (1987). The id, the ego, and equal protection: Reckoning with unconscious racism. *Stanford Law Review, 39,* 317–388.

McIntosh, P. (1989). White privilege: Unpacking the invisible knapsack. In H. S. Shapiro, M. C. Davis, & P. Fitzpatrick (Eds.), *The institution of education* (6th ed., pp. 215–218). Boston, MA: Pearson.

Pease, B. (2010). *Undoing privilege: Unearned advantage in a divided world.* London, UK: Zed Books.

Pedersen, P. (1995). *The five stages of culture shock: Critical incidents around the world.* Westport, CT: Greenwood Press.

Solórzano, D. (1998). Critical race theory, racial and gender microaggressions, and the experiences of Chicana and Chicano scholars. *International Journal of Qualitative Studies in Education, 11,* 121–136.

Solórzano, D., Ceja, M., & Yosso, T. (2000). Critical race theory, racial microaggressions, and campus racial climate: The experiences of African American college students. *The Journal of Negro Education, 69*(1/2), 60–73.

Suárez-Orozco, C., & Suárez-Orozco, M. M. (2001). *Children of immigration.* Cambridge, MA: Harvard University Press.

Takimoto Amos, Y. (2003). Navigating marginality: Searching for my own truth. In G. Gay, (Ed.), *Becoming multicultural educators: Personal journey toward professional agency.* San Francisco, CA: Jossey-Bass.

Chapter 10

Engaging Intercultural Communication

41. Cultural Perspectives of Political Understandings

Regina Williams Davis, Ph.D.

In the field of Communication Studies, the interview is a qualitative research tool for data gathering to uncover beliefs, attitudes, political views, and worldviews. The questionnaire may be used as a device to initiate an experiential focus of where understandings or misunderstandings of culture, politics, and diversity in terms of race, social class, ethnicity, culture, alternative life styles, religion, gender, exceptionality, and the "other" intersect; and how these understandings are communicated and transmitted across generations.

People who are perceived as different are likely to experience bias and differential treatment as well. Most people do not realize they perpetuate bias through communication. What better time in life than being a college student to grapple with these complex notions of culture, communication, and politics?

For many who study issues of racism, social class discrimination, misogyny, and other forms of bigotry, they often believe that ineffective communication (verbal and nonverbal) exacerbates these longstanding problems. Effective communication must be adequately addressed when seeking to reduce misunderstandings about culture and its impact on politics. Most political issues may seem simplistic because they are communicated in a 10-second soundbite to persuade or dissuade the listener quickly, when the essence of the issue is much more complex than a 10-second soundbite or even a 140-character tweet.

Using an interview for promoting the understanding of how people may communicate the manifestations of "isms" in conjunction with the political discourse of race, social class, gender, special needs, religious differences, and alternative lifestyles is an assertive approach toward "staring these issues in the face"; looking at oneself in the mirror; and effectively learning the intensity of the deep-seated roots of cultural incompetence. This exercise is a critical component of cultural communication and learning to see where the student interviewer has misunderstandings. The student interviewers should and must feel something from this experience and should be prepared to write about it.

Monkey Business Images/Shutterstock.com

The interview has statements that express variations in culture, religion, and language to help demonstrate how individuals can be perceived as self-contradictory in their understandings. Some examples may be:

1. "I believe in a woman's right to choose; yet, I do not believe in the right to bear arms."
2. "I don't believe in big government. Government needs to be small and less regulatory; yet, I believe that a constitutional amendment should exist to ensure that marriage is only recognized between one man and one woman."

Hopefully students will gain insight and understand effectively what marginalized populations all too often experience in America. Preparing future voters and public servants to represent a more varied population than ever before in the history of this country is the impetus for encouraging college students to interview individuals, tabulate their data, and discuss the results in class.

When conducting these interview sessions, individuals are often reluctant to share their true feelings and beliefs when in group settings. Therefore, it is essential that individual meetings are conducted in a quiet and comfortable environment. The person you are interviewing should feel relaxed and that they can trust you. Please keep your personal opinions to yourself and minimize facial expressions that may convey a nonverbal message. Remember, we all have bias and personal preferences. The potential for future success of today's college student can be impeded by allowing the baggage of racism, sexism, social class bias, or other prejudices to continue and manifest.

Using the data collected from the interview to start hard conversations about culture and politics will only be the beginning. Self-talk will continue as students, professors, and the individuals interviewed reflect on their initial responses to some of these prompts. This exercise may be life changing.

Key Terms

Bias, Cultural Groups, Culture, Communication Competence, Decode, Diversity, Dual-perspective, Encode, Ethnocentrism, Fields of Meaning, Globalization, Intercultural Business, Intercultural Communication Competence, Political Views, Qualitative Research, Worldview

Key Concepts

Intercultural communication is transactional, a process, systemic, dynamic, contextual, and symbolic.

The steps toward developing intercultural communication competence include self-awareness, developing a dual perspective, active listening, and cultural difference.

Application Activity: Curious Cultural and Political Communication: An Interview

Objective

This assignment will help you realize that communication behaviors and beliefs across ethnicity, race, and culture have heavy influences on the direction of the political climate. As future voters, public servants, and leaders, you will be responsible for interacting with a wide variety of people. It will be your responsibility to develop cross-cultural skills in communicating with them.

Directions

Conduct **two separate** interviews (each separately). Please be sure to conduct one interview with someone who is ethnically similar to you and a second interview with someone of a different ethnicity. You will ask your interviewees a series of questions listed on the following questionnaire. Record their actual responses. Do not change their words. What the interviewee says is what you should report, regardless of the harshness of the content. Your task is to record their responses, organize the results, and then prepare a narrative to reflect the data that you've collected. The data, tabulations, results, and narrative must be typed and double-spaced. Charts and graphs are encouraged!

INTERVIEW

Section I. Questions on American Culture

1. What is your understanding of our social welfare system?

   _____

   _____

2. What group do you believe receives the majority of services?

   _____

   _____

3. Name two minority groups in the United States.

   _____

   _____

4. Name two minority groups in Canada.

   _____

   _____

5. What is the largest minority group in California?

   _____

   _____

Section II. Cultural Practices (You select a minority for the interviewee)

1. What types of foods do you commonly eat? What types of foods do you perceive are an untrue stereotype for your ethnicity?

   _____

   _____

2. What types of music do you commonly listen to? What types of music do you perceive are an untrue stereotype for your ethnicity?

    _____

    _____

3. What types of clothes do you commonly wear? What types of clothing do you perceive are an untrue stereotype for your ethnicity?

    _____

    _____

Section III. Personal and Political Responses

1. What is your understanding of liberalism? (Explain)

    _____

2. What is your understanding of conservatism? (Explain)

    _____

3. Should a naturalized citizen be allowed to become President of the United States?

    a. Why?

    _____

    b. Why not?

    _____

4. Should an American-born Muslim be allowed to become President of the United States?

    a. Why?

    _____

    b. Why not?

    _____

5. Should a person with a physical disability be allowed to become President of the United States?

   a.   Why?

   _____

   b.   Why not?

   _____

6. Should an atheist be allowed to become President of the United States?

   a.   Why?

   _____

   b.   Why not?

   _____

7. Should a racist be allowed to become President of the United States?

   a.   Why?

   _____

   b.   Why not?

   _____

8. Is there any group in particular that irritates you?

   a.   Why?

   _____

   b.   Why not?

   _____

9. Demographic Information on Interviewees (Please record the information requested below for each interviewee)

   a.   Age of your interviewee _____

   b.   Sex of your interviewee _____

   c.   Ethnicity of your interviewee _____

   d.   Level of education of your interviewee _____

   e.   Social class of your interviewee (according to interviewee) _____

   f.   Range of geographic experience of your interviewee _____

   g.   Has been outside of the state _____

   h.   Has been outside of the region (southeast) _____

   i.   Has been outside of the country _____

MINI QUIZ

10. True or False: Nonverbal communication is the one aspect of communication which is consistent across cultures.

11. Multiple Choice: Cultural groups share

    a.   Values and beliefs
    b.   Attitudes
    c.   Traditions and norms
    d.   All of the above

12. Fill in the Blank: _____ is a process where you really attend to the messages of another person and interact with them to analyze your understanding.

13. Essay: Think about your future career goals. Explain how your understanding of intercultural communication, your personal political view, and personal bias may influence your ability to communicate with others.

42.   The Japanese Business Card Exercise

by Daniel Richardson

When discussing intercultural communication, you may find some unique differences in areas of communication that may seem very small with little impact. Simple etiquette is one of these areas. To demonstrate this to my students, I have them participate in "The Japanese Business Card Exercise." The exercise is dramatically acted in my classroom as follows:

1. I ask two student volunteers to leave the room with me. I explain the exercise to them.
2. When we return, I explain to the class that these two students are two Americans attending a business-networking event. The two students meet and exchange business cards (I provide the cards). The students glance at each other's business cards, have a short conversation, and one student mentions their company has a new website. The second student pulls out a pen, crosses out the original website on the face of the business card, and writes in the new website address before putting the card into their pocket. (All this behavior would be considered acceptable [not polished perhaps] in our western culture.)
3. For the second scenario, I explain to the class that one student is a Japanese businessperson and the other person is an American businessperson at this same networking event. The two students meet and exchange business cards. The American glances at the Japanese card and waits while the Japanese businessperson takes time to read and absorb the information on the American card. A short conversation ensues and the Japanese businessperson mentions their company has a new website. The American whips out a pen and starts to write across the face of the business card. The Japanese businessperson protests and the American responds, "It's okay. I do this all the time." and proceeds to write in the new website before stuffing the card into their pocket.
4. The epilogue is that the Japanese businessperson excuses himself/herself and does not speak to the American again or take their phone calls after the event. The American is puzzled and asks a friend who is more knowledgeable about Japanese culture if they did anything wrong. The friend explains:
    a. Merely glancing at the business card without reading and absorbing the information is considered rude.
    b. Stuffing the business card into your pocket is considered extremely offensive.
    c. Writing across the face of the business card is viewed as a direct insult.

5. When the American businessman says they don't understand why making an important correction on the face of the card would be insulting, the friend says, "Permit me to demonstrate the equivalent behavior in our culture." He takes out a pen and starts writing across the face of the American businessman (I make sure the students don't actually touch each other).
6. "Now do you understand," the friend begins. "Would you do business with me after I just wrote across your face?"
7. "Heck no!" the American businessman retorts.
8. "Well, in Japan, the business card is an extension of the individual and writing across its face would be like writing across your face," states the friend.

I like the experiential component of the exchange because my students are able to understand the level of insult being offered in a way that is difficult to grasp with mere explanation. Sensitivity to intercultural communication and nonverbal messages across cultures will help minimize such misunderstandings in real life situations.

43. In Black and White: Race and Communication

by Myra Shird

Overview

Communication patterns also differ by cultural affiliation and race. Cultural groups share speech codes: distinct system of communication rules, norms, and patterns that guide their communication behaviors. These speech codes differ by race, causing interracial tensions. Making an effort to learn about other cultures to check our understanding before jumping to conclusions will help us to be more effective in our personal, social, and professional relationships.

Objectives

1. To learn the guiding principles for assessing communication differences among races.
2. To become more aware of the differences in communication patterns between the Black and White Race.

Attention-Getter

Activity 16: Is All That Passion Necessary?

A. Ask the class if they have any examples of the differences in the way Black people speak, compared to White people?

(There are differences in their posture and passion.)

i.e., Black people often tend to

- ▶ use religious/spiritual terminology,
- ▶ sound preachy,
- ▶ be animated,
- ▶ get confrontational,
- ▶ be assertive, and
- ▶ raise their voices.

i.e., White people seem

- ▶ less passionate,
- ▶ softer spoken,
- ▶ matter-of-fact and
- ▶ appear to be more practical.

How can you as a public speaker use this information?

Supporting Materials

PowerPoint's, Activities 16 and 17

General Outline

In Black and White: Race and Communication

Preview

- ► *Guiding Principles*
- ► *Communication Patterns by Race*

Guiding Principles

Different Does not Equal Wrong

Identifying differences in communication patterns among different cultural groups is not judging which group communicates better.

- ► Cultures are Dynamic.
- ► Racial identities are not static.
- ► To be Black or White today is different than fifty years ago.
- ► Cultures change as they respond to the world and people around them.
- ► Definitions of race change.
- ► Cultural Competence is a Process.

To learn how to communicate effectively with people from a different background requires

- ► Time
- ► Effort
- ► An open mind
- ► Self-discovery
- ► and a little discomfort

Learning about Others Helps Self-Understanding

- ► A personal encounter with another culture brings out the assumptions we had about that culture that we were not aware of.

Apprehension about Racial Differences is Normal

▶ Feeling self-conscious about encountering another culture is normal.

▶ Although race does not define a person, attitudes, values, and beliefs of our racial culture do influence communication patterns.

Communication Patterns by Race

Language Use

▶ Black people tend to be creative with language and use words and sayings that have specific meanings to other Black people.

▶ A shared code that reinforces a shared identity.

▶ White people tend to use language literally.

▶ The use of words that have a specific dictionary definition.

Sequencing

▶ Black people tend to organize their ideas in a web-like or circular fashion.

▶ White people tend to organize their thoughts in a linear fashion.

Eye Contact

▶ Both Black and White people tend to interpret eye contact the same way in some ways.

Direct eye contact

▶ Honesty and respect.

▶ Lack of direct eye contact.

▶ Lying or hiding something.

▶ Some Black people tend to maintain direct eye contact while they are speaking, and look away when listening.

▶ Some White people maintain eye contact while listening and avert their eyes while speaking.

Emotional Expressiveness

▶ The use of inflection, vocal range, rhythm, emphasis, and tone when speaking.

▶ Blacks tend to be emotionally expressive in their speech and value authentic displays of emotion in public.

▶ Whites tend to be more reserved in their speech and value self-control in public.

Taking Turns

- ► Who speaks and who listens in a conversation.
- ► Whites tend to believe in taking turns.
- ► Blacks allow the most vocal person to speak. They also accept interruptions.

Assertive Language

- ► Black people tend to use assertive, powerful language.
- ► White people tend to use softer tones, and less assertive language.

Topics of Conversation

- ► White people tend to believe that asking another person about jobs, family, or other personal topics is a friendly gesture.
- ► Black people tend to believe such personal topics are inappropriate.

Similarities

- ► Black people and White people share 99.9 percent of genetic make-up.

44. Rebas and Cronis: An Intercultural Communication-General Simulation Model

Andrea Patterson-Masuka, Ph.D.

Goal

This culture-general simulation activity will be used to focus the student's attention on how stereotypes are developed, barriers created, and misunderstandings grow exponentially. This cross-cultural activity will allow students to examine their own bias and how they perceive differences, and motivate them to rethink their behavior and attitude toward different cultures.

Rationale

Using the simulation model of instruction, students will experience and understand how their culture, stereotypes, and attitudes influence their behavior.

The goal of this simulation game was to build awareness of how cultural differences can impact our attitudes and perceptions of others. Motivate students to revaluate their actions and attitudes towards others. Allow students to think about their own bias.

Consider how stereotypes are developed.

Materials Needed

Red and green self-adhesive stickers.

Direct Explanation

Students will understand and develop the concept of cross-cultural sensitivity. This is the important ability to recognize differences and similarities between cultures and to understand how social and cultural realities affect the personal and professional attitudes and practices of individuals and organizations (Landis & Bhagat, 1996).

Students will gain a deeper awareness of the following:

1. The labels and stereotypes we assign to others can impact how we feel about others, what we expect from them, and ultimately how we interact with them through nonverbal and verbal communication.
2. The importance of developing in a multicultural society to develop intercultural communication competence and develop cross-cultural skills.
3. Develop an awareness of cultural sensitivity. This is the important ability to recognize differences and similarities between cultures and to understand how social and cultural realities affect the personal and professional attitudes and practices of individuals and organizations (Landis & Bhagat, 1996, 87).

Directions for Assignment

Phases	Actual Model	Lesson Presentation
Phase 1 Orientation	Prepare the broad topic of the simulation and the concepts to be incorporated into the simulation activity at hand. Explain simulation and gaming. Give overview of the simulation.	Today we will explore the powerful impact that culture has on our lives. I will ask students to close their eyes, visualize a judge, a chemist, a public school superintendent. I will then process the focus activity. I will ask them with their eyes closed to raise your hand if you saw an Hispanic judge, a Black psychologist, or an Asian public superintendent. I will ask them to open their eyes and look around. I will explain to the class that we all see people through our perceptual filters which affect our behavior and attitude towards people from other cultures. We make people decisions every day— whom we talk to, spend time with, ignore, etc., avoid. We put labels on people, a judge should look like this, a school superintendent should look like this, a psychologist should look like this. Today, we will participate in an experiential exercise designed to simulate interaction between members of a different culture. A simulator is a training device that closely represent reality but in which the complexity of events can be controlled (Joyce, Weil, & Calhoun, 2004, 327). This activity is a simulation game. It is a simulation because it models reality and a game because (1) the participants agree to abide by a certain set of conditions in order to create an experience. And (2) inefficient means of communicating are incorporated into the rules (Shirts, 2004).
Phase 2 Participant Training	Set up the scenario (rules, roles, procedures, scoring, types of decisions to be made, goals). Assign roles Hold abbreviated practice session	1. Set the Scenario You will pretend that you will be members of two different cultures, The Rebas and the Cronis. You will not know the rules and customs of the other culture, but they will be interacting with one another. You have been at Reba/Croni School all day. Classes are over for the day, it is now social hour. Today, the Cronis will be joined by several people from a different culture. This is your time to socialize with each other and to get to know the new people. Try to find out as much about the visitors as possible. As you mingle, remember the characteristics of your own culture. Remember you must abide by the rules in your culture.

Phases	Actual Model	Lesson Presentation
		2. Assign Roles
		One half of the class should receive a red sticker (Reba), and one-half of the class should receive a green sticker (Croni).
		They should wear their stickers on their forehead so they can easily recognize which culture each person belongs to once the interaction occurs. Note: Since the Croni culture has gender-specific behaviors, it is important to have males in the Croni culture. Assign stickers with that in mind. (One and Two were reversed in class due to the limited time for presentation.)
		3. Hold Abbreviated Practice Session
		Students should then go quickly to their assign rooms to practice the rules of their culture. The instructor and an assistant should move from one group to the other to help them learn the rules of their culture. Students should be standing to learn their rules.
		Distribute the appropriate handout and read it aloud. Demonstrate the cultural behavior after the role is read. (Switched due to time constraints.) Usually they are a bit confused and shy to be demonstrative, but learning their behavior is an important part of the success of the exercise.
		Practice cultural behavior 5–7 minutes (due to time constraints). This step should take 15–20 minutes, during the actual simulation.
Phase 3 Simulation operation	Conduct game activity and game administration. Obtain feedback and evaluation (of performance and effects of decisions.) Clarify Misconceptions. Continue Simulation.	The two separate cultures should be led to the same room. The room should have ample room for rapid movement. (The boys will be chased.) *(Unable to obtain feedback and evaluation of performance, clarity misconceptions, etc., due to time constraints.)* This portion of the simulation should take 20–40 minutes, depending upon time constraints. The minimum amount of time is at least 20 minutes. It takes the students about 5–10 minutes to immerse in their culture and interact with the other culture.)

Phases	Actual Model	Lesson Presentation
		Note: Be sure that the groups maintain their culture while the new visitors are in their midst. Sometimes, as the game continues, they get caught up in the confusion and conflicts they have encountered with the other culture and they forget about the behaviors they should demonstrate.
Phase 4 Participant Debriefing (Any or all of the following activities).	Summarize events and perceptions. Summarize difficulties and insights. Analyze process. Compare simulation activity to the real world. Relate simulation activity to the real world. Relate simulation activity to course content. Appraise and redesign the simulation.	**Summarize events and perceptions.** Stop the simulation. The students should sit with their cultures. Ask the two cultures to describe the other group using only adjectives. Select one person from each group to come to the chalkboard and write the descriptions the students provide. (You are likely to hear words such as pushy, noisy, snobs, etc. Then have a group member read their culture sheets aloud. See guided discussion questions in the lesson plan section in the packet.) The number of questions and the type depends upon your specific objectives. Basic questions: (1) Describe the people from the other culture. How are they different from you? **Summarize difficulties and insights.** (2) What problems did people from your culture encounter when interacting with the other group? (3) How did you solve these problems? How did you feel in the other culture? (4) How did you respond to the other culture? **Relate simulation activity to the real world.** (5) Ask students when might these types of situations occur in the real world? (6) Are there some analogies to some of the things you experienced during your first month at a new school or when you visited a different region of America or a different country?

Phases	Actual Model	Lesson Presentation
		Relate simulation activity to course content.
		(7) How can we improve the ways we relate to people whose traditions and customs are different than ours?
		Ask students to brainstorm in small groups for about 10 minutes. Then have the group come back to share their responses.

You Are a Reba

(Red Culture)

You are <u>very friendly.</u>

You love to talk, and you put your face <u>very close</u> to the face of the person you are talking to.

The most insulting thing to you for a member of another culture to say the first word in a conversation (even if it is hello). If this happens, you <u>hiss at the person</u> and walk away without talking.

However, if a Reba gets in the first word, the conversation will be fruitful and pleasant.

You are very informal. You prefer to <u>call people by their first names.</u>

You believe that speaking to people makes them feel welcome, so you like to talk to lots of people, but you <u>do not talk to anyone for very long.</u> You move on to another person.

You never pass up an opportunity to touch others with a warm gesture, such as a pat on the shoulder or back, a hug, or a caress. (No handshaking though. That is too distant.)

You are interested in family background. You love to talk about your parents, siblings, even distant relations, <u>but never about yourself.</u> (That would be too vain.)

If someone asks you something about yourself, you talk about yourself in a whisper, rather than in a conversational tone, but when you are talking about others in your family, you raise your voice and talk with enthusiasm.

You Are a Croni

(Green Culture)

In Croni culture **boys are the weaker gender. They are protected by the girls.**

Croni boys may talk to other Croni boys, but they **do not make eye contact with or talk to alien girls. They only talk to them through their protector.**

It is very **insulting for an alien girl to speak to a Croni boy. If this happens, he screams and runs away.**

You prefer to **stay with other Cronis.**

You like to **keep at least an arm's length distance between you and the person with whom you are speaking.**

You **do not make eye contact when talking with anyone.** That is considered rude.

Before you begin taking, you **cross your arms in front of you and keep them there** until you finish the conversation.

You prefer **formality** when you speak to people, so you use **Mr. Mrs. or Miss when addressing someone ex. Mr. Mike, Miss Susie, etc., and you say, yes sir, no ma'am, etc.**

The traditional greeting in your culture is **to touch your elbow to the elbow of the person you are greeting. Any other type of physical contact is considered impolite.**

In Croni, it is important to know background information about people, **so you ask lots of personal questions** (age, birthdays, family information, school, hobbies, favorite foods, etc.

Bibliography

Banghart, F., and Trull, Jr. (1973). *Educational Planning.* McMillan: New York.

Bernstein, S., Scheerhorn, S., and Ritter, S. (2002). Using simulations and collaborative teaching to enhance introductory courses. (college level teaching strategies). *College Teaching,* 50(4), 9. Retrieved from Infotrac Web: Expanded Academic.

Joyce. B., Wed, M., and Calhoun. E (2004). *Models of Teaching,* 7th edition. Allyn and Bacon: Boston.

Landis, D., and Bhagat, R. Eds. (1996). *Handbook of Intercultural Training: 2nd edition.* Sage Publications: Thousand Oaks, CA.

Lopez, A. (1999). Pretending for real. (simulation games are gaining popularity as educational tools.) [Electronic Version]. *UNESCO Courier* (3), 14. Retrieved from Infotrac Web: Expanded Academic.

Shirts, R. (1975). A taxonomy of simulation related activities. [Electronic version]. Retrieved March 27, 2004. from http://www.simulationstraingsystems.com/articles/taxon_rel.html.

Shirts, R. (1975). Ten mistakes commonly made by persons designing educational simulations and games. [Electronic version]. Society for Academic Gaming and Simulation in Education and Training Journal. Retrieved from http://www.simulationstrainingsystems.com/articles/ten_mistakes.html

Sprague, H. Inventory of Hunches. Retrieved from http://www.simulationtrainingsystems.com/articles/inventory.html.

Spectre, M., and Prensky. M. Theoretical underpinnings of Games2Train's approach. Retrieved from http://www.games2train.com/site/html/theory.html.

Appendix A

Organizational Assimilation/Socialization Reflection Activity

by Elizabeth Jeter

Step One: Pick a work experience—paid or volunteer—you have had with an organization, preferably one you had in the past.

Step Two: Answer the following interview and demographic questions (Myers & Oetzel, 2003, p. 455) about that work experience.

Interview Questions

1. Do you feel more like a part of the company than you did on your first day here?
2. What do you think changed?
3. Do you remember any situation or particular time when you felt that you were becoming a part of the company?
4. What did others (coworkers, managers, or your subordinates) say that might have helped you to feel this way?
5. Do you believe you felt differently toward the company and your fellow employees after that time?
6. How so?
7. Do you think you can tell when a new employee has assimilated into the company? What might that person or their coworkers do that might clue you into whether or not that person has become a part of (name of the company)?
8. Can you think of someone who hasn't really assimilated into the company?
9. What might that person or their coworkers do that might clue you into whether or not that person has become a part of (name of the company)?
10. How does a new employee know when they have begun to "fit in" here at (name of the company)? What might their co-workers say that indicates their acceptance?
11. What would someone who had "fit in" do or say that would be different from someone who had not?
12. What strategies did you use to integrate into the company?

Demographic Questions

1. How long have you worked for (name of the organization)?
2. What is your position?
3. How long have you been in that position?
4. Do you supervise other employees? How many?
5. Your age?

6.   What is your ethnicity?
7.   What is your sex?

Step Three: Answer These Additional Questions

1.   Did you experience any challenges or conflicts involving coworkers and/or organizational rules, policies, or procedures?
2.   If yes, how were these challenges or conflicts resolved?
3.   Would you have done anything differently in response to the challenge or conflict?
4.   If yes, what would you change to have a better outcome?

Step Four: Gather any other relevant information from that experience that can help interpret and contextualize your responses to the interview and demographic questions. For example, interview coworkers or review performance evaluations.

Step Five: Review your responses. What are the memorable messages? Where are the turning points in events? What are similarities and differences among the information? What patterns emerge? Reflect on these observations and patterns by writing notes.

Step Six: Write a one-page or more essay about your experience. Reflect on what insight you can gain from this activity and how you might apply that insight in the future.

Contributors

Editors

Regina Williams Davis, Ph.D.
North Carolina Agricultural & Technical State University

Dr. Regina Williams Davis is a professor at the North Carolina Agricultural and Technical State University faculty where she is currently the Interim Chair for the Department of Liberal Studies and Foreign Languages. Additionally, as a tenured faculty member in the English Department, she delivers courses on persuasion, ethics, argumentation and debate, small group communication, and intercultural communication.

Dr. Williams Davis has published seven books, eighteen book chapters and essays, and nine abstracts on Communication, African American Youth Identity and Family; she is the co-author of The Instructor's Manual for Communication Voices, which made the best seller's list for Historically Black Colleges and Universities.

Andrea Patterson-Masuka, Ph.D.
Winston-Salem State University

Andrea Patterson-Masuka earned her M.A. and Ph.D. from the University of North Carolina at Greensboro in Education Studies with a specialization in Cultural Studies. She is an Assistant Professor in the Department of Communication and Media Studies at Winston-Salem State University. She teaches intercultural communication, interpersonal communication, group communication, and the basic communication course. Her research interests are in intercultural communication, critical pedagogy, social justice, and the basic communication course. As a former journalist, she has co-edited three books and published several essays on intercultural communication, racism, and the basic communication course.

Chapter Contributors

Debashis "Deb" Aikat, Ph.D.
The University of North Carolina at Chapel Hill

A former journalist, Debashis "Deb" Aikat has been a faculty member since 1995 in the School of Journalism and Mass Communication at the University of North Carolina at Chapel Hill. An award-winning researcher and teacher, Aikat theorizes on social media, global communication, news media, and the future of communication.

Dr. Aikat's research interests range across the mass media. His research has been published in book chapters and refereed journals such as *First Amendment Studies, Health Communication, Global Media and Communication, Electronic Journal of Communication, Popular Music and Society, Convergence: The International Journal of Research into New Media Technologies* and publications of the Association for Computing Machinery, Microsoft Corporation, and the International Radio and Television Society (IRTS).

Dr. Aikat worked as a journalist in India for the Ananda Bazar Patrika's *The Telegraph* newspaper from 1984 through 1992. He also reported for the BBC World Service. Aikat earned a Ph.D. in Mass Communication and Journalism from Ohio University's Scripps School of Journalism in 1995. He completed in 1990 a Certificate in American Political Culture from New York University. He lives in Chapel Hill, North Carolina, USA.

James Nesmith Anderson

James Nesmith Anderson is a writer currently living in North Carolina. He lived in South Korea for two years and plans on returning in the near future. He is also a co-leader of *Disruptive Voices,* a Seoul-based collective working for advocacy for sexual assault survivors and affirmative consent.

Winsora Blanford, Ph.D.

Winsora Blanford is currently an independent scholar, who researches the intersection of education, trauma, and violence. After a career as a criminal justice professional, she became a professional academic advisor. Her education includes an undergraduate degree in psychology, a graduate degree in counselor education, and a Doctor of Philosophy Degree in Education and Cultural Studies.

Brian C. Blount, Ed.D.
Winston-Salem State University

Dr. Brian C. Blount is an associate professor and department chairperson in the Department of Communication and Media Studies at Winston-Salem State University. He specializes in electronic media and digital convergence. He graduated from North Carolina Central University with a Bachelor of Arts in English, Media, and Journalism. He earned his Master of Arts in Instructional Design and Educational Media from North Carolina Central University. He completed his Doctorate of Education degree in Agricultural Communications from North Carolina State University. He completed media management programs at Harvard University and Cornell University. He worked in the field of broadcasting for 10 years and worked as a former radio engineer and producer for several radio and television stations in North Carolina before moving into higher education.

Yea-Wen Chen, Ph.D.
Ohio University

Yea-Wen Chen (Ph.D., University of New Mexico, 2010) is an Assistant Professor within Scripps College of Communication, School of Communication Studies at Ohio University, Athens, Ohio.

Stephanie Sedberry Carrino
The University of North Carolina at Greensboro

Stephanie Sedberry Carrino is a Research Associate and Grants Manager for the Physics Education Group at the University of North Carolina at Greensboro. She has 20 years' experience teaching at the college level, most recently at North Carolina A&T State University where she taught in the Speech Program for 12 years. She has a Master's Degree in Speech Communication from the University of North Carolina at Chapel Hill, and is a doctoral candidate in Educational Studies at UNCG. Her research interests include educational philosophy and technology.

Sandra Crosier, M.Ed.
Retired, Texas Tech University, University of Kansas

Sandra Crosier holds a Masters in Teaching English as a Second Language (ESL). She has lived and taught in Thailand, Iran, and Japan and has traveled widely in Asia and Europe including a bicycle trip of about 1,000 miles through Italy, France, England, and Ireland. She taught ESL for 10 years in public schools in Lawrence, Kansas, and at both the University of Kansas and Texas Tech University (TTU). She is now retired from TTU where she last served as Director of Study Abroad from 1994 to 2014.

Joe DeCrosta, Ph.D.

Joe DeCrosta, Ph.D. holds a B.A. in Communication from Rutgers University, an M.A. in International Communication from American University, and a Ph.D. in Communication and Rhetorical Studies from Duquesne University. He has worked as a university administrator in the field of international education for 20 years. Dr. DeCrosta believes that although the act of intercultural communication can often be confusing and challenging, authentic dialogue requires us to create meaningful experiences out of our interactions with others from various ethnic, national, and cultural backgrounds. As a professional in the field of international education, Dr. DeCrosta has worked with students from a number of cultural backgrounds and nationalities, and has encouraged U.S. university students to take advantage of study abroad opportunities whenever possible; such cross cultural experiences can often shatter our preconceived notions about cultural others with contrasting belief systems, and ultimately impact the ways in which we communicate in every aspect of life. Dr. DeCrosta has experienced the phenomenon of culture shock himself.

Chrys Egan, Ph.D.
Salisbury University, Salisbury, MD

Dr. Chrys Egan earned her Ph.D. in Communication from Florida State University and is an Associate Professor at Salisbury University in Communication, and Gender and Sexuality Studies. Her scholarship examines the intersections of interpersonal relationships with popular culture. She serves as a conference co-chair to the Popular Culture Association in the South, and the International Leadership Association's Women and Leadership Affinity Group. Book publications include: *Family Communication: Theory and Research* (Pearson) chapter; *Communication Research Instructor's Manual* (Pearson); *The St. Martin's Guide to Public Speaking Student Workbook*. Journal publications appear in: *The Free Speech Yearbook, Studies in Popular Culture, Journal of Popular Culture, Iowa Journal of Communication*, and *Gender in Management: International Journal*. Her leadership and civic engagement work involves gender and family issues, and community wellness. She is also a professional fitness instructor and mother.

Suresh Gopalan, Ph.D.
Winston-Salem State University

Dr. Suresh Gopalan is Professor of Management and MBA program coordinator at Winston-Salem State University. Originally a native of India, he has lived in the United States for the last 26 years. He has earned a Bachelor's in Communication from Loyola College, University of Madras (1983), a MBA from the University of Southern Mississippi (1986), and a DBA from Louisiana Tech University (2000). Prior to his tenure at WSSU, he worked at West Texas A&M University and Columbus State University. His teaching and research interests are in the areas of International Management and International Business and Strategy.

Amanda Gunn, Ph.D.
Denison University, Granville, OH

Amanda Gunn focuses her teaching and scholarship on the development of relationships and communities through engaged communication. Specifically, she explores questions of marginality, voice, and empowerment in a variety of communication context including interpersonal, small group, and organizational. She completed her BS at Appalachian State University, and her MA and PhD at the University of North Carolina at Greensboro.

Gladys Exum Huggins, Ed.D.
Winston-Salem State University

Dr. Gladys E. Huggins is an Associate Professor in the Department of English at Winston-Salem State University, where she teaches writing and literature courses. Dr. Huggins has taught at Winston-Salem State University since 2003. She has assisted students in higher education in developing their academic skills for more than thirty years, and she has a strong interest in creative writing.

Elizabeth H. Jeter, M.A.
University of South Florida

Elizabeth H. Jeter (M.A., University of North Carolina at Greensboro) is a doctoral candidate at the University of South Florida. She is an organizational communication scholar, with additional interests in intercultural and applied communication. Her current research focuses on interorganizational collaboration and change in law enforcement efforts against human trafficking.

Anna K. Lee, Ph.D.
North Carolina A&T State University

Dr. Anna K. Lee is an Associate Professor of Psychology at North Carolina Agricultural and Technical State University in Greensboro, North Carolina. She received her Bachelors of Science degree in Psychology from Southern University and Agricultural and Mechanical College in Baton Rouge, Louisiana, and her Masters and Doctor of Philosophy degree in Social Psychology from Howard University in Washington, DC. Her research interests include investigating the influence of race and racism on wellness within the Black community.

J. Maria Merrills, Ph.D.
Winston-Salem State University

Dr. J. Maria Merrills is Assistant Professor of Liberal Studies at Winston-Salem State University. She holds a Master's Degree in African-American Literature and a Ph.D. in Educational Studies. Her research interests include digitization and its impact on Africana learning, culture, popular culture, and social justice. She has written articles focused on African American preferences in online learning. She has also written and produced plays and web shows focused on African American culture such as *A Date with Destiny* and *Seeing Faith*.

Soncerey L. Montgomery Speas, Ph.D.
Winston-Salem State University

Dr. Soncerey L. Montgomery Speas received the Bachelor of Arts from North Carolina State University, the Master of Arts from the University of North Carolina-Chapel Hill and the Ph.D. from the University of North Carolina-Greensboro. Currently, Dr. Montgomery Speas is an Associate Professor in the Department of Communication and Media Studies at Winston-Salem State University. She is the author of *The Heart of a Student: Success Principles for College Students* and the founder of "Success with Soncerey" business ventures. Dr. Montgomery Speas is a proud member of Delta Sigma Theta Sorority, Inc. and is actively involved in her community.

Leonard Muaka, Ph.D.
Winston-Salem State University

Leonard Muaka is Associate Professor of English and Swahili at Winston-Salem State University, where he teaches courses in linguistics, English, African literature, and Swahili language and culture. His main research interests include youth language, discourse analysis, language ideology, and language acquisition. He also leads a study abroad to Kenya and Tanzania every summer that focuses on language, culture, and politics of the East African region.

Christine L. North, Ph.D., MPH
Ohio Northern University

Christine is Associate Professor of Communication at Ohio Northern University. She has taught classes in Mexico, Costa Rica, and Spain, and regularly works in rural Dominican Republic with student groups and educating students about responsible aid and the issues associated with voluntourism and short-term mission work. Her work in public health and interest in international cultures and settings has exposed her to many of the unintended consequences that often occur when well-meaning people take part in aid projects without adequate cultural knowledge and understanding about the people and places with whom they interact.

Daniel Richardson
North Carolina A&T State University

Daniel Richardson has been an adjunct instructor of Speech Communication at North Carolina A&T State University since 2009. He is also a successful entrepreneur having owned and operated several successful businesses including a speed dating franchise and a concierge service. Prior to coming to North Carolina A&T State University, Richardson served as an adjunct instructor of Speech Communication at Winston-Salem State University from 2005 to 2012 and earned an O'Ki fellowship while working there. He received his M.A. from the University of North Carolina at Greensboro in 1995 and was a 1994 John Robinson Fellow.

Richardson is single and has two dogs who are in many ways his children—Shadow, a four-year-old white German Shepherd and Lily, a four-year-old Black and Tan Coonhound.

Juan A. Rios Vega, Ph.D.
Davidson College

Juan A. Rios Vega is an adjunct faculty at Davidson College, NC. He teaches Latino/a Education in the U.S. His research interests include English Language Acquisition, Multicultural Education, Critical Race Theory, Latino/a Critical Theory, Social Justice in Education, and Latino masculinities.

James A. Schnell, Ph.D.
Ohio Dominican University

Jim Schnell, Ph.D. (Ohio University, 1982) is a Professor in the Department of Communication Studies at Ohio Dominican University. He retired from the U.S. Air Force (Reserve), after 30 years of service in the U.S. intelligence community, at the rank of Colonel—with his final 14 years as an Attaché to China. He was the Lead Social Scientist for the Army Culture & Foreign Language Directorate between 2010 and 2013. Schnell is a Fulbright Scholar, completed three Visiting Fellowships at the East-West Center in Honolulu and was a visiting scholar at Ohio State University. He has taught at universities in the U.S., China, and Cambodia and has 15 books in print, over 70 book chapters and journal articles published, and delivered over 150 conference presentations.

Abhijit Sen, Ph.D.
Winston-Salem State University

Abhijit Sen is a Professor in the department of Communication and Media Studies at Winston-Salem State University. He teaches international communication, media criticism and media writing courses. He does research on global communication and cultural issues. His other research interests are in semiotics and film criticism. His scholarly papers have been published in *Media Asia, Journal of Development Communication, Global Media*

Journal, Observatorio, Proteus, and others. He received his doctorate from University of Maryland, College Park, his masters from Fairfield University, and his bachelors from Calcutta University.

Nathaniel Simmons, Ph.D.
La Salle University

Nathaniel Simmons (Ph.D., Ohio University, 2014) is an Assistant Professor within the Department of Communication at La Salle University, Philadelphia, Pennsylvania.

Omar Swartz, Ph.D.
University of Colorado Denver

Omar Swartz (Ph.D., Purdue University, 1995; J.D., Duke University, 2001, *magna cum laude*) is Associate Professor of Humanities and Social Sciences at the University of Colorado Denver. His areas of research and teaching are law and diversity, mass media law, cultural criticism, and philosophical problems in the social sciences. He is the author or editor of 12 books and nearly 100 essays, book chapters, and reviews.

Tanya E. Walker, Ph.D.
Winston-Salem State University

Tanya E. Walker is an Assistant Professor in the Department of English. She earned a Ph.D. in English from Howard University with a specialization in African American literature. Her scholarly interests include black women writers, contemporary drama, and black speculative fiction. Her current research project is titled *Revisiting the Tragic Form in African American Women's Drama* and focuses on dramatic depictions of rape and black female sexuality. Additionally, Walker is a member of Sigma Tau Delta International English Honor Society and Delta Sigma Theta Sorority, Inc. She is the mother of her 10-year-old son Ayo.

Sheila Whitley, Ph.D.
North Carolina A&T State University

Sheila Whitley has 31 years of experience in higher education. She began her career in 1984 as a visual communications specialist in Agricultural Communications at NC A&T State University. In 2001 she accepted a full-time teaching position in the Department of Journalism and Mass Communication at NC A&T State University. In 2012, Whitley became associate chair in the department.

Her research interests include the scholarship for teaching, curriculum development, and learning and student success. Additionally, she has numerous photographs published in magazines, textbooks, and other publications. Whitley has several essays or published in textbooks or aired on a local radio station.

Whitley received her Ph.D. in Curriculum and Instruction with a focus in Higher Education Administration for the University of North Carolina Greensboro, Greensboro, North Carolina; Master of Arts in Educational Media from the Department of Library Science and Media Studies, Appalachian State University, Boone, North Carolina; B.A. in Radio, Television and Motion Pictures from the University of North Carolina at Chapel Hill, Chapel Hill, North Carolina; and an A.A. Literary from Wingate University, Wingate, North Carolina.

Sheila Whitley was born and grew up in High Point, North Carolina.

Student Essays

Jennifer Evens, Student
Winston-Salem State University

Jennifer Evens is an interracial Floridian born and Carolina raised student at Winston-Salem State University. She is a sophomore and is a biology and chemistry minor. She hopes to use her knowledge that she earns in school to get into medical school and to become a pediatrician. Prior to coming to Winston-Salem State, she attended Davie County High School to which she graduated in 2013.

Lan Jin, Student
Purdue University

Lan Jin is a doctoral student at Purdue University. Her research currently focuses on consumer behavior and health communication, particularly on intercultural communication, mental health of immigrants, and health disparities.

Dongjing Kang, Student
Ohio University

Dongjing Kang is a Doctoral Candidate within Scripps College of Communication, School of Communication Studies at Ohio University, Athens, Ohio.

Ronell Miller
North Carolina A&T State University

Ronell Miller is a Junior International Management student from Los Angeles, California. He is a Multicultural Ambassador for the 2014–2015 school year, President for West Coast Aggies, and a Residential Assistant. He strives to live a diverse life every day. Ronell has an explorer's personality. Doing and learning new things is one of his passions; he believes that if you're doing the same thing with the same intent you are wasting time. One of Ronell's strengths is that he is an adaptive chameleon on the move, so you might say he is unpredictable.

Matt Parmesano, Student
Winston-Salem State University

Matt Parmesano is a junior mass communications major at Winston-Salem State University. He has always been into sports and writing, so he put two and two together and is studying to become a sportswriter. He's from Walkertown, N.C., a small town just six miles east of WSSU, and has been working at the Winston-Salem Journal since he was a junior in high school.

Keon Pettiway, Student
North Carolina State University

Keon Pettiway is a Ph.D. candidate in Communication, Rhetoric, and Digital Media at North Carolina State University.

Eric Magruder Price II, Student
Winston-Salem State University

Eric is a junior Sociology major at Winston-State University. A native of Washington, DC, Eric's interests include a passion for the field of Higher Education, as he intends to work on the collegiate ranks as Student Affairs Administrator, helping the underprivileged to matriculate through college.

Sydney Silverthorne
North Carolina A&T State University

Sydney Silverthorne is a non-traditional transfer student at North Carolina Agricultural & Technical State University. In the fall of 2015 she will receive her bachelor's degree in speech communications. Along with continuing her education at NC A&T, she is the mother to Sean, her six-year-old son and a full-time associate with an apartment management company in Greensboro, NC. Sydney is also a veteran. She served in the United States Army as an active duty soldier from August 2007 to August 2012, with one tour to Iraq in support of Operation Iraqi Freedom/New Dawn. When Sydney is not working or in class, she enjoys spending time with her son, eating out at nice restaurants, and going to the movies.

Qinghua (Candy) Yang, Student
University of Miami

Qinghua (Candy) Yang is a doctoral student at the University of Miami, with research interests in health and intercultural communication. Her work has appeared in leading peer-reviewed journals including *Computers in Human Behavior*, *Health Education*, *Journal of International Consumer Marketing*, and *Journal of Communication Media Studies*, and been presented for a number of times at major academic conferences, such as NCA, ICA, and AEJMC.

CPSIA information can be obtained at www.ICGtesting.com
Printed in the USA
LVOW02s1113080815

448837LV00005B/15/P